A12900 351085
ILLINOIS CENTRAL COLLEGE
PS3511.A86Z947
STACKS
Faulkner's narrative,
A12900 3510
P9-DNC-301

Faulkner's Narrative

Faulkner's Narrative

BY JOSEPH W. REED, JR.

NEW HAVEN AND LONDON
YALE UNIVERSITY PRESS, 1973

Grateful acknowledgment is made to Random House, Inc. for permission to include selections from the copyrighted works of William Faulkner.

Published with assistance from the foundation established in memory of Philip Hamilton McMillan of the Class of 1894, Yale College.

Library of Congress catalog card number: 72-91304
International standard book number: 0-300-01590-9

Designed by Sally Sullivan and set in Linotype Baskerville type.
Printed in the United States of America by Vail-Ballou Press, Inc., Binghamton, N.Y.

Published in Great Britain, Europe, and Africa by Yale University Press, Ltd., London. Distributed in Canada by McGill-Queen's University Press, Montreal; in Latin America by Kaiman & Polon, Inc., New York City; in Australasia and Southeast Asia by John Wiley & Sons Australasia Pty. Ltd., Sydney; in India by UBS Publishers' Distributors Pvt., Ltd., Delhi; in Japan by John Weatherhill, Inc., Tokyo.

To Marion Fred
Sam Chris

"The best game of all, the best of all breathing
and forever the best of all listening"

Contents

Acknowledgments ix

Editions Cited xi

1 "One Single Urn or Shape" 1

2 The Short Fiction 12

3 *Sanctuary* 58

4 *The Sound and the Fury* 74

5 *As I Lay Dying* 84

6 *Light in August* 112

7 *Absalom, Absalom!* 145

8 Uncertainties: *The Unvanquished* and *Go Down, Moses* 176

9 Faulkner's Failure: *Intruder in the Dust, Requiem for a Nun,* and *A Fable* 201

10 Snopes 218

11 The Search for Freedom 258

Appendixes 283

Index 289

Acknowledgments

Wesleyan University has supported this study by sabbatical leaves, a moonlighting arrangement, research grants, and its student aide program. Other student labor was paid for by the Work Study Program of the Office of Economic Opportunity. The students of English 275, 249, 227, and attendant tutorials have seldom bored me, usually instructed me, and frequently contributed directly to this study. I must name James B. McEnteer, Larry D. Carver, Jules Landsman, Richard A. Hood, and Samuel T. Barnett III because I can point to their individual contributions, but it is unfair to single out any without thanking all. Frank G. Levering, Wesleyan '74, assisted with the proofs; Ellen Gates D'Oench, '73, prepared the index. John Peyton Crigler III, Wesleyan '69, my research assistant for three years, has read, criticized, taken notes, researched, encouraged, and contributed to the book at every stage.

My colleagues have listened patiently and Larry P. Vonalt, Richard M. Ohmann, Richard P. Wilbur, Carl A. Viggiani, Louis O. Mink, James L. Steffensen, Jr., Thomas G. Henney, and Richard S. Slotkin have responded to particular queries, although some may not have realized it at the time. Paul Horgan and F. D. Reeve gave the manuscript a particularly valuable early reading and Travis R. Merritt did so at a later stage. Irving Howe and David L. Minter made valuable suggestions for final revision. I am deeply indebted to the careful readings and suggestions of Wayland Schmitt.

The portrait sketch of Faulkner by Peter Hurd is used by the kind permission of its owner, Paul Horgan, and of the artist. Quotations from Faulkner are made by arrangement with Random House, Chatto E. Windus, Ltd., and Curtis-Brown Ltd.

All I know about narrative I have learned from my wife, Kit Reed, and from her fiction, and they began this book. I am responsible for its miscalculations, excesses, and errors.

J. W. R.

Middletown, Connecticut
1972

Editions Cited

Reference is made to these editions parenthetically by cue-title:

Absalom	*Absalom, Absalom!* (New York: Random House, 1936).
As I	*As I Lay Dying* (New York: Random House, 1957; new collation by James B. Meriwether).
Fable	*A Fable* (New York: Random House, 1954).
GDM	*Go Down, Moses* (New York: Random House, 1942).
Hamlet	*The Hamlet* (New York: Random House, 1940).
Intruder	*Intruder in the Dust* (New York: Modern Library, 1948).
Light	*Light in August* (New York: Modern Library, 1968).
Lion	*Lion in the Garden: Interviews with William Faulkner 1926–1962,* ed. James B. Meriwether and Michael Millgate (New York: Random House, 1968).
Mansion	*The Mansion* (New York: Random House, 1959).
Reivers	*The Reivers* (New York: Random House, 1962).
Requiem	*Requiem for a Nun* (New York: Random House, 1968).
S&F	*The Sound and the Fury* (New York: Random House, 1946).
SS	*Collected Stories of William Faulkner* (New York: Random House, 1950).
Sanct.	*Sanctuary* (New York: Random House, 1959).
Town	*The Town* (New York: Random House, 1957).
Univ.	*Faulkner in the University, Class Conferences at the University of Virginia 1957–58,* ed. Frederick L. Gwynn and Joseph L. Blotner (Charlottesville, Va.: University Press of Virginia, 1959).
Unvanq.	*The Unvanquished* (New York: Random House, 1965).

1 "One Single Urn or Shape"

Q.: Do you like myths, Mr. Faulkner?
Faulkner: I like myths because they are about people.

Lion in the Garden, *p. 284*

If Faulkner had, like Keats, outlined his theory in deeply felt personal letters, or, like Yeats, concealed it behind a mystical beard, or even, like Henry James, embodied it in a series of controlled and immaculately ordered essays, the theoretical basis of his art would by now have been well established. That what there is of it was manifested in spontaneous answers to somewhat rambling and thickheaded questions has brought critics to transfer this thickheadedness to his answers and to assume that there is little or no theory to be had. Faulkner's consistent concern at Nagano, Virginia, and West Point with craftsmanship, narrative, unity, and form has been ignored for the most part in a rush to point out his self-contradiction and his various poses.

There are, of course, contradictory masks and poses to be had in plenty, a different one for each situation. At Nagano Faulkner is a national representative, Mr. American Literature, replying to questions as if from an answer sheet prepared in advance, dealing out automatic responses as if he were Robert Frost in a freshman class on metaphor. At Virginia there is a strong element of pipe-chewing, let's-show-these-academics-a-thing-or-two philistinism. At West Point Faulkner's answers seem almost as calculatedly decorous as his three-piece suit, bowler, and stick are for Cartier-Bresson's portraiture. In each of these encounters and in most of the interviews collected by Meriwether and Millgate, the rhetorical situation is that of the lion unwilling, beleaguered by questions he has heard before, giving responses he's a bit tired of or indulging in the whimsy of invented or artificial answers.

Yet we must take these poses seriously if we are to deal with Faulkner's fiction, even as we must take seriously all of Lord Byron's poses if we are to deal with his poetry. They reveal essentially two warring impulses of self-depiction: either to chew the pipe and play the gentleman dirt-farmer and guts-writer, denying that he ever saw a theme or a symbol, or to play the academics' game and outdo them, to answer the wildest question with a paradox or deeper meaning which has just occurred to him, and to run to the barn with it. Both are whimsical extremes of a central serious concern. Faulkner had submitted himself to the questions of Virginia or Japan or of the schoolboy reporter on vacation because he felt that his answers might serve writers: "The contribution would come out of my experience as a writer, as a craftsman, in contact with the desire of young people to be writers, to be craftsmen" (*Univ.*, p. 12). Craftsmanship, unity, integrity, the "one single urn or shape" (*Univ.*, p. 65) is at the center of every interview, and it is partly because we are unwilling to accept the simplicity of this center that we mistake the man for a mask and the mask for a man.

> I wrote for the sake of writing because it was fun. . . .
>
> I'm a story-teller. I'm telling a story, introducing comic and tragic elements as I like. I'm telling a story—to be repeated and retold. I don't claim to be truthful. Fiction is fiction—not truth; it's make-believe. Thus I stack and lie at times, all for the purposes of the story—to entertain. [*Lion*, pp. 255, 277]

The root of Faulkner's art is just what he says. He had heard well-told stories that were worth repeating and he wanted to be able to tell some of his own. To tell them well was a more complex matter, but the aim was almost simplistic: the communication of pleasure to a reader.

> Well, the writer, actually, that's an obligation that he assumes with his vocation, that he's going to write it in a way that people can understand it. He doesn't have to write it in the way that every idiot can understand it—every imbecile in the third grade can understand it, but he's got to use a language which is accepted and in which the words have specific meanings that everybody agrees on. [*Univ.*, pp. 52–53]

> Let him remember that a novel is to create pleasure for the reader. The only mistake with any novel is if it fails to create pleasure. That it is not true is irrelevant: a novel is to be enjoyed. A book that fails to create enjoyment is not a good one. [*Lion,* p. 280]

This is the external sanction out of which all standards, controls, and rules grow. Both the anecdotalist and the novelist must try to seem to be uncalculating (for that is part of the game), but both must design and plan for the reader's pleasure. This pleasure can be a complex, elaborate response (hunting for symbols, Faulkner admits, can be a legitimate pleasure of fiction, *Univ.,* p. 121), but pleasure must be there.

The reader's pleasure depends most heavily on identification of himself with characters. He must find "flesh-and-blood people that will stand up and cast a shadow" (*Univ.,* p. 47). Message or idea is secondary. In making an extreme case for his primary aim, Faulkner sees these two ends as mutually exclusive: "I don't believe any writer is capable of doing both, that he's got to choose one of the two: either he is delivering a message or he's trying to create flesh-and-blood, living, suffering, anguishing human beings" (*Univ.,* p. 47).

I dwell on this series of rather obvious assertions to emphasize what Faulkner said he was *not* doing and the proper precedence he suggested for the several things he was doing. Idea or message could not come first—the people and what they did had to. This led him to insist that his process of composition always had a clear point of genesis—a human germ of narrative: "The story can come from an anecdote, it can come from a character. With me it never comes from an idea because I don't know too much about ideas and ain't really interested in ideas, I'm interested in people, so what I speak from my experience is probably a limited experience" (*Univ.,* p. 19). Genesis varies from story to story and from interview to interview ("He usually begins with a character and just starts writing," *Lion,* p. 17), but the literary germ most frequently cited is an almost visual image of a character imprisoned in a fleeting moment. The most celebrated of these is, of course, Caddy and her muddy drawers: "An image, a very moving image to me was of the children. . . . And it took the rest of the four hundred pages to explain why she was brave enough to climb the tree to look in the window. It was an image, a picture to me, a very moving one, which was symbolized by the muddy bottom of her drawers" (*Univ.*, p. 31). He tries to maintain the element of primitive mystery in the image as he releases the character from that moment and invents moments to precede it and moments to follow.

> There's always a moment in experience—a thought—an incident—that's there. Then all I do is work up to that moment. I figure what must have happened before to lead people to that particular moment, and I work away from it, finding out how people act after that moment. That's how all my books and stories come. . . . I like to tell stories, to create people and situations. But that's all. I doubt if an author knows what he puts in a story. All he is trying to do is to tell what he knows about his environment and the people around him in the most moving way possible. [*Lion*, p. 220]

But the mystery is balanced on the other side by the pragmatic builder of narrative, applying calculated pressure to the germ to transform it into narrative and to transfer elements of the real world into the fictional: "There's a case of the sorry, shabby world that don't quite please you, so you create one of your own, so you make Lion a little braver than he was, and you make the bear a little more of a bear than he actually was" (*Univ.*, p. 59). This is the lying and stacking he refers to, the adjustment of elements of our world to fit them to the particular world of their particular fiction:

> Beginning with *Sartoris* I discovered that my own little postage stamp of native soil was worth writing about and that I would never live long enough to exhaust it, and by sublimating the actual into apocryphal I would have complete liberty to use whatever talent I might have to its absolute top. It opened up a gold mine of other peoples, so I created a cosmos of my own. I can move these people around like God, not only in space but in time too. . . . I like to think of the world I created as being a kind of keystone in the Universe. [*Lion*, p. 255]

The statement is a perfect example of the way Faulkner's masks can get in the way. "Sublimating the actual into apocryphal" develops his central aim, but almost immediately after that comes the heady generality, Faulkner's bromide, to dilute such revealing particular details. The relationship of the individual to the universal is a central element in Faulkner's theory and in his fiction. But this statement is not so much directed at describing his fiction as it is at rendering a self-image, and as always Faulkner gets hung up between seeing himself as an inspired writer bursting with literature and seeing himself as a tireless craftsman, building his box. The first of these images led him continually into universal generality, in a development which reached its peak (or nadir) in the Nagano sessions. Coupled with a weakness for rhetoric, this tendency leads him to embrace any convenient squashy generalization and let a rolling period carry him down a peroration into the "anguish of man." His rhetorical temptation to universal platitude is similar to Gavin Stevens's or Thomas Carlyle's.[1] It is possible to salvage what lies behind the empty phrases of some of these universal bromides only by fastening upon his tougher statements about particular methods or techniques.

When supported by internal evidence from his fiction, such descriptions of the detailed processes of narrative make a convincingly coherent theory. The first principle is derived from the idea of a "story worth repeating": any box-builder can borrow from any other box-builder to make his own.

> No, I use materials at hand. [*Lion,* p. 277]

> The writer . . . is completely amoral. He takes whatever he needs, wherever he needs, and he does that openly and honestly because he himself hopes that what he does will be good enough so that after him people will take from him. [*Univ.,* pp. 20–21]

> Read, read, read. Read everything—trash, classics, good and bad, and see how they do it. Just like a carpenter who works as an apprentice and studies the master. Read! You'll absorb it. Then write. [*Lion,* p. 55]

There is a pragmatic, catch-as-catch-can quality to this:

> I would say that the writer has three sources, imagination, observation, and experience. He himself doesn't know how much of which he uses at any given moment because each of the sources themselves are not too important to him. That he is writing about

1. In order to explain Boswell's biographical genius, Carlyle constructs a rhetorical frame which leads to one "great secret." When he finally arrives at it, it is nothing more than "the secret of an open, loving heart."

> people, and he uses his material from the three sources as the carpenter reaches into his lumber room and finds a board that fits the particular corner he's building. [*Univ.*, p. 103] [2]

The extension of the metaphor makes clear the precision involved: what comes first is the precise element, the moment, the specific narrative at hand, "the particular corner he's building." What is casual is the availability of materials in his resources. There is precision in the selection of materials and their appropriateness to the "corner," as well as the corner's place in the total shape of the work when constructed: he "finds a board" to fit the moment, not vice versa.

The carpenter metaphor occurs to Faulkner because he looks back on some books in his career which he feels were good and some which were not; those which were not still had their unseen value to him later in what he learned from them and carried with him: "That one [*Mosquitoes*], if I could write that over, I probably wouldn't write it at all. I'm not ashamed of it, because that was the chips, the badly sawn planks that the carpenter produces while he's learning to be a first-rate carpenter, but it's not a—not an important book in my list" (*Univ.*, p. 257). As the metaphor develops, offhand references to stopgap or jerry-built construction gradually evolve into allusions to the technique of an accomplished craftsman: "I just try to drive the nails straight so the cabinet comes out right. . . . I write about people. Maybe all sorts of symbols and images get in—I don't know. When a good carpenter builds something, he puts the nails where they belong. Maybe they make a fancy pattern when he's through, but that's not why he put them in that way (*Lion*, pp. 48, 61). The "fancy pattern when he's through" refers not just to critical assessment or symbol-hunters, but to Faulkner's own sense of the quality and "rightness" of the completed work; "where they belong" is structural: a concern for the central narrative purpose.

The metaphor of the adaptable craftsman—the "quickest tool to hand," "the nearest hammer" (*Univ.*, p. 3), the "lumber room of his memory" (*Univ.*, p. 72), "whatever tool that he thinks will do most to finish the picture which at the moment he is trying to paint" (*Univ.*, p. 39)—runs throughout the interviews, so that eventually

2. Here again the precision of the particular is undercut by a long descent which follows, ending, expectedly, in the "aspirations, the troubles, the anguishes, the courage, and the cowardice, the baseness and the splendor of man, of the human heart."

Faulkner has applied it to almost every element of technique and subject-matter: allusion, humor, tragedy, comedy, message, rhetoric, character, violence, sensationalism, symbol, injustice, and inhumanity (*Univ.*, pp. 3, 6, 9, 24, 39, 49, 72, 84, 177, 239; *Lion*, p. 61). Aptness and flexibility are the constant impulse to the metaphor: "the tools which seemed to me the proper tools to try to tell" (*Univ.*, p. 9), "the facet of the character which I needed at that particular time to move the story I was telling" (*Univ.*, p. 24), "just what he needs for that moment" (*Univ.*, p. 259). And that moment is the point of genesis described earlier—the moment for which the carpenter needs all these tools to build the "corner" or the "box" in which to catch those "flesh-and-blood" people, "shown for a moment in a dramatic instant of the furious motion of being alive, that's all any story is. You catch this fluidity which is human life and you focus a light on it and you stop it long enough for people to be able to see it" (*Univ.*, p. 239). Storytelling is the means to the end of universal truth, and his respect for his means or his tools is so great that, fortunately, Faulkner here falls short of his usual platitude and instead dwells upon the truth of particular individuals and the apt selection of the narrative urn or shape to fit this truth. But the tools are not the end: always, "the carpenter don't build a house just to drive nails. He drives nails to build a house" (*Univ.*, p. 50).

My contention is that, as carpenter, Faulkner saw himself as he saw Cash Bundren: a careful craftsman, conscious of the need for calculation and design, resourceful in adapting available materials. But he could not candidly admit to this resemblance for a number of reasons—not the least of which was, again, that conflicting image he had of himself as the humane man of letters. Cash, especially as seen in his first section in *As I Lay Dying*, is somewhat heartless, cold, and unconcerned. Faulkner had to—and wanted to—keep concern for humanity at the center of his work. Too often he had been charged with the distortion of this central concern with gothic grotesques and Southern naturalism; the image of Cash, the calculating craftsman, was as much a distortion. So dispassionate and rationalistic a self-image would overturn the proper precedence of means and ends, and this precedence was the chief point of Faulkner's carpenter metaphor in the first place. Flesh-and-blood people are the substance, aim, and end of fiction. Anything else—symbol, message, humor, violence, even narrative design—were but means to that end. Tools had to be mastered and used with skill, but a tool was not a heart.

The metaphor of cabinetmaking craftsmanship makes clear that what he is trying to tell is more important than how it is told, but at the same time, it makes clear that what is being told may be so elusive that it will defy the telling if the shape is miscalculated or the box clumsily built As the writer improves or gets older, his skills at fabrication improve (not necessarily his wisdom, despite another of Faulkner's favorite bromides), the mastery of the tools becomes more and more important. His clearly established hierarchy of ends and means perhaps explains something about the strange curve of his career: early blurting-out, later experiment in narrative and consciousness, and finally, as experiment gives way to confidence (or, in a different view of the career, to a fear of decline in his powers), the release of open narrative. With Faulkner the telling never becomes the tale (except perhaps, in a very complex way, for *Absalom, Absalom!*) but the design of the telling continually determines secondary fictional effects: timed revelations determine thematic use of time; ease of narration can be the result of control or profusion of metaphor; compelling fate can be the by-product of a complicated narrative strategy, perhaps adopted in the first place only to build the "particular corner."

The external sanctions (pleasing his audience by carefully calculated storytelling and doing justice to his subject) and the internal demand (pleasing himself by doing a craftsmanlike job) may come into conflict in a given work. Here too he sets up a proper order of importance.

> That may be the reason that a man has to rewrite and rewrite—to reconcile imagination and pattern. Of course, any work of art in its conception when it reaches a point where the man can begin to work has got to have some shape, and the problem then is to make imagination and the pattern conform, meet, be amicable, we'll say And when one has to give, I believe it's always the pattern that has to give. And so he's got to rewrite, to create a new pattern with a bulge that will take this bulge of the imagination which insists that it's true, it must be. [*Univ.*, p. 52]

The work has "some shape" at its conception. In designing the "single urn or shape" to fit the "particular corner" Faulkner adduces some rather strict generic limits.

> We'll assume that a novel has set rules. [*Lion,* p. 56]

> I think that anything that can't be told in one standardized book is not a novel. That is, it can't follow the fairly rigid rules which —in which a novel has got to be compressed to be a novel. . . . The more or less rigid pattern which a novel has got to conform to . . . to fit into that form to give the pleasure which doing a complete job within the rules of the craft demand. [*Univ.,* pp. 107–08]

This passage speaks of the Snopes trilogy, a fiction too long for a single novel, here termed "chronicle." The novel by contrast must have compression, "unity and coherence, the proper emphasis and integration, which a long chronicle doesn't have" (*Univ.,* p. 108). This coherence is also contrasted with the "too loose. . . . mass of stuff," the "series of events" (*Lion,* p. 56) which he finds in *Huckleberry Finn.* Another exclusive category—a genre—is the story-series, "too episodic to be what I considered a novel" (*Univ.,* p. 252).

He has even sharper lines for the short story and such a perfectionist goal that he finds little of his work that measures up to the standard he sets.

> In a short story that's next to the poem, almost every word has got to be almost exactly right. . . . I mean by that the good short stories like Chekhov wrote. That's why I rate that second [to poetry]—it's because it demands a nearer absolute exactitude. You have less room to be slovenly and careless. There's less room in it for trash. . . . It's got to be absolutely impeccable, absolutely perfect. [*Univ.,* p. 207]

> "I never wrote a short story I liked." He didn't like "The Bear"? Yes, but he didn't call that a short story. A short story is 3,000 words or less. Anything more is, well, a piece of writing. [*Lion,* p. 59]

Brief narratives demand perfection; with greater length, standards relax, become "fairly rigid" or "more or less rigid." Condensation (although his early reviewers would never have believed it) is for Faulkner a constant ideal of quality and generic consistency ("My way made a better story. . . . It makes the story seem a little more condensed," *Univ.,* p. 236). An early assertion that "a book of short stories should be linked together by characters or chronology" (1931; *Lion,* p. 13) enforces the high priority he gives to internal consistency. The ground rules balance pleasure for the reader, justice for the subject, and satisfaction for himself.

If the hierarchies and the "proper orders" of Faulkner's statements have here been correctly abstracted (that is, if I have done it without making him illegitimately responsible for my thesis) then it is apparent that there is a clear integration in Faulkner's fiction between how the story is told and what it means. If the chosen narrative method succeeds—builds just the box to contain just that genetic moment, and the moment before and the moment after—or even if it only constructs properly the "particular corner at hand," then the strategy and structure Faulkner has chosen to reveal or enclose the moment, or the box he has chosen for a particular set of "flesh-and-blood" people, must necessarily be crucial to our understanding of his fiction. One does not have to invoke some kind of mind-reading of the author's frequently irrelevant intentions to be able to distinguish between the narrator's functions as storyteller and as seer, so that it will be, I hope, apparent that narrative design and strategy (those qualities in which Faulkner was pleasing himself) take some of their aims and directions from the thematic and human force of the fiction. And, as I have suggested, strategy can determine timing, atmosphere, character, metaphor, and theme. Thus perhaps finite means of narrative strategy and design can be used by the critic to examine infinite ends of theme and substance.

Yet these "tools" and strategies have come in for remarkably little critical discussion—far less than the meanings, forces, and shapes of the "flesh-and-blood" living people which they control and enclose. Perhaps the most important reason for this is that narrative is exceptionally difficult to discuss without either lapsing into words of one syllable and invoking the Makars and bards or resorting to squirrelly diagrams in an attempt to describe variations in voice. Discussion of narrative tends to be impressionistic and can never claim to exhaust its subject, since, like language, its infinite variety is its chief beauty—or even to explain its own end, since the burden of art in the fiction lies beyond its narrative, which is only its means. Thus a critical judgment of narrative quality—the assertion that one narrative is "better" than another, can only be made in respect to its function, never in any absolute sense.

I am, nevertheless, going to attempt to discuss narrative. I cannot claim even to exhaust the available patterns in a single author. What

I have here is what has emerged from my reading of Faulkner's individual fictions and whatever general rules can be adduced to join one work to others in a common practice. To this I add some evolutionary estimates of the changes in narrative attention and design which develop as Faulkner's career proceeds. Theory of narrative in this study, then, is less an attempt to deal with narrative in general than it is an attempt to find a place to start discussion leading toward, as Addie Bundren says, a shape to fill a lack or fit a need.

In order to discuss narrative at all, I have had to resort to some abstraction of means from ends and, ignoring my own caveat, to employ words of one syllable at times and indulge in squirrelly graphs at others. Throughout I have had to emphasize minor technique and detail beyond major import and meaning, and I have been forced to subjugate whatever full-formed responses I have to the total impact of a story or novel to the more careful, isolated, and hence abstracted consideration of its purely narrative structure, strategy, and device. The abstraction becomes less extreme as the study progresses because I can build on reference to schemes and devices already discussed and because of the increasing complexity of the narrative strategy as Faulkner's career advances. I overstate, of course: one of the advantages of a study of narrative is that the act of telling embraces eventually all the attendant resources of literary effect. Discussion of narrative most frequently leads to lesser included systems and rather infrequently becomes an exclusive or self-sufficient pattern or grid. And, of course, as it was Faulkner's chosen center, it has primacy in being what *he* thought he was doing most of the time, no matter whether he called it "entertaining," building a "box," or plumbing the depths of the "anguishes, the courage, . . . the baseness and the splendor of man, of the human heart."

2 The Short Fiction

In Faulkner's short fiction the metaphor of the adaptable craftsman has its most readily apparent application. We can watch him developing the "germ" for "A Rose for Emily," for instance—the gray hair on the pillow—putting pressure on it to produce the moments leading up to it and the implications which follow from it, building just the "box" or "corner" which fits it perfectly. On the other hand, to think about *The Sound and the Fury* or *Absalom, Absalom!* as some kind of well-wrought box doesn't clarify much. With Caddy's muddy drawers as "germ" the process is more confused because the narrative is longer, more complex because every "corner" leads into another; the narrative strategy becomes difficult to see as a whole because it is made up of so many narrative tactics. The development of the young Thomas Sutpen at the big front door is even more difficult to see as it grows through the narrative because this is treated less as an aim—an ever-present "germ"—than as a starting point. Such boxes are master achievements of a developed craft, Duncan Phyfe highboys of narrative, marvels of detail, veneer, inlay, finishing, the harmonious mixture of different materials, while the short stories are the napkin rings or tie-racks whacked out in seventh-grade manual training.

The analogy is too extreme. *The Sound and the Fury*'s complexity is not adequately spoken to by the design and finish of a Phyfe, nor is the subtlety of workmanship of "Emily" or "Dry September" properly conveyed by the crudeness of the napkin ring. But the point of the analogy is clear: tools are used and materials cut and finished in a clearer, simpler, and more overt manner in the smaller than in the larger product. Criticism of the smaller, then, might lead to principles for clarification of the larger.

Faulkner calls "A Rose for Emily" a ghost story because he wants to emphasize the story's simplicity. The label has done the story a disservice, not because it is inaccurate but because it implies that "Emily" can be dismissed with Faulkner's approval as "gothic" or "a simple little horror." This is not so much unfair to "Emily" as it is to the ghost story as genre and the mastery and technique necessary to make its simplicity work.

The ghost story is an almost perfect instance of collaboration between Teller and Hearer—an instance the more readily available to us because most of us have experienced it in the oral tradition. Even the most casual Teller of an improvised ghost story wants (and needs) belief in his events, so he must have verisimilitude; he wants (and needs) suspense, so he must—in order to resolve that suspense and complete the pattern, give us satisfaction—have a climax. The Hearer must be enabled to predict the climax, since that is half the fun of suspense, but the Teller must be able to suspend it from the Hearer until he wants to spring it. The rules for casual storytelling here carry over almost directly into the generic rules for formal fiction of the supernatural. The heart of the ghost story is suspense and the essence of suspense is order. Revelations are controlled, our involvement and identification are managed, we are led along.

The telling of such a story in the first person (witness Poe or almost any fantasy up to and including *Gulliver's Travels*) supports all these desires and needs of the Teller. The Teller's involvement in the events, because he is here now, with us, telling it, makes us believe. His voice gives the tale verisimilitude—but the first-person voice also calls upon empathy—our identification with his hopes, fears, emotions, and concerns. We grant him cooperation by being scared and by being controlled, and he calls upon our fears and desires for fear on the one hand and upon our reason and our scientific ability to explain away our fears on the other. The two chief components of the ghost story are death and decay in the Subject—set at greater distance from the Hearer than in most other stories—and our sense of empathetic participation as Hearers with the Teller.

I emphasize the desire for fear and horror, the Hearer's demands. To submit to a ghost story is to want to be frightened or horrified as surely as to submit to a shaggy-dog story is to want complications and incredible, illogical connections, and to submit to any joke is to want to laugh. We move in the Teller's chosen patterns because we have entered into a contract with him to be frightened, to join with him in obtaining evidence. We grant belief, insist on our disbelief, need and demand a conclusion or resolution to the pattern of mounting horror and final denouement.

These demands determine some generic characteristics: simplicity, verisimilitude, and precision in suspense that is almost mechanistic. All the shotguns must be fired in the proper order and the narrator must play it straight. The rule of the shotgun is simple and mechanical: if the Teller drags an object into view it must be used. We must both be allowed our anticipation—be given everything that would enable us to figure it out for ourselves—and be granted its fulfillment—the comfort of expectation satisfied or the happy surprise of expectation overturned. The Teller must play according to the rules. Generally speaking (Mr. Albee to the contrary), shotguns ought not to become popguns. Faulkner is more than fair in "Emily." He gives us every opportunity to anticipate his denouement, in theme, in the peculiar time sequence, even by direct suggestions. The shotguns (the poison, the smell, the graying of her hair, among others) are all in a row.

The standard thematic trappings of the ghost story are laid out in the first paragraph, which has a death, a funeral, and a fallen monument. They become even more overt in the second: a house that had "once been white," encroached upon and obliterated by garages and cotton gins, now in decay; and again, the death of Emily, the names in the cemeteries, the anonymous graves of soldiers. The love of death, the love of the gruesome, the smell of death and decay are all contrasted with love of life and love for love; the isolation of Emily's decay is contrasted to the community of the life of the town, its busy curiosity.

The other necessary element is apparent very soon. The story is told by an unspecified first-person speaker, apparently an individual, but one who always speaks as *we*. He gains our allegiance gradually, beginning with "our whole town," then moves on to "we believed," or "people in our town." There is a strong infusion of *we*s near the end of part 2, and some in part 3. At the beginning of part 4 a rhythm is established which drives to the climactic string of twenty-nine *we*s in the last two sections. And this empathetic participation with the narrator keeps us from anticipating the specific death and decay of the climax: we join with him to amass evidence, evaluate gossip, draw conclusions, reject suspicions. We elect as our own his view of Emily (or as he always puts it here, *our* view, the collective view of the town).[1]

But in this process we are given every opportunity to take another point of view. Subgroups within the town join the narrator or disagree with him: "the young," "the old," "the men," "the women," "ministers and doctors," "law and force," "the Board of Aldermen," then "some of the ladies," "some of the men," finally "daughters and granddaughters of Colonel Sartoris's contemporaries." The groups are definite, their characteristic opinions are cited, and we can agree or disagree with them. If we elect to join the narrator even though other opinions are open to us, we are free to do so in the way that the man called up from an audience is free to choose any one of a number of cards from the hand of a magician. Faulkner directs the choice. We join the narrator not just because of the automatic alliance of the first person (all those appealing *we*s) and not just because of our desire for fear, but because he makes sense, because he is tough-minded, because his imagination and expectation seem more objective than the other options offered us. He sifts evidence and imagines disaster, horror, decay, and death, and we need to complete the pattern in a culminating disaster. Cassandra is appealing not just because she is here now, or because she is tough-minded and says it well, or because she turns out to be right: she is appealing because she sees the horror and in response to her we yearn to get to the horror.

The peculiar time scheme supports this alliance. Shifts in time call upon us as readers to share—eventually almost to create—a memory. First there are three shifts back to the beginning of the chronological sequence: we begin the story at the death, move back to 1894, then to the "smell," and finally to Emily at thirty. Then we move forward in time in ten much less abrupt, much more natural jumps. Naturally we remember what we have been told of events during our backward movement, and we join the narrator in mutual memory as we move forward: Emily at thirty, with her father, with Homer, with the servant, with the taxes, and so on. But as the web of incident becomes more complex, we supply conclusions based not only upon

1. What follows is, in part, parallel to the discussion of this story in Cleanth Brooks and Robert Penn Warren, *Understanding Fiction* (New York: Appleton-Century-Crofts, 1943), pp. 411–12. I deal with the first-person plural narrator in considerably more detail.

our induced memory but upon our suspicions and fears formed by landmarks in the narrative (such as the smell) by our sense of the decline in Emily's life and of the general movement toward horror. Ground is covered twice not just for the sake of familiarity, to make us inseparable from the people of Jefferson, but for the ominous and inexorable function of repetition in foreshadowing disaster. This is sometimes combined so effectively with false temporary conclusion (for instance, that the smell was a dead snake) that we are for the moment fooled. But we retain our faith in the narrator because his general tendency is downhill toward disaster, and even if he slips now and then into optimism or into a simple explanation for something that turns out to be most complex, he has clearly separated himself from the saccharine, sentimental, or romantic conclusions of "some of the ladies" and other groups. A "dead snake" is tough-minded; in a thematic sense it *is* a dead snake that makes the smell.

Finally a sociological pattern supports the story's impetus. I have never been very impressed by the arguments of that school of criticism—perhaps best and worst represented by the final *TIME* cover story on Faulkner—which holds that Faulkner spent his life understanding the South in the manner of a data-gatherer, that Jefferson is Elmtown or Middletown in Transition, that Faulkner's sexual grotesques taken as a group form some sort of fictionalized Kinsey Report, or that Emily and Homer, if we *really* understand the story, make some sort of allegory for the South and the North. Faulkner is an artist, not a census-taker, and to read his books for what they have to say about the South is, for me, a kind of intellectual embezzlement—somewhat like using a copy of *Hamlet* to solve a crossword puzzle.

Nevertheless, social attitudes are an inescapable part of Faulkner's subject matter. His characters tend to be fully formed: they not only have noses and skin colors and clothes, but social classes, snobberies, prejudices, and confusions. Miss Emily is of the "high and mighty Griersons," who always "held themselves a little too high for what they really were." As "the last Grierson," she was formed in an aristocratic ethic which, for instance, "would not think seriously of a Northerner, a day laborer." Emily was "a real lady," and the process of the story, our yearning for disaster, our empathy with the attitudes of "our town" is in part our resentment of this "high and mighty," "real lady" aristocracy. Once we as readers are joined with "our town" in empathy—once we adopt a few attitudes, some mem-

ories, and some suspicions, the attitude of "the ladies" and "the old people" becomes our snobbish monkey's paw—when they say she is high and mighty, *we* will tend to agree, even though we will not say it aloud. They can regard her aloofness as a choice not to be of *us,* as a haughty disdain, and we can half believe them even though *we* —the tough-minded, objective *we*—wouldn't have come right out and said it.

That Emily is isolated, that she is high and mighty, becomes an element in a folk-myth of hybris. Tragedy does not deal with noble figures just so that we can say "If it is thus even for him, how will it be for us?" but so that we can yearn for the leveling which results from disaster. Horror will make equals of us all. And our relish for each disclosure of decay, initiated by the ghost-story pattern and cultivated by narrative empathy, is given immense force by this desire for equalizing the mighty or the isolated or the odd—a force which we later look back on with added horror because of what we have become in so desiring decay, helping it along. *We* surrounded Emily with attitudes which isolated her and perhaps forced her desperate love and its extreme end.

The metaphors of the story move beyond their atmospheric support of the aura of death and decay to emphasize this isolation. The house, "lifting its stubborn and coquettish decay above the cotton wagons and the gasoline pumps," with its "cupolas and spires and scrolled balconies in the heavily lightsome style of the seventies" (*SS,* p. 119) is an emblem of this isolation: Emily is a still point in a rushing world, isolated by time, by fashion, by encroachment. The first, unforgettable physical description ("She looked bloated, like a body long submerged in motionless water, and of that pallid hue. Her eyes, lost in the fatty ridges of her face, looked like two small pieces of coal pressed into a lump of dough," *SS,* p. 121) is followed by less and less direct description. But as the story advances Faulkner transforms her by metaphor, by figures which increasingly objectify and distance her. The metaphors' vehicles are human stereotypes or objects seen at a distance, awe- or worship-inspiring. In the window she is an "upright torso motionless as that of an idol," then "a slender figure in white" (*SS,* p. 123), later "like a girl, with a vague resemblance to those angels in colored church windows—sort of tragic and serene" (*SS,* p. 124). She has a "lighthouse-keeper's face" (*SS,* p. 125), and a "face like a strained flag" (*SS,* p. 126). Finally she becomes, in the window again, "like the carven torso of an idol in a niche" (*SS,* p. 128). This distancing clearly completes the pattern established in the manipulated allegiances of narrative empathy: there is now the *us* of the narrator, the *almost us* of the town's subgroups, the *almost them* of the visiting cousins, Emily's father, Homer Barron, and the silent (and more than a little spooky) servant, and the *them* of Emily: object of our attentions, subject of our fears, idol of our hope for decline and decay.

The alienation of *them* by *us* is completed by our final guilt at the end of the story. We get into the house—as "most of the women" were dying to do at the beginning. As caretakers of a kind of public probity, of the tradition, duty, care, and hereditary obligation of Miss Emily and all she stands for, we seek out that "one room in that region above stairs . . . which would have to be forced" (*SS,* p. 129) and so complete is our cooperation, so headlong our relish for the horror beyond, that we not only force it without once questioning *why* it must be forced, but we participate in the violence which forces it—we literally break down the door. We find a tomb, a rose color, a frozen moment like Miss Havisham's bridal chamber, and in perhaps the most brilliantly economic instance of Faulkner's exercise of stopped-action description, the things we see are frozen each for a moment like stills spliced into a movie. Faulkner and the narrator pile horror upon horror in a tour de force of climactic revelation. We see the man himself; then that he is "in the attitude of an embrace" (*SS,* p. 130); then that he is in a nightshirt; then the indentation of a head on the second pillow; finally a long strand of iron-gray hair; the "germ" is the ultimate climax. It is a climax similar to the end of Beethoven's Third: we think he can't keep it up and then he delivers yet another blast. The last shotgun is triggered by the last word of the story.

A little shocker, an exercise in Southern gothic which simultaneously defines the mode of Southern gothic, replaces its predecessors and tops all subsequent attempts at its horror. It is also a tour de force of narrative which moves the story far beyond the impact expected of a short story, not just through thematic power, but because the consistent interplay of themes of death and decay and counter-themes of romance and love support and are supported by the carefully calculated narrative strategy: an active engagement by the reader, empathy which amounts to participation, an eagerness for denouement which begins as a formal and conventional response and ends as participatory guilt and conviction. We brought Emily to this end as surely as "our town" did, because we elected to be of that town, to have its memories, to patronize Miss Emily, to envy her standing and long for her fall, to drive finally with violence into the secrecy of her tragic isolation.

Viewed in one way, this "corner" is built almost mechanically, calling upon the conventional forms and responses of the nineteenth century; but seen in another way, the calculation and construction of the story is by no means simple. Faulkner involves us in a complicated initiation into a group by means of calculated alienation from other groups and an elaborate shuffling of chronology. Then a classic reversal worked on our empathy with the no-nonsense Teller brings us to a sudden identification with the Subject. Empathy with "our town" is instantly converted to empathy with the hitherto distanced individual. Thus our conventional response of empathy with the first-person narrator is only a prelude for our ultimate response to the isolated Subject. Conventional empathy is used to introduce unconventional reversal.

Most of the central concerns of narrative strategy can be seen in "Emily," although some are here in rather crude form: managed and variable narrative distance, the cultivation of variant empathies, the function of time and timing (including the relationship of present events to the burden of the past), technique as denouement. The way they all function together determines a complex narrative "plot" of strategy, characterization, rendering, metaphor. The indeterminate ends of meaning are manipulated by the calculation of determinate means.

Given his "germ," Faulkner was faced with the problem of where to stand and how much to tell. Just the simple choice of where to stand offers a plethora of options. Some of these slight variations—like the Japanese sex manual with its stick figures or contorted artist's lay-figures to detail the varieties of position—are less productive of understanding or pleasure than of abstraction and ingenuity. The test comes to be what slight variation, the angle of an elbow or the turn of a foot, can produce what can be called and numbered a new position, while true variety, the aim of description in the first place, gets lost in the boring enumeration of slight and essentially meaningless variation. There are a finite number of narrative positions: narrator dominant, subject dominant, and so on. But more important than the slight variations of method and the possibilities of classifying them are the possible combinations of psychological connection and distance between the Teller, the told, and the told-about. These determine the story: connections of sympathy, empathy, and identification; distances of the same sort and, in addition, those of mode, tone, formality, irony, humor, and style.

"Emily" is an extreme in the manipulation of these psychological distances, but having its extreme before us may make it simpler to trace the central narrative concerns. Most important in the story—a side-effect of the decision on where to stand—is the use of the group or community and its relationship to the isolated individual. Faulkner without a group is without a point of reference essential for his most effective narrative. Yoknapatawpha provides not just a useful and convenient "cosmos," as he said, but a readymade set of groups for experiments in interaction between them and individuals, in the parochialism or universality of limited environment, in shared and unshared human values. The group can be a family or a family with its retainers (as the Bundrens, the Compsons, and the Sartorises); or it can be a whole town (sometimes with the heavy guidance and interpretation of an elite group), as in "Hair" or *Light in August;* or it can be a combination of family, town, and savants, as seen in *Absalom, Absalom!* or the Trilogy. There are smaller, more special units—the hunting camp of *Go Down, Moses,* the Indians of the short stories, the fliers of the World War I stories, or even veterans in general as they line up against the civilian world. Even two-man alliances, such as Shreve and Quentin, the "contemporaries," or Cass Edmonds and Ike, can take on some of the functions of group.

Once the group is set up a variety of possibilities is open: the individual can be isolated by his own group (Eula, Quentin, Caddy, Darl, Minnie of "Dry September"), or if he is an outsider, he can be isolated by the insiders (Temple, Joe Christmas, Flem). Faulkner can calculate his narrative to develop either our kinship with the group majority against the isolated individual (*us* versus *them* in "Dry September" or the Trilogy) or, by showing that majority for what it is, to attract our sympathies to the isolated individual (*them* versus *us* in "That Evening Sun" or *Light in August*) or, as in "Emily," he can develop both alliances in sequence. Our relationship to the in-group or to the one isolated may be varied and manipulated with almost infinite variety by the method Faulkner chooses to spin out the story, his decisions on what to tell, where to stand, what intermediary voices he as Teller chooses to interpose between himself and us or between Subject and Hearer.

To be brought into the group (as a character within a story or as a reader being cozened into an empathetic relationship) is to be subjected to exposition in lieu of initiation: information and background are the ritual. Such initiation is a part of a larger function of initiation in Faulkner's fiction. Initiation can be device, strategy, theme, metaphor, or theory of fiction, or it can combine several of these functions. To realize the variety of these interactions, compare the initiation of Temple Drake, Joe Christmas, or Shreve with that of Ike McCaslin.

There has been almost too much thematic discussion of initiation in *Go Down, Moses* and especially in "The Bear," but perhaps the process is less apparent in *Light in August* or *Absalom, Absalom!* Compare for a moment the overtly thematic initiation in *Go Down, Moses* with that of *Absalom, Absalom!* Ike's initiation by Sam Fathers into the ways of the woods is far less subtle than Bon's initiation of Henry, the exposure of his "photographic plate" in the silken chambers of New Orleans. But more subtle still is Quentin's initiation of Shreve to the whole Sutpen saga and Shreve's initiation of Quentin to the full implications of their collaborative invention. I digress here from the smaller "corners" of short fiction, but I think it is important to emphasize just at this point some of the distant and thematic implications of the simple and technical matters at hand. Narrative strategy is not just a tool: in the case of initiation it is frequently the embodiment of theme.

Even beyond this, initiation has a special meaning for the whole of Faulkner's fiction. The canon can be seen as in-group initiation: if you've read one story or novel, you might as well go on to read all the rest. The carryover of theme, character, and event between one and the next provides a residual effect and gives the initiated reader the advantage over the uninitiated. This accounts in part for all those Faulkner handbooks: to follow characters from one book to another one needs, apparently, a DeMolay or a Chi Psi ritual handbook. The assumption is that every story or novel can count on its function as a small piece of a big puzzle. I don't mean to suggest Malcolm Cowley's view of the canon, the "planks cut from the still living tree," because I have some strong reservations about the formal difficulties which arise from that view. Rather I would suggest that although we want to know everything about the postage-stamp of native soil, we need not be told it right away. This can be a strong incentive both to encyclopedic and familiar telling and to active, attentive, and patient hearing. The story or novel seeks its formal unity and structure on its own, but the habits and conventions of Faulknerian narrative can develop and build from story to story and from novel to novel.

"A Courtship," for instance, develops the "our town" technique in a reminiscent framework and counts on a certain amount of allegiance to the insiders, or enough desire for information about insiders to get through the story. "This is how it was in the old days, when old Issetibbeha was still the Man, and Ikkemotubbe, Issetibbeha's nephew, and David Hogganbeck, the white man who told the steamboat where to walk, courted Herman Basket's sister" (*SS*, p. 361). The introit has a double function. Each story must start, proceed, and end on its own in order to be a story. To catch the reader off guard with facts or events alien to him is to induce strong suspense in him because he will naturally want to fill in ellipses. In this respect, the opening is an assumption of a kind of prior knowledge, a beginning in the middle of things, the suspense by omission characteristic of almost all of Faulkner's fiction. But in the scheme of the whole group of Indian stories (a group that has some trouble hanging together because of internal inconsistency), the opening is an invitation to work upon prior knowledge, to have a comfortable feeling of recognition and familiarity. The steamboat is a catchword, the Indian names perform not only their alliterative and rhythmic function but also their function as cues in the chronicle. "A Courtship" operates with the aura of a golden age somewhat tarnished by realistic detail. Faulkner's Indians always do. They are never seen in their prime, in a state of noble simplicity, but are always at one stage or another of a decline into cultural assimilation. Casting backward in search of purer ideals results only in the certainty that one would have to cast even farther backward for true purity. This kind of reminiscence is more productive than any of Faulkner's rueful reminiscences of World War I (this is what they were and because of this they became what they are).

But this reminiscence is not without the strong sense that a time even only slightly less corrupt was better. Quentin Compson is the reminiscent onlooker for "A Justice" and he seems almost an irrelevant choice. The standard question asked of exposition, "Why are you telling me all this?" gets a heavy accent on the *you* when we first read this story. We can easily shrug off the question by reflecting on the small population of Yoknapatawpha in 1931 when Faulkner wrote the story: he needed a boy, Quentin was the boy he knew best. In his continual return to Quentin, though ("That Evening Sun," *The Sound and the Fury, Absalom, Absalom!*), as in his returns to Gavin Stevens, V. K. Ratliff, and Lucas Beauchamp, there is more than a little suggestion of fondness—not of Hemingway's fond need for Nick Adams, which is primarily subjective, but of a delight at the flexibility and variety in his objective characters as created. There is also the suggestion of the initiation and carryover principle I have described. Quentin lets Sam Fathers tell the bulk of the story (as in "Centaur in Brass," a hint that the story is somewhat uncertain where it is going) but at the end there is a statement which clarifies not just the peculiar choice of narrator but a more general essential in Faulkner's fiction.

> We went on, in that strange, faintly sinister suspension of twilight in which I believed that I could still see Sam Fathers back there, sitting on his wooden block, definite, immobile, and complete, like something looked upon after a long time in a preservative bath in a museum. That was it. I was just twelve then, and I would have to wait until I had passed on and through and beyond the suspension of twilight. Then I knew that I would know. But then Sam Fathers would be dead. [*SS*, p. 360]

To hear about the old time from a participant and to be able to understand it all at once is a dream only fiction can accomplish. The problem of reminiscent narrative and contemporary understanding is involved in "That Evening Sun," all of the Indian stories, *Absalom, Absalom! Go Down, Moses,* and *The Reivers* (a partial list). Narration—the telling and the hearing—is only a first step. One man's narrative is only a first step. Understanding depends on the fusion of this first step in the Hearer with the total image of the action as it emerges from the story. The Indian stories generally are an exercise in the unsaid, in compression, elision, cultural distance, and the excerpted legend. Putting this particular tale in Quentin's mouth fuses its meaning to his life but to a certain extent suspends it from us.

But there is an even subtler thematic function in this initiation. The end and aim of Faulkner's telling is not just that we be manipulated by the particular story in just the way he wants so as to give his "germ" maximum impact, nor even just that we become familiar citizens of his county moving among all those people with ease and understanding. Initiation is not just manipulative tactic or technique of inductive orientation but an introduction to a way of reading human actions, an introduction to a function of literature as Faulkner sees it. Revelation of what who did when and what resulted, no matter what its thematic point, is maybe not as important to Faulkner as is the whole process of curiosity, skill, and delight in the Teller, and receptivity, demand, and ratiocination in the Hearer. Both Teller and Hearer must be the best of gossips—not just in the usual sense of communication and characterization but in the sometimes neglected analytical function of gossip. The best of gossip, as well as "the best of all listening," is directed not just at the exchange of information but at the understanding of character, action, motivation, and structure. What the Hearer can put together from what the Teller gives him so that he can make it fit with everything he knows already is a difficult function of narrative manipulation. The story as told is a part of this suspension of meaning, the narrative presence's gathering of information which leads to the story is a part. The various meanings which different Hearers take away from a given story demonstrate that a story is a suspension of fake facts, a framework of possible readings, a net in which to catch meaning rather than just a compendium of fake fact, reading, or meaning itself.

This use of clever gossip and collective consciousness is seen in two "gossip" stories. In "A Bear Hunt" the "our town" function is performed in shorthand. The introduction comes from an unspecified voice and joins us to the town's concerns; this acts as a frame for the tale told by Ratliff about Lucius Provine. The opening gently leads us as outlanders into the story, fills us in on details we might not get otherwise, in a familiar, let-me-show-you-around-town way. Then the personality does the rest. Ratliff, more than any of Faulkner's other characters, is both narrative technique and "our town" personified. He has more than a little of that characteristic of the Southern woman Faulkner dwells on in Rosa Coldfield and Tennessee Williams dealt with dramatically in Amanda Wingfield—the indiscriminate, overliteral mind, a mind careless but far from ignorant of our sense of what is essential and relevant. Ratliff, like Rosa and Amanda, toys with these senses, but unlike them he controls his digression. He uses his advantage of information to cultivate our sympathy, he infuriates us with digression just long enough and then he plays his ace. His storytelling depends upon the assumption that his hearers have a common background of information and that Provine is known to them. Like Faulkner, he is willing to cheat a bit to improve his story.[2]

As it turns out, Ratliff alone could not accomplish what this story aims to do. He needs the "our town" introduction to provide a connection which could only appear there. The anecdote of the celluloid collars connects the apparently irrelevant Old Ash to the hiccup-cure and makes the story's climax possible. It would have spoiled Ratliff's (and Faulkner's) story if Ratliff had been the one to tell us about that bit of ancient history, but his collaboration with the "our town" introduction makes possible suspense and its resolution. Faulkner designates Ratliff to build this particular corner, but there is a part he can't complete without the help of an undesignated narrative presence.

"Hair" seems at first to work on the "our town" framework; it even has a hint of the "Emily" subgroups ("Some said that Susan was a niece. . . . Women mostly, these were," *SS*, p. 131). But it turns out to be dependent on the "our town" assumptions of familiarity without the "our town" initiation which compelled us through "Emily." The narrator (unspecified, but almost certainly Surratt-Ratliff again) addresses us as familiar Hearers but feels no obligation to bring us up to date, because "Hair" is a story of outlanders. We are expected to know Ratliff's informants and to be quite concerned with which of them told him which part of what he knows ("Maxey told me. No; it was Matt Fox, the other barber, told me that. He was the one," *SS*, p. 132). Ratliff pushes the process of information-gathering to the surface to cultivate our familiarity, our empathy, our alliance. But here, unlike "A Bear Hunt," the confident, familiar teller is outfoxed. Hawkshaw-watching is similar to Emily-

2. The first time he tells it, his words on seeing Provine return are, "Well, you ought to be satisfied. You done run clean out from under them." When he comes back around in his narrative to that moment again, he says, "Anyway, you done run out from under them hiccups" (*SS*, pp. 67, 76).

watching in that it produces some of the same desire for downfall (if not disaster) in the barber's long courtship. But instead of drawing our desires through to disaster and resultant guilt, here Faulkner surprises us with a reversal, demonstrating again the flexibility of the "our town," *them–us,* in-group–outlander technique. At the end, with Stevens holding the final piece of information which will complete the story, Ratliff runs through his (and our) ending as we might expect it to work out at its worst: " 'Only the girl went bad on him,' I said. 'Forty-five's pretty late to set out to find another. He'll be fifty-five at least by then' " (*SS,* p. 147). The Stevens mannerisms, overextended and perhaps tedious in the Trilogy, here work perfectly to maintain suspense. Ratliff is confident in his information, ready to give it, to make ironic comment upon it, ready to draw the story to the ending he has made for it; and he is a perfect foil for Stevens, who is saving for his last line the information which will blow Ratliff's whole theory sky-high. Our favorite guide turns out to be a faulty witness. Hawkshaw gets the girl and the end doesn't surprise but gratifies: it proves Ratliff wrong in his "realist" assumptions—assumptions characteristic of his manner but not of his sympathy, characteristic of the worst of our fear–desire for downfall—and we are pleased when they turn out to be groundless. The conclusion of the story gratifyingly defies the premises of its method.

The flexibility inherent in this technique does not, perhaps, need to be underlined. The familiar community interlocutor can encourage our adoption of the town's point of view and gain all the benefits which are to be had from collaboration and joint discovery ("Emily," "A Bear Hunt"), or he can assume we need no introduction and move along with us, comfortable in his assumptions, only to overturn our expectations as he, Faulkner's intermediary voice, turns out to be wrong. "Hair" is a prime example, but this function of "faulty witness" is also seen in "the investigator from Jackson" in "The Tall Men," in Bogard's condescension for the young "navy egg" in "Turn About," and (rather crudely handled) in Jarrod of "Dr. Martino." A combination of both these functions of "our town" is essential to the peculiar rhetorical use of groups in *Light in August* and one of the central structural characteristics of the Trilogy. Familiar interlocutors bearing the truth become faulty witnesses and vice versa. "Our town" can be either (or both) comforting community and crucible for evil.

The use of gosssip as the backbone of these stories is acknowledgment of Faulkner's roots in the oral tradition. Not only is storytelling fertile subject matter and mode for the fiction, but as his comments in *Faulkner in the University* and *Lion in the Garden* suggest, it is the theoretical basis of his idea of the function and uses of fiction. This could seem to be no more than the guff of his gallus-snapping persona until one realizes how far gossip and anecdote can carry one into the functions of narrative technique.

Any cliché-collector listening to a group of gossips can come up with evidence that both Teller and Hearer in informal storytelling have some of the same rules and responsibilities as the formal artists of fiction and some of the same possibilities of multiple technique and variations in combination. The informal storyteller's asides reveal his concerns: "But what you have to know first . . ." is a concern of exposition; "You should have seen the expression on his face . . ." for rendering and characterization; "I shouldn't try to do *him,* but I will anyway" for characterization in dialogue or first-person narration. Rendering of physical reality comes in with "You had to be there . . . " or "Right there on the table in front of me was . . ."; timing in "There was a long pause . . ."; "Imagine my surprise . . ." gives a hint of need for empathy; and "I've spoiled the punchline . . ." or "I ruined it . . ." or "But I just gave it away . . ." are admissions of the failure of narrative strategy or suspense-plotting. The Hearer's interjection of "You must be lying . . . ," "I don't believe it . . . ," and "It's like a novel . . ." verify the dignity of the Teller's contribution to the bare bones of his story; "What's the point? . . . ," "Oh, get on with it . . . ," "But I thought you said . . ." are all the severest critiques of the Teller's skill; but "Meanwhile what was *x* doing?" "How did it all end?" "What time of day was it?" or "And then what happened?" can be the eager cries of a Hearer in pursuit of the oral anecdotal art, testimony that the Hearer's demands function in and form any story that is told. "If you see him, get *him* to tell it . . ." is an admission that literary skill is involved even in ephemera such as this, and that some Tellers are better than others. The clichés "spinning it out," "running it into the ground," "going on and on," "sketching in the background," and taking "all the parts when he told it" are testimony to the connection between martini-holders and lyre-thumpers.

Most of the simple variations of technique are available to the informal Teller, too, at least with the more skillful (or the more affected) practitioners. First-person imitation, third-person distance, and mixed technique for difficult subject matter can be heard here and there. What I would emphasize, even for such rudimentary narrative, is that telling is always a two-way street. In third-person narrative there is not only, from the Teller's side of things, the directions of narration:

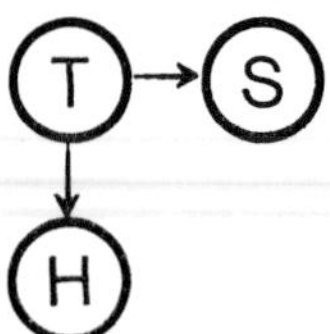

but, from the Hearer's side, the directions of attention, demand, and control:

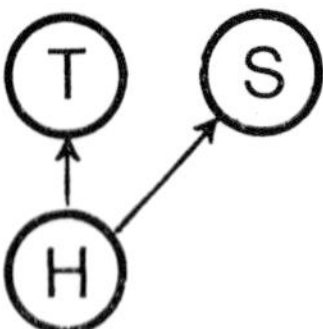

In first-person narrative, similar lines influence the telling and what is told:

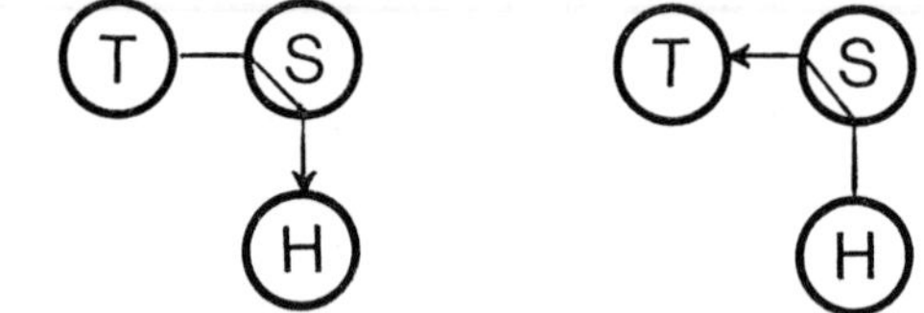

These are the standard shapes. If we were to move from simplistic anecdote to rather more sophisticated written narrative, even the simplest story, "A Rose for Emily," starts to take on the complexity of a flow-diagram.

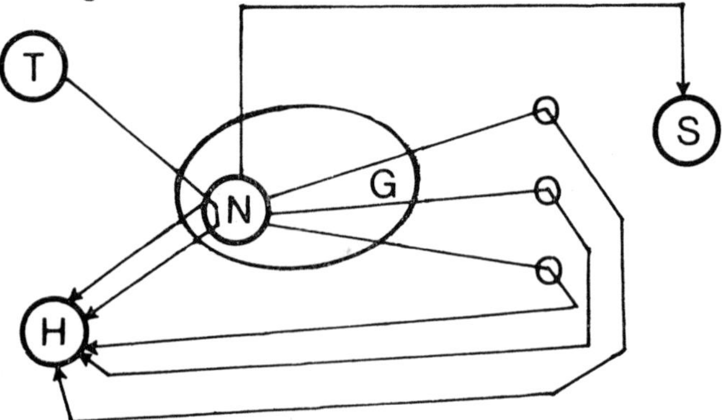

A diagram to cover all of the narrative resources, devices, and tools of *Light in August* would be hopelessly complex, and a full treatment of *Absalom, Absalom!* would probably resemble one of those twenty-foot-long diagrams of the history of the world drawn up to justify the Scriptures. But it is clear that *Absalom, Absalom!* depends upon Hearer–Teller exchange. The novel, whatever its complexities, explores the necessity to tell, the compulsion to alter in the hearing, and the resultant obligation to order and understand the various altered versions. It is Faulkner's prerogative to choose the optimum terms of suspension, revelation, connection, overtness, allegory, and given meaning—to suspend the action in just the amber which will best promote not necessarily our understanding but our fascination. Hair, straws, dirt, grubs, worms can become jewels and objects of our fascinated examination and reexamination when suspended in the clear substance of contrivance, arrangement, voice, Teller, and Hearer. Surrounding and suspension is all. "A Justice" would not work if told to Ike McCaslin (whom we might well expect in the framing) because Quentin's final observation belongs peculiarly to that hope for perfection which finally leads to his despair. It must come to one imprisoned by time. And that it is conveyed to us by him colors our perception and memory of the story.

The point I am making, of course, is not that the narrator must be wondrously skillful in managing all this, but that description of the possible varieties is not as important as is a recognition of the complexity of the psychological variations in the exchange between Teller, Hearer, and Subject which attends all of them.

The Teller must hold the Hearer's attention or the Hearer will find an excuse to get another drink (or in literature, close the book or walk out of the play). He finds his appeals for such attentions somewhere between the fantasy of total invention and the bare but demanding minimum of the imitation of life. Both sides—the holding of the Hearer's attention by the Teller and the Hearer's demand of the story from his Teller—are in productive tension; neither can exist without the other. The Teller decides what to tell and what not to tell, but the Hearer must be considered at every point: he demands the story he is told as surely as the audience demands the play it is given and imposes all of the limitations, obligations, and necessities of genre on that form.

Although we are accustomed, because of the real presence of the audience at a play and the traditions of drama criticism, to grant it the Hearers' powers of generic determination, a similar acknowledgment in fiction is more difficult. The critic is immediately tempted to commercial snobbery (familiar in Faulkner criticism from implications that Faulkner was writing *for* the *Saturday Evening Post*) and to move immediately from the author's general intention to give pleasure into the designation of particular intentions for given stories or devices.

In a very strong sense, the Hearer-Teller pattern is not as much of an abstraction of Writer-Reader as the difference between the words might suggest. For Faulkner, "hearing" is less an analogy than it is a simplified description of a part of the narrative process. If Faulkner's insistence that he is only a "storyteller" is to be credited ("I'm telling a story . . . thus I stack and lie at times, all for the purposes of the story—to entertain"), then some of the functions of Hearer, clearly, are transferred to Reader. Some, of course—the immediacy of response, the Hearer's actual presence—will not apply to the "story" on a printed page, but it seems hardly necessary to appeal to more of Faulkner's "theory" to suggest that his first consideration is for the Reader in devising a narrative line or designing a narrative strategy. He wanted as much of the immediacy of hearing as possible to carry over to reading. The directness of his design, the strong (perhaps his strongest) root of his narrative in the oral tradition, in tale-swapping and gossip, all testify to this.

The functions of the group and its gossip, of initiation and carry-over, have carried us perhaps too far. A more fundamental question involved in "where to stand" is the basic choice between first- and third-person narration. It would be absurd to suggest that Emily Grierson tell her own story: for Faulkner's reversal and our ultimate guilt to operate she must be isolated and distanced. The choice of first or third person is more subtle than this suggests, though. First-person narration is a form of entrapment. The Teller, by moving into the Subject's mind and voice, submits to an imprisonment: he agrees to see and hear and tell and think nothing more than the Subject can see and hear and think, to tell nothing that could not have come out of his mouth.

Quentin Compson makes his other appearance in the short fiction in "That Evening Sun," and the method as well as its subtle adjustment to the substance and theme is carefully chosen. There is a reminiscent third-person framework, here apparently introduced for the sake of the atmospheric detail it contributes: it not only sets the story firmly in a semirural, agricultural period of social transition but also in a specified moment in the life of "our town." This is the story of a passing, a twilight—an ethos still surrounding the newly freed slaves. The reminiscence introduces a dated portrait of the Compson children as a group, and the dated quality of the portrait implies their passing as a unit—the passing of the family as a whole and of each in turn. Quentin's aim in his telling seems not so much to initiate us into any of this but, rather, to further his own initiation in a sense: to reconstruct perfectly a moment out of the past that he can then use to inform his present.

The first paragraph suggests a golden age—that we will very quickly pass to a simpler time. There is again encroachment, as in "Emily," but here it is machines and their products ("to make room for iron poles bearing clusters of bloated and ghostly and bloodless grapes," *SS*, p. 289). In the rest of the story Quentin strives for total recall; he pushes to recapture the tiniest detail in rendering the story of Nancy, searches for that simplicity, that perfect whole moment now safely sealed in the past, so that he may perhaps use it to explain what he and Caddy have become. In striving for such detail, he must become the young Quentin. He consciously adopts the persona of himself as a child so that the game will work, attempting to see and report the events as they were and as he was, rather than as they seem to the reminiscent eye: "Caddy said. . . . Nancy said. . . . Jason said. . . ." (*SS*, p. 290).

Faulkner often uses the child's restricted understanding in the short fiction, but here it contrasts to the reminiscent framework to give it far greater impact. The point of "That Evening Sun" is not that Quentin's restricted consciousness cannot see the point of the story, but that Quentin can now see everything of what, at the time, he saw almost nothing. He tells the story knowing the outcome of the Compsons (most intensely, of Caddy) and the import of Nancy's troubles, obscure to the children at the time. The force of the story is not just in what it tells, but in Quentin's obsession with its details. He dwells on each little point in his abstraction, his attempt to realize perfectly that time of innocence now lost. "Dilsey was still sick in her cabin. Father told Jesus to stay off our place. Dilsey was still sick. It was a long time. We were in the library after supper" (*SS*,

p. 292). Repetition and simplistic statement reproduce the breathless immediacy of young Quentin reporting the past as it happens, but they also represent the older Quentin, striving to get the sequence absolutely straight, filling in every detail. There is one curious lapse into his older voice:

> "Jason!" mother said. She was speaking to father. You could tell that by the way she said the name. Like she believed that all day father had been trying to think of doing the thing she wouldn't like the most, and that she knew all the time that after a while he would think of it. I stayed quiet, because father and I both knew that mother would want him to make me stay with her if she just thought of it in time. So father didn't look at me. I was the oldest. I was nine and Caddy was seven and Jason was five. [*SS*, p. 294]

But at the end of this passage he forces himself back into his adopted persona, determined to stay firmly within the ken of the young Quentin. The concentration of the narrative (somewhat similar to Ratliff's intensity when he means for us to ally ourselves with him and the town) here works as an incentive, not necessarily to join Quentin, but to share the intensity of things felt without knowing exactly where they will lead us and without understanding the obsession of their intensity.

The children's arguments and actions in the story begin as an "outside event"—familiar to any reader of fiction: one track of two or more simultaneous events of which the other seems at the time more important. They are irrelevant to what is happening at the center of the story, but they accidentally or innocently play and comment upon the dialogue of the central story, with Quentin—the ironic intercessor—never pointing out the irony, because it is vital to his aims to abstain from narrative interference. Only Caddy asks the right questions (which for Quentin as he reminisces must be an ironic commentary on her later development), but she does not know what they or the answers (when she gets answers) mean.

The children's arguments become more central as it becomes clear that this "outside event," has gained the upper hand. Nancy is dependent upon the children; their chatter is vital to her because their whims can determine whether or not she will be left alone. As soon as they realize this, Jason's habitual blackmail ("He cried until mother said he couldn't have any dessert for three days if he didn't stop. Then Jason said he would stop if Dilsey would make a chocolate cake," *SS*, p. 299) is topped by Caddy's subtlety: "We ought to go. . . . Unless we have a lot of fun' " (*SS*, p. 303). For Nancy this is a cruel threat because she believes it balances her between life and death.

The meaning of the story does not lie within the story as told but beyond it, somewhere in the contrasts and similarities between the children's arguments and the adults' concerns, between Quentin's reminiscent constructed innocence and his ironic commentary upon his current self, between the way in which white men use Nancy and make her a potential victim for Jesus and the children's use of Nancy when they sense she is desperate for their presence. Those contrasts convey fear, subtle cruelty, and unspoken terror, and these emotions combine with the story's obsessive narrative tone for an intense impact. The story is a brilliant example of the use of conventional narrative manipulation to achieve an unconventional end in indeterminate meaning. Faulkner uses "square" narrative devices to produce a very modern and indeterminate result.

The story is dramatic because so much of it depends on suspension and interpretation—our own understanding as readers and our reading of the story in the light of what we know of Quentin and the Compsons—and because so much of the story depends on that space between the adults' and the children's levels and on their dependence upon each other. But to appreciate the importance of the first-person method, try to imagine the story for a moment done as a drama. The reminiscent frame sets Nancy's dependence in a simpler time, when the issue of the white man's sexual use of black women is clearer and more overt but still not in the period of slavery, when it would become simply a cliché or an atrocity story. The reminiscence also renders in shorthand all of the distance between the Compsons as a unit and the Compsons in disintegration and between Quentin as a bland (but not, perhaps, an innocent) participant and Quentin as an ironic reconstructor. The story is a net designed for the purpose of suspending Nancy's ineffable isolation, and it does its job more clearly and more surely as designed than it could have in any other technique or any other form. With perhaps nothing to fear (the story never tells us if Jesus is in that ditch) [3] Nancy is the subject of per-

3. Apparently not, since she survives to care for the Gowan Stevenses' child in *Requiem for a Nun*.

haps the most intense fear in Faulkner's fiction, at the mercy of Jesus but, perhaps worse, subject to the whims of the Compson children.

Reminiscence, frequently criticized as Faulkner's failing, is here clearly used as a tool rather than just as a habit of mind. In "A Bear Hunt," reminiscence was a form of historical exposition, a means of bringing us into "our town." For "A Justice" it is one horn of a complex theoretical dilemma of fiction's ways of meaning. But in "That Evening Sun," reminiscence forces us with Quentin to try to know the unknowable and think about the unthinkable. Without the framework, Quentin's purpose would be unknown; without his purpose we could not find our way to the crux of the story, suspended in the distance of the undetermined. Faulkner *did* dwell on the past and he *did* have a nostalgic weakness, but in each of these stories, the backward glance is not taken just to be able to wallow in the past, but because that backward glance builds a particular "corner" for the essence he seeks. Reminiscence is, of course, a rich source of thematic meaning, but its essential function in narrative strategy ought not to be overlooked. Tool becomes meaning in such a way that it is impossible to assume that reminiscence is for Faulkner nothing more than habit or neurosis. The telling is part and parcel of what gets told.

Faulkner's child-narrators have been subject to similar confusion between habitual subject and useful tool. The children of his fiction have been justly praised; sometimes innocent but always unashamed, they represent at once his accuracy of transfer in consciousness and voice, and they represent, I suppose, his place in the mainstream of American writing—in what Fiedler calls the American child's garden of terrors, immature sexuality. But more important, they supply him with a battery of narrative tools. Vardaman, Ike and Lucius Priest, and their counterparts in the short fiction emphasize that the place and size of the child is as important as his voice and eye.

"That Will Be Fine" is perhaps the simplest example. What the child does not know acts as the end for the narrative means his age and limited understanding provide. His view is limited and the adult's world is excluded from his consciousness because he is too small, his angle is wrong and he is obsessed. This child is an exception to our more-or-less automatic identification with a child-narrator: he is a money-grubbing monster, with scarcely a hint of dawning consciousness. The story might, in other hands, have fallen into all the sentimental traps of nostalgia for its own sake, Penrod and Uncle Rodney, but instead the dominance of the boy's obsessive subjectivity, the clarity and unity of his total materialism—as only a child can be totally and irrevocably materialistic—obviate this possibility. Unpleasant things are happening, but the boy is completely unaware of them, lost in dreams of nickels and dimes and quarters. He himself is blind to the hints he gives us of the serious complications of Uncle Rodney's life, but we can read them clearly. Whether Rodney is killed or only maimed at the end of the story, the "side of meat" we see makes sharply real the consequences of the child's hitherto comic strivings after profit and turns the end of the story into a black sequence of sardonic cruelties. The adults, with a great deal more gusto than seems necessary (they continue to be heard in the comic mode even when the events have turned serious) deceive the child about the results of his actions. He waits for Christmas as he did at the beginning of the story, but with a much greater danger now of immediate disillusionment and sudden bitter maturity.

"Two Soldiers," "Shall Not Perish," and "Shingles for the Lord" all have similar aims—the suspension of remarkable events in the midst of commonplace routine. The former two are perhaps too gimmicky for serious discussion (read at our distance from World War II, the first is almost icky), but "Shingles" cannot be dismissed so easily. Somewhere between the adults' childishness about deals and swaps and the child's competence and familiar acceptance there is a gentle commentary, never overt, on business itself. The child understands work units and dog units and the system (*SS*, p. 29) and is as capable a narrator of the trading and deals as any adult. The only thing he lacks is a clear view of his father's excessive pride.

Flat descriptive sequences (*SS*, pp. 31, 33) frame the central action even as in "Shall Not Perish," but here the contrast is not between the simplicity of the everyday and the excess of the adults' wordy response to grief, but between the everyday of the work units and the extraordinary of the fire. The child has a mastery of both and can accept both in an immediate rendition which enables him to see as he would see and at the same time to show us what we want to see. I dwell on this in some detail because the child's view, the flat, stopped-action narrative of sudden event, is not just a hallmark of Faulkner's adeptness at role-taking but a characteristic of much of his action narrative in general.

> He laid back on the bar and this time it got a holt. It wasn't jest a patch of shingles, it was a whole section of decking, so that when he lunged back he snatched that whole section of roof from around the lantern like you would shuck a corn nubbin. The lantern was hanging on a nail. He never even moved the nail, he jest pulled the board off of it, so that it looked like for a whole minute I watched the lantern, and the crowbar, too, setting there in the empty air in a little mess of floating shingles, with the empty nail still sticking through the bail of the lantern, before the whole thing started down into the church. It hit the floor and bounced once. Then it hit the floor again, and this time the whole church jest blowed up into a pit of yellow jumping fire, with me and pap hanging over the edge of it on two ropes. . . . I don't remember climbing down. Jest pap yelling behind me and pushing me about halfway down the ladder and then throwing me the rest of the way by a handful of my overhalls, and then we was both on the ground, running for the water barrel. [*SS*, p. 39]

The tone of the passage is that of the child's acceptance of what happens. Observation of detail, selection, and relevance are integral functions of the way children see because they are more excited by just seeing and saying than adults are. But beyond that there is a gratified urge for adventure—something is really happening, not anything very good for anybody, but it's happening, it's happening right now, and that's different and exciting. It comes through the child's eyes and is directly set forth in his words, and each loving second separates itself from the next in discrete, orderly, stopped-motion detail. This sense of adventure is set against the everyday as the boy watches Whitfield's baptismal garment burn (*SS*, p. 40). The event of the burning cuts across the everyday and becomes a passing away of things, in which the child can almost understand the end involved in what is ending, but cannot keep from cherishing the excitement of the action involved in the ending while it is going on, so that he must isolate each precious moment of the burning, as he has of the fall of the lantern. This is connected to meaning: the garment is immanent in the world of belief—this too shall pass away. We are returned to something like the inexorable progression in "Two Soldiers," but here it leads to an endurance beyond any familiar progression or process.

> But there was something that even that fire hadn't even touched. Maybe that's all it was—jest indestructibility, endurability—that old man that could plan to build it back while its walls was still fire-fierce and then calmly turn his back and go away because he knowed that the men that never had nothing to give toward the new one but their work would be there at sunup tomorrow, and the day after that, and the day after that, too, as long as it was needed, to give that work to build it back again. So it hadn't gone a-tall; it didn't no more care for that little fire and flood than Whitfield's old baptizing gown had done. [*SS*, p. 42]

The existence of the church stands beyond the adults' work-units, dog-units, deals, and manipulations which the child has so surely mastered; and the contrast between the everyday and the frantic action of the fire, when cast in the child's narrative, reveals this in a way the same story told by the father never could have. Again I emphasize the tool represented by the child and his stopped-action narrative rather than the meaning he may impart. The point is not that the child's view has been captured by the narrative, but that Faulkner has calculated this narrative as a means to a more complex meaning without once carrying the boy's words beyond his understanding.

The "Two Soldiers–Shall Not Perish" child is just at the point of perceiving some adult complexities; the narrator of "Shingles" has passed through that stage but redeems his adult consciousness of complexity with an unexpected return to the child's excitement of innocence. In "That Will Be Fine" the child is brought just to the point of revelation but left there, uninformed, because Faulkner's strategy of narration finds more profit from the unknowing opposition of innocence and experience—even rather cruel dwelling on the blindness of innocence—than it could by carrying the child through to the next stage. This denouement is more acute in imperfect realization than it could have been had it been worked out to the full.

Each of these narrators demonstrates a very different use of the same basic narrative premise. The child sees action plain and delivers a flat, literal record of everything he sees as it happens, becomes a part of the process of seeing, because he is seeing the event and rendering it for its own sake. He renders transparently, with no adult bias to come between us and what is happening. This would be quite enough to satisfy Faulkner's first aim in fiction, the reader's pleasure, but he uses the child for much more. The child is in a situation which must end (he'll grow up, or find out, or be disillusioned). Sudden reversals are the rule rather than the exception, and since the reader from his own experience anticipates these sudden reversals, the threat of reversal can be almost as effective as reversal itself. This sure reader-identification is more automatic than any other. For the "our town" alliance to succeed there must be all sorts of feeding, coddling, and cultivation, even to achieve an artificial kinship. Few of us share Mississippi or even the South, and not all share the small town with Faulkner, but everyone comes from childhood. Our identification with the child's narrative is the natural by-product of the similarity between his childhood and ours, his adults and ours, his feelings and ours. And in most of these stories the involvement that comes from this empathy with the Subject is enforced by our involvement in their direct rendering of unassimilated, unquestioned action, a factor which also contributes to the success of *The Unvanquished,* the Trilogy, and *The Reivers.*

This tool, like the others, has thematic dividends. The child can transmit even what he cannot understand—and more. He can see without knowing ("That Will Be Fine"), know without seeing (Vardaman), feel without experiencing (Benjy), or experience without feeling (Joe Christmas), because of the double world he inhabits where everything is the wrong size for him and the rules make no sense. That children are archetypes of innocence is much less important than this pragmatic and technical flexibility they offer as narrative tools.

Probably the richest employment of these technical and thematic devices is seen in the child-narrator of "Uncle Willy," a story which also raises another essential strategic function. This boy has already passed from innocence to experience as the story begins. The opening lines crystallize the boy's—and the story's—awareness of both sides, both child's and adult's, innocent and experienced.

> I know what they said. They said I didn't run away from home but that I was tolled away by a crazy man who, if I hadn't killed him first, would have killed me inside another week. But if they had said that the women, the good women in Jefferson had driven

> Uncle Willy out of town and I followed him and did what I did because I knew that Uncle Willy was on his last go-round and this time when they got him again it would be good and forever, they would have been right. Because I wasn't tolled away and Uncle Willy wasn't crazy, not even after all they had done to him. . . . I went because Uncle Willy was the finest man I ever knew, because even women couldn't beat him, because in spite of them he wound up his life getting fun out of being alive and he died doing the thing that was the most fun of all because I was there to help him. [*SS*, p. 225]

This is simple, almost classic suspense by omission. But in "Uncle Willy," the child's impatience with his elders' assumption of his innocence gives us in the opening a sense of a more complex kind of adult cruelty than that of "That Will Be Fine," a condescension which talks down to the child's assumed innocence even as it is making the wildest assumptions about the adult "reality" of the situation.

As the story advances we make some comfortable assumptions drawn from previous experience with "our town." We respond conventionally to "the women, the good women in Jefferson" with a stock Huck Finn response. But then we are informed, rather matter-of-factly, that Uncle Willy is not just a run-of-the-mill ne'er-do-well but a dope addict. We have to adjust our response—not to "the women, the good women," but to Uncle Willy and the boys. We become more objective about the narrator—increase our distance from him—because we can't maintain the stock response he seems to expect. The tone of the narration differs from that which will characterize the "simple non-virtue" of *The Reivers*. This narrator lacks Lucius Priest's wholehearted delight and mixes what remains of our conventional natural empathy with the boy together with some rendering straight out of nightmare. The boy himself could have come from the pages of Thomas Bailey Aldrich; but his ideal —Uncle Willy—is out of Edgar Allan Poe.

> We had a league of three teams in town and Uncle Willy would give the prize, a ball or a bat or a mask, for each game though he would never come to see us play, so after the game both teams and maybe all three would go to the store to watch the winner get the prize. And we would eat the ice cream and then we would

> all go behind the prescription case and watch Uncle Willy light the little alcohol stove and fill the needle and roll his sleeve up over the little blue myriad punctures starting at his elbow and going right on up into his shirt. [*SS,* p. 226]

The child accommodates both of these visions with no difficulty, even as he can jump from the metaphor of his teacher's joke on April Fool's Day directly into Darl Bundren's departure for the insane asylum (*SS,* p. 228).

The last third of the story (as Willy is reduced from a dope addict to an alcoholic) gives up this mixed vision and adopts something much easier—a Faulkner stock figure and a literary cliché—perhaps because Willy was so appealing to that part of Faulkner which goes all squashy about individual independence. The Poe-Aldrich complexity returns only at the end in the triumphantly ambiguous metaphor:

> Because the dying wasn't anything, it just touched the outside of you that you wore around with you for comfort and convenience like you do your clothes: it was because the old garments, the clothes that were not worth anything had betrayed one of the two of us and the one betrayed was me, and Papa with his other arm around my shoulders now, saying, "Now, now; I didn't mean that. You didn't do it. Nobody blames you." [*SS,* p. 247]

Perhaps the clothes are those of the appearance of childhood, the assumptions of the adults throughout the story, that the child had been "tolled away," robbing him of whatever will he had in the matter. Or perhaps, in more difficult terms, they refer to Willy's use of the child—that Willy didn't confide in him and didn't take him along in the airplane because he was only interested in the child as a tool—that, in other words, Willy's interest in him was just what the adults had assumed. The clothes of childhood had betrayed him even with Willy.

Narrative strategy has found a new kind of suspension for this complex "corner." We are subjected by the story's assumptions to just the same adult, know-it-all assumptions that the child must suffer. But we are first the child, then the adult, then the child again. The puzzle of the first paragraph is solved in the last paragraph's ambiguity: the boy assumed that Willy saw him and prized him for what he was—a peculiar mixture of youthful eagerness and mature disregard for public mores; but the final paragraph reverses this. Willy had used him and assumed too much on his innocence. Suspense by omission here accomplishes a reversal of theme. We thought the story was one thing and it turns out in the last paragraph to be quite another. And yet more than that: the denouement of the story is accomplished by a solution of the narrative strategy.

I do not suggest that my peculiar reading is the only possible reading of the story—or that any special understanding of narrative is essential for the story to work. The plain events work well enough to give pleasure without any need to appeal to a complex reading of the "plot" or rhetoric of the narrative scheme. But for a moment, take another of Faulkner's stories—a much simpler, far more gimmicky example, "Artist at Home." It seems to be not much more than a cliché at first glance, but on further examination it is perhaps as close to pure narrative experiment as any of Faulkner's other stories. The tone of the opening is elusive—it seems always just about to judge the writer ironically, to take to task the everyday round of teas and autographs and nonwriting and tickety-boo farmhouse, to work satirically, but it continually slides away from the comment the reader expects. As the triangle of the writer, the poet, and his wife develops, the previously objective narrative presence unexpectedly begins to address us directly: "Now get this. This is where it starts" (*SS*, p. 634). Narrative distance narrows suddenly.

> She is watching him. Then she turns, walking fast. He follows, doping along a little behind her, so that when she stops in the shadow of a clump of bushes, with her face all fixed, he stands there like this dope until she touches him. And even then he doesn't get it. She has to tell him to hurry. So he gets it, then. A poet is human, it seems, just like a man. [*SS*, p. 636]

The events move into the present, apparently into *our* present. The supposedly disembodied narrative presence takes on personality. "But that's not it. That can be seen in any movie. This is what it is, what is good" (*SS*, p. 636), and two pages later the writer has begun to write the story as he enacts it. Life moves faster than fiction and it's hard to get it all down; but he works at it.

> And what was it he had been writing? Him, and Anne, and the poet. Word for word, between the waiting spells to find out what to write down next, with a few changes here and there, of course,

> because live people do not make good copy, the most interesting copy being gossip, since it mostly is not true. [*SS*, p. 644]

"Artist at Home" is, we finally conclude, the story its central character is writing. "Anyway, here's the rest of it, what they did next" (*SS*, p. 645). The denouement is the product of a gradual solution of the puzzling narrative tone in the opening. Beyond that, the denouement, the solution of the story, if it is to have a solution at all, is a joke on the Hearer. What seemed at the outset to have been rather shallow third-person satire has become the self-irony of a first-person involvement. In "Uncle Willy" the "plot" or rhetoric of narrative depended upon a sudden widening in the distance between us and the narrator. In "Artist at Home" this same distance must, for the effect of the story, be just as suddenly narrowed. The two stories argue for much more than Faulkner's fine discretion for narrative economy. They suggest again that the best of Faulkner depends not just on the story told or the framework used to tell or the economy of either, but on a peculiar Teller-Hearer collaboration: a consciousness of the artifice of narration is involved with the delight in hearing something told really well. Faulkner enjoys devising the best means for his substance, but we can miss the full effect of substance if we are unconscious of the tools and skill he employs in getting it told, or if we forget that we as Hearers participate with him from the other end in constructing the artifice he chooses.

The orders of such comparatively simple first-person alliances are matched in the third-person narrative but further complicated by the freedom and range of the third-person narrative presence. Here is found the liberty which the Teller's imprisonment in the Subject's head denies in the first person. The Teller can vary his voice while remaining more or less objective about Subjects (or, at least, never resorting to the first person) and can do this in a variety of ways. His relish or distaste for the story he is telling, his fluidity or crabbed stumble, the delight with which he tells it or his halting horror as the Hearer drags it from him, comprise the first range of variety. The Teller can vary his rhetorical position and mode. He can be the fly-on-the-wall, machinelike recorder of events and dialogue (still retaining his all-important determinant of selection and timing), or he can be the angry and vengeful narrative god, sitting in judgment on his characters and directing the forces he subjects them to. Another full range of choice is available to him in making the physical surroundings for the Subject, in arranging patterns of imagery, ways to say things which neither he nor his narrative presence can afford to say directly and overtly. He can use everything from the most elusive imagery to the construction of a complete world, with its own moral, physical, and coincidental law.

The contrast of the third-person narrative is perhaps made clearest by reference to yet another story of a child, "Barn Burning." The first-person stories narrated by children all depict a stasis in development. The child at the end of "Shall Not Perish" is capable of not much more than the child at the beginning of "Two Soldiers." His fundamental allegiances have not changed, his understanding has deepened only a bit. "That Evening Sun" has development only by virtue of reminiscence, and in "Uncle Willy" development occurs between the time of the events and the narrator's present: neither has internal development. "Barn Burning" is Faulkner's triumph of internal development in the child, and he could not have brought it off in the first person. Again the problem is where to stand. A first-person solution would have severely limited "Barn Burning"; instead the third-person with a strong point of view is combined with rhythmic interruptions of objective narration and dramatic dialogue, and all of this is set within an elaborate series of time devices.

The story begins in a powerfully rendered synaesthesia of hunger ("smelled . . . knew he smelled . . . could see . . . his stomach read . . . knew he smelled . . . intestines believed he smelled . . . smell and sense . . . of fear . . . of despair and grief, the old fierce pull of blood," (*SS*, p. 3). The continuously sliding perception and the run-on style give us not just an intense introduction to Sarty but instant identification and empathy with him: he senses things with the wrong organs because of his intensity and he transfers this intensity directly to us. We quickly discover that it is not just the product of hunger or deprivation but of an attempt to distract himself—he is taking his mind off the serious proceedings of the justice of the peace to escape a process he does not want to be involved in: "He could not see the table where the Justice sat and before which his father and his father's enemy . . . stood, but he could hear them" (*SS*, p. 3). Rendering, point of view, locating, and some exposition are all poured out at once. But even before we can take all this in, the trial turns to the boy. The intense, almost expressionistic rendering of the boy walking beneath the "palpable weight" of the faces (*SS,* p. 4) his fear of the Justice and his fear of his father, and the fragment of internal monologue in dialect seem perfectly natural because we share his intensity, his place. All of the third-person devices to promote vicarious empathy have been brought into play. A bit of objective narrative ("The boy said nothing," *SS,* p. 4, line 31) follows the first few questions, but it is immediately broken into by another spot of internal monologue (*"Enemy! Enemy!"*). There is an omniscient narrator only until some other arrangement can be made. Sarty, by a narrative trick which the story's donnée forces Faulkner to invent, is made capable of being his older self. A reminiscent voice appears, somewhat similar to the older Quentin of "That Evening Sun"; it can sense from afar the complexities and implications of what is going on in the story. This peculiar narrative freedom not only provides a productive solution of "where to stand" (as the boy himself crowds out the narrative presence), but makes the boy's escape believable. The older self, by giving us a sense of what Sarty is to become, makes him seem more capable of breaking free, and by demonstrating his complex response to "the pull of blood" later in life, also makes him seem worthy to break free.

The next step in Sarty's cyclic world after the trial is the family's move in the wagon, with the mother-of-pearl clock that will not run. Faulkner chooses this for the first of a series of time-distortions which forms the story's reminiscent framework. It is a simple turn of phrase ("in later years . . . still later"), but it gives the short story some of the scope of the novel. Faulkner, as if he were Dickens with a Pip, can now call upon the boy's eventual judgment, can see the childhood event from a distant mature vantage. The first instance is cast in the voice of the narrative presence ("it was exactly that same quality which in later years would cause his descendants to over-run the engine," *SS,* p, 6), but on the next page, to describe his father's "niggard" blaze Sarty moves through a series of jumps forward to arrive at a fully matured judgment. Even as the background established in exposition for a character informs every moment in a story for that character, so do Sarty's future views form present moments for him. The evolution of his at first dialectal monologue (*"And I will have to do hit,"* *SS,* p. 4) into what eventually becomes pure Faulknerese (*"Maybe it will all add up and balance and vanish—corn, rug, fire; the terror and grief, the being pulled two ways like between two teams of horses—gone, done with for ever and ever,"* *SS*, p. 17) are foreshadowing of his eventual maturity. But even more than this, the mature judgment (as in "That Evening Sun") sharpens and objectifies the conflict at the heart of the story and our mixed responses as adults and as empathetic images of the boy. The central conflict between the "old fierce pull of blood" and societal responsibility becomes overt as his father asks his defensive rhetorical question, " 'You were fixing to tell them. You would have told him' " (*SS*, p. 8). Now the boy says nothing, but "Later, twenty years later, he was to tell himself, 'If I had said they wanted only truth, justice, he would have hit me again.' " (*SS*, p. 8).

Perhaps it is too direct, too overt a bit of message-mongering to be much praised, but the next use of the device enriches the contrast: "They went back up the road. A week ago—or before last night, that is—he would have asked where they were going, but not now," (*SS*, p. 9). From these two fragmentary projections we know that the process of decision has begun. The boy's minimal awareness that something did not fit into his pattern of recurrence (that his father would strike him and pause to explain why) has brought him to a vague state of distrust. Experience has not yet told him what he must do, but the tiny disturbance in the chain of recurrence has triggered a new internal time-scheme. Discretion is necessary because he recognizes the handicap of being young, the light weight of his few years—weight enough to keep him from accepting the cycle as immutable, not enough for him to try to change it.[4]

The story's clear rhythm corresponds to this cycle of family. The long run-on flows of prose come at points of great pressure.[5] The final passage moves into the incantatory, idyllic prose style of the

4. There is an overt statement of the function of physical weight in maturity in *The Reivers*, p. 48: "There is no crime which a boy of eleven had not envisaged long ago. His only innocence is, he may not yet be old enough to desire the fruits of it, which is not innocence but appetite; his ignorance is, he does not know how to commit it, which is not ignorance but size."

5. At the beginning, to establish us with intensity inside Sarty's head (*SS*, p. 3), to follow his father's movement out of the story (p. 5), to describe the wagon (p. 6), to share Sarty's first view of the deSpain house (p. 10), and to follow his father's movement into it (p. 11), to mark the beginning of the final burning (pp. 20–21) and follow the action of Sarty's escape (pp. 22–23), and finally to share Sarty's vision of his father's disappearance (pp. 24–25).

opening of "The Bear," to deal with the freedom, the peace which lies outside the frantic circle of recurrence. It contrasts with the claustrophobic, hungering, sensual run-on paragraph which begins the story, making clear the line between imprisonment and freedom. Dialogue alternates with narration, too, and the rhythm of this is as repetitive and inexorable as the cycle of burning-trial-moving-offense-burning. The story's argument that trust in society is a natural sense is perhaps unbelievable in detail, but because we have arrived at this natural sense even as Sarty did and have been helped along the way by both his participant and his reminiscent selves, the argument is compelling. Whether this has succeeded depends more on the calculation of narrative strategy and the manipulation of narrative distance than it does on how right or true the story is in theme or substance. The design of the telling is the design of the story.

A first-person solution here would have destroyed the story's point, would have limited it, as it would have first of all introduced a classic problem of narrative: why is he telling us all this? In the first person, Faulkner couldn't have managed the time distortion, the sense of cyclic time played against Sarty's double (participant and reminiscent) time unless, as in "That Evening Sun," he had chosen a reminiscent first person, in which case he would have sacrificed (as he did in that story) the immediacy of the boy as participant. And Sarty, after all, is no Quentin. From the little we know about him in later life (he does not show up to perform in the Trilogy) he would not have been capable of carrying the unstated irony which accompanies the reminiscence of "That Evening Sun"; [6] much less would he be interested in reconstructing in such compulsive detail this moment out of his past. Perhaps more important to the story's impact, however, is the sense "Barn Burning" gives of the process of becoming: initially the boy is an object moved by his world, then he becomes sentient, capable of understanding some of the world. Eventually he breaks free. Had the story been trapped in the pure subjective, this would have been lost.

Third-person narrative is not, of course, just a device for escaping subjective imprisonment, nor is it always even that. The varieties

6. There's a good chance, of course, that he would be just as incapable of some of the complexity of diction and syntax Faulkner gives him in the reminiscent voice.

of distance and flexible subjectivity available in the third person give it a potential for an almost infinite number of individual experiments ranging from the omniscient puppeteering to the other extreme of near-dramatic objectivity. The Teller does not need to take the Subject's voice in order to deal with his mind. He can hint at, guess about, or paraphrase the mind without using the voice at all, or he can interpret the smallest impulse that puts an expression on the Subject's face. Retaining all the ranges and varieties of his own voice (relish, rhetoric, rendering) he can move into and out of the Subject's consciousness, and as long as he retains his respect for the Hearer's sensibilities—has an eye to the rightness, necessity, relevance, and measure of what he is up to—he is free. This respect, though, is essential, for here is found the most common cause of blunder, miscalculation, and overexpenditure. Teller can play upon consciousness after consciousness, now become god, then fly; mind-read and proclaim objective innocence; manipulate time, distance, universal law, person, and voice with the ease (and far more effect) than the moviehouse organist at the mighty Wurlitzer of our youth. But he can do this only so long as his story—and even more important, his Hearer—demands it and permits it. Again appropriateness and measure of means to ends are the prime rules.

"Red Leaves" demonstrates such a productive mixture of modes. The story of the pursuit of an Indian chief's black bodyservant begins like Sam Fathers's narration of the tale of Herman Basket, with an attempt to induce some of the effects of legend by stylistic shorthand: "The first Indian said. . . . the second said" (*SS*, p. 313). The objective narration of background seems to move in the direction of Conradian godlike omniscience ("like carved heads on a ruined wall in Siam or Sumatra, looming out of a mist. The sun had done it, the violent sun, the violent shade," *SS*, p. 313), but Faulkner's narrative presence never quite follows through with overt thematic interpretation. The Conradian element instead develops, most appropriately, into something more like anthropological objectivity. One aim of the story is a comparison of two cultures. The narrative presence gives us a quick trip through the past. Part 4 reverses this objective movement and throws us into the consciousness of the runaway bodyservant in an intense rendition from his point of view. The contrast drawn at the beginning of the story—between red culture and white—is reversed as the cultural description becomes relegated to the background and we concentrate on the black's attempted escape. His intense fear depends upon subjective involvement even greater than that with Nancy in "That Evening Sun." Once again, as with Nancy, there is no need to follow this character out to his end in escape or death because it has become irrelevant to the story. The black has "run well" and is still running, and has run up against an absurd inevitability of belief, law, culture, and determination which are not his but which will kill him. The story has chosen a mixture of tools to accomplish an end which could not have been predicted from its beginning. As we were reading, the narrative strategy has made us different from what we were at the outset.

The third person is a more fertile field than first person for narrative experiment, but I would stress that in all these experiments, even the more extreme, experiment is not undertaken for the sake of experiment. Faulkner tries out this and that, but not so much to see how it works as to show that it *does* work. Experiment is not a path to invention but rather a means of exploration and experience. He devises the narrative shape to fit the shape and demands of the substance; he does not endow a narrative shape with substance to demonstrate the flexibility of his art, or his ability at tour de force, or his fancy footwork.

This is a difficult point to prove, but take for a moment a narrative road not taken (at least in the short story): the third-person narrative at its impersonal extreme, the almost purely dramatic rendering of, say, Salinger's "Uncle Wiggily in Connecticut" or "Just Before the War with the Eskimos." Faulkner was no dramatist. The dramatic portion of *Requiem for a Nun* is as unsatisfactory as Robert Browning's dramas, and for some of the same reasons. The speeches in it are repetitive representations of hesitation (hesitancy to tell a secret, tell the truth, face up to it), comments on this hesitation, and variations on the form of open-letter soliloquy. He depends heavily on stage directions: the movement and meaning they convey is more important than the speeches themselves, which ought to be the heart of the conflict and the drama. The pseudo drama of *As I Lay Dying* is not even as dramatic as O'Neill's *Strange Interlude* because the surface action cannot stand on its own—the undercurrents are all. I suspect it might not even make a good film without heavy adaptation. There is good drama in *The Reivers, Light in August,* and *The Town,* but it tends to be found in scenes in which characters who are present talk about those who are not. It is exposition rather than drama. The point is that Faulkner cast *Requiem for a Nun* as a drama not to show that he could do it (for I suspect that from the absence of dramatic tendencies in the short stories he knew he could not) but because it was an experimental solution to the narrative problem of that book's germ—a solution similar to the more complicated one he found for *Sanctuary.* Problem-solving is the impulse, not self-demonstration. Faulkner needed the added dimension of consciousness provided by the first person or more flexibly by the subjective point of view in the third person. He needed the alliance and the isolation that a group will provide but that two characters will not. He needed an element of artificiality in speech (even as Boswell did in the *Life of Johnson* to "Johnsonize" Johnson), which can sound absurd when spoken (witness the last reel of Clarence Brown's film of *Intruder in the Dust*). He needed the complex resources of fiction because he could not master the simple resources of drama.

"Mule in the Yard" is perhaps a good test-case for both of these points. Much of the story is dramatic in the sense that it is the stage-directions and the setting, the performance and the atmosphere which give the speeches of the story their life: action becomes vital because of the tangible presence of atmospheric setting—the mist from which the mule emerges and into which it disappears. The immobile fog is contrasted continually with the frantic action—and the frantic conniving—at the center of the story.

> That's why it was not cold: as though there lay supine and prisoned between earth and mist the long winter night's suspiration of the sleeping town in dark, close rooms—the slumber and the rousing; the stale waking thermostatic, by re-heating heat-engendered: it lay like a scum of cold grease upon the steps and the wooden entrance to the basement and upon the narrow plank walk which led to a shed building in the corner of the yard: upon these planks, running and still carrying the scuttle of live ashes, Mrs. Hait skated viciously. "Watch out!" old Het, footed securely by her rubber soles, cried happily. "Dey in de front!" Mrs. Hait did not fall. She did not even pause. She took in the immediate scene with one cold glare and was running again when there ap-

> peared at the corner of the house and apparently having been born before their eyes of the fog itself, a mule. It looked taller than a giraffe. Longheaded, with a flying halter about its scissor-like ears, it rushed down upon them with violent and apparition-like suddenness. [*SS*, p. 250]

"Mule" is intensely visual: the apparently coincidental fog and the apparently disconnected action eventually connect to the frantic trading and speeches, the concentrated human relationship between Snopes and Miz Hait. Snopes is bested in a deal by the end of the story, and this is not to be expected. The surrealistic movement of the mule and the women and the accidental burning of the house are not just "outside events," but elements in a metaphor for the strange machinations of Snopes and the strange death of Hait. This world is a blank mist until an apparently arbitrary or coincidental manifestation emerges, violently scurries about, and fades again. Results and reactions are seen in the foreground; motives and strategy remain shrouded. This narrative technique and thematic pattern come to be of major importance in the Snopes Trilogy in the "shaking bushes" of V. K. Ratliff's whodunit pursuit of Flem. But more important to the immediate point, factors and functions of drama are subsumed in a story which only fiction (or perhaps film) could realize. Experimental combinations of rendering, outside event, arbitrary surprise, stage-direction, and the flat depiction of action baldly discovered are called for by the substance, theme, and meaning. Strategy is far from simple and clearly experimental. The means serve the end: narrative device is bent to shape the substance, not vice versa.

I find the highest reach of the confident use of third person in "Dry September," one of Faulkner's most rigidly controlled stories. Much of that control is exercised by the calculated choice of narrative strategy. It begins in an intensity of rendering similar to that in "Barn Burning" with some of the same productive confusion. But here instead of confusion of the senses and consciousness, there is aesthetic confusion of tenor and vehicle, of rendering and theme.

> Through the bloody September twilight, aftermath of sixty-two rainless days, it had gone like a fire in dry grass—the rumor, the story, whatever it was. Something about Miss Minnie Cooper and a Negro. Attacked, insulted, frightened: none of them, gathered

> in the barber shop on that Saturday evening where the ceiling fan stirred, without freshening it, the vitiated air, sending back upon them, in recurrent surges of stale pomade and lotion, their own stale breath and odors, knew exactly what had happened. [*SS*, p. 169]

The heat, dust, and airlessness encourage the fire of rumor as surely as do Minnie Cooper's age and isolation. The objective, almost dramatic scene in the barbershop is broken only twice by the narrative presence, once to report, "His name was McLendon" (*SS*, p. 171), and again to report that the third speaker "too had been a soldier" (*SS*, p. 172). Sleeves are dragged across faces, "the air was flat and dead. It had a metallic taste at the base of the tongue" (*SS*, p. 173). Dramatic scenes, action narrative, subjective analysis here and throughout the story continually find their center in the hermetic, motionless, heated atmosphere of the title.

Part 2 begins with "She was . . . ," the kind of explanatory background we might expect from garrulous Ratliff, leaning forward in "Hair" to give us another plum, but here it is without that mediating and ameliorating first-person familiarity. It is an almost militant objectivity, pushed to an extreme, almost, as if to contrast with the barbershop bonhomie of "Hair." The bond of the barbershop here cements a lynch mob; the community's concern for its inhabitants here only alienates and isolates Minnie. The boundary of the small town, in other stories marking the closeness of familiarity, here turns everything sour, septic, promotes rumor, and makes inevitable the violence of reaction.

The introduction of Minnie employs intimacy, not intimacy with her consciousness but rather the one-sided intimacy of the anatomist or the abnormal psychologist. Objectivity will not relax into sympathy, empathy, or even an appeal to us to see her side of things, much less to adopt her point of view. The narrative takes her vital signs—age, residence, daily schedule, annual schedule, back to her daily schedule—whips us through her manner, family background, appearance (as she ages rapidly before our eyes) her social standing, her life schedule. At this point in the dissection there are four cuts forward in time on a single page. Her face is like a mask or flag, and we are told "the town began to see" (*SS*, p. 174), but without that appeal for our empathetic participation in the town which characterized "A Rose for Emily." Here the town is a witness, as the narrator is, dispassionate but not really neutral. The narrator takes into account some of the strong judgments of the other townspeople: "They would tell her about him, about how well he looked, and how they heard that he was prospering in the city, watching with bright, secret eyes her haggard, bright face" (*SS*, p. 175). But the narrative neither accepts nor rejects their attitudes. It takes them in, along with everything else, with the same chilling objectivity.

Part 3 moves back to the action narrative where 2 left off, and we return to the center: "The day had died in a pall of dust; above the darkened square, shrouded by the spent dust, the sky was as clear as the inside of a brass bell. Below the east was a rumor of the twice-waxed moon" (*SS*, p. 175). Natural beauty caught in the bell image is combined with immutable entrapment: the dust is a pall and the square is "shrouded" with "spent" dust, echoed by the exhaustion and impotence of the "twice-waxed moon," itself an echo of the "rumor" of the first paragraph of the story. The passage takes these details beyond stark atmosphere into incantatory legend: the time is set for an event, the characters are in place and not all of them are human—there is an immanent vitality in objects. They move in like guards to prevent escape: "A rutted lane turned at right angles. Dust hung above it too, and above all the land. The dark bulk of the ice plant . . . rose against the sky. . . . He hurled the car up and slammed to a stop, the headlights glaring on the blank wall" (*SS*, p. 176).

Faulkner advances this movement another step with visual enforcement similar to that of "Mule in the Yard": the atmosphere becomes not only instigator of events and participant but dramatist too: "Dust lay like fog in the street. The street lights hung nimbused as in water" (*SS*, p. 176). The underwater effect takes on malevolence on the next page: "The wan hemmorhage of the moon increased. It heaved above the ridge, silvering the air, the dust, so that they seemed to breathe, live, in a bowl of molten lead" (*SS*, p. 177). There are no other living creatures near, not even their sounds—nothing but the "faint ticking of contracting metal about the cars." The atmosphere has become the mover of characters, the objects have become a chorus to an inevitable end. The actions are not as important (in fact they are deemphasized) as the forces which gather upon them and produce them: "Behind them the sourceless lights of the second car glared in the dust. Presently McLendon turned into a narrow road. It was rutted with disuse. It led back to an abandoned brick kiln—a series of reddish mounds and weed- and vine-choked vats without bottom" (*SS*, p. 179).

Hawkshaw escapes this impetus but once he has subtracted himself from the mob (and that not without some damage), he cannot affect it. "The dust swallowed them; the glare and the sound died away. The dust of them hung for a while, but soon the eternal dust absorbed it again. The barber climbed back onto the road and limped on toward town" (*SS*, p. 180). He enters and has no effect, then leaves, halting. Individual action seems to be as irrelevant here as appeals for empathy.

Part 4 advances us farther than 2 into Minnie's mind: "Her own flesh felt like fever" (*SS*, p. 180). And the dust invades Minnie's world. She seems to be moving on a crest with the dust and heat—she is "in the center of the group," she has regained the eyes of the "coatless drummers in chairs along the curb. . . . even the young men lounging in the doorway" (*SS*, pp. 180–81). If there is human motivation at all in this story, this is perhaps what motivates her. They no longer distinguish her from other habitual objects and she has to be noticed.

Any break in objectivity comes only in metaphors in this section: the picture show is "like a miniature fairyland with its lighted lobby and colored lithographs of life caught in its terrible and beautiful mutations." But such distanced judgments of the narrative pale beside the true intimacy now of the intense point of view. We are within Minnie: "Her lips began to tingle . . . it would be all right . . . could hold back the laughing so it would not waste away so fast and so soon. . . . against the silver glare and the young men and girls coming in two and two against it." The picture show is brighter, more human, but it parallels the compelled action at the ice house and brick kiln: the headlights glare on the blank wall, the screen glows silver; the men were moved, impelled; the silver dream accumulates "inevitably on and on" (*SS*, p. 181). She begins to laugh, and the shock of the laughing brings the narrative sharply back to dramatic rendition. The end of this section returns to the doubts of the first: " 'Do you suppose anything really happened?' " (*SS*, p. 182).

The final section is recessional, moving away from the impulse after the catastrophe. McLendon's violence against his wife is real, conventional, and therefore not of much interest to him. It is automatic and reflex. He moves to the "screened porch" of the "birdcage" that is his house and trap. He reaches to the heat and we move, as we knew we would, back toward the legendary force of the atmospheric center as he stands panting against the dusty screen: "There was no movement, no sound, not even an insect. The dark world seemed to lie stricken beneath the cold moon and the lidless stars" (*SS*, p. 183).

The story is as rigidly controlled by its narrative strategy as the town is controlled by the dust and heat. Comment is rare. It comes only in metaphor and in the tone of the close observation of Minnie, so that it stands in strong contrast to the predominant disciplined objectivity. The construction is circular in the whole and section by section. In part 1 we begin and end in atmosphere, in 2 in description; 3 is circular in theme, metaphor, and atmosphere, 4 in locale, 5 in entrapment. The heat, the enclosure (bell, water, lead, picture show, birdcage), and circular structure are metaphors for the entrapment which moves the action. The compulsion in the characters is produced by the pressure of entrapment. Minnie's is released in hysteria, McLendon's in violence. Hers completes her already effectual isolation, McLendon's fails to release or complete anything. He perhaps finds some momentary outlet in his leadership of the group, some release from the birdcage of his civilian home and his wife's patience, perhaps some in the extraordinary deed which he envisions his action to be, but he is nevertheless just as trapped at the end. Hawkshaw is completely frustrated as he sees his deeds fall short of the impulse of his words. Only Minnie completes anything. By attempting to put herself back in the picture in a town in which she has become invisible, she removes herself completely from human contact: poor Minnie becomes crazy Minnie.

This is the most claustrophobic of Faulkner's fiction, in which atmosphere, metaphor, theme, character, structure, merge in frustration, compulsion, entrapment, and isolation. And all of this is under the control of a disciplined narrative strategy. What we see, what we feel, to what we relate and from what we are distanced is controlled by the telling, the strategy of Teller for Hearer. In this story narrative control moves beyond device, beyond simple questions of where to stand or empathetic attachment into a combination of almost Aeschylean artistry, involving distance, control, compulsion, dissective objectivity.

In the short stories Faulkner seems to be exploring the limits of technique and the necessary balances between substance and presentation, between meaning and suspension. Among other things, this concentrated mass of innovation, experiment, "corner-building," argues rather convincingly that some of the cherished pedagogical assumptions about narrative are false. First person is not necessarily the shortest distance to the heart, and third person does not necessarily provide the greatest distance or coldest objectivity. Nor can distance in narrative be measured simply in the extent to which a third-person narrative adopts the point of view or thoughts of a character or characters. Faulkner is clearly closer to Sarty Snopes than to Minnie. But what of the distance between Teller and Subject in "Elly" and "Turn About," and the difference between these two? We get more from within the mind of Elly than from within that of the Coxswain, but the narrator (by virtue of the strategy of the faulty witness) is closer in understanding to the "navy egg." We are closer to Mrs. Hait in "Mule in the Yard" than to the bodyservant of "Red Leaves," even though the latter includes a lengthy, intensely empathetic experience within his mind. An omniscient narrator comments in both "Victory" and "Artist at Home;" but by virtue of the device of synchronous composition, the narrator in "Artist" *is* his own subject, whereas the narrator of "Victory" is at an almost coldly objective distance.

A mixture of methods in the third person can discover remarkable depths in a simple situation ("Barn Burning") or show the shallowness of apparently complex substance ("Doctor Martino"). When technique serves only itself it can reveal nothing more than its own failure to deceive. When it becomes a part of the substance of a story it can produce the empathy and the experience of the best of fiction in the brief compass of a short tale. Systems of any sort can lead only to complete understanding of the mistakes of failed fictions, not to the heart of the mystery of good fiction.

Yet there is an element in such discussion that is bound to displease our literary sensibilities: where is the art in such mechanical manipulations? R. P. Blackmur has dignified this as "executive technique," but why should the organist be praised for the organ's built-in flexibility? The hard fact is that such mechanical manipulation is as essential to the narrative of *Finnegans Wake* as it is to that of *Peter Pan.* Narrative design can be no more than an automatic organ stop, a mechanical end in itself, or it can be (as with Faulkner) not just a means to an end but the central and abiding concern of the fiction, ruling and determining other concerns. Faulker establishes this in his theoretical utterances and mumblings, and he documents it in every short story and novel he ever wrote.

This is not to say that Faulkner produced only marvels of the narrative art—he sometimes failed—or that he thought of narrative as a game or a combination of gimmicks. The "one single urn or shape" was not just a way of saying one gimmick, or indeed, of saying *one* in any sense that is simple. He meant the particular, unique urn or shape which approached perfect realization of the "moment" which was the genesis and the life of a particular story.

This is something like theatrical lighting—noticed only when it is wrong. When Faulkner fails at devising such a shape, we know it immediately because the urn or shape—the story's device, in other words—stands out from its substance. The mode dwarfs the moment and becomes the first and only impression we have of the story. Reading such a story can be like reading Donne's "The Flea" as he gives over his poem in order to win the argument with his mistress, or watching Hawthorne scrabbling around, willing to do *anything* to end *The House of the Seven Gables.* Once fiction fails this way, Faulkner loses interest in it and the reader knows it: "Fox-Hunt," "Pennsylvania Station," "The Brooch," the lassitude of *Soldier's Pay* all proclaim this kind of failure. His "carpenter" theory excuses these as bad pots from the wheel, poor furniture for the local market.

But other failures do interest Faulkner—not those in which the technique has slipped or the shape been miscalculated, but those in which the best he could devise, the right urn or shape or nails or lumber captured part of the moment but could not exhaust the whole. The urn or shape contained the "germ" but fell short of complete realization of the moment, partly because the urn or shape (as in *The Sound and the Fury*) was so effective a medium that it released more than he knew was there, and there was no end to it. The tendency (so frequently overstated by both critics and Faulkner) to make a pretty cover for the pot or to slather the cabinet with varnish and put it out for sale should not be confused with his faith in the urn or shape and his frustration at the fullness and complexity it sometimes realized or set free. Nor should it be confused with the human inability (more frequently stated by him as his "failure" as an artist) to realize all the potential nuance and subtlety that art had released.

3 *Sanctuary*

To me it is a cheap idea, because it was deliberately conceived to make money. . . . I tore the galleys down and rewrote the book. It had been already set up once, so I had to pay for the privilege of rewriting it, trying to make out of it something which would not shame The Sound and the Fury *and* As I Lay Dying *too much and I made a fair job and I hope you will buy it and tell your friends and I hope they will buy it too.*

Sanctuary, *Introduction, 1932*

Faulkner's statement in the introduction to the Modern Library issue of *Sanctuary* is an apologia. He indicates a tension between temptation and duty: "a cheap idea" had to be made into "something which would not shame" his work. The novel itself perhaps falls between stools in much the same way, but it falls with a bang, triumphantly true to that tension and consequently true to itself alone. It is no more written with the left hand than Graham Greene's "entertainments" are. Behind the dirty leer of the persona he has adopted for the introduction is still Faulkner, telling a story, planning effects, and, in this phase of his career, spending most of the time calculating technique.

The "cheap idea" is undeniably there. The substance of the book is chosen for sensational shock. But Faulkner in an interview identified sensationalism as secondary.

> I would say, if he is creating characters which are flesh-and-blood people, are believable, and are honest and true, then he can use sensationalism if he thinks that's an effective way to tell his story. But if he's writing just for sensationalism, then he has betrayed his vocation, and he deserves to suffer from it. That is, sensationalism is in a way an incidental tool, that he might use sensational-

> ism as the carpenter picks up another hammer to drive a nail. But he doesn't—the carpenter don't build a house just to drive nails. He drives nails to build a house. [*Univ.*, pp. 49–50]

Here, quite literally, the objects of the book—the corncob, the cosmetician's plug of wax which pops out of the hole in Red's forehead, the two lovebirds cut up with the scissors and the half-grown kitten, even Popeye himself, an object fashioned of stamped tin, old auto parts, and a cigarette—are the raw materials which challenge Faulkner's technique to combine them in such a way that they will not "shame." His response to the challenge is a mixed narrative which explores not just the uses of sensational objects but of narrative techniques usually thought of as "cheap," techniques which emulate and imitate various patterns drawn from popular media and the oral tradition. But the disciplined stylistic and narrative control which unifies the mixture of imitations and the complex, multilevel structure are rather expensive ideas. Quite apparently money alone was not a good enough reason to write the book, in spite of the gallus-snapping, hard-bellied persona of the introduction. What began as a cheap idea did not emerge as a cheap book. *Sanctuary* cannot be dismissed as a potboiler. But its simple (or cheap) origins, its chronological place, and the overtness of its strategy make it ideal as a starting point for an examination of the function of narrative pattern in the novels.

Leslie Fiedler holds that the book is not just the "darkest of all Faulkner's books" but "the dirtiest of all the dirty jokes exchanged among men only at the expense of the abdicating Anglo-Saxon virgin."[1] Either Fiedler hasn't paid much attention to the jokes he's heard or he's heard pretty bad ones, because the book fails in just this respect: it will not become pornography and its generic structure refuses to conform to that of the dirty joke. Certainly the corncob, the corncrib, elements of Tommy and the deaf-and-blind old man emerge from the same great mass of popular oral material as the hillbilly jokes of the twenties and thirties (perhaps most concretely remembered in the old *Esquire* hillbilly cartoons or in the gradeschool ditty, "We Mountaineers, we have no fears"), that vein Erskine Caldwell mined so tirelessly. But again these are objects rather than stories. In technique, only chapter 21, the tale of Virgil

1. *Love and Death in the American Novel* (New York: Criterion, 1959), p. 312.

Snopes and Fonzo, fits the pattern of the dirty joke, but even it omits the punchline. The novel is not so relentlessly directed as a dirty joke must be, in which everything must be constructed to serve the climax. There are elements of that strangely antijoke form of joke, the shaggy-dog story, in Temple's wanderings about the farm, but even shaggy-dogs must have a punchline, and this has none, unless it is the corncob, so carefully put off for fourteen chapters and 220 pages until it can be introduced in evidence at the trial. The pursuit of Temple fits more surely into the genre of the euphemistic semipornography of pulp fiction of the twenties and thirties, teasing and teasing up to an encounter, and then throwing in a lot of colorful writing for the "Afterwards as they lay together" section. Here again it is a truncated imitation, for the tease is surely there, but we are led to an encounter and then denied it, and even the "afterwards" is delayed. As dirty joke or as pornography, *Sanctuary* is like another feature of the Japanese sex manual printed on tissue paper. Male and female figures can be superimposed one on the other, but it's not printed dirty—you make it dirty yourself.

The humor in the semipornographic imitation of pulp is the humor of excess, the nervous laughter of Grand Guignol or effective melodrama. This contrasts with another kind of humor in the book, the high-class one-liners of Miss Jenny's scenes. The world Horace re-enters in chapter 3 is that of high drawing-room comedy. Jokes may be made about lack of manhood, but they are in the vein of *The Country Wife,* not the Travelling Salesman. Miss Jenny perhaps reaches her highest point of successful and witty—but inhumanly distant—commentary on the lowlife of the present by another device of Restoration wit: using the past as a weapon to beat the mores of the present with. The present somehow threatens to soil her. And we discover in the process of the book that this is a true threat. She maintains the only position of true safety in the world of *Sanctuary.*

Experiments in imitation and emulation go beyond structural and narrative similarity into a combination of character-cliché, situation, and narrative technique. Here and there is an unmistakable odor of old newsprint, a suggestion of tabloid journalism which finally comes to full force in chapter 31, the story of Popeye. Its form is as old as journalism itself—the formative years or the confessions of the condemned criminal, a form which has changed little between the *Newgate Calendar* and the current copy of *Midnight.*

The dancehall sequence before Red is killed, Temple's ride into Memphis, and some of Ruby's autobiographical narration of her loyalty to Lee are so strongly redolent of popcorn and gummy folding seats that there can be no mistaking either the atmosphere which holds the vision or the cliché counterparts for the characters—flaming youth at the dancehall, the tart with the heart-of-gold, the moll faithful to the end outside the walls of Sing Sing Prison—all come from Hollywood. Perhaps this is why in spite of sleazy adaptation the second film of *Sanctuary* had moments of power. Even if Popeye is transposed into a devilishly attractive Candyman in Yves Montand and the whole movie is an insult even to *Sanctuary,* all the film clichés are there set down in order, and the book's movie must coalesce here and there with the movie's movie. Some of the passages which seem to have been clipped from second features could not, of course, have been done by Hollywood of the late twenties, even though movie censorship had not yet become very forceful. These must be credited again to a source common to both, pulp fiction. The somewhat antiquarian sensationalism of too much alcohol and lost women on a steady diet of gin is rather thin stuff for the appetite of a sensationalist of the sixties or seventies, but these and white slavery—all calculated forty years ago to produce a shock in us as readers which we can't quite manage any more—emerge from the backgrounds of cheap fiction and its high moralistic tone. It's possible that the aging decline of the book's shock value in the years since publication has made it possible for us to see the design more clearly. Now that we can no longer dismiss it with confidence as Faulkner's dirty book, we can no longer accept Faulkner's claim for it as a "cheap idea."

It is as American as apple pie and as violent as it is American. But not all of this Americanism is simple imitation in "period" manner. One of its imitational forebears moves beyond contemporaneous life to a much deeper and perhaps even more useful source of violent narrative. The land is hostile and there are Indians here, bent on their own odd designs, weird rites, and curious religious practices. The similarity to narratives of Indian captivity is apparent when the book is compared to "Red Leaves," and Temple is put in the place of the black bodyservant of that story in her cultural contrast to her captors, in her pursuit, in her peculiar helplessness. She has nothing to do with their aims, but she has stumbled among them and is now subject to their laws and customs. The pattern is even clearer if Temple is compared to women of the early captivity narratives.[2] Among the Indians the captive first sees her captors as devils; then sees them become evil men and finally they become mere functions of their alien society. Popeye's development from his early monosyllabic replies through his comparatively garrulous responses in Memphis to the almost humanizing explanation for his evil in genetic and environmental abnormality (chap. 31) parallels this. Captivity can include a process in which the captive passes through cultural shock into an adjustment of his values to those of the alien society, almost acceptance and liking (a friendly squaw like Ruby, a change in one or another devil into something human), and then becomes, in turn, alienated from his own society. The process must end in self-condemnation in the narrative of Indian captivity, especially under the Puritan ethos of the parent society. The captive was a sinner when she was captured (because she was a good Christian woman, and all good Christian women are self-accused sinners), she was brought to captivity for her sins, while in captivity she sinned more (by adapting herself to the company of the godless heathen), so that after her rescue she looks back upon her behavior in captivity with mixed feelings which can result in a misanthropy similar to the disaffection for humans Lemuel Gulliver felt in order to justify his affection for Houyhnhnms. There was a corresponding condemnation of her by her native society and suspicion or even accusation of cohabitation with the savages.

In *Sanctuary* the judging function of the Puritan ethic is supplanted by several sets of standards against which Temple may be judged—the tone of moral indignation transplanted from pulp fiction, the disapproval of the Miss Jennys of the world of Jefferson or of the society of "respectability" which her father the judge represents. The structure of captivity narratives can fall, as in *Sanctu-*

2. See, for instance, Mrs. Mary Rowlandson's *The Soveraignty and Goodness of God,* 1682, in *Narratives of the Indian Wars,* ed. Charles Lincoln, 1907; or Cotton Mather, *A Brand Pluck'd out of the Burning,* 1692, in *Narratives of the Witchcraft Cases,* ed. G. L. Burr. My discussion here owes much to Richard S. Slotkin and his study of preliterary American literature, *American Myth: Regeneration through Violence* (Middletown, Conn. Wesleyan University Press, 1972).

ary, into two parts: the capture and the adventures and adjustments in captivity, and the sometimes parallel narrative of the beginning and execution of the rescue process.[3] The full pattern of cultural assimilation, alienation from her own society, and disaffection is only completed in *Requiem for a Nun,* but the tensions unresolved in Temple here are strikingly similar to those of the original captives.

Sanctuary, then, moves in patterns borrowed from both deep and shallow sources: from the deep, a pattern of mounting terror first at the fact of captivity, then at the failure to try to escape. Running parallel to this is the arbitrary, hard-edged, nervous quality of tabloid journalism in some parts and pulp-fiction in others, directness which makes no apology for its literary forebears, overt imitation which cultivates the appearance and effect of unrefined arrangement and unpolished contrast. From second-feature movies come the isolation of the observing eye—its distance from human concern—the arbitrary sequence, the harsh lighting, the black-and-white, third-person objective qualities. In combination, all of these make up a narrative which may be ridiculed while it is being read, and which certainly never measures up to Faulkner's work at the top of his form, but which rests in the memory more securely in the manner of powerful myth than does any of his other works.

Why it falls short of the novels of the main range is more difficult to resolve. Why does such careful calculation and skillful pastiche fail to satisfy as one reads along? I think it is because Faulkner breaks one of his own rules in this book. *Sanctuary* is calculated to serve the reader, both in individual effect and in driving narrative impetus, but in *Sanctuary* Faulkner was willing to sacrifice total entertainment—his central aim in pleasing the Hearer—in order to please himself with harsh impact and unrelieved hopelessness. The book carries us along and delivers sometimes more than it promises; but it refuses to satisfy our need and desire for a place to stand, an undamaged ideal, even a hint of the hope of human efficacy. There is no Ishmael, and *Sanctuary* as a result is more of an object like Popeye than it is an experience shared.

3. Whether Faulkner knew any of the original captivity narratives is another question. Certainly the Indian stories demonstrate more knowledge of white narratives of Indian behavior than they do Indian narratives. "A Bear Hunt" offers another parallel of captivity, albeit involving latter-day Indians.

The book is moved by almost objective contrasts. The narrative is split between the enclave and the town, Frenchman's Bend—Memphis and Jefferson, the captors and the captivity, and the rescuers' success and failure. The division is made sharply by chapters: Frenchman's Bend–Memphis, 1–2, 4–14, 18, 21, 24–25, 31; Jefferson, 3, 15–17, 19–20, 26–30. The parts of each are continuous from the end of one section to the beginning of the next, with convergences of the two narrative lines in 1–2, 23, and 27. The arrangement has the force and impetus of a tight end-plotted nineteenth-century novel, with its immediate transitions and an almost creaky overtness of device. It is a powerful but strongly artificial structure.

But within this simple and rather blunt general structure there is great variation of effect. Neither of the two lines is stylistically continuous: rather the immediate material at hand determines the immediate treatment for each section. Chapters 1 and 2 balance a nightmare world with an obliviously self-indulgent Horace and introduce the oddly indifferent element of Nature which becomes so important to the moral structure of *Sanctuary*'s world. Chapter 3 returns to Jefferson, Horace assumes his normal role (without the nightmare manner and the loquacious confessions of 1–2), and Faulkner's chronicling manner, the *Sartoris* style, takes over. Basic relationships are set forth in the tracing of Horace's dead-level normalcy. Temple's nightmare, chapters 4–14, is marked by a rigid control of diction and by a dreamy, seemingly pointless wandering about of the characters. Theme and rendering weave in and out of this. The switches between one point of view and another and the switches between point of view and objective omniscience are frequent, apparently ruled by the same arbitrary lack of aim as is Temple herself. Then back in the world of the rescuers (15–27) we see the less safe and secluded precincts of society, the operations of the law and order necessary to support 3's aura of comfort and seclusion. The town, the crowds, the functions of society here contrast with the oblivious heaven-tree. Back with captivity at the whorehouse, 28 switches into cinematic, swift narrative and tangible effects. Popeye, once out of Frenchman's Bend, becomes more of a character and necessarily more of a human being. But Faulkner wants it both ways: the world of the whorehouse must be shown to be depraved because he is counting on that old shock value of white slavery and too much gin; but the tone of these chapters insists as strongly that they are the affectionate memoir of a closed society, humanizing the necessary evil in their characterization. There is a glimpse of Oxford (and another tonal and stylistic shift) in chapters 19–20. The dirty joke (21) of Fonzo and Virgil ties ends together too—the pair enforces both the affectionate memoir in their humor and the white slavery wickedness in their innocence—and manages to get us back to Temple. Then the mixture of Snopes's low comedy and Horace's tension between two worlds and 22 returns to the death-row romanticism introduced in the heaven-tree. The first person is dominant in 23; back at the whorehouse, chapters 24–25 return to the cinematic for the death of Red; 26 returns to the town's ineffectual, wandering crowds; 27–28 are Perry Mason. The town and Horace are contrasted in 29, a contrast embodied in the sudden climax of the lynching of Lee, but 30 returns to the *Sartoris* style of 3. Chapter 31 is the tabloid treatment of Popeye, saying more than it tells but explaining less, sharply shifting at the end into a Jamesian mode for Temple in the Luxembourg Gardens.

The overwhelming impression is mixture rather than harmony in the combined movements of the two narrative lines. Nature, in loving and sometimes fulsome description, contributes to this confusion. The descriptive passages seem almost independent of the narrative which surrounds them, and so invite the reader to make them into a pattern or a comment upon the human events they watch over. Almost every section of the book has such a passage, with certain significant exceptions. As sun sets at Frenchman's Bend, Nature disappears, not to reappear until the following morning (Chaps. 7–10). It disappears again from the chapters which relate the rape in the corncrib and the departure for Memphis (13–14) and again for Red's funeral and the chapter on the prosecutor and Temple's testimony (25–28).

The book's opening description introduces Nature's complexity of functions.

> The spring welled up at the root of a beech tree and flowed away upon a bottom of whorled and waved sand. It was surrounded by

a thick growth of cane and brier, of cypress and gum in which broken sunlight lay sourceless. Somewhere, hidden and secret yet nearby, a bird sang three notes and ceased.

There is more here than visual background. The undisturbed quality of the sand and woods suggests pastoral, but the sourceless sunlight is a neutral, rather ominous note. The bird is more ominous than neutral. If we pursue that bird in a few more passages it becomes more puzzling than ominous:

> The bird sang again, three bars in monotonous repetition: a sound meaningless and profound out of a suspirant and peaceful following silence which seemed to isolate the spot, and out of which a moment later came the sound of an automobile passing along a road and dying away. . . .
>
> Now and then the bird sang back in the swamp, as though it were worked by a clock; twice more invisible automobiles passed along the highroad and died away. Again the bird sang. . . .
>
> Benbow heard the bird again, trying to recall the local name for it. On the invisible highroad another car passed, died away. Between them and the sound of it the sun was almost gone. . . .
>
> Popeye went on, with light, finicking sounds in the underbrush. Then they ceased. Somewhere in the swamp a bird sang. [*Sanct.*, pp. 2, 3, 5, 116]

Once the bird seems worked by machine, but bird and machine are equally present and ominous and equally neutral. Nature surrounds human actions but keeps its distance. The isolation which either sound provides is clearly now not the isolation of pastoral but rather of false pastoral, less a purifying return to nature than a terrifying distance from anything to which one can call for help.

Neutrality gives way to threat as the book proceeds. Both at Frenchman's Bend and in Jefferson architecture or trees are continually drawn up in silhouette against the sky (pp. 6, 20, 22, 40, 42, 133, 230). This is still neutral, flat, featureless, but it seems to threaten enclosure—something of the threat inherent in expressionist stage decor, the psychological threat of exaggerated height.

Popeye's fear of the woods, of trees, his terror at the owl, all hold out hope that a natural adversary will appear to confront his machine monstrosity. But this is sucker-bait. The natural landscape, from the very outset, takes on attitudes and poses, but continually denies our hopes for any natural solution to anything.

The slain flowers, the delicate dead flowers and tears. . . .

That country. Flat and rich and foul, so that the very winds seem to engender money out of it. Like you wouldn't be surprised to find that you could turn in the leaves off the trees, into the banks for cash. That Delta. . . .

Above the cedar grove beyond whose black interstices an apple orchard flaunted in the sunny afternoon. . . . In a sombre grove through which the breeze drew with a sad, murmurous sound. . . .

Beyond, she could see a weed-choked slope and a huge barn, broken-backed, tranquil in sunny desolation. . . .

Between the sombre spacing of the cedars the orchard lay bright in the sunlight. . . . She walked right through the barn. It was open at the back, upon a mass of jimson weed in savage white-and-lavender bloom. . . . Then she began to run, . . . the weeds slashing at her with huge, moist, malodorous blossoms. . . .

Out of the high darkness where the ragged shadow of the heaven-tree which snooded the street lamp at the corner fretted and mourned. . . .

The outer darkness peaceful with insects and frogs yet filled too with Popeye's presence in black and nameless threat. . . .

The splotched shadow of the heaven-tree shuddered and pulsed monstrously in scarce any wind. . . .

The last trumpet-shape bloom had fallen. . . . They lay thick, viscid underfoot, sweet and oversweet in the nostrils with a sweetness surfeitive and moribund, and at night now the ragged shadow of full-fledged leaves pulsed upon the barred window in shabby rise and fall. . . .

The ragged grief of the heaven tree would pulse and change, the last bloom fallen now in viscid smears upon the sidewalk. . . .

A narrow street of smoke-grimed frame houses . . . set a little back in grassless plots, with now and then a forlorn and hardy tree of some shabby species—gaunt, lopbranched magnolias, a stunted elm or a locust in grayish, cadaverous bloom—interspersed by rear ends of garages. . . . [*Sanct.*, pp. 15, 16, 47, 49, 108, 135–36, 143, 148, 149, 160, 169]

Fecund, somber, sad, tranquil, savage, malodorous, peaceful, it flaunts, frets, mourns, pulses monstrously, depicts ragged grief, is forlorn, hardy, stunted, cadaverous. It is neither Eden nor Arcadia but rather a self-dramatizing, self-indulgent, helpless hodge-podge of pathetic attitudes, incapable of helping anything or anyone. It overdramatizes itself and its surroundings and does nothing. It is neither the maimed wilderness familiar from Faulkner's favorite theme of human nature's destructiveness, nor is it an ironically sunny backdrop for man's failure at natural dignity. It can slash out or mourn, it can perform a dazzling series of emotional impersonations, but these mean less than its impotent omnipresence. It is there. It sits. It watches. But it is intent only upon its own cycles and survival, its own strange and distant melodrama, not upon anything human going on against it, beneath it, or nearby. It is powerless to comment on anything but itself, and even these comments fail in self-consistency. The impotence is most clearly established in two passages at the center of Temple's ride to Memphis.

> She sat limp in the corner of the seat, watching the steady backward rush of the land—pines in opening vistas splashed with fading dogwood; sedge; fields green with new cotton and empty of any movement, peaceful, as though Sunday were a quality of atmosphere, of light and shade—sitting with her legs close together, listening to the hot minute seeping of her blood, saying dully to herself, I'm still bleeding. I'm still bleeding. . . .
>
> It was a bright, soft day, a wanton morning filled with that unbelievable soft radiance of May, rife with a promise of noon and of heat, with high fat clouds like gobs of whipped cream floating lightly as reflections in a mirror, their shadows scudding sedately across the road. It had been a lavender spring. The fruit trees, the white ones, had been in small leaf when the blooms matured; they had never attained that brilliant whiteness of last spring, and the dogwood had come into full bloom after the leaf also, in green retrograde before crescendo. But lilac and wistaria and redbud, even the shabby heaven-trees, had never been finer, fulgent, with a burning scent blowing for a hundred yards along the vagrant air of April and May. The bougainvillea against the veranda would be large as basketballs and lightly poised as balloons, and

looking vacantly and stupidly at the rushing roadside Temple began to scream. [*Sanct.*, pp. 163–64]

The indifferent neutrality of nature is enforced by the transformation of the city. We might expect a Popeye-city filled with monstrous grotesques. What we get has some elements of machine-change horror, but for all that it is happier than we anticipate (or would hope for if we were trying to construct an allegory of the machine versus nature). There is an almost transcendent quality of the magical:

> . . . a low doored cavern of an equivocal appearance where an oilcloth-covered counter and a row of backless stools, a metal coffee-urn and a fat man in a dirty apron with a toothpick in his mouth, stood for an instant out of the gloom with an effect as of a sinister and meaningless photograph poorly made. From the bluff, beyond a line of office buildings terraced sharply against the sun-filled sky, came a sound of traffic—motor horns, trolleys—passing high overhead on the river breeze; at the end of the street a trolley materialised in the narrow gap with an effect as of magic and vanished with a stupendous clatter. . . .
>
> They could hear the city, evocative and strange, imminent and remote; threat and promise both—a deep, steady sound upon which invisible lights glittered and wavered: colored coiling shapes of splendor in which already women were beginning to move in suave attitudes of new delights and strange nostalgic promises. Fonzo thought of himself surrounded by tier upon tier of drawn shades, rose-colored, beyond which, in a murmur of silk, in panting whispers, the apotheosis of his youth assumed a thousand avatars. . . .
>
> Between them low, far lights hung in the cool empty darkness blowing with fireflies. [*Sanct.*, pp. 169, 233, 279]

The opposition is not Nature versus Machine or Popeye versus Nature. Beauty can emerge anywhere, and it doesn't matter. A man is executed unjustly for a crime he did not commit and it is followed by a display of blooming in nature. The man guilty of that crime is executed for another crime *he* did not commit and the blooming in nature follows just the same. The city, home of the Machine, can be a wonderland. The wilderness, home of Nature, can be a nightmare.[4]

The imagery of the book supports these conclusions. Nature images are used to depict humans: the baseball game is "marsh-fowl disturbed by an alligator, not certain of where the danger is, motionless, poised, encouraging one another with short meaningless cries, plaintive, wary and forlorn" (*Sanct.,* p. 43). The coeds Horace meets in the station are like "identical artificial flowers surrounded each by bright and restless bees" (p. 202), and later "like honey poured in sunlight, pagan and evanescent and serene, thinly evocative of all lost days and outpaced delights, in the sun" (p. 206). As the book closes in the Luxembourg Gardens where Temple sits in triumphant ambiguity, the description combines nature images applied to the human scene with direct description of Nature robbed of its natural qualities.

> It had been a gray day, a gray summer, a gray year. . . . From beyond the circle with its spurious Greek balustrade, clotted with movement, filled with a gray light of the same color and texture as the water which the fountain played into the pool, came a steady crash of music. . . . In the pavilion a band in the horizon blue of the army played . . . while the twilight dissolved in wet gleams from the branches, onto the pavilion and the sombre toadstools of umbrellas. Rich and resonant the brasses crashed and died in the thick green twilight, rolling over them in rich sad waves. . . . Beside her her father sat . . . the rigid bar of his moustache beaded with moisture like frosted silver. She closed the compact and from beneath her smart new hat she seemed to follow with her eyes the waves of music, to dissolve into the dying brasses, across the pool and the opposite semicircle of trees where at sombre intervals the dead tranquil queens in stained marble mused, and on into the sky lying prone and vanquished in the embrace of the season of rain and death. [*Sanct.,* pp. 378–80]

The ambiguity, the failure of nature and surroundings to govern anything in the slightest, and Temple's return to her beginning in indifference are all complete. Neutrality passes into self-dramatization and back to neutrality again. Temple's volitionless movement

4. Throughout the book there is a matching ambiguity in images of light. Light keeps falling on Temple as if in rays of hope, only to prove false, and tunnels of trees turn out not to be as ominous as they promised to be.

through the book is the source of the waves of accidence which destroy people, but she enters as an accident-prone innocent, proceeds into the maelstrom, and emerges at the end with some of that innocence (or at least a neutrality similar to that of Nature) intact.

When Popeye spits twice into the spring an expectation is aroused, and when he is terrified by the woods and the owl the expectation is strengthened. But like most of the expectations in the book, it is introduced just so that it can be overturned. We expect that the comfortable town, as safe as Aunt Jenny's distance from humanity, with its garden and October blooms and rose-colored shades, will provide the proper antidote for the poison of the enclave at Frenchman's Bend. But it turns out to have a poison of its own, more deadly because it disguises arbitrary accidence with certainty, establishment, and calm. When it is a comfy old sofa that conceals the remorseless fang, what greater terror can Popeye's grotesquerie conceal? The conventional order of things, society as refuge, community as rescuer, is overturned because the conventional order of things is in collaboration with nature: it takes poses and does nothing. Our expectations are as sure as our confidence that the cavalry, pennons flapping and bugles calling, must pour over the crest of the hill. Horace is good at heart and is the only conscience-armed instrument of the society. We expect that, as in Perry Mason, five minutes before the end of the program, as Hamilton Berger's eyes widen and his jaw drops, the witness will break down under his steely cross-examination and confess all, clearing all those people (including the defendant) who have been busy looking guilty as sin throughout the trial.

But the cavalry does not come and the witness is the steely one. Horace is betrayed by his sister, a mainstay of the same conventional order. When she goes to the district attorney for personal reasons, to extricate herself and Horace from damaging involvement, the district attorney goes to the Jew Lawyer for personal reasons, to win the case and gain political advantage, and the Jew Lawyer goes to Temple (here the direction of all these movements becomes clear) for the same reason Popeye does, because she has something he needs. We know that the good people will triumph. Temple crouches in the gas station, and there are good people on the road and all around her: someone will notice and then the people will stop this rape or theft or corruption or white slavery. But all those good people passing in and out of the scene, as obedient as the chorus in a Verdi opera, are no more effectual than the blind old man at the farm, who can only be affected by what he puts into his mouth.

The pattern is the same in Nature. Inexorable accident wins out over that rather lovely presence as surely as it does over the enclaves. Isolated incidents and personal aims must win out over the society of massed mankind. Nature is always present and usually lovely. Society, cities, Popeye, machines, all tarnish and blight it—but *it doesn't matter* because Nature has no force even at its full strength, other than its power to distract. Accidental injustice is followed by celebratory blooming and accidental justice is followed by an equally celebratory blooming. The people go to church, the people wander in Memphis and Oxford, the people assemble and look at Tommy's corpse. The people are as immanent and ineffectual as Nature.

The impact of both Nature and the people is dependent for narrative force upon contrasts which arouse expectation and end in defied expectations and denied hopes. The characters are groping and accidental, and their groping arouses more ridicule than empathy. If Horace is the hero, then the hero must fail, like the hero of *Paradise Lost.* Even worse, he is so feckless, so impotent (Faulkner used him as an emblem of impotence in *Sartoris*), that he must continually seem less interesting than his adversaries.

But Popeye is an even clearer case in point. The introduction of Popeye's biography in chapter 31, so late in the game, is a fictional device with a twisted purpose. It is a hangover from the conventional novel, a device of characterization designed to further the plot. There, the character who has appeared innocent and holier-than-the-hero has his past set forth in such a way as to cue in all of our unresolved questions of plot. But Popeye has clearly been wicked all along, and here we get not just instances of past wickedness, but genetic and environmental excuses for his development, and finally an ameliorative intimacy and humor in death row.

The section must throw the reader completely. Popeye looks like an antihero—but not exactly. The device finally forbids even comparatively sophisticated expectations: if the owl and the woods won't strike him down, then at least he can survive and, like The Mummy or Dracula of the horror movies, live on to be wicked once again. The reader is right here to resent the complete overturn of his expectations, however arcane those expectations may be. But I think

Faulkner knew what he was doing, too. In a world in which Popeye is king and overturn is the rule, the law of psychological and sociological development can hold no more precedence than the laws of Nature or of man. The section comes on like explanation or even denouement, but its effect is only to accentuate accident, as explanation becomes excuse and excuse dissolves in enigma. The joke is, in one sense, a novelist's joke on us: the veil is lifted and what is revealed is more puzzling than what we had before. In another sense it is a rendering of a cosmic joke: all of our systems for explaining evil away by finding human cause or tracing environmental development fail. Their failure is as sure as that of the heaven-tree, the redbud, the dogwood and trial by jury.

Manipulated effects and reversed sympathies are combined in such a way that in the end Faulkner, as he overturns expectation after expectation, deprives us of essential balance. We can no longer find a horizon of morality or satisfaction or empathy, as character after character fails to confront the evil. In the distance, rising over the heads of Hogarth's grotesques and poverty and cruelty, there is the hint of an ideal to steer by. A row of overturned expectations must lead to some steadfast cliché or the expectations will cease to seem overturned. The reader is in free fall. *Sanctuary* in its defiance of expectation, its ideal of reversal, its carefully calculated distance from human feeling, refuses to introduce a necessary isle of repose. Because of this it is more exciting in memory than while it is being read. Its characters stand in the memory and their myth is true at a distance. We believe in them because we believe in what we have been through in the experience of their events. But the book while we were reading it denied us empathy, denied us a place to stand, denied us all our essential comforts, and manipulated us so frantically that we could not believe it while it was happening.

Faulkner did not make the same mistake twice any more than he wrote the same book twice (even *Big Woods* is a different book made of old parts). *Light in August* has Lena and Byron, *Absalom* has Judith and even Quentin, and the later books are firmly in the control of *us* figures, firmly in the hands of men rather than gods. Trees act like trees and mobs are generally brought to their senses by an obliging *us*-surrogate. Only here is coldness uncompromised, objectivity heartless, the performance more important to Faulkner than the audience.

4 *The Sound and the Fury*

Then they talked about what they would do with twenty-five dollars. They all talked at once, their voices insistent and contradictory and impatient, making of unreality a possibility, then a probability, then an incontrovertible fact, as people will when their desires become words.

The Sound and the Fury, *p. 136*

Perhaps the most consistent answer to any of the questions continually put to Faulkner was his very characteristic tracing of the genesis of *The Sound and the Fury*. The most concise form appears in an interview with Cynthia Grenier in 1955:

> It started out as a short story about two children being sent out to play in the yard during their grandmother's funeral. Only one of the little girls was big enough to climb a tree to look in the window to see what was going on. It was going to be a story of blood gone bad. The story told wasn't all. The idiot child had started out as a simple prop at first as a bid for extra sympathy. Then I thought what would the story be told like as he saw it. So I had him look at it. When I'd finished I had a quarter of the book written, but it still wasn't all. It still wasn't enough. So then Quentin told the story as he saw it and it still wasn't enough. Then Jason told the story and it still wasn't enough. Then I tried to tell the story and it still was not enough, and so I wrote the appendix and it wasn't enough. It's the book I feel tenderest towards. I couldn't leave it alone, and I never could tell it right, though I tried hard and would like to try again though I'd probably fail again. It's the tragedy of two lost women: Caddy and her daughter. [*Lion*, p. 222]

Although this and its variants provide the most legitimate impression of Faulkner's view of the primacy of narrative selection, as annotation to *The Sound and the Fury* it is perhaps a bit misleading. Our idea of the action in that book is formed by combining subjective views of objective reality: the continual sensual present of Benjy, the persistent theoretical or conceptual past of Quentin, and the improvised pragmatic future of Jason. But we do not emerge from the book with just a combinative effect or a triangulation of a central truth by point of view, as Faulkner says, but with these *and* the results of a powerful interaction: between characters, between characters and narrator, between characters, narrator, and reader. The book is shaped by mimesis, metamorphosis, choice at every point; by the combination of these forces in us and the juxtaposition of narratives in the characters.

The novel lies beyond what any of the individual sections can give us. If it is the story of Caddy (the little girl with the muddy drawers), then Benjy's section is a draft, Quentin's a revision, Jason's a sequel, section 4 an anticlimax, and the 1946 appendix an anti-anticlimax. If it is the story Faulkner says he was trying to tell, "of two lost women: Caddy and her daughter," then the protagonists are always beyond the limelight—Caddy only seen as what her brothers' affections and hatreds make of her, Quentin a shadow crawling through a window, hating one brother and being annoyed by another. The sections do not add up to a narrative whole, nor are they equivalents as Faulkner suggests: 1 does not equal 2, 3, or 4; 1 + 2 does not equal 3; 1 + 2 + 3 does not equal 4, and the narratives of all four do not trace the story that emerges on the edges of each of the narratives. The parts are not enough to make the whole.

This could be said, of course, of almost any novel: *Clarissa* is both more and less than the sum of the letters—but I stress the point because the effect of the book is the result of a very different process of combination and suggestion than any of the rest of Faulkner's work, and instructively different from that of *As I Lay Dying, Go Down, Moses,* or *The Town.* These differences have something to do with the reason that Faulkner describes *The Sound and the Fury* as "a failure" and *As I Lay Dying* as a "simple *tour de force.*"

Benjy's narrative seems to be purest obfuscation to start with, but like a doublecrostic, it gets much easier toward its end. The symptoms of this are familiar to students and teachers of the book: the chronology is deliberately jumbled (although it contains a better coverage of the time span of the book than any other section), and the leaps between present and past are too simple for us to grasp at first because we are too complicated in our fictional expectations. There is a great distance of empathy: Benjy's mind is not our mind and we cannot shift quickly enough or simply enough from perception to memory to pain. Then there are added confusions of naming and names: caddie-Caddy, Quentin-Quentin, Jason-Jason, Maury-Benjy. The point (beyond the evident fun Faulkner is having leading us into and out of the maze) has something to do with the end of the Compson line—name-confusions similar to a Hapsburg genealogical chart signify inbreeding and the last gasp of aristocracy—but beyond that, Faulkner wants to emphasize the distance between Benjy's consciousness and ours, a distance never really bridged until section 3 with Jason, because Quentin confuses reality and illusion as surely as Benjy does immediate and distant, smell and love, then and now.

But the alien in fiction quickly becomes familiar. One day is not that much different from the next to Benjy's view, so we move between what appears to be an ordinary present to various extraordinary days which have broken his pattern. We move easily because the triggers are immediate and habitual once we find out what's going on. A convenience of his perception is that it takes in all spoken words although it understands only some names. Within the segments of his narrative he is rigidly chronological and outlines everything, so that, in segments, his narrative gives something like the result of a completely objective third-person. He records as a fly on the wall or a hidden camera would. His rudimentary thoughts interrupt recording only as a rather reluctant narrative presence would interrupt his story—in Benjy's case, some perceptions interfere with what is being said. In other words, if we can put aside for the moment what Faulkner says about it, Benjy comes first not just because he casts the reader adrift but because he gives him a place to stand. His narrative is more significant as clarification than as obfuscation. The section contains many more germs of Quentin's, Jason's, and the third-person narrative of 4 than do any of these other sections. And even when his several pasts fade into the light of common day in the segments of the present, his narrative has a tangible power. In one way or another that day calls up all of Benjy's losses: Caddy, the fire, his castration, everything but the shapes of sleep. Even in action, as Quentin (closely parallel to Caddy in Benjy's view, in spite of her lack of affection for him) makes good her escape, the day of the present level turns out to be uncommon for the movement of the book.

Quentin's way of seeing things is as difficult as Benjy's in its own way, but where there has been a simple explanation for some of Benjy's confusions (his automatic associational triggers for the past, the handle of the stove which burns him when he watches the fire there), there is not always for Quentin. The effect of Quentin's narrative is more an effect of the past than Benjy's. Benjy's structure makes the past present, Quentin's seems to make the present past. There is less dialogue, more internal construction, as Quentin is eager to put even the most immediate moment behind him—the blood oozing from his finger, the smell of gasoline. We find some help in the connections to Benjy's events—Caddy's perfume, their mother's camphor handkerchief, the night of the sassprilluh, going back on the train for Christmas—but perhaps more important than the factual connections is one similarity of mind: when Quentin moves into the past he seems almost to take on Benjy's way of perception. Travel into memory is not automatically triggered but obsessively intrudes. The past keeps interrupting Quentin in units of perfect chronological order, units which he can suspend when the present is pressing, but which return in sequence as soon as he gets distracted. To his odyssey to the bridge is appended the memory of Harvard and the memory of home; upon the memory of home hangs his reconstruction of the past when, even as in "That Evening Sun" he is partly compelled and partly anxious (for the sake of understanding) to construct a whole out of the fragments which continually impinge themselves upon the present. Beyond this reconstruction is another level of memory, remembered within the past (the muddy drawers are here) and even beyond that an imagination formed of that memory, which takes his real conversations with his father and remakes them into imaginary conversations, working on real events which he improves with invention: real love which he wants to have been incest, failure which he wants to become unforgivable sin, disappointment which he hopes to make into despair.

He does not wander from one level to the next just because this is the way his mind works: he is driven from level to level. Confusions about the Italian girl and Caddy illustrate distance between Benjy's and Quentin's dislocation. Caddy's wedding, the perfume which so offended Benjy, kissing Natalie, Dalton Ames—all of these keep interrupting his self-obliterating day. As Dalton Ames intrudes more and more, Quentin is driven into unpunctuated prose. The memories and memories of memories mount up until he finally decides to have it whole, and we move into the central reconstruction of his conversation with Dalton Ames and Caddy, fully realized down to the minute, so fully realized that it makes irrelevant his life on the present level, and he moves out of his dreams into reality by striking Gerald. This is not a case of his dramatic awakening to what a fool he has been, not an awakening of embarrassment, but a clear transition out of the past because he has come to the climax and can now let it alone. He has made a whole past by turning upon fragments which pursue him like furies and making them into a whole. It has given him assurance over his doubts, despair out of his fragmentary regrets. He can now become a true "temporary," go back to the room, clean up, and arrive at three-quarters past the hour with the absolute purity of the absolutely arbitrary.

To take another view of Faulkner's "failure," it is perhaps not his failure at each of these sections in turn, one after another, nor his failure at integrating the whole, but his inability to make Quentin's narrative work in tandem with the other three sections, a failure to keep Quentin from dominating the whole. Readers tend to fasten upon Quentin because he offers them the most of hard-core "meaning." They cannot identify their thoughts with Benjy's, and the two later sections seem to dwindle off into the everyday: the comic, the gothic, the religious.

Quentin speaks too much in the fashion, with all the commonplaces of twentieth-century anxiety, so that readers are drawn to make him the center of the book and then to be disappointed in the rest of it. With this emphasis it becomes a failed conventional book. It seems to me that it is much more credibly seen as a flawed unconventional book.

Benjy's first-person narrative takes us out of our normal sympathies and fictional empathies, preoccupations upon which the effect of a first-person narrative normally depends, which it cultivates, by which it seduces. It subjects us to an entirely new mode of perception. It is not because it is a tale told by an idiot that we are jolted, it is that the idiot's tale so perfectly orders the perceptions, associations, and thematic relationships, makes them so inescapable, that we forget our normal stock sympathies and participations in the fictional world and move in a different step. We do not "become" Benjy because that would betray the peculiarity of his pattern, the subtlety of the free associations which connect sections, so clearly his and his alone. We don't identify closely enough with him and his patterns to become anything like him. The section is less a realistic rendering of the author's adoption of Benjy's consciousness than it is an exercise in the control of limited language to a poetic end. The construction is as "literary" as chapter 33 of James's *Golden Bowl,* yet it spins itself out with the ease of the babble of Benjy's mind. The different step in which we move is timed to a literary or poetic end rather than to that of a precise representation of consciousness.

Then comes Quentin: a theme-dominated, conventionally self-indulgent first-person narrative which calls up all of our conventional responses to the confession. Moving from Benjy to Quentin is not the same as shifting from one narrator to the next in Kurosawa's *Rashomon,* that is, from one sensibility met in us by one kind of empathy, to another consciousness met by the same kind of empathy. *Rashomon* moves from one Quentin-appeal to the next Quentin-appeal, from one conventionally shared set of experiences to the next similarly shared. To come to Quentin from Benjy is to return to the narrow world familiar to us from most other first-person fiction: the intimacy and participation of a shared confessional. I would emphasize the *narrow.* This is not to say that Faulkner wants us to have no sympathy with Benjy or that he wants us to adopt Quentin's assessment of reality or events as his own or our own, but is only a comment on the kind of variety involved in the use here of several first persons.

Jason is more complex. His narrative seems to appeal to the same sort of stock response demanded by Quentin and granted to him by us. But the subtle differences turn out to be significant. Jason's observations come down squarely in the present, and he is never confused about what is the past and what is the present. He's telling us—and his observations have less of the power of confidential confessional; we seem to be listening to a side of the story rather than participating in the consciousness. That his narrative is heard is emphasized by the way we hear "Once a bitch always a bitch" (*S&F,* p. 198), by his ritual storyteller's repetition of "I says." [1] Benjy was a transparent narrator—dialogue came directly from the speaker to us without the intercession of a Teller because Benjy could not understand what was said. For Quentin, dialogue was a kind of intrusion—something essential to a reconstruction of the past but not necessarily essential to his narrative—he brought it up for his own purposes, signified by the frequent omission of the notation of speakers. Jason is dependent upon public acknowledgment of his cleverness. Perhaps he is not really speaking out loud (certainly he is not "telling" in the same way Ratliff "tells" "Hair"). But after Benjy's narrative is reviewed by him and directly perceived by us, Quentin's thought by him and felt by us, Faulkner builds upon the heard-spoken qualities of Jason and adds humor.

We want to see things Jason's way because he tells it the way it is. He is amusing, tough-minded, funny, ironic. There is a part of us (as we shall discover in a different way in *As I Lay Dying*) which likes his cynicism, is relieved by his pragmatism. The strongest shift between Quentin and Jason is between conceptual and pragmatic, as the strongest between Benjy and Quentin is between seen and felt. Pragmatism and flexibility have undeniable appeal. Noah's wife in *The Deluge* raises some pertinent earthy questions for her other-directed spouse and she is the freshest breath of air in British drama up to that point because she cuts through the other-worldly domination. She may be wrong, but we *needed* that. The narrator and his group in "A Rose for Emily" are undeniably wrong, but we join him because he seems to know what he is doing; he has confidence, objectivity, and support in numbers. Like the non-Bundrens' in *As I Lay Dying,* Jason's line of narrative is strung somewhere between *them,* the observed (in this case the disintegrating Compsons) and *us* as observers. One of the early effects of his narrative is to attempt to dissociate himself from the isolated and join the crowd, to disown *them* and become *us.* In other words, Faulkner counts on Benjy to dislodge us from our stock fictional foundations, counts upon Quentin to make us comfortable again in a customary fictional response, then uses this established response (first-person involves us in spite of ourselves) and curries favor with us, seduces us, suckers us in with

1. This was called to my attention by a postgraduate student from Japan in one of my seminars. He had exceptionally good English but said that "I says" puzzled him and asked why Faulkner had used it so often for Jason.

our human desire for relief, for a realistic view, for a practical attitude. It doesn't matter at first whether Jason is right—he has his eyes open, he's a realist. Dilsey *could* get on the nerves—to say nothing of that incredible mother—and Benjy *is* an idiot. He drools; he's out of a menagerie. The household is a sideshow. We've come this far in the book without taking much stock of things as they are, what this family is really like, and then Jason comes along and conducts a guided tour of the madhouse.

We must pay for seeing things Jason's way, of course. He's a monster, and by subjecting ourselves to his story, by seeing things his way, we must become monstrous too. The hangover from the rather heady wine of apparent objectivity is discovering what we have become in the process. Because the character is an almost perfect example of Faulkner's suspension, he not only gives us his version of what his family is like, but within that version also gives us himself—like Chaucer the pilgrim or Lemuel Gulliver, his objective assumptions are not only objective but distinctively his. Our natural tendency to sort and sift evidence makes several piles. What we think is true (it corresponds to other evidence—in this case it fits with what we have found out from Benjy or Quentin), what we think might be true (it's news to us—we want to believe it because it is practical, sensible, realistic), and what we reject (that's just the way Jason sees it, he's paranoiac, he's a monster). The first and second of the piles grow fast early in Jason's section, the third becomes overwhelmingly large near the end. Detailed evidence of Jason's cruelty comes late, although evidence of petty chicanery is spread throughout. His cruelty to Luster with the tickets and to Quentin with the threats is much worse than any of the lying, cheating, or physical violence earlier. He emerges in stages like Mr. Hyde in the movies: first he simply conveys the other side of the story and adds humor; then he becomes Jason the sadist, the pathetic investor, the hopeless employee, and wanders into his brief flirtation with the past (somewhat in Quentin's manner); then we see Jason Connubial, Jason the Victim, Jason the Cruel, down to the final scene with his mother, and we leave him, *solus* in his room with his ill-gotten gold.

I dwell on Jason at such length because I think our responses are important in this book and our response to Jason is the most complex of any of the four we are called upon to make. Our response to Benjy must be new with this book—we have seen something like it (but not at all exactly like it) in any attempt at stream-of-consciousness. We are familiar in poetry with the dreamlike qualities of pure perception divorced from cognition and intellection, but the response called up by Benjy is not parallel to any conventional or familiar fictional response. Quentin calls forth the opposite response. Ah. Here we are. We know about this kind of thing. Jason's section seems to continue in this groove of the familiar, and we do not know we are involved in something different until it is too late and we have become Jason, or at least enough like Jason to give us pause. We observe Benjy in safe abstraction. We follow Quentin over the parapet because we've done it before—with Werther, with Childe Harold, with Trigorin, with whom you will—and it hasn't really hurt us. But the final failure of identification with Jason is more significant than our stock identification and self-destruction with Quentin. We stop short after a bit because his function in the novel has been achieved only when we make the decision to quit "following" him in the same sense, and by then it's too late. We have become Jason in a way different from the way in which we became Benjy or Quentin. Difficult or impossible metamorphosis first, not quite brought off, even by brilliant conception and evocative, poetic, patterned rendering. Easy metamorphosis second, managed by conventional, theme-dominated ramble. Damning metamorphosis third, achieving its purpose in the middle of things when we call a halt to the proceedings, make him *them* in spite of his efforts to become *us,* and observe what kind of a thing *us* really is.

Giving over subjective parochialism, Faulkner turns to the third person to finish the novel. The final section must be third-person for some of the same reasons that have determined the other tactics of the book. We as readers now need absolute objectivity. We need day-to-day. We need chronology. We need dynamics of the parts interacting. We need the peace of a story told straight out. We need the kind of whole world we have been denied. We came for a story and have put up with bits, glimpses, flashes, and parts, and now we want our sugar cube or our carrot or our fish.

Our fish is an odd one. Just because it has become a third-person narrative, we think, does it then *have* to be mundane? Breakfast at the Compsons. The everyday, fully rendered, minute-by-minute, word-by-word narrative comes on like a brick wall to the subjective momentum built by the other sections (a momentum which seems to have decreased from the beginning, but which is nevertheless noticeably stronger at the end of the Jason section than at the beginning of the last section). Here we are, and there can be no mistaking about time, place, and every single event. Why?

I think Faulkner wants to deal with Dilsey and to give us a dose of Mrs. Compson, and to begin to make a whole. The Auden poem about the Old Masters—a foreground filled with the mundane, with Icarus barely visible—comes to mind. What is happening is the *last* of the first and the last. Quentin is gone. Jason's future has been forestalled. But the daily round goes on. Dilsey sees the last, but it's not over yet, and won't be for some long, sad time. The dramatic, melodramatic action is here immersed in the expected, habitual, everyday; and if the third-person stops us short or at least slows us down and brings us back to dead level, it is in part because the book is dealing in terms of convention. The poetry of Benjy's perception, the tragedy of Quentin's obsession with theory, the comedy of Jason's business-as-usual all derive from a grounding in the mundane—but all rise through the several consciousnesses to a realization (in both senses: the fulfillment of the whole design of the book and the perception and understanding of individuals) which is the stuff of high art. Once we have been through those consciousnesses and participated in those imprisoned realizations, we have been multiplied ourselves—not by identifying with any of them, necessarily, but by trying and failing to identify, by identifying too easily, by identifying and discovering that we cannot go on. A new response is called forth from us here: as we have perceived through the power of poetry, through the stock convention of participation in a confession as it is forming itself, as we have been transformed by the objective powers of ironic practicality, we now must apply all three to the dying fall—the long, continuing dying fall—of the mundane spinning out of the lives, rendered without these transcendental insights. The Compsons are tragic not because of what they are or what they have been, or even because we have been each of them and are now none of them, but because our objectivity has been made subject to each of their consciousnesses in turn, and now we are deprived of any but have possession of all.

5 *As I Lay Dying*

That's a simple tour de force. *I took this family and subjected them to the two greatest catastrophes which man can suffer—flood and fire, that's all.*

Faulkner in the University, *p. 87*

Well, I judge my books by how much work and agony went into 'em. Something like As I Lay Dying *was easy, real easy. A* tour de force. *It took me just about six weeks (With a grin). I could write a book like that with both hands tied behind my back. It just came all of a piece with no work on my part. Just came like that. I just thought of all the natural catastrophes that could happen to a family and let them all happen.*

Lion in the Garden, *p. 222*

As I Lay Dying is a peculiarly moving book. Even readers who think it is a botch and teachers who teach it against their will find themselves puzzling over the novel's simple emotional power. The individual consciousnesses of the Bundrens are brought together by the process of sharing and keeping, by their exchange of ways of seeing and knowing, by a gathering of disparate desires along a common axis of things shared. These define the central unity. Things unshared—style, individual knowledge, or insight—define the individuals. But each individual's version of things shared, held in common, defines the individual too. The reader cannot stay wholly isolated from this. As the novel moves from the complexity in one individual's haunted consciousness and its invisible ghosts toward the comparative unity of shared consciousness, the reader must be drawn in too. We eventually share Cash's pride in his box, with Jewel we sacrifice the horse, with Dewey Dell we seal ourselves off in a hermetic circle, with Vardaman we drill the holes, and with Darl we burn the barn.

Yet Faulkner calls it "a simple *tour de force*." Faulkner's peculiar understanding of tour de force is a complex matter better deferred for the moment,[1] his insistence that this complex book is simple offers one clue to it. The substance is simple and its treatment is not; more than that, the simplicity of the characters and their adversary emerge with such clarity only because of the complexity of the narrative tactics and design. The ending of the novel and its ambiguity—part comedy, part tragedy—make no sense at all if they are not a part of the context of the novel's beginning and the rhythm and sequence of its middle.

The fifty-nine first-person segments of the book are doubly alternated, individually and by group. The narrative is passed back and forth between various Bundrens, and these "exchanges" within the family are in turn alternated with those of outside observers or witnesses. The pattern of alternation is complex, depending on both subtle juxtaposition and grand pattern. One narrator's segment can build on preceding sections cast in his voice, relate to the sections which surround it, or build a pattern for the book as a whole. The frequency with which any single voice is heard is almost entirely a function of the controlling pattern of empathy: there is more of Darl and less of Jewel because Darl is more important than Jewel in every way, to the design, to our alliance with him, to all the functions of becoming and shaping which are at the center of the novel. But that there is so little of Jewel enforces another pattern—he might be reduced by more words, he is more present in our imagination *because* of his few words—and this carries us back to Addie's observation on the distance between words and doing.

Beyond the simple matter of frequency, sections are ordered to form complex sequences, apparently determined by a uniform controlling design. Any single segment may share and continue what comes before it or contrast sharply with it or what comes after: the choice is determined by what the book's design needs for immediate combination or contrast or for more remote thematic threads and cohesive sharing. Darl and Vardaman tend to appear together (especially in the sequence of the fire, *As I*, pp. 196–216) [2] because they have the most to share with each other. Between Vardaman (p. 239)

1. See chap. 11.
2. I quote from the edition of *As I Lay Dying* listed on p. xi, and I give name or initial of narrative consciousness with page number.

and Darl (p. 243) there is an almost perfect continuation of style and substance. Vardaman attempts to concentrate on his loss of Darl by dwelling on certain constants (*Darl is my brother. . . . my brother he went crazy,*" pp. 241–42), and he is echoed almost perfectly by Darl's exercise in split personality as his outward self regards his inward in the same tone, the same style, in the present tense, with the same anxiety to figure it out. Three consecutive sections which form a clear sequence are Darl's description of the circle of light around the lantern which ends with the "is-not-is" calculations of the strange room (pp. 71–76), Cash's "I made it on the bevel" (p. 77), and Vardaman's "My mother is a fish" (p. 79). Cora precedes Addie because of what Addie is going to reveal to us and Whitfield follows because of what she has revealed. Juxtapositions for thematic contrast are seen in Dewey Dell's self-concern (DD, p. 56) and Vardaman's objective logical progressions which reconstruct his mother (V, pp. 62–64), or in a similar contrast (here probably a contrast for relief rather than for impact), as Tull (pp. 65–70) follows Vardaman (pp. 62–64) and Tull (pp. 80–89) follows Vardaman (p. 79).

Contrast and combination in the sequences and relationships formed by individual sections relate more to the book's strategy of alliance—the way we perceive the events of the book—than they do to the rendering or impact of the events themselves. Individual events treated by individual voices become in sequence a compound of common experience, then gradually through shared effort become a common cause. The book hovers on this balance for only a moment and then, broken by Darl's action in starting the fire, dissipates back into individual, disparate voices and actions and meanings. It is this force in the combinations which moves the narrative beyond the reach of any single voice and beyond the simplicity of "this family and . . . the two greatest catastrophes which man can suffer."

The novel's narrative rhythm supports this force; it is in part dependent upon chronology, events, and the Bundrens' adversaries of fire and flood. Transitions between sections form a pattern of acceleration as the book advances. Cursory examination of the transitions reveals a pattern of increasing frequency: more happens, more time passes per section as the novel progresses. Preceding Addie's section (pp. 3–160), overlapping connections outnumber any other form of transition; following her section there are more time lapses than anything else. Overlap dominates in the preparations for the journey and the journey as far as the river. Time lapse dominates once the river is reached.[3] The narrative impulse of the book reflects a gathering of forces, consolidation and acceleration to the end (almost a downhill run), felt perhaps most strongly in those sections in which the river is crossed and the barn burned.

But more important to the book's rhythm than this progression is the alternation of the family's voices with those of observers outside the family. What had to be held off in *The Sound and the Fury* until section 4 can here be distributed throughout the novel so that it continually balances the family's testimony: we get the objective outsider's view early and continually. There are two long passages (of eight sections each) in which only Bundrens speak, one of which precedes and begins the journey and the other of which leads up to and includes the fire. But beyond these two passages the family is regularly interrupted by witnesses who can never suffer what they suffer, sink to their misery, or rise to their triumph. They provide a continual objective commentary on the book's subjective center in the family without ever compromising first-person consistency.

The scheme used for "Emily" gives some indication of the complexity here: there is *them* (the Bundrens), *almost them* (Whitfield and the Tulls), *almost us* (Peabody), and *us* (Armstid, Moseley, and Macgowan). The isolation of all the Bundrens corresponds to Emily's isolation. But within this general isolation there are seven individual kinds: Addie at the far extreme, in ultimate isolation; Darl (like Minnie in "Dry September") about to remove himself from the scene; Vardaman, isolated in the helplessness of childhood, and so on down the line to Cash, perhaps just about to move toward *us*. The whole family is isolated from society by its mad journey, and individuals within the family are isolated from others in the family. In "Emily" the narrative strategy forced us to adopt the *us* of the narrator as our own view: we joined forces with him to share a common view. When the *us* turned out to be wrong, we perceived not just our failure, but the way in which we made Emily Grierson become *them*. In *As I Lay Dying* non-Bundren witnesses provide us with a collective objective vision to set against the combined subjective of the family. Our allegiances are stretched even farther. We have the same impulse to join *us* that we had in "Emily," but here there is both a

3. These and other structural relationships are perhaps clarified schematically in Appendix A.

stronger and an easier empathy with the individuals of the family (by virtue of the first person) than there ever was with Emily. As the narrative passes from family consciousness to objective witness, from *them* to *us,* we become accustomed to a rhythm in which one relieves the other: what was shocking transition in *The Sound and the Fury* between first-person subjectivity and third-person objectivity here becomes an expected progression.

The alternation of insider and outsider corresponds to the line between comedy and tragedy. As objective observers, we can see with the non-Bundren witnesses the grotesque comedy of the Bundrens' dogged and and naïve isolation. Darl's consciousness in his first section, the distracted concentration of his ironic vision, makes commonplace actions become an abstract dance. Vardaman's excessive logic, his adult seriousness, are comic. Dewey Dell's simple dependence is comic. Cash's literal response to the question of how far he fell is comic. But they are comic only as long as we see with Moseley's or Armstid's or Peabody's eyes. The pageant-wagon of the coffin is a comic grotesque only as it can be seen or smelled from a distance. Once we are involved participants in the family, even though our participation is tenuous—no more than an involvement with the shifts of first-person empathy—we must share individual compulsion, isolation, and ultimately tragedy. We continue to view the same objects, but our attitudes toward those objects, our participation with them and judgment of them, continually alternate between ridicule and respect.

Shifts of narrator, alternation from inside the family to outside and back again, establish the basic rhythm of the book. Both rhythm and sequence establish a general sense of flux. What happens to us in the novel happens because of where we have been and what we have seen, where we are and what we see. From Darl's almost autistic observation of Jewel in his first section we move to Cora's cakes; by the time we return to Darl he has changed, the book has changed, and we have changed. This sort of thing could be said, of course, of any novel. Faulkner's indication of the novel's "germ" better defines this particular sense of flux. The "germ" was not a source-point (like the muddy drawers of *The Sound and the Fury*) or an end-point (like the gray hair of "Emily") but a progress—the Bundrens confronted with every catastrophe he could think up: family, fire, and flood. This is consistent with the book's determined immediacy. That the Bundrens lack the Compsons' sense of the past assures immediacy.

The Compsons' world has but to decay and the Compsons to respond to that decay; we have but to respond to them responding and to section 4's objective picture of the slow but endless dwindling out into time. Throughout *As I Lay Dying* the characters respond to what they are now, expressed in an intense first-person narrative. Only what they have been—their immediate individual memories—and what they are or want to be now can inform their lives. The novel suspends unity between diffusion and decay, suspends momentary articulation between feeling and disappointment: but it must first construct the entity before it can trace its dissolution. Love—just a word to Addie (a shortsightedness which leads to much of the suffering of the book) is a part of this construction; poetry and poetic abstractions, formed by individuals or by their sharing, are others. A questioning of the locus of individual identity, of the ways identity can change when it interacts with others, is another part. The difference between experienced, shared, or observed suffering, an acute questioning of the relationship of the subjective and the objective, is the aim of the whole construct.

This questioning has its center in our relationship as readers to the events of the book. I have already alluded to the ambiguous attitudes which the insider–outsider alternation produces in us in terms of the novel's comedy and tragedy. Beyond this there is a complex alternation of individual empathies. Our Ishmael is not constant. The ordering of the narrators forces us to adopt Darl as home base because he is the first to speak and most frequently returns. Once we have done this, his view becomes our norm—his prophecy, his poetry, his abstraction become our habit of thinking against which some other characters' modes seem to work as deviants while some (such as Vardaman's) seem to support the center. Darl's sections act in some of the same ways that strongly directed point-of-view does in a heavily controlled third-person narrative, or as the control of our empathy does in "Emily." It is somewhat similar to the appeal of the conventional first-person but is not, as Quentin's is, dependent upon a cliché response to self-conscious confessional. Darl does not confess so much as he observes; self, others, world, shapes, are given almost equal value. He offers the most information, the most familiarity, the voice to which we are most accustomed. His sections are the occasion of our greatest temptation to join the family. We adopt him as guide.

Prescience is one of his modes, and the power of his voice for us, its sureness in our allegiance, perhaps explain how Faulkner can get away with the prescience, a violation of conventional narrative. As our guide he is superhuman in a sense, a god, like the omniscient narrator in the third person. Darl is a poet and a master of abstraction: he must know these things. His prescient narrative tells us what we want to know. We have no reason to doubt the details of what he gives us, so we accept his version.

When Addie's section comes along (the central shock of the book, since she speaks from a face drilled full of holes and only lightly covered with mosquito bar) Darl's prescience has accustomed us to violation, so we accept another—consciousness from beyond death. Addie's living physical presence rendered in the deathbed scenes have been prelude to this; her almost wordless communication with Cash; Cora's, Darl's, Anse's memories of her, lend credence to extrasensory perception. We suspend our disbelief more willingly because of the power of what she says, because of the way her words organize action, theme, and image. But in part we suspend our disbelief unwillingly and unconsciously because we need to escape from the physical horror of the action of the book to a level of human ideal dignity, and we think for a moment that in her consistency, in the strength and rebellion of her credo, we may find a moral center for the book. Perhaps her voice is innocent of the horror even though her corpse is at its center. For the moment she takes over and becomes the center of the book.[4]

But because she is dead and because as we move farther along we become aware that not just her corpse but her voice have imposed the ghastly trip on the family (she is not only conscious that it is a revenge but exults in it) we do not shift our center of feeling completely. Our moral center and our center of consciousness remain with Darl. We persist and are condemned and committed with him, as he attempts to bring to an end this pageant wagon of desire, aspiration, petty revenge, maiming, death, and horror. We want to burn it, with Darl we try to burn it, and in the act our madness and his are discovered at once, because the pageant won't be stopped, and

4. If Addie's section is taken as the midpoint (actually it is about two-thirds through the book in terms of pages and almost exactly at the two-thirds mark in terms of sections), there are eight direct chronological connections preceding her section, five sections with no connection, sixteen involving an overlap in time, and four involving a lapse of time. Following Addie's section there are four direct, three unconnected, two overlapping, and seven time-lapses.

the desires, aspirations, revenges must endure or even triumph, together with the broken leg, the sacrificed horse, and the face full of holes on the soaked and rotting corpse.

Darl couldn't have solved anything except a problem of illusion had he succeeded. Cash would still have been maimed, Anse would still have gotten his teeth and his wife and his gramophone, Dewey Dell would still have discovered she was doomed to the intrusion inside the circle which Addie before her both loved and hated, Jewel would still have been without his horse, and Addie, although removed beyond the realm of still-suffering flesh, would not have seen the fully ironic conclusion of her scheme: that her wish expressed to accomplish covert revenge had resulted in the welding of her family into a vital unit, then in the mutual destruction of individuals within the unit, and these together in the elevation of the whole caravan to a level close to tragedy.

The central alliance with Darl defines the patterns of "becoming" in much the same way that the acceleration of transitions between sections sets the rhythm of narrative. His opening section casts us into the familiar pattern of suspense by omission. We are outlanders moving into a strange mind, and we discover that that mind not only sees odd things—apparently irrelevant things—but sees them in a peculiarly detached and humorous way, not only sees them himself but imagines how they must appear to someone somewhere else. The seeds of his final split between objectivity and subjectivity are already present.

> Jewel and I come up from the field, following the path in single file. Although I am fifteen feet ahead of him, anyone watching us from the cottonhouse can see Jewel's frayed and broken straw hat a full head above my own. . . . When we reach it I turn and follow the path which circles the house. Jewel, fifteen feet behind me, looking straight ahead, steps in a single stride through the window. Still staring straight ahead . . . he crosses the floor in four strides . . . and steps in a single stride through the opposite window and into the path again just as I come around the corner. In single file and five feet apart and Jewel now in front, we go on up the path toward the foot of the bluff. [Darl, pp. 3–4]

Our immediate attempt to define this style and manner leads to an attempt to get at Darl's way of seeing things or to discover why he is seeing these things and not others. In *The Sound and the Fury* we were cast adrift in an alien perception which immediately marked itself as alien. Darl's by contrast is alien in ordinary ways—we know his particular peculiarities gradually, even as our allegiance is cultivated, only by successive exposure.

In the second section we pass from Darl to Cora, outside the family, who begins her narration in total, nonstop preoccupation and obsession, an overliteral tracing of a series of apparently irrelevant encounters having to do with cakes. The cakes are a red herring —they figure in the story but do nothing to advance it—but the discussion of them does much to advance Cora's momentary importance. She turns out to be far from the center of the book, but from all we know at this point she is as central as Darl is. In other words, we enter both minds with equal unfamiliarity, without prior assumptions. The jerky rhythm of section-to-section progress becomes smoother only after we have been through about four of Darl's sections. The effect of this lurching advance is to sharpen contrast between sections, cast us adrift in a world in which we can't tell the difference between molehill and mountain, and then gradually to relieve us with reassuring returns, allegiance-building repetitions, and the comfort of growing familiarity.

This diffuse introduction is matched by disintegration at the end of the book. The fire divides as surely as the river united the Bundrens. Darl seeks his final solution in the burning, Dewey Dell finds out and tells Vardaman not to tell (not to tell something which he fails to comprehend), Jewel risks his life to thwart Darl's solution. The journey marks time until something can be done about the hurts—Dewey Dell's pregnancy, Cash's leg, Jewel's back, Anse's teeth, and Darl's madness. Then Dewey Dell betrays Darl and moves off on a tangent to try out an abortive medicine she knows will fail, Cash turns his attention from the confusing issues of Darl's insanity to the gratifying conclusion of Anse's desires, Vardaman gets no train but some bananas, and life goes on. Diffusion, concentration, diffusion: we drift out of the book on side-issues, even as we drift in.

The concentration—the coming together in the middle—is more complex. Our growing familiarity, the progress of our initiation and our empathy with Darl, account for some of it; but the sharing processes in which the members of the family come together and begin to move as one is most difficult to define in concrete terms. Darl on the edge of the river (D, p. 134) marks an important moment in this cohesion. Quotation from the book would not serve my point, because excerpting destroys the strong sense one brings away from this section that the members of the family and the functions of their natural adversary are both coming together at once. The members of the family look at each other or watch each other or probe; the elements roll by: trees, river, logs mixed in a constant yet everchanging whole. There is an earlier such moment as Darl and his brothers carry out the coffin (D, pp. 91–93). All of the disparate responses to the making of the coffin unite to carry it out of the house: Cash's precision and planning, Jewel's daring, and Darl's dreaming and perceiving are all brought to bear on a single immediate problem, and instead of remaining a trio of assonant responses, Darl's less practical approach acts in mediation between Cash and Jewel so as to bring harmony, as surely as his mediation between Vardaman and the world brings a momentary peace.

Another such moment occurs when Darl, miles away in the wagon, reconstructs the deathbed, and his rendering of it invokes individual encounters between various members of the family, charts individual relationships and then group temper in a cohesion of love, hate, respect, and attention which make the action and narration of this section a microcosm of the book's structure (D, p. 46). Addie is surrounded by her family. She looks at Anse, out the window at Cash, at Vardaman, does not look at Anse, and then dies. Dewey Dell cries, Vardaman stares, Anse leans. In the wagon Darl speaks to Jewel. Back at the house Cash enters, Anse stands, Cash looks, does not listen. Dewey Dell does not move—and so on. In another section, just after the river crossing (D, p. 149), the wounded Cash is surrounded as Addie was, and the various members of the family look and do not look, speak and do not speak. Each of these is the book's central gathering and cohesion in small. Members of the family individually examine, wonder about, make metaphors for, see, fail to see, look at, refuse to look at, are threatened by, and threaten each of the others in turn.

This coming together is organic, fused by the common enemy of the river and the common goal of the burial, dispelled by the fire and the reemergence of all the individual aims as they reach Jefferson. It is bound to be of short duration because of the nature of individual human mutability, but it is dazzling in its triumph at the center of the novel. Individual and group, word and deed, thought and action, the shared and the unshared, the subjective and the objective, come to a point of balance and then fall away again into separation and imbalance. As Cash puts it: "It's like there was a fellow in every man that's done a-past the sanity or the insanity, that watches the sane and the insane doings of that man with the same horror and the same astonishment" (C, p. 228). The summary is not just applicable to Darl but to everyone in the book. We see Cora's obsession becoming insane, Anse's rationalization becoming self-delusive, Peabody's expertise about hill people becoming misguided. We regard Vardaman's drilling of his mother's face as irrational but right from his point of view at the time, Jewel as isolated but righteous in his insistence on privacy, Addie as inflexible but strong in her credo, Dewey Dell as obsessed but human. Each is suspended between sane and insane, between private and public, between doing and words, between kindness and cruelty, and each swings from pole to pole as the book proceeds. And the tremendous moment of coming together, of becoming one, after it has hovered for a moment, drifts off on the opposite swing, the one becomes many once again, involvement becomes unconcern, tragedy is reduced to comedy, and the extraordinary moves back to the terrible doing that runs along the earth.

"Becoming" is the subject of *As I Lay Dying*. The change that takes place between beginning and end, then, is far less important than multiple continuing experience in the middle—because the narrative design determines that it will be so. But a merely schematic sense of these processes of "becoming" is inadequate. It can give an abstract satisfaction for our sense of form, but scheme is too static for the heart of this book. Details of allegiance and alliance—small fluctuations of inner resource, small alterations in perception and being and becoming, are essential to an understanding of the novel's narrative design. Its concentration on inside-outside, individual-group, participant-observer, produces a particularly complicated strategy of empathy, in which details of metaphor and of logic in the characters' individual formulations become functions of narrative design.

The book is as image-dominated as Quentin's section of *The Sound and the Fury,* and the central theme of the individualized habits of shaping and forming all answer to Cash's reflections on madness: "That's how I reckon a man is crazy. That's how he cant see eye to eye with other folks" (C, p. 223). Seeing, looking at, watching, of course, relate directly to the insider-outsider, objective-subjective questioning. The images for eyes assume prominence very early in the novel but not in the disconnected showmanlike way familiar from Faulkner's other fiction (the lumps of coal in the dough of "Emily" or the rubber knobs of Popeye). The coherence of the references makes clear that they are clues to a most important pattern. On Addie's deathbed her eyes are the last living part of her (Peabody, p. 43), although certainly not the last part of her to die. The light in them is internal. Once they go blank for Cora (p. 9), but generally they are a source of light—"two candles" that "gutter down into the sockets of iron candle-sticks" (Cora, p. 8), "lamps blaring up just before the oil is gone." She shoves at Peabody with them (p. 44); "all her failing life appears to drain into her eyes" (D, p. 46), and just at the moment of physical death "her eyes, the life in them, rushing suddenly upon them; the two flames glare up for a steady instant. Then they go out as though someone had leaned down and blown upon them" (D, p. 47).

Dewey Dell's eyes lack the internal source, but the idea of the offensive weapon continues: "if her eyes had a been pistols, I wouldn't be talking now" (Samson, pp. 108–09).[5] Tull repeats Peabody's description of Addie and sees Dewey Dell's eyes "kind of blaring up and going hard" (T, p. 118). Even Anse, when Addie first knew him, had been known to drive his eyes at her "like two hounds in a strange yard" (Ad, p. 163). Jewel, by contrast, never reveals himself this way: his eyes are "like wood set into his wooden face" (D, pp. 4, 17, 173), and in the most bizarre rendition of impassivity, "Spots of white paper pasted on a high small football" (D, p. 203). Addie's internal source is not there. There is more than a hint here of Jewel's function in the book as object, the cynosure of other eyes. Eyes are not Jewel's chosen weapon. He reflects other light, somewhat dully, which goes along with Darl's dismissal of his consciousness, that he "knows he is, because he does not know that he does not know whether he is or not" (D, p. 76).

Anse "gazes out over the land" (D, pp. 16, 17, 19), but Darl's eyes are so full of the land that "the land runs out" of them (DD, p. 115). Vardaman's by contrast seem not to contain but to be empty and

5. Darl says they are "watchful and repudiant" (p. 102).

awaiting something: "his round head and his eyes round" (D, p. 46), "round and black in the middle like when you throw a light in a owl's face" (T, p. 66), "his eyes and mouth three round holes" (D, p. 210). They are waiting to be filled, perhaps even as Addie's new "eyes," the holes Vardaman adds with the auger, are.

Passion in Addie, prescience in Darl, fear in Dewey Dell, impassivity in Jewel, and determined innocence in Vardaman are borne out by the rest of the book but indicated in the imagery—not just in the way Darl sees things, but his way shared by others, taken over by strangers, shared oddly on all sides. And seeing is but one form of sensing, one analogue for point of view or for the function of point of view in this book, the commentary on becoming, and on the distance between the objective and the subjective. There is a similar sharing in the perceptions of Cash's carpentry: Darl, Jewel, Dewey Dell, and Vardaman can hardly get away from the sound (pp. 5, 13, 15, 19, 25, 49, 51, 57, 58, 63). Individual rendition varies ("Chuck. Chuck. Chuck," "One lick less," "like a dog outside the house," "coming dark along the ground," "Sounds like it is asleep," and Darl, Vardaman, and Tull share "snores"). Cash as he works is seen by both Tull and Darl as craftsmanlike, like a "jeweler" working "glass" or "gold" (D, p. 74; T, p. 82; D, pp. 4, 150), but Darl finally settles upon a repeated image with distinct sexual implications of an automatic machine "going up and down above the saw, at the bleeding plank" (p. 62), the "pistoning edge" of the saw (p. 72), moving "up and down, in and out of that unhurried imperviousness as a piston moves in the oil" (p. 73). The concentration upon the object and work on it makes the coffin a locus for ways of sensing, as inescapable for us as it is for them. It is made with care because a book of this title must have a coffin at its center, and responses to its making contain both the individuality and the common core which are the poles of the book's central tension. Surrounding it and its making with a shared attitude of unshared responses is a way of rendering the shared and unshared responses to Addie, responses to her departure and her legacy of determination, the complex individual relationships she had formed inside and outside her family. The sound of the coffin triggers Jewel's image of himself and his mother alone on the hill, the sealing of the coffin advances Vardaman's logical positivism, and, carrying it farther, Darl's speculations about fullness, emptiness, and common effort, and the whole enterprise makes articulate Cash's definition of the forces of this world arrayed against the builder.

All of this is predictable: as the book is about death, so will the coffin take primacy, even as that the Bundrens are hill people determines that their metaphors will concentrate upon natural or agricultural objects. Jewel is a snake, a leech, a hawk, a racehorse, a bulldog, his shaved neck a white bone, his face the "pale green of cow's cud" (pp. 12, 13, 89, 208, 225, 38, 91). Cash is an owl (p. 102), Dewey Dell a wildcat (p. 227). Anse is a scarcrow (p. 69), an "old tall bird" (an image shared by Addie and Darl, pp. 162, 154), an owl (p. 48), and his hand a claw (p. 51). For Dewey Dell, Tull, and Darl he is a steer, right after the maul hits it or standing knee-deep in an upended pond (T, p. 69), or "failing" (D, p. 154). Addie's hands are roots of "gnarled inertness" (J, p. 15, D, p. 50), rotten bones (D, p. 48), and of course a fish and a horse (pp. 79, 89, 95, 187). Each is remade for a moment by the observer into a frozen objective image, which reveals as much about the observer as about the subject. The most inimical images are applied to natural forces: rain like buckshot (D, p. 72), "sweat" of the river (D, p. 134), and the force in the river, like "hands . . . prodding at bones" (D, p. 151). The catalog adds up to less than one might want it to, perhaps, until one realizes the rather unpredictable function of all these metaphors, the emphasis of grotesque distance, corresponding to the tension between our subjective empathy with the Bundrens which leads to a perception of tragedy and our objective ridicule which leads to a sense of them as comic. That the vehicles of these metaphors are rather unattractive is perhaps the result of our lack of familiarity with such simple lives. One measure of the force that the grotesque takes on in the book can be accounted for by the distance between our sensibilities and experience and those of the Bundrens. And one measure of how well the empathy structures and the narrative and metaphorical devices work together is that the resolution of this tension achieves such unconscious emotional force in the book's remarkable impact.

The balance of the symbols, shapes, and metaphors follows directly from the concentration on eyes, through seeing and hearing, into a dynamic and shaping sense which involves forming and ideas of form. And here we come to an even more important alliance than just our alliance of familiarity with Darl. His is the most consistent development of shapes and formulations in the book, an ever-shifting but coherent development of seeing, sensing, and shaping for understanding. Faulkner's tendency to freeze action in time or to examine characters in the midst of a violent action can be expected to produce reference to artifacts, but Darl's tendency to abstract everything solidifies this tendency into a strong conscious pattern of images connected to the arts. There is some drama, as Cash shapes "with his empty hand in pantomime the finished box," (D, p. 47) and we watch the fire "through the dissolving proscenium" of the barn door (D, p. 211). Painting and sculpture are more frequent. Addie is (for Cash) a "picture of all time" in Darl's telepathic vision (D, p. 47), the chips of the coffin "look like random smears of soft pale paint on a black canvas" (D, p. 71), Cash's hair is "plastered in a smooth smear across his forehead as though done with a paintbrush" (D, p. 149). Jewel and his horse are "two figures carved for a tableau savage in the sun" (D, p. 12); he is a "flat figure cut leanly from tin" (D, p. 208), recalling "Barn Burning," *SS*, p. 10, or *Sanctuary*), one of "two figures in a Greek frieze" (D, p. 211), or "as though carved squatting out of the lean wood" (D, p. 221). Addie is "like a casting of fading bronze" (D, p. 50), and Anse "a face carved by a savage caricaturist" (D, pp. 73–74), "a figure carved clumsily from tough wood by a drunken caricaturist" (D, p. 156). Darl's sculptural vision becomes architectonic in the fire: "The front, the conical façade with the square orifice of doorway broken only by the square squat shape of the coffin on the sawhorses like a cubistic bug, comes into relief" (D, pp. 208–09). That Darl perhaps might never have seen a painting, much less a "cubistic bug," has become at this point in his prescience only a quibble. His shaping imagination is capable of almost any form, almost any design or abstraction that is relevant, except a design which would give him a sense of that which might limit his shapings, that which most threatens him—the line between sanity and insanity, a line which, ironically enough, Cash has to contribute from his orderly mind. This is not meant to suggest that Darl lacks order in his, but that his is the order of an artist, in which one shape suggests another and a formulation advances out of one system into another.

Darl's need to give shapes and forms to what he sees is parallel to everyone else's strong general tendency toward abstraction—not necessarily abstraction as sophisticated or as intricate as Darl's, but abstraction nonetheless. The idea of form is reduced to the almost visible but certainly tangible. Particular shapes are frequently drawn from the forces that move the Bundrens in the book: earth, air, fire, and water. For Vardaman shaping is a function of air or lack of it: sound moves faster because the air has moved out to make room for the rain (V, pp. 53–54), the dust sucks down the road, following the departing air (V, p. 54). In the corn crib he couldn't breathe because the rat was "breathing up all the air" (V, p. 62), which is, of course, a central postulate to his metamorphosis of his mother, and his ventilation of the coffin. For Dewey Dell the shaping force is a dark wind. It rushes past her breast (DD, p. 59), the "dead air shapes the dead earth in the dead darkness" (DD, 61). Her version of Vardaman's concern for air is a wind, somehow connected with time: *"I knew that something was passing but I couldn't even think of time then . . . I knew that something was it was wind blowing over me . . . like the wind came and blew me back from where it was I was not blowing the room . . . and all of them back under me again and going on like a piece of cool silk dragging across my naked legs"* (DD, pp. 115–16). She is more conscious of time because of the pregnancy. As it now constitutes a threat to what she has been, it takes on the power of shaping.

Darl sees both of these forces, and adds to them those of the light's shaping, the river's shaping, the rain's shaping, the fire's shaping, and the mind's shaping. His extended rendering of the work on the coffin by night is a product of a circle of light cast by the lantern, the shadows of moving figures within that circle the product of it and the encroaching darkness, lantern and darkness working together to create the action. He ends this section with thoughts on sleep and a discourse on emptying the mind of thought so that it may be filled with sleep, then moves to the implications for *is/not-is* which that emptiness and that fullness convey: "when you are emptied for sleep, you are not . . . when you are filled with sleep, you never were" (D, p. 76). Jewel "cannot empty himself for sleep because he is not what he is and he is what he is not." As he works on this he perceives another shaping force outside the house, "the rain shaping the wagon," which brings him into considerations of the relationship between time and ownership and thought and possession. The whole passage demonstrates the difficulty of extracting a single strand from the weaving of elements in the book. Individual alliance, sequential rhythm, diffusion and coalescence, seeing and sensing, knowing and shaping, image and fact are continually present, are all continually not only dynamic but organic, never *is* but always becoming, made to seem tangible and substantial by the central tension and strategy of the novel.

The continual concern for emptiness and fullness emanate from Addie's theories of how words and names "fit," that words are "just a shape to fill a lack," that Anse is nothing but contained molasses, "the shape and echo of his word" (Ad, pp. 164–66). But hers is less a shaping imagination than it is an imagination of shapes. Where Darl is dynamic, up-and-doing in his shaping, she is passive and static. He creates forms in motion, she stops motion in form; he begins and sets free, she ends and limits. In Addie's section the dominant mode is geometrical: circles, verticals and horizontals, diagonals, and curves are the objects of the controlling collective metaphor. In order to talk about these each character develops his own logical system of definition, reasoning, and justification, following Darl's lead in argument based in *is, is-not,* and *was.* The conclusions that these various individual logics make possible provide judgments of identity, cause, fate, isolation, and the nature of time.

The circle is rooted in Addie's section:

> I would think that even while I lay with him in the dark and Cash asleep in the cradle within the swing of my hand. . . . Anse or love: it didn't matter. My aloneness had been violated and then made whole again by the violation: time, Anse, love, what you will, outside the circle. Then I found that I had Darl. At first I would not believe it. Then I believed that I would kill Anse. It was as though he had tricked me, hidden within a word like within a paper screen and struck me in the back through it. [Ad, p. 164]

For her the circle is the self and that part of the self (Cash) which lies within the swing of the hand; the aloneness and isolation of the self inside the biological entity can be intruded upon by conception but not by the impregnation which brings it about. Dewey Dell sees the circle in a similar way—with similar shock that this last best constant in her life has been encroached upon:

> It's like everything in the world for me is inside a tub full of guts, so that you wonder how there can be any room in it for anything

> else very important. He is a big tub of guts and I am a little tub of guts and if there is not any room for anything else important in a big tub of guts how can it be room in a little tub of guts. . . . It's because I am alone. If I could just feel it, it would be different, because I would not be alone. But if I were not alone, everybody would know it. . . . He is Lafe and I am Dewey Dell, and when mother died I had to go beyond and outside of me and Lafe and Darl to grieve because he could do so much for me and he dont know it. [DD, pp. 56–57]

As seen here, intimations of fullness and emptiness work into this general pattern. The fullness which Darl empties into the strange room is a fullness of self, as real and tangible to him as the guts in Dewey Dell's metaphor and the more perfect geometry of Addie's concentric, overlapping, tangential, and separate circles. But Darl's vision moves in accord with the flux of the book, in tune with the power of moment-by-moment shaping—the confusion and the power of life. Addie's moves according to her need for a neat ending ("A man cannot know anything about cleaning up the house afterward," Ad, p. 168) and what must lead to it. She is subject to the force of forms, but lacks the power of forming. She perceives the stasis of plan, scheme, and conclusion, but can gain none of Darl's freedom of the forming imagination. About the family Addie is as settled as Cash is about his coffin. He knew what he was doing, he did it, and there it is. She knew at every point, kissed them (or not) and put them there, and there they will remain. Cash's plan for the coffin cannot accommodate the holes Vardaman drills in it, making a mockery of his careful calculation of seepage, or of so simple an accident as putting Addie into it upside down so as not to spoil her wedding dress ("if they want it to tote and ride on a balance, they will have," C, p. 90),[6] to say nothing of Darl's burning. Flux challenges stasis and now and again—even when it doesn't win out—demonstrates that it is the more powerful, more flexible rule of life.

The ever-increasing circle of buzzards swinging high in the air (D, p. 98, V, pp. 185, 187), though, is a reminder that stasis and static forms have power in their persistence. A circle, a fixed plan, motivated this journey: the circle perpetuates Addie after death. Her plan for the journey—her revenge—is not accomplished in the way

6. The passage breaks off at this point.

she intends, and certainly it does not take the form of a triumph of self; but her force which began the action on the road continues to impel that action throughout the book, and the circle of buzzards is certainly one among several things which impel Darl to the burning. Stasis has an immanent power.

Verticals and horizontals are not stated quite so subtly. Again the source of the theme is in Addie's section. The spring down the hill, Addie's quiet place, bubbles "up and away" (Ad, p. 161), she hears the wild geese "going north and their honking coming faint and high and wild out of the wild darkness" (Ad, p. 162). The explication of this comes later in the section:

> And so when Cora Tull would tell me I was not a true mother, I would think how words go straight up in a thin line, quick and harmless, and how terribly doing goes along the earth, clinging to it, so that after a while the two lines are too far apart for the same person to straddle from one to the other; and that sin and love and fear are just sounds that people who never sinned nor loved nor feared have for what they never had and cannot have until they forget the words. Like Cora, who could never even cook. [Ad, pp. 165–66]

It would make a pretty diagram if it worked so simply—if all doing crawled along the earth as Dewey Dell feels sound does (DD, pp. 57–58), as the whole wagon-pageant does, if all of Darl's abstractions and words flew straight up as he feels voices do (D, p. 19) or as the sparks of the barn do. But although Addie's pattern is used by Darl, Anse, Cash, and Dewey Dell, none of them uses it in just her way. For Anse, the upright is immobile and the horizontal is flux:

> And it fixing to rain, too. I can stand here and same as see it . . . a-shutting down behind them like a wall, shutting down betwixt them and my given promise. . . . A-laying there. . . . I told Addie it want any luck living on a road when it come by here, and she said, for the world like a woman, "Get up and move, then." . . . because the Lord puts roads for travelling: why He laid them down flat on the earth. When He aims for something to be always a-moving, He makes it longways, like a road or a horse or a wagon, but when He aims for something to stay put, He makes it up-and-down ways, like a tree or a man. . . . Because if He'd a aimed for

> man to be always a-moving and going somewheres else, wouldn't He a put him longways on his belly, like a snake? It stands to reason He would. [An, 34–35]

Since Anse is "dead," the only alternative he sees to "doing" is not-doing. He applies this logic of alternatives to the intrusion of the road, the outside moving into his world, and in his blindness fails to see any other possibility for the vertical. He is consistent throughout: his anxiety to get the work done is an eagerness for others to move; his desire for the trip, although he represents it as respect for Addie's wishes, is only a necessary trip out in order to come back with something—Mrs. Bundren and the teeth—which will make staying put more easeful (even as he consented to drive four miles out of his way to get Addie in the first place). Moving is asking for trouble: the vertical stationary is where man belongs.

For Cash, both vertical and horizontal are vital, but he calculates them in terms of stress: standing produces vertical stress, lying down produces "sideways" stress, and corpses produce diagonal stress. Unlike Anse he prefers none of these over the other but calculates the distinctions between them because foreknowledge of physical laws is part of his craftsmanship. His "bevel" is not just good construction but good insurance against the slanting attraction of animal magnetism and the vertical force of the earth and of water. The diagonal moves between vertical and horizontal, as a coffin is a compromise between a house and a bed (the vertical force of the sinking earth and the "sideways" force of the prone body, plus the diagonal force of animal magnetism). His calculation is thwarted because it cannot anticipate human accident.

Darl, Dewey Dell, and Vardaman are also conscious of the diagonal—but with a difference. Diagonals surround the Bundren house: "the top of the barn comes swooping up out of the twilight" (V, p. 53), "the sky lies flat down the slope, upon the secret clumps" (DD, p. 61). Slopes and diagonals threaten them: "Then I can see the slope, feel the air moving on my face again, slow, pale with lesser dark and with empty seeing, the pine clumps blotched up the tilted slope, secret and waiting" (DD, p. 59). The diagonal is not only the unknown, but (and here they differ from Cash) the unpredictable: "Jewel carries the entire front end alone, so that, tilting as the path begins to slant, it begins to rush away from me and slip down the air like a sled upon invisible snow, smoothly evacuating atmosphere in which the sense of it is still shaped" (D, p. 92). Jewel (in the dream on the slope with his mother), Vardaman (with the barn roof he could almost leap through), Dewey Dell, and Addie all refer in passing to slopes and hills, but only Darl seems to try to understand this middle way of the diagonal. He sees it in the river: *"What had once been a flat surface was now a succession of troughs and hillocks lifting and falling about us, shoving at us, teasing at us with light lazy touches in the vain instants of solidity underfoot"* (D, p. 140). Later he arrives at a theory of origins, made of the same stuff as Addie's master-theory of words and doing but with a conclusion which contradicts hers: "Life was created in the valleys. It blew up onto the hills on the old terrors, the old lusts, the old despairs. That's why you must walk up the hills so you can ride down" (D, p. 217). He sees a threat inherent and has worked out his solution using the same premise as Addie (how terribly doing runs along), but he has arrived at a more disengaged conclusion, one which does not compel him to exclude or limit possibilities but simply comments upon the qualities of what he finds. There are dark forces, but he will ride them out. Continual advance is a part of his formulation; hers is nonproductive movement.

The curve is almost entirely Darl's image and has to do with time. It begins in the circle—the wheeling buzzards: "Motionless, the tall buzzards hang in soaring circles, the clouds giving them an illusion of retrograde" (D, p. 89)—as if the circle which survives from Addie's pattern, the reminder of her negotiations and arrangements "inside the circle" can really drift into the past, as if there is some hope that time will heal these wounds of the present. Darl returns to them later in the journey but sees not even the illusion of retrograde now: "High against it they hang in narrowing circles, like the smoke, with an outward semblance of form and purpose, but with no inference of motion, progress or retrograde" (D, p. 216). A good part of the horror of the journey for Darl is that it will not end—that time has somehow been abolished or become confused with space—that the confusion of the two is one of the causes of the journey's pain: "Vernon still stands there. He watches Jewel as he passes, the horse moving with a light, high-kneed driving gait, three hundred yards back. We go on, with a motion so soporific, so dreamlike as to be uninferant of progress, as though time and not space were decreasing between us and it" (D, p. 101). At the river he takes up the image of a looping cord, trying to articulate the previous groping guess at the nature of the family's suspension in time:

> The river itself is not a hundred yards across, and pa and Vernon and Vardaman and Dewey Dell are the only things in sight not of that single monotony of desolation leaning with that terrific quality a little from right to left, as though we had reached the place where the motion of the wasted world accelerates just before the final precipice. Yet they appear dwarfed. It is as though the space between us were time: an irrevocable quality. It is as though time, no longer running straight before us in a diminishing line, now runs parallel between us like a looping string, the distance being the doubling accretion of the thread and not the interval between. [D, p. 139]

The diminishing line running straight before was the endless road, like ribbon on a spool (D, p. 38). The river's intervention across this constant diminishing line distorts both dimension and measurement: the members of the family are no longer separated by the distance which the river puts between them but by the irrational time it will take to cross that distance. Darl's image of the doubling accretion of the loop is made concrete in the rope in the river: "We submerge in turn, holding to the rope, being clutched by one another. . . . We touch and fumble at one another's extended arms, letting ourselves go cautiously against the rope; or, erect in turn, watch the water suck and boil where one of the other two gropes beneath the surface. Pa has come down to the shore, watching us" (D, pp. 151–52). The river is a distortion of distance into time, the river is a transformation and inversion of the normal forces of gravity and air and wind and light, so that to enter it is to enter an alien world.

This new geometry has echoes, of course, in Addie's calculations. Her love for Darl or Cash was not a question of their distance from her but of when they arrived on the scene. Her dismissal of the other children ("I gave Anse Dewey Dell to negative Jewel," Ad, p. 168) is a distancing determined by her experience up to that point and not a measure of her relationship to them. She cannot perceive that their relationship to each other is a continual becoming—that Cash can't wait to build the coffin, that Anse sends Jewel and Darl off for that final three dollars, that Darl has read Dewey Dell's condition.

Time and timing have replaced distance, and to get back to the nearness which mere distance would give them, it is also necessary to cross the river, to go through the flood and the fire, to join in the common enterprise designed by Addie as revenge on Anse but in a mysterious way thwarting her revenge, working to undo the complexity of the looping strings of the time relationships between members of the family. The dichotomy between distance and time recalls Addie's own statement of the vertical and horizontal: "how words go straight up in a thin line . . . and how terribly doing goes along the earth . . . so that after a while the two lines are too far apart for the same person to straddle from one to the other." The growing gap between distance and time and the way that one has begun to take over the functions of the other have brought Darl to an impasse.

Finally he takes the ribbon-spool, doubling thread, safety rope idea as a refuge. Confirmation of its powers would at least be a consistent replacement for the confusion of opposing forces and contradictory powers: "How do our lives ravel out into the no-wind, no-sound, the weary gestures wearily recapitulant: echoes of old compulsions with no-hand on no-strings; in sunset we fall into furious attitudes, dead gestures of dolls. Cash broke his leg and now the sawdust is running out. He is bleeding to death is Cash" (D, pp. 196–97). This is wishful thinking. Lives don't and lives won't. Cash is not bleeding to death, the sunset won't arrive. Even Darl recognizes this a page later: "If you could just ravel out into time. That would be nice. . . . if you could just ravel out into time" (D, p. 198).

Distance has been obliterated on the journey by time, but time has not taken over firmly enough or clearly enough to solve anything. The fire is, in Darl's terms, the only possible ending which can cut through the looping strings of time—cut short the suffering. Compelled by Addie's patterns, pursued along by the reminder of Addie in the buzzards and the remains of Addie which generate their atmosphere, the air the Bundrens must breathe, Darl dreams of ending it all at once, of sending it straight up, like words in a thin line, but better than words, leaving only the ash behind, free of the smell, the buzzards, the road, the pursuit, the suffering.

All the Bundrens use both shape and geometry: some share meanings for given shapes, some of the meanings (such as Darl's curves) are highly individual. To trace thoroughly the arguments arising out of the considerations of shape, form, vertical, horizontal, would be repetitive and perhaps to no great purpose, because these arguments are filled with the kind of productive ambiguity which makes reading of the book so rich. But more important than the specific arguments are the conclusions the arguments reach, the self-definition which the various narrators achieve in argument, and these are closely connected to what motivates or necessitates such argument in the first place. All the Bundrens use variations on the same logical system, but all come to the logical system seeking different ends, and the ends they find are predetermined by the ends they seek.

Jewel has no need of such questioning because he "knows he is, because he does not know that he does not know whether he is or not" (D, p. 76). But that this limitation (among other things) confines his testimony to one section does not deny his force in the book. He is the object of Darl's, Vardaman's, Dewey Dell's, Anse's, and Cora's analytical appraisal. He is the volition, the vitality, the potential which, like his horse, make their own pattern and impact in the world but do not impose an intellective pattern. This very lack of curiosity, in fact, his satisfaction with how things look and what he knows, is what drives him into fantasy on the subject of his mother. Lacking Cash's system and Darl's dreams, lacking any means to question what is, he resorts to what is not in an attempt to come up with a metaphor for his love for his mother:

> If it had just been me when Cash fell off of that church and if it had just been me when pa laid sick with that load of wood fell on him, it would not be happening with every bastard in the county coming in to stare at her because if there is a God what the hell is He for. It would just be me and her on a high hill and me rolling the rocks down the hill at their faces, picking them up and throwing them down the hill faces and teeth and all by God until she was quiet and not that goddamn adze going One lick less. [J, p. 15]

Exclusive rights to his mother are what he wants and what move him, but we never get much farther than this statement, a testimony in ellipses. Apparently he feels that his death in one of the two accidents would have carried him to a position of greater potential for action or at the very least a position more removed from the staring bastards, closer to exclusive possession of his mother. There is power in his section that comes from a kind of frustration—as if Darl had been represented in the book only by his first section. Jewel seen by others is spirit, vitality, *animus,* but what comes through his own voice is resentment—not paranoiac resentment like Jason's, but simple, blind, let-me-alone resentment, a ruling passion which determines the connections between his feelings in the section and explains his ellipses. His trading of the horse in order to free Addie's corpse from the staring bastards is a surrender of one exclusive ownership to serve another exclusive ownership and is one of the great sacrifices of the book. We have no access to it in words or explanations—it is simply there. Jewel's argument—if it can be called argument—is similar: negative in structure, uncohesive in form, neither self-serving nor open to the world but hermetically sealed in frustration.

Cash reasons from options, and tends to make his choices according to known laws. He is misrepresented by his first section (which has also misled some critics). His reasoning is narrow but surprisingly efficient. It develops over the course of the book so that by the end it has taken over at least some of the mediational functions of the now-absent Darl. This is a change perhaps brought on by suffering or even by a need to fill a lack. Except for the first section—that list of cold forces and stresses—his voice perhaps most closely approximates a norm of associational thought in the family, a middle ground which tries for less, settles for less, is more cautious, and survives in the end.

Dewey Dell attempts to define her biological self in relation to Lafe, Peabody, and Darl by use of *is* and *is-not* (DD, pp. 50, 57, 58, 115, 116). She doesn't finish sentences, rushes from one clause to the next with ellipses which represent her proccupation with her worry and her fear, even as Jewel's argument represents a mind that has never made the connections. She reasons from an internal conviction arising from biological necessity, and from this manages to bring forth a fully formed universe with herself at the center and to construct a fate from an arbitrary gamble with chance. Her style is of rushing obsession, as Jewel's is of enclosed resentment.

Anse indulges in self-centered reasoning which is essentially historical. His sections are almost oral in their delivery, in their apparent need to explain his plight to a real hearer—spare, self-justifying rationalization which keys in almost perfectly with his dialogue as reported by the narrations of others. His troubles come after the road, therefore the road must have brought them. Darl says he thinks he must believe it himself, but it is as childish—without the innocence—as Vardaman's argument which establishes that Peabody killed his mother.

Vardaman works on inclusive–exclusive deduction to arrive at the most startling metamorphoses of the book in an attempt to replace his mother (V, pp. 52, 55, 63, 79, 95) and he goes through a similar process in an attempt to define himself in relation to Cash's pain and Darl's madness (V, pp. 186, 200, 205–06, 239–42). Pure deduction and negative induction represent the limitations of his experience, but his limitations are more complex than Dewey Dell's because of the complexity of childhood, of pure argument without experience. His blindness is excusable because of the innocence with which he employs it. Vardaman is also too insistent that precedence means cause and subsequence means effect (although he is not as exclusively dependent upon this kind of argument as Anse is), and he is driven to false conclusions by the crucial necessity of putting *something* into the gap caused by his mother's death. He is like an unstable atom: something is missing and has to be replaced. He depends upon argument more than any of the other members of the family except perhaps Darl. He does not argue to justify but to remake. Besides, his absurd conclusions (that his mother is a fish and that crazy is farther away than Jackson) seem less and less absurd as the book proceeds.

Darl's argument has some of the same innocence: he makes Addie a horse, argues against fate, re-makes time, questions essence and almost everything else that comes along. He is open to everyone else's possibilities since he is the bearer of everyone's secrets through the processes of prescience and telepathy, but he also contributes a new term to the form of argument: to *is* and *is-not* he adds *was* and brings *was* back around to question present existence (D, p. 76). His reason for argument also differs from many of the arguments of the book in that it is not self-justifying. Darl does not undertake it in order to re-make the world to suit his life but in order to try to make the world resemble what it is. His argument leads ultimately to irrational violence, but even this conclusion is not self-justifying or self-serving so much as it is undertaken to free other sufferers. His is the argument most open to suggestion and most closed to rationalization. His particular dislocation manifests itself in a lack of interest in how things look and a preoccupation with essence—why things are, what they really are. And the burning of the barn is a natural conclusion to a covert train of argument Darl has pursued from the start of the book.

Addie, by contrast, accepts things as they are, or rather more precisely, solidifies them as she thinks them to be and expects them to remain. Her experiential justification springs from grounds similar to Anse's, but her apologetics is more refined, her case for utility more sound. Her section is frankly a credo and well organized to convince: this is how it happened, that is what I have decided and this is what I have done—quiet, assured, confident, and a bit imperious. Her argument, though, so moves to the central issues, images, and movements of the book that it becomes the theory to beat: it is so central that it challenges the rest of the book to provide a complex answer better than her simple pattern.

But her credo, even with the power of its poetry, ultimately cannot dominate the complex of action and interaction, thought and heroism, prescience and calculation, absurdity and dignity set in motion by her death and her wishes. It has to fail, not because it is unsound but because it is too inflexible. She expects her family to remain what she has ruled them to be ("I gave Anse Dewey Dell . . ."). Like Ike McCaslin she has forgotten about love—that she does not need the word love is less important than that she has lost—or never had—love for most of her family. Like Sutpen she does not allow for organic interaction but expects everyone to remain isolated (as she has) inside the circle. Like Quentin's, her structure is too profoundly cold, too absolute to become true, too rigid to be human. Her design defies the development of sharing and cannot even predict the unity they reach by the river. She denies words, and as we read her section the book seems to support this denial, by statement from beyond death and by her sure conviction of the superiority of doing.

The whole book finally denies this denial of words. Without the shaping power of abstraction that makes possible Darl's metaphors, his escape from his present reality, his becoming, the book would be a bore. Without that product of words that is fiction—the grand abstractions of selection, characterization, juxtaposition and rendition of consciousness, and, most important, the calculation, arrangement, and narrative strategy which determine our dynamic and organic involvement in emotional response—the Bundrens would remain in the vestibule of the uncreated. If doing and being could not have been indicated in words, if there had not been a triumph of words and their abstractions, this slough of experience and doing could never have been dignified. "Just going to town. Bent on it. They would risk the fire and the earth and the water and all just to eat a sack of bananas" (T, p. 133).

6 *Light in August*

Well, a man's future is inherent in that man. . . . That is, . . . there is no such thing as was. *That time* is, *and if there's no such thing as* was, *then there is no such thing as* will be. *That time is not a fixed condition, time is in a way the sum of the combined intelligences of all men who breathe at that moment.*

Faulkner in the University, *p. 139*

Memory believes before knowing remembers. Believes longer than recollects, longer than knowing even wonders.

Light in August, *p. 111*

Light in August is character-dominated as is no other of Faulkner's books—not even *The Sound and the Fury* or *As I Lay Dying*. One result of this is that each character carries his own structure with him and to a certain extent imposes it on the book. The structure of the whole cannot completely rule any of these individual narrative patterns, yet the whole is clearly greater than the sum of its parts: an explication of these individual patterns is not a decent explication of the book, and some strong general narrative forces have no root in the individual patterns. The enigma of *Light in August* is the relationship between these individual worlds and the book's cosmic forces. Individual worlds, islands of privacy, exist side by side for a time, then impinge on each other or interpenetrate. Some are kept private longer than others, only to be smashed into each other finally. The book has thus been taken to be compound rather than complex; in Malcolm Cowley's terms, it "combine[s] two or more themes having little relation to each other." [1]

I think that the tracing of narrative strategy can make more sense of this than any thematic system. This multiple progress of all the pri-

1. *The Portable Faulkner* (New York: Viking, 1946), p. 18.

vate, segregated parts and their violent conjunction brought about by the force of the whole makes, for instance, an elaborate proliferation of time schemes: the small time scheme for each character must govern that private world until the grand time scheme of the whole book seizes it. In *The Sound and the Fury* the past was the inherited burden of group and of individual. In *As I Lay Dying* the function of the past was reduced to little more than individual memory: each narrator's past operated according to his own rules, sometimes breaking out to affect his or someone else's present, but in every instance each was far less significant and far more securely individual than any of the individual parts in *Light in August.* Here the past is central: individual freedom or compulsion is primarily determined by a character's success or failure in dealing with his past—in coming to terms with the unspoken or, frequently, the inarticulate residue of what he has known, believed or done. And this past more or less determines his present.[2] Characters who can successfully integrate what they have been into what they are now manage to escape. Of those who cannot, some smash themselves up when their present meets another's present or when their *was* begins to constitute for them a *must be:* Hightower finds a happy entrapment by submitting himself to a chosen past, selected to replace and supplant permanently his present.

All the issues of the book—of past and present, of individual and group, of cosmic and human cause—emerge from those multiple functions of time, or in one way or another from the two quotations set as epigraph to this chapter, from man's "inherent" future or from memory believing. But no overview comprising a single unifying theme or narrative strategy will "solve" the whole or unify its disjunctions. Even the "solution" of a part is illusive because that part's identity is in continual flux, subject to change as the book progresses because of its dynamic relationship to other parts and the dynamic tension of the whole. Either the whole or another part can at any time rather arbitrarily change it or determine its fate.

One third of the book narrates events of the deep or intermediate past, and all of this is manifested in the pasts of individuals: Joe, Joanna and her family, Lena, Hightower, the Hineses. Each of these

2. Cf. *As I Lay Dying:* Darl's momentary concern with the relationship between *is* and *was* is far less important than his continual concern with *is* and *not-is,* with essence, with the problem of formulation or articulation.

is rendered in a different way and comes upon us rather unexpectedly. We move to Joe's past earlier than we expected (if we expected it at all). Lena's past is continually present because she is pregnant—everyone infers a simple past for her and that is not far from the truth. Joanna tells Joe about her past in the middle of the book's arbitrarily timed but strictly chronological tracing of *his* past. The narrative deals with four levels of time: present, imperfect, the deep past, and an intermediate level between the historical chronicle of the deep and the almost-immediate of the imperfect. The passage tracing the Burden family history which begins in objective narration and passes into Joanna's narrative to Joe is cast in the deep past in a style resembling the disconnected objectivity of the *Dictionary of American Biography*. Hightower's childhood (in chapter 20) is also of the deep past, but it is cast rather as a reverie of memory. Joe's deep past (say, everything up to Bobbie) is more objectively narrated than Hightower's, but it never approaches the coldness of the Burden section. The intermediate past (Lena's family, Hightower and his church, Joe's "phases" with Joanna) is also subject to considerable variation in tone and style.

The point is that we are led to believe that all this has relevance to the present moment, but we are given no warning when the next time shift may come. The narrative presence seems to accept as his donnée that his sense of timing is unquestionable and he need not consult our comfort or our wishes in the matter.

No past in this book is safely sealed off from the present. Hightower's past continually rises to the surface to haunt him in the present and to allow Faulkner to connect him with Joe and Joanna on the level of plot. Doubts about Joe's race haunt the book, partly imposed by his own internal doubts and habitual action in the present and partly trailing him out of the past in what people have heard. Because the barrier between the present and the past is so thin, the plot cannot be charted in proper Dickensian patterns of early incident and late significance: for individuals the past is never really gone—there is no such thing as *was*—but for the whole, the reader never knows whether what is past will stay safely sealed away or will erupt into the present. Hines behaves like a proper Dickens character, popping up when least expected with an identifying phrase out of the past ready on his lips. But McEachern, abandoned on the schoolhouse floor, doubtfully dead, a much more likely subject for coincidental resuscitation, never returns. Character dominance and arbitrary accidence combine to create a strong sense of doubt in the reader. Accidental triggers rouse the past, chance encounters rule the present. They never establish *Sanctuary*'s cosmos of accidence but, enforced by narrative momentum, they become by the end a web of inevitability.

This pattern of individual parts, the arbitrary eruption of pasts into presents, is set within an even more puzzling chronological scheme in the whole. Take *Sanctuary* as a point of reference. There Horace gives us exposition as he wanders into the Frenchman's Bend enclave and gives us more exposition when he gets back to Jefferson. We return to the enclave for the Perils of Temple and the narrative proceeds to shift back and forth between the outlaw camps of Frenchman's Bend/Memphis and the law and order of Jefferson, in the conventional manner of a gangster movie or western of the thirties. *Light in August* defies such an order. It opens with a narrative neither puzzling in its content nor expositional in its intent: the essentially static action of a character who later seems rather tangential. We move by what seems to be an accidental train of narrative association through Byron Bunch and Gail Hightower to Joe Christmas. There is frantic and unexplained action. Then we backtrack into the past of Joe Christmas, a character who has not concerned us for the first quarter of the book. We finally find connections between these disparate elements when we are more than halfway through, and then they are not conventional connections but only happenstance encounters. The Lena thread is tied up, the Christmas thread is brought to a dramatic end, we pause for more character exposition with Hightower, and then Lena and Byron move us out of the book. Disjunction here goes far beyond just a confused chronology or overturned conventional expectations. The reader has to become content to move where and when the author chooses, give himself up to a flow of characters, events, information, and encounters, and to draw his meanings and arrive at his responses where he can. Action, drama, or the conventional involvement of plot will not carry him comfortably along.

This narrative unconcern, the Teller's apparent lack of concern for the Hearer, is also present in the book's most puzzling time device, the arbitrary switches of tense from present to imperfect and back again. We might well expect such alternation to resemble the relationship between deep past and immediate narrative (as might a chronological narrative reordered to satisfy requirements of suspense and calculated revelation: this is what happened and this is how that motive originated). If the alternation of tense were arranged systematically around the arbitrary locus of the column of smoke from the Burden house, for instance, the story might be narrated in the present as it advanced from that point and in the imperfect for events leading up to that point. Instead we find that shifts between present and imperfect (in chapters 1, 2, 14, and 18) are from the very outset almost completely arbitrary.[3] Since this switching accomplishes no locating purpose it must be for effect, to enhance immediacy and dramatic closeness.[4] The use of the present tense (especially in returns to the present from dominant imperfect) slams the reader up against the action. Switches back and forth also lead to a peculiar uprooted quality, and this enforces the narrative power of moments of crisis such as the pursuit of Joe and Byron's pursuit of Brown.

But beyond this there is a more important function more closely related to the book's other time disjunctions. Once we as readers discover that we can function in the uncertain fluctuation between present tense and imperfect, we begin to get the idea that there is little difference between them: that pasts tend to persist in the present; that a past which has risen to the surface of the present several times becomes a stronger past and tends to convert a future *might be* into *must be;* that recurrence is a pattern in which it doesn't much matter where you stand because it's the same all the way forward and all the way back. Switches back and forth not only level distinctions between past and present (the past is present and the present is never really past), but suggest to us that for an individual, time might work in both directions. We can thus seek an explanation for the confus-

3. Chapter 1 moves three times into the imperfect (it begins and ends in the present), chapter 2 three times into the imperfect and once into the intermediate past. Chapter 14 moves twice into the present for Joe's point of view, and for the rest of the pursuit is cast in the imperfect. Chapter 18, moving among Brown's, Byron's, Lena's, and an objective point of view, begins in the imperfect and ends in the present with nine shifts in between, at one point shifting three times on a single page (p. 415). Chapter 20 has a pattern of switching similar to chapter 1—six shifts away from a beginning and end in the present; but here they are shifts into Hightower's deep past.

4. Such emphasis perhaps was intended to compensate for some of the vivid intimacy Faulkner had lost by abandoning the first-person narrative for this novel. This would connect the device to another similar attempt at intimacy in the frequent direct quotations of consciousness (see pp. 121–33).

ing, apparently arbitrary present in the incoherent, chaotic, inarticulate past. At the same time the narrative strategy invites us to look forward to the unforeseen results of tiny impulses started in the past.

Finally there is the contrast between our sense of time and distance at the beginning and at the end of the book. The novel opens in Lena's journey, timeless and distanceless because of her nature and her present condition. Ponderous moving and apparent non-moving here are contrasted to inexorable, inevitable movement at the end. From the pursuit of Brown through the death of Joe the book is compulsively driven to its conclusions, emanating from The Player's movements and culminating in Grimm's killing of Joe. The early concentration on present tense has already been accounted for in the way Lena's *is* presents her *was* to all who see her. But there is a further explanation: both Lena's helplessness as isolated stranger, subject of the town's sometimes cruel and automatic care, and her character of patient and timeless endurance are essential at the outset, both to define her place in the book—as a possible Ishmael—and to make believable her attraction to Byron. The downhill narrative propulsion at the end can also be accounted for, because Joe's *was* becoming an *is* necessitates a *must be,* and as it does the narrative gives over its arbitrary switches from tense to tense and takes up the inexorable drive to its fated end. The Player steps in.

But The Player has always been there. In our sense of the whole the omnipresence of the past and the narrative presence's omniscience about it, the Teller's apparent disregard of our sense of order and expectations, and the book's rather chilling objectivity have all been preparations for him, or perhaps even extensions of him back into the novel. He is the logical conclusion, the personified agent of all the habits to which the book's strategy has been accustoming us. And in the "Emily" sense, he is *us*: we, because of what the book's patterns of objectivity, justice, and accidence have instilled in us, have become The Player as surely as it is we who break down the door to Emily's room.

Seen in terms of the triple issue I have posed—time, individual, cause, and effect—the book's rather intimidating time disjunctions make sense. Each narrative device responds to the immediate need, whether of part or of whole, and the disjunction between part and part or part and whole are illusory. Eventually everything in the book responds to the story's necessities. The novel as a whole moves forward chronologically (rather slowly because so little of it narrates the immediate action at hand), and each of its discrete parts tends backward, from accomplishment to source. Lena enters the book pregnant; we learn how she got pregnant and begin a search for the father. We then see Hightower in deep isolation and examine the events which led to that isolation. We see Hines without knowing who he is, then see him nearly mad and move back to a point which precedes our first encounter with him to look for the sources of his madness. The burning house appears in the narrative before the crime does, Byron's weekend concerns appear without an explanation for them (Faulkner never really gets back to this), and Christmas's wanderings just prior to the killing of Joanna are traced before we see any of the causes for his fitful "thinking" or his psychosis. Later we know Lena has given birth before the birth is narrated, and know Christmas is dead before we have met his killer or traced his pursuit. And just before the end, we are given a yet more remote past for Hightower—the backward look itself looking backward. We might well expect to find such omissions and reversals at the beginning of the novel since Faulkner's opening move is so frequently suspense by omission; but the reversals begin early and persist throughout. None of Faulkner's other books—not even *Absalom, Absalom!*—reveals so consistent a set of reversed parts.

We are able to move through all this with comparative ease, in part because of the narrative landmark of the burning Burden house. It stands as a pillar in the center of the book, and the remotest reaches into the deep, the intermediate, or the immediate past are never far away from that mark. As with the house, all paths, figurative, narrative, and causal, lead there.

I have charted the relationship between parts and whole first in time schemes because our deep involvement in the book while we are reading it so peculiarly distracts us. The introduction of Lena sets up a red herring which, if we happily pursue it, can bring us to disappointment in the end. Even concentration on the central part, the narrative thread of Joe Christmas, is a disservice to the whole because it denies the significance of his dynamic relationship to the book's world; concentration on him can distract us from the greater effect of the chilling cosmos the whole novel embodies. Relating the parts to each other without undervaluing any of them is difficult but I think essential. Part of this depends on the double sense of time—cause can be traced forward or backward.

Each character sets off concentric waves, some of them out of his past, some from his present, and these waves meet the waves set off by others, resulting themselves in more complex waves. Small and harmless actions, moving through different individuals and their differing systems of values, become larger and larger, out of proportion and unrecognizable from their origins in force and result. The hermit, the eccentric, the outlaw—each moves and is moved in a private dance called by elaborate combination with the private dances of others.

A similar law works in the opposite direction: an unremembered action, an answer, a word deep in the past can prove to be the root cause of a complex response or violent action erupting in the present. Every individual is a puzzle, a set of nested Chinese boxes of cause and motive. *Light in August* gives us appearance first, the outside box, then a groupthink analysis by the town or another group, and then by stages seems to move us toward the heart of the final box. The explanation of this final root cause is not given; frequently it is resolved in action rather than in cause or motivation, but this, too, in its own way, builds the novel's power.

A colleague once said to me that he liked *Light in August* because it was the greatest study he knew of the origins of evil. I agreed at the time and still agree, but more and more wonder which origins of what evil. Both Joe's self-pursuit and the town's pursuit of Joe produce evil but are not themselves its cause. Each individual pattern, its particular residue of memory, knowledge, belief, abstract system, can be benign in private but in combination with just the right pattern in another provide a formula for malignancy. Some benign residual patterns can even operate for good in combination with others. Lena's particular state and pattern call forth Byron's protection and (in spite of his own defensive patterns) his love. His love in turn conditions his response to others and his appeal to Hightower to leave his isolation.

But those individual patterns which contain adaptations of rigid abstract systems tend to become malign when they combine with others. Hines's compulsive poison and his and McEachern's private and individually manufactured hells of Calvinism contribute to Joe's eventual poisonous combination with Joanna. Hines returns and triggers malignancy in others. But to say that Joe's crime is the product of his reaction to their Calvinism is simplistic. Personal adaptations of almost any institutional or abstract form can be equally poisonous: the Calvinist work-ethic, prostitution, motherhood (or foster-motherhood), community pride, racism, benevolent uplift, moralistic self-degradation. Each is more or less benign in itself, but when cultivated by rigorous personal adaptation and met with just the right combination in another individual, any of these can lead to evil.

Joanna's carpetbagger and reformer instincts, far from evil in themselves, become evil when they rather than her human feelings determine her relationship to Joe. They interpose external forms (even as MacEachern and Hines interpose their individual adaptations of Calvinism) as a substitute for human flexibility. The form of automatism promoted by abstract ideals, the hardening of responses and feelings into habits or reactions, is one of the chief subjects of the biographical digressions. Joe throughout his affair with Bobbie takes on more and more automatic patterns of behavior: to avoid being looked upon as an outsider he takes on protective coloration which will make him less conspicuous in the diner; he develops affectations in smoking and wearing his hat which bring him closer to Mame and Max. But these are secondary adaptations and he the experimental subject for the primary adaptations and automatic reactions in others. Thus adaptations or cruelty in others conditions in Joe a stock response to every contact until he finally finds all the shapes of his past—of kindness, of feeding, of love, of evangelical attempts at redemption, of racial attitudes—in the body of one woman and can kill them all once and for all by taking off her head.

Reciprocal interaction is the key to the fictional realization of all this and to the particularly flexible third-person method which Faulkner adopts as its essential narrative medium. The processes of cruelty are almost always dependent upon reciprocal fear—in the dietitian, McEachern, Bobbie, Joanna, in Lena and Burch. The tension in these confrontations is not just between subject and object, but between what the character knows and cannot know, between what he remembers and does not remember, what he knows and what he believes, what he thinks and what lies too deep for thought. The rhythm and frequency of third-person variation is capable of a much more delicate and sensitive response to momentary vacillation, the tiny vibration between appearance and consciousness, than is that of the first person.

The dietitian sequence seen only through Joe's eyes could never have revealed the dietitian's essential fear. Joe fears punishment for eating the toothpaste. The dietitian hasn't even noticed. She fears exposure and dismissal if Joe reveals something he cannot reveal because he hasn't noticed and is too young to understand. Joe rendered in the first person would have sacrificed the reciprocity of fear, the intense way in which the object of fear is played against the fearing sentient being.

A great deal of *Light in August* is devoted to the momentary examination of just what *As I Lay Dying* had to omit: the immediate response of consciousness to consciousness, the slippage between assumption or formulation of one consciousness about another, and what is actually going on inside another.

In casting this book in the third person rather than the first Faulkner did not want to sacrifice all the immediacy just to gain total objectivity. He salvages some of the first person's immediacy by switching into present tense but, more important, by a peculiar device designed to render thoughts and point of view. The framework for this is set forth early in Lena's journey:

> From the corner of his eye he watches her profile, thinking *I dont know what Martha's going to say* thinking, 'I reckon I do know what Martha's going to say. I reckon womenfolks are likely to be good without being very kind. Men, now, might. But it's only a bad woman herself that is likely to be very kind to another woman that needs the kindness' thinking *Yes I do. I know exactly what Martha is going to say.* [*Light,* p. 10]

The first quotation in italics of Armstid's "thinking" is at a level just below speech, more or less formulated for speech. The second (in single quotation marks) lies at a lower level, more articulate as it appears here than the thought it represents (as in "Barn Burning," *SS,* p. 10). The third, again in italics, returns to the level just below speech but incorporates a conclusion formed at the lower level. This is a very simple example of the 322 similar patterns in the book (see Appendix B), but it represents well the typical movement of even the most complex pattern. Complexity increases as the book proceeds. Joe has more instances of "thinking" than anyone else; Hightower is next with a more continuous development between one "thinking" and the next; Byron's are more infrequent but seem to move deeper in these isolated instances.

The venture into Lena's consciousness which opens the book is an example of the way in which Faulkner brings a comparatively simple device to complexity by its conjunction with other narrative devices. The first pattern (1) is an inner soliloquy very much in her style and speech, but speech repressed. This is followed by a second version coming from somewhere a bit deeper in the consciousness. Lena has come a long way and is farther from home than she has ever been. This could have been handled more efficiently by Faulkner in a bit of mind-reading by the narrative presence, but he chooses this more complex way because Lena's process of thought carries a meaning beyond its substance. *Is* and *was* are mixed for Lena Grove. The present dominates in her own mind but those who help her see her in terms of her past. Lena's pregnancy represents a past of which she has been made innocent by the man's abandonment and her simpleminded search for him. People treat her kindly because they believe in her condition (*was* surviving in *is*) as surely as they reject Joe Christmas because of what they believe about him, that is, that he is black. The whole opening section represents Lena's attempt to impose a *was* on what for her is a continual present of squeaking wagons. By showing her inability to do so, Faulkner demonstrates in short compass something essential about her.

The next three instances (pp. 3–4) reflect her innocence but, more important, her fatalism, which, rather strangely, is one thing that makes the present so dominant for her. All three of these "thinkings" are out of the past, and her thinking carries us back there so she can tell us about it as if she were still in that time. But her consciousness as she tells us is only of the present ("If it had been this hard to do before," p. 4). She amplifies this with "my hearing before my seeing" (p. 6). Since the noise forms her consciousness of the wagon, it seems that she was in it half an hour before she got in, and after she gets out, will in that sense continue in it for another half-hour. The present encloses her in the repetition of faces, kindness, wagon squeaks. The present encompasses both the past (her "thinkings" on pp. 3–4) and the future, which she develops by a fantasy of happiness, the vicarious adaptation of what Lucas Burch, she feels, will be thinking: "I will be riding within the hearing . . . before his seeing. He will hear the wagon, but he wont know, so there will be one within his hearing before his seeing. And then he will see me and he will be excited. And so there will be two within his seeing before his remembering" (p. 6). The fantasy is generous and more than a little innocent, but this is Lena's characteristic mode. Faulkner soon contrasts this unseen generosity to the unseen stock cruelties which lie behind Armstid's and Varner's kind words. But generally her effect on others produces good. Everything in Lena that is of the present causes the characters she meets to re-examine their pasts and try to change them: Byron gives up Saturday nights for her; Lena as catalyst brings Hightower to re-examine his place in the town and his isolation and to be tempted to change some of his *was* rules: to consider again having a woman in the house, to sally forth again as midwife, tempting all that old trouble, finally to realize fully his past.

All of this could be seen as a rather clumsy way to introduce a consciousness, pushing Lena's essential innocence so hard. But Faulkner has also involved us in Lena's sense of time and change: even as she adopts Burch's consciousness she further explicates her own. In the "hearing-seeing" relationship there is the suggestion of a Darl-like formulation, never developed fully, but perhaps completed in another individual, when hearing jolts Byron out of his dream of love for Lena the virgin and he sees Lena in labor. For Byron Lena represents so certain an *is* and so hopeless a *was* that he is able to suspend her from both *was* and *will be,* a suspension not broken until the baby is born and Byron is faced with a reassessment of what she has been and what he must become.

Faulkner's desire for unity and coherence in the pattern is not as strong as is his desire for truth to individual response. When Byron comes to that moment of reassessment, his mind works in its own way, one not so much marked by a literary mode common with Lena's, the similarity of his "thinking" patterns to hers, as it is by individual and immediate response to his situation. His pursuit of Brown in chapters 17 and 18 demonstrates some of the same volitionless movement as Joe does at points of decision, something of that same mental numbness which follows points of realization: "And then, just outside the cabin door where he had stopped, he heard the child cry once and something terrible happened to him" (p. 377). This is the echo of Joe's fears as he "waited for what came next," and the echo is repeated again for Byron in chapter 18 ("his insides were afraid that . . . something terrible would happen," pp. 394–95). For Byron the present is his involvement with Lena (signaled in the text by the repetition of "Byron Bunch knows this"). For Hightower and for us, Byron's past is that enigmatic cause of his weekend hegira. The town sees Byron's present as his job, and they don't know or care if he ever had a past. We never find out much about the past, and he abandons it completely when he meets Lena and is thus able to break free of whatever obligation it had imposed upon his present.

The surface similarity between Byron's and Joe's premonitions, far from enforcing the dominance of a common fate or even a common consciousness, suggests instead that even fate is individual. Byron's premonition does not prove true. "What came next" offers him a path for escape because his realization is not tragic but almost comic. It involves the adjustment of a dream to conform with present reality: "It was like for a week now his eyes had accepted her belly without his mind believing. 'Yet I did know, believe,' he thought. 'I must have knowed, to have done what I have done: the running and the lying and the worrying at folks.' . . . Yet still he did not believe" (p. 377). Byron has planned, assessed, calculated—all hermetic "thinking" directed to the end of serving and saving Lena. The narrative presence steps in with a metaphor for this:

> He was working fast, yet thinking went slow enough. He knew why now. He knew now that thinking went slow and smooth with calculation, as oil is spread slowly upon a surface above a brewing storm. "If I had known then," he thought. "If I had known then. If it had got through then." He thought this quietly. . . . "Yes. I would have turned my back and rode the other way. Beyond the knowing and memory of man forever and ever I reckon I would have rode." But he did not. [*Light,* pp. 378–79]

Joe's "thinking" is hermetic, but by contrast it is internally, not vicariously, compulsive. Byron has moved to complete his relationship with Lena, but it fails to satisfy his premises or resolve his identity. Thus for him the process cannot end with simple realization: he must carry the realization back to his former assumptions and change them.

> *It was not until . . . I heard her and saw her face and knew that Byron Bunch was nothing in this world to her right then, that I found out that she is not a virgin* And he thought that that was terrible, but that was not all. There was something else. . . . *I'll*

> *have to tell him now. I'll have to tell Lucas Burch. . . . Why I didn't even believe until now that he was so. It was like me, and her, and all the other folks that I had to get mixed up in it, were just a lot of words that never even stood for anything, were not even us, while all the time what was us was going on and going on without even missing the lack of words. Yes. It aint until now that I ever believed that he is Lucas Burch. That there ever was a Lucas Burch.* [*Light,* p. 380]

"Thinking" about himself has been prevented by the surface calculation he has devoted to helping Lena, and by believing. Now both are called into question by the believing he has failed to do. The surface has been enough to lead his memory, his knowing, and his believing into falsehood, to protect him from the danger to his self-esteem which lurks in "thinking" about himself. His volitionless movement responds to external necessity—helping Lena. He has been kept from Joe's kind of "thinking," from Joe's self-compulsion by a false believing, which has made it possible to lie, meddle, and care in a way which Joe's self-thought would have cut short. In other words, he has been in love.

Realization has come to him by way of the external, unavoidable, and incontrovertible fact of a noise and a sight, and it has brought with it a question about the basis of his action, meddling, compulsion, and love. When the adjustment comes it is not *anagnorisis* but inverted *anagnorisis*—essentially comic because it permits him to restore his order and to pass out of time and distance (in chapter 18) and back in. Then (free of this false pattern of believing) he can escape the book into some kind of future with Lena.

> The world rushes down on him like a flood, a tidal wave. It is too huge and fast for distance and time; hence no path to be retraced. . . . It is as though he has already and long since outstripped himself, already waiting at the cabin until he can catch up and enter. *And then I will stand there and I will. . . .* But he can get no further than that. . . . He does not give up, however, *Even if I cant seem to get further than that. . . . And then I will. Look at her. Look at her. Look at her.*— [*Light,* p. 418]

He gets no farther because what lies beyond is a leap of faith and a breaking of his accustomed pattern. He must move forward from realization to action—to make another try at what has been based in a false belief, and to have the courage to replace it with real belief.

Hightower's pattern at a similar point of realization results in entrapment. He begins (chapter 20) in a comfortable retrospective mood, shifting into his deep past: "Thinking goes quietly, tranquilly, flowing on, falling into shapes quiet, not assertive, not reproachful, not particularly regretful" (p. 461). But the quiet and comfortable (somewhat self-condemning) process hits a snag, and the narrative presence steps in with a metaphor: "Thinking begins to slow now. It slows like a wheel beginning to run in sand, the axle, the vehicle, the power which propels it not yet aware. . . . The wheel of thinking slows; the axle knows it now but the vehicle itself is still unaware" (p. 462). For Hightower the past is present in the rushing hooves every evening. He fled the present and the community that surrounded him to seek his present isolation in the cultivation of that past. The town thinks Hightower's past is what they said of him then that made him what he is now. And to Hightower the town is his *was,* as he is theirs. It is safer for both that way.

But now when he throws himself the old sops they don't work. He wants to continue to conceal from himself that his martyr's exile from the church was simply self-indulgence.

> "But I was young then," he thinks. "I too had to do, not what I could, but what I knew." Thinking is running too heavily now; he should know it, sense it. Still the vehicle is unaware of what it is approaching. . . . "It is any man's privilege to destroy himself, so long as he does not injure anyone else, so long as he lives to and of himself—" He stops suddenly. . . . He is aware of the sand now; with the realization of it he feels within himself a gathering as though for some tremendous effort. Progress now is still progress, yet it is now indistinguishable from the recent past like the already traversed inches of sand which cling to the turning wheel, raining back with a dry hiss that before this should have warned him [*Light,* p. 464]

His agony comes in the slow process of realizing what he is thinking, of seeing the false thinking within it. Again the narrative renders this by a collaboration between the narrative presence's mind-reading and direct quotation of "thinking." Byron's realization came on the instant and made all of the difference at once, to be consolidated only by the slow process of reassessment after realization. Hightower's is strongly contrasted to this.

> Out of the instant the sand-clutched wheel of thinking turns on with the slow implacability of a mediaeval torture instrument, beneath the wrenched and broken sockets of his spirit, his life: "Then, if this is so, if I am the instrument of her despair and death, then I am in turn instrument of someone outside myself. And I know that for fifty years I have not even been clay: I have been a single instant of darkness in which a horse galloped and a gun crashed. And if I am my dead grandfather on the instant of his death, then my wife, his grandson's wife . . . the debaucher and murderer of my grandson's wife, since I could neither let my grandson live or die . . . " The wheel, released, seems to rush on with a long sighing sound. . . . It is going fast and smooth now, because it is freed now of burden, of vehicle, axle, all. [*Light,* pp. 464–65] [5]

The wheel freed can move on to Byron and Lena, to Grimm and Christmas, the last two faces confused in his mind. He utters a final lament ("I wanted so little. I asked so little. It would seem . . . ," p. 466) [6] and the wheel turns on, on its own, because Hightower is back with the "whipping ribbons . . . and eager lances." His realization is tragic because he cannot use it to move beyond himself but instead falls back into his earlier fantasy. The last glimpse of him, objectified in his window, a bandaged head upon the twin blobs of his hands, as distant from life (although perhaps not from self-knowledge) as Emily, "like an idol in a niche," is as poignant as anything in Faulkner.

In Hightower protection of the self has taken precedence over all. He has broken some of his resolutions of self-protection and ventured out, but where Byron's realization ends in escape, Hightower's must end in entrapment. Hightower has been trapped in a dream of harmless insignificance, Byron has believed in a dream of altered reality. Hightower's fall from the dream must be to a horrifying realization of self-deception, while Byron can escape by reassessment. Hightower comes to realize that he is what he was

5. The first two ellipses are indicated in Faulkner's text.
6. Ellipsis indicated in Faulkner's text.

and what all before him have been, Byron that he can be what he is willing to be. We leave Hightower as an object, in a present dominated by a past. We leave Byron as a man in a *will be* formed of his past and his present. The "thinking" device finds its poetic statement and its major force in Joe Christmas. All other patterns of "thinking" are less absolute—controls for the compulsive and absolute integrity of his pattern: "Memory believes before knowing remembers. Believes longer than recollects, longer than knowing even wonders. Knows remembers believes a corridor" (p. 111). This is not just an overt statement of this most effective narrative device but its organizing principle. Memory is inarticulate and can believe without formulating. Belief contains the sense of both a leap of faith and a false self-deception. The inarticulate operates before the articulate takes over, and can persist even when the articulate has taken over some of its functions. *Before* gives memory not just chronological priority but primacy of incidence: it not only precedes the remembering of knowing in the child, but can also be dominant later, can cause knowing to be ineffectual ("longer than recollects, longer than knowing even wonders"). Memory can reach farther back in time than knowing, and can last longer—can outlast even knowing's failure to recollect, wondering why it does not.

This formula can be made to approximate roughly Wordsworthian categories: an infancy of direct sensations whose residue forms memory, a childhood of knowing and conning another part of facts and external truth, the youth's believing and the adult's remembering. But to make Faulkner's formula fit into such a rigid schematic pattern is neither necessary nor particularly useful (and commits the critical sin of preferring systematic arrangement to sense.) Faulkner needs only a limited system, to define the rough limits of these words (memory, believe, know, remember) and some others (think, see, say), so that he can then count on them to operate by controlled diction.

The main aim of the verbal limitation is to get at the central fact of the character of Joe Christmas: he is ruled by inarticulate memory. He knows, remembers, forgets, builds up self-knowledge and self-definition in a system of recurrence and repetition. Darl in *As I Lay Dying* sought freedom by trying to get away from time and distance formulation in an attempt to get at what *is* as contrasted to the appearances of what *is-not.* Joe is caught by the recurrence of what *was* and what *is,* and this forms his knowing, believing, remembering, being, doing, and necessity. Recurrence supports and feeds his remembering (which in some cases involves forgetting), his knowing (which is sometimes only formulation to replace a lack of knowing), and his believing (which, as with most believing, often involves a condition contrary to fact). The repetition and recurrence of what *was* in what *is* produces a necessary belief in (and indeed a strong likelihood of) what *must be* ("He was waiting for the rest of it to begin; the part that would not be pleasant, whatever it would be," p. 156; *"Something is going to happen to me. I am going to do something"* p. 97).

For Joe the past is what he was then—not big enough, not sure enough, not adapted enough. The present is thinking, believing, remembering—everything that has accrued to him from encounters in his past. *Was* for him is an ever-present recurrence demonstrated in physical fact by the return of Hines to his life, proved to Joe's own satisfaction by the uniformly stereotyped behavior of his women. *Was* is constant. Women (in a sense, always the same woman) are always a part of his *is.* He defines himself in terms of what she *is,* but first makes her become what other women have been to him. He has lost the power to escape from this form of dependence. For the town, Joe's past is a stereotyped offense of race and his present a stereotype of the mad-dog fugitive killer. It manufactures this by combining its stock reaction to his blackness with its stock reaction to Joanna's reforming zeal. For the town, the perfect victim has met the dream aggressor.

In Joe's patterns of "thinking" we see most clearly that the technical device is a continual response to narrative need, the same need to which the time disjunctions responded: there is no such thing as *was;* every moment of the present and every moment of action involves a deep residue of reference, connection, and even determination from the past. With Joe, Faulkner concentrates on the notion of the experience or fact he has forgotten (in the sense that he cannot call it up consciously) that still operates on his consciousness. Faulkner is trying to get at something that lies deeper than telling. We know but Joe does not what is determining many of his momentary movements and responses. Almost everything of significance that happens in the novel is the product of subverbal (or at least unspoken) weighing, calculation, or arrangement.

Joe's "thinking" falls into so many different patterns that any discussion which did not replicate the length and thickness of the novel would do a disservice to its subtlety and nuance, but a most representative sample can be found in his relationship with Joanna. The end of chapter 10 brings Joe to this final, decisive liaison. But already in chapter 5 (paralleling the general outlines of effect-to-cause movement in the book) we have observed Joe's wanderings just before he gets back to the matter of Joanna. Then in chapters 6 through 8 we accumulate data with him, watch the formation of a consciousness and objectively retain all—some of which he subjectively forgets, slurs over, and obliterates. In chapter 8 (the encounters with Bobbie) recurrence begins, and represents not just an input of experience but also the inductive process in which experience and recurrence operate in rapid mutual acceleration. The residual product of earlier input begins to determine new input. For instance, in his scene with Mrs. McEachern after striking down her husband (pp. 194–96) Joe performs and uses the words he might in a condemnation of Bobbie which could follow her refusal of him (if he ever got the chance to play out that condemnation). The combination of experience-input and repetition-echo results in a reaction which is already almost predetermined by the previous input. Lena is immersed in the process of travel, which obliterates time, distance, *was* and self. Joe is immersed in the process of recurrence which makes all of these one and determines his response. Perpetual warfare with his current woman involves continual warfare with himself as he watches, helpless, voluntarily moving again into a cycle, knowing his adversary must in the end win out but defying her nonetheless. He quite literally sees himself as object, even as he hears his mouth saying, sees his hand hurling the dishes against the wall, as he sees himself moving back to try the kitchen door again when all he really wants to do is get away (pp. 261, 224). He is rendered will-less by the process, because inasmuch as he is rootless and a fugitive he exercises free will. As experience accumulates, so must his fatalism. Joe in a sense makes the web himself by his initial judgment of his women and the performance determined by that judgment. Casting the various women always in the archetypal role imprisons them and him in a web of preordained action. In Joanna he finds the perfect adversary, one who matches each of his archetypal expectations with a stock response of her own, so that although she continually fulfills the role he casts her in, she does it in a perfect way which he has not met before. She draws him on by the fascination of her variety (she is a combination of all of her predecessors) and perfectly satisfies his expectation of the archetype.

At the end of chapter 10 he is already trapped.

> He did not know that he had even wondered or tasted until his jaw stopped suddenly in midchewing and thinking fled for twenty-five years back down the street, past all the imperceptible corners of bitter defeats and more bitter victories, and five miles even beyond a corner where he used to wait in the terrible early time of love, for someone whose name he had forgot; five miles even beyond that it went *I'll know it in a minute. I have eaten it before, somewhere. In a minute I will* memory clicking knowing *I see I see I more than see hear I hear I see my head bent I hear the monotonous dogmatic voice which I believe will never cease going on and on forever and peeping I see the indomitable bullet head the clean blunt beard they too bent and I thinking How can he be so nothungry and I smelling my mouth and tongue weeping the hot salt of waiting my eyes tasting the hot steam from the dish* "It's peas," he said, aloud. "For sweet Jesus. Field peas cooked with molasses." [*Light*, p. 217]

When Joe connects field peas and molasses with Mrs. McEachern, he infers the next step in the recurrence, saying that he won't be trapped, that he is under no necessity to love—but what he thinks he's saying is "won't eat." With Joanna he says he won't eat, won't love, won't go to school, won't pray—establishes a series of final lines of defense and then successively finds a rationalization for retreat from each one, largely because Joanna's patterns of attack demonstrate such variety and so surprise his suspicions and satisfy his imaginations of disaster. Possibly he might even have found a retreat from her praying, had she not pulled a gun on him. Joanna's patterns of memory, believing, knowing, remembering are operating in just the way which foreordains a conclusive end for Joe's patterns of recurrence. So the gun—perhaps a gun from the Sartoris duel—must be pulled, and Joe, to complete his own internal patterns, must kill her.

After the rather overt tracing of the process of recurrence and recapitulation in chapter 10, the narrative changes its method. The recurrence and the complexity of responses to experience are assumed, and Joe's experience with Joanna is developed with all the narrative richness of mixed chronology, variant focus and individual confusion.

Chapter 11 opens with a passage which firmly establishes the relativity of time in this part of the narrative.

> By the light of the candle she did not look much more than thirty, in the soft light downfalling upon the softungirdled presence of a woman prepared for sleep. When he saw her by daylight he knew that she was better than thirtyfive. Later she told him that she was forty. "Which means either fortyone or fortynine, from the way she said it," he thought. But it was not that first night, nor for many succeeding ones, that she told him that much even. [*Light,* p. 219]

The first sentence takes up where the preceding left off. Then we move in a series of time shifts which dissolves our attention to chronology, so clearly built up since the beginning of chapter 6. "It was a year after he had remarked without curiosity the volume of mail which she received and sent" (p. 220). The text is studded with references to particular times or periods of time and the relationships between one and the other, but order is gone. "And when he entered the house at night it was as he had entered it that first night; he felt like a thief, a robber, even while he mounted to the bedroom where she waited" (p. 221). That moment most beloved of trash fiction, the moment of first physical contact, is slurred over here, so that we are never quite sure when it happened. Joe's childish defiance of her "manlike surrender" clearly follows this first experience; his almost volitionless decision to "blow" and his subsequent return to the kitchen with the food-throwing follows on that, so that the general chaos is interrupted by passages of chronological order. Chronology is conceived of in a filmic way: it is here out of focus and there in focus, depending on the function of the particular moment—whether the event is to be dealt with in terms of the preceding narrative or in the more general terms which apply to the progress of the new connection, the new adversary, the new cycle. The distance serves narrative necessity by getting out a lot more exposition than Faulkner has the leisure to cover (point by point). In the midst of the general, rather distant narrative of the "three phases" Faulkner can insert the chronicle of the Burdens, then casually give us the impression that Joanna has recited all this, or something like it, to Joe.

The product of this development of the "thinking" patterns is a rich narrative of consciousness—consciousness which seems at times to be nothing much more than a surface level of twitches and knee-jerk survival, at others to go to the depths of now-forgotten patterns which form Joe's later actions. The process begins at a distance. Joe is an object of town curiosity, seen at a distance shoveling sawdust across the way. We move closer and see him in a series of enigmatic, almost autistic reactions, then become intimate as only a thoroughgoing chronological biography can make us intimate, watch him moment by moment and through a summary of a long period of development given in short compass. Then we see him pursued, get even deeper objective origins (in chapters 15 and 16). His end is at the greatest distance. We hear about it at the end of chapter 18, follow his pursuit in 19—when he is nothing more than a glint of handcuffs in the distance, again the fugitive outlander over there across the way, as he began—and finally we see the bleeding corpse. Except for that last-minute closeup, he has returned to his original state of the stranger.

Only we, like Hightower, cannot forget. We know too much. Faulkner has taken an impossible case for sympathetic attachment and empathetic participation and has not only made him accessible but has made the outside world of the town (which we accept at the outset) foreign to us because of our association with the outlander. This characterization is tour de force in the highest sense of his use of that term—tour de force which involves not just knowing what you want to do and then doing it, but stacking the deck at the outset against doing it, and involving all of the techniques of fiction to overcome the stacked deck. The time disjunction subjects us to both the compelling immediate effect of narrative details and the thematic results produced by narrative strategy. We begin in ponderous moving/not-moving and end in inexorable propulsion. The variety of our developing responses to Lena, Byron, Hightower, and especially to Joe—from objectivity through intimacy and back to objectivity again—moves us deeply into the individual power of parts without dissipating the overpowering effect of the whole.

One familiar narrative structure of this whole is yet to be discussed: our relationship to the town. It brings forth its consciousness in a complex imitation of the patterns of "thinking" familiar in individual consciousnesses. The residual patterns of the members of the community are generalized at the fire as a macrocosmic personality. Individual patterns of automatic reaction become as one. When community personality meets with the force of an abstract ideal in Percy Grimm everyone can embrace it because of their automatism—Grimm justifies their fears and at the same time can seem to represent a call to higher action, while still permitting them to retain their cherished modes of individual respectability and behavior. The macrocosm can become a whole by gaining in Grimm the will and force which they as individuals would never have known: with Grimm, the archetypal blind conscience, they can become as one for the pursuit of Christmas, the archetypal foe.

The subtle development of this needs to be traced in detail. Chapter 1 establishes basically the same pattern we saw in *As I Lay Dying*. Lena, wrapped in her subjective oblivion of time and distance, totally preoccupied with her search, is regarded by Armstid and Varner in much the same way Armstid and McGowan regard the Bundrens. They feel superior to the outsider in their experience and the innocence they assume for her along with several false attitudes which are functions of the archetypal role they have cast her in. Varner even reads Lena's mind, and the narrative presence immediately provides us with a correction to this reading, indicating that Lena is even more innocent than Varner had assumed, and that the process of community concern rests on a rather shaky foundation of assumptions and unsuccessful sympathetic identification. The community is in trouble from the beginning, then; it can neither appeal to our sympathies nor demand our adoption of its attitudes. It is unworthy of them because it is essentially mistaken.

In chapter 3 Hightower's career is followed in a narrative pattern strongly reminiscent of the pattern in "Emily." The subgroups are present but they have a less significant function here, only to illustrate the unanimity of the community's attitude. There is no central sensible, tough-minded observer as in "Emily" to which they can react by contrast.[7] The community displays uniform smug-

7. The subgroups here, with the number of times each is mentioned, are: the town, 6; people of the town, 1; people, 2; they, 18; some, 1; the church, 1; the

ness and misunderstanding at every level, acts upon attitudes rather than feelings, and consequently our opinions are neither engaged nor directed. They may be trying to enlist us, but because we see them objectively we will not share their attitudes or finally their guilt. The "elders" here put us off almost as much as the "party of masked men," partly because of familiar associations from experience and from other literature, but the novel seems not to be manipulating even this distaste.

Chapter 4, operating within the small subgroup of the men at the sawmill, contains perhaps our strongest invitation to join the town. Byron's point of view and statement, assessment, observation, are alternated with those of individuals and groups at the mill. All are clearly directed against Christmas and Brown as outsiders, and in this unanimity of opinion and the strong temptation to join in the camaraderie (compare similar feelings of kinship in the groups of "Hair," and "A Bear Hunt") we are for the first time persuaded toward alliance.

The effect of this persuasion, however, is gone by chapter 13, after we have been through Joe's biography and autobiographical commentary. After we have seen this complexity, beside which the simplicity of the town's attitude to an "outsider" is an absurdity, the possibility of an alliance with them is gone. In chapter 13 the town has become an attitude-machine for the production of damaging oversimplifications. At just this point the narrative presence announces quite clearly where all this ambiguity has been leading us. "Within five minutes after the countrymen found the fire, the people began to gather" (p. 271). They come together in a passage heavy with atmosphere, filled with the detailed treatment of small-town passage and flux which marks similar passages in *Sanctuary* and *Intruder in the Dust*. They are not gathering to serve as an obedient chorus or as atmospheric background but rather to provide the omniscient narrative presence with the materials for a thematic statement.

> She had lived such a quiet life . . . that she bequeathed to the town in which she had been born and lived . . . a kind of heri-

---

congregation, 2; members of other churches, 2; men, 4; women, 3; a woman, 1; elders, 6; neighbors, 2; old men, 3; old people, 1; old ladies, 1; ladies, 4; everyone, 2; Memphis reporters, 1; cameraman, 2; loafers, 3; party of masked men, 2.

> tage of astonishment and outrage, for which, even though she had supplied them at last with an emotional barbecue, . . . they would never forgive her and let her be dead in peace and quiet. Not that. Peace is not that often. So they moiled and clotted, believing that the flames, the blood, the body that had died three years ago and had just now begun to live again, cried out for vengeance, not believing that the rapt infury of the flames and the immobility of the body were both affirmations of an attained bourne beyond the hurt and harm of man. Not that. Because the other made nice believing. Better than the shelves and the counters filled with longfamiliar objects bought not because the owner desired them or admired them, could take any pleasure in the owning of them, but in order to cajole or trick other men into buying them at a profit; and who must now and then contemplate both the objects which had not yet sold and the men who could buy them but had not yet done so, with anger and maybe outrage and maybe despair too. Better than the musty offices where the lawyers waited lurking among ghosts of old lusts and lies, or where the doctors waited with sharp knives and sharp drugs, telling man, believing that he should believe, without resorting to printed admonishments, that they labored for that end whose ultimate attainment would leave them with nothing whatever to do. And the women came too, the idle ones in bright and sometimes hurried garments, with secret and passionate and glittering looks and with secret frustrated breasts (who have ever loved death better than peace) to print with a myriad small hard heels to the constant murmur *Who did it? Who did it?* periods such as perhaps *Is he still free? Ah. Is he? Is he?* [*Light,* pp. 272–73]

This is a remarkable passage of condemnation, almost vituperation. It has two foundations, one in our understanding of Joanna built up in preceding chapters and another in an ironic statement of the distance between the town's false beliefs about Joanna and its contented hypocrisy about itself. The narrative presence is able to convey both the town's developing point of view of belief and his own ironic denial of the validity of this belief. The machinelike professional or vocational functions of individuals in the town (their adaptations of system) have so far supplanted humanity that their reaction is not feeling but rather outrage on Joanna's behalf (secretly, because she has attained peace, the narrative presence tells us). The fire is an excuse for a momentary escape from the unsatisfying mechanism their passionless and soulless pursuits have forced them into. The passage is a denunciation, self-contained on one page, of the emptiness of man's usual workaday pursuits and the hypocritical excuse this emptiness provides for his madness in crowds. It is as bitter a reading of human motivation as is to be found in Faulkner, and it rules all of this book's prior references to community.

The narrative presence has been unequivocal throughout. When Varner attempts to read Lena's mind, the narrative presence steps in to tell us, "She is not thinking about this at all" (p. 23). He reminds us again, about Byron, "Man knows so little about his fellows. In his eyes all men or women act upon what he believes would motivate him if he were mad enough to do what that other man or woman is doing" (p. 43). He then goes on to assert that no one (certainly not his landlady) knows of Byron's life beyond his work. Mechanics and automatism have supplanted human relationships. Each man moves in his own track until he happens to draw the attention of the mob. Then it moves toward him, not to care or help but to destroy. Behavioral mechanism is suggested in another of Byron's observations on Hightower's progress: "As though, Byron thought, the entire affair had been a lot of people performing a play and that now and at last they had all played out the parts which had been allotted them and now they could live quietly with one another" (p. 67). Byron also suggests that only he knows why Hightower sits in the window, that the town does not know that he sits there or know that Byron knows. As it turns out, even Byron does not know what Hightower sees from the window.

But failed knowledge is less important than failed caring. Byron observes of Brown: "The thing was, there was no reason why he should have had or have needed any name at all. Nobody cared, just as Byron believed that no one (wearing pants, anyway) cared where he came from nor where he went nor how long he stayed. Because wherever he came from and wherever he had been, a man knew that he was just living on the country, like a locust" (p. 33). There is a kind of resigned inevitability in the town's insistence on the uncaring automatism of its behavior: "Then the town was sorry with being glad, as people sometimes are sorry for those whom they have at last forced to do as they wanted them to" (p. 64). Individuals are caught each in his own, largely self-made, pattern, and the community is caught in a pattern of automatic recurrence of boredom and automatic relief in righteous outrage. The stage is set for a terrible collision.

> Later, as the town quieted for the night, . . . Grimm's platoon began to drop off too. He did not protest, watching them coldly; they became a little sheepish, defensive. Again without knowing it he had played a trump card. Because of the fact that they felt sheepish, feeling that somehow they had fallen short of his own cold ardor, they would return tomorrow if just to show him. . . .
>
> Somehow the very sound of the two words [Grand Jury] with their evocation secret and irrevocable and something of a hidden and unsleeping and omnipotent eye watching the doings of men, began to reassure Grimm's men in their own makebelieve. So quickly is man unwittingly and unpredictably moved that without knowing that they were thinking it, the town had suddenly accepted Grimm with respect and perhaps a little awe and a deal of actual faith and confidence, as though somehow his vision and patriotism and pride in the town, the occasion, had been quicker and truer than theirs. His men anyway assumed and accepted this; after the sleepless night, the tenseness, the holiday, the suttee of volition's surrender, they were almost at the pitch where they might die for him, if occasion arose. They now moved in a grave and slightly aweinspiring reflected light which was almost as palpable as the khaki would have been which Grimm wished them to wear, wished that they wore, as though each time they returned to the orderly room they dressed themselves anew in suave and austerely splendid scraps of his dream. [*Light,* pp. 431–32]

A system is accepting converts and they will be able to move in a dance called not by themselves but by something higher. Community has finally taken its final shape. After starting as something we could almost share, passing through a stage which invited our conventional disapproval of its conventional smugness, it has passed from the dissatisfying mechanism of individual tasks into the terrifying form of the collective individual, happily donning the uniform of an adopted system, an adopted ideal, an adopted force, more attractive than individual feeling because it is potent, committed, idealistic—more dangerous for the same reasons. We have known that the town was capable of this since chapter 4, but only now does the full impact of that capability emerge. Then it was only a crucible for the production of frustration. Now it is a power unto itself.

Percy Grimm's individual destiny has just the characteristics which make it perfect for combination with the community's. His past never was—or rather he manufactures a past out of what he wasn't, repairing the lack of the war out of due time, now, in the present. His present, then, is a recompense for what his past failed to supply. He is madder than McLendon of "Dry September" in that he is trying to recapture what he never had in the first place. He is somewhat similar to Hightower: both are what the community has made them; in both a lack in *was* has led to a failure of *is*. But Grimm is striving to change the town's memory of him, and Hightower is striving to remain safely within the memory the town had made of him. Grimm, unlike Hightower, is the collective individual in small, seeking gratification in recapturing a power he never had. Thus the pattern of his part of the narrative corresponds so closely to the pattern of the whole that he operates the way we expect characters in novels to act, as functions of the advance of the whole (unlike Joe and Lena and Hightower).

The narrative, then, does not attempt to form an alliance between us and community. Yet in the confusion of conflicts between individual parts and collective whole our first instinct is to find a safe alliance or identification—someone to act as our locus if not as our guide. In *As I Lay Dying* we could elect to adopt Darl as guide to both general complexity and difficult individual relationship. He failed in the end and was carted off, but he served the purpose for most of the book. Here no one gets quite far enough away from involvement in events (as Darl does there through formulations and his dedication to abstraction) to act as our constant guide, or even to provide some indication of a direction to follow. Byron comes closest because he has greater objectivity about himself than the others. In chapters 17 and 18 this objectivity is called into question and he finally proves it to have been self-deception, but his questioning process even here is more objective than anyone else's.

Lena, of course, is the most consistent force in the book, but we cannot accept her as guide because we cannot share enough of her approach to things—we don't know what it is.

But we need a guide for *Light in August* because, with the mixture of subjective intimacy and objective coldness, we have been given no consistent pattern of *us* and *them*. We at least tentatively empathize with Lena and Byron: Byron as perfect expositor delivers exposition to Hightower, the perfect straight man for exposition, and the burden of exposition is one of the constant characteristics of narrative locus of the *us*-surrogate. The man with the facts not only attracts our identification with him as he is delivering them but makes us tend to look to him in the future for more explanation. And this is a book in which eagerness for explanation, or expectation that explanation is possible, is one of the reader's most strongly felt responses. That Lena and Byron escape from the town and, to a certain extent, from its guilt and the local web of inevitability, gives them the added attraction of Ishmaels. And as with Ishmael, personal peculiarities or moments of doubt are less significant for us in the final accounting than is the fact of escape.

The Lena–Byron portions then make one locus. Hightower serves as mediator of action between this group of actions and some actions even more remote than his own, with Byron acting as information-giver and Hightower as Hearer. We can assert from this a rather clumsy order for our identification with the book's actions—a division of individuals into us-figures, mediator, and others: one part to share with us and provide for our escape, connected through another part to the more remote events of Joe Christmas.

But the trouble (and here the complexities of our several relationships to individual characters and their individual narrative patterns are most apparent) is that we spend so much of our time caring about and empathizing with Joe. He can't be our guide, but he is our center: we cannot escape with him but we find ourselves caring most about his fate. We can measure some of this strange empathy by the distance we feel from Byron when he shows marked indifference to Joe in trying to protect Lena. Even the characters in the book who are able to care cannot care for Joe or affect what must be for him. They can listen and sometimes comprehend, but they can never understand or enter into his situation.

We can—more than Byron or Hightower, and more important,

more than Joe can. We can see the structures, archetypes, and individuals which must attract him, reject him, spell his doom, because we hold (by virtue of what his part of the narrative has given us) more knowing than he can call up by remembering. Compare what we share with Joe with the way we came to share the collective memory in "Emily." There we move backward in the narrative in three steps and forward in ten, so that by the time we return to the present we have not only been given the memory but have been taken up in some of the processes of remembering. Here we build up experience as Joe does, but do so in very short compass, so tangibly and with such compression that it is possible for us to remember everything—even some that he forgets.

We know in abstraction and retain all. Joe knows in totality and retains only shapes and repetitions. Byron knows of Joe what he hears. The town knows next to nothing and supplies its lack with ready-made archetypal beliefs about what it thinks he is—a nigger and a mad-dog killer. Again the central pattern seems to return to knowing and not knowing (as in the community's knowledge), the distance between what is and what is thought to be, the town's objective formulations from appearance and Joe's subjective compulsion from his past.

This split between *us*-surrogate and the book's strongest empathy does not help to resolve its unity. The independence of the progress of individual parts from the progress of other parts and from the progress of the whole will never, of course, yield a perfectly gratifying unity. This lack of schematic unity is surely part of its conscious design: part of the book's impact rests on the failure of its cosmos to provide unity for anything but disaster.

The solution of the problems of the rather enigmatic ending helps a bit. If we can connect even the surface of the Byron-Lena-Hightower events to the Christmas events we will have something. But there is a problem in even this minimal unity of surface: If Christmas exists only to bring Hightower to self-realization, then he died in vain, since we never find out if that realization is significant or just a momentary interlude before another surrender to the mad galloping hooves. The failure of this surface connection provides a clue: if the book is seen as a double structure on the surface, one part leading up to the death of Joe and the other to the birth of Lena's baby, some rude unity emerges. Byron and Hightower are the mediators—Byron because he must get involved with Joe's problems in order to help Lena, Hightower because the town's pursuit of Joe is parallel to his exile by the congregation and because he involuntarily becomes involved with Joe's end. The birth of Lena's baby is, of course, connected by Mrs. Hines with the birth of Joe, but this is just frosting on the cake in the manner of Faulkner's other rather offhand Christ-parallels.[8] The birth releases Brown and frees the Hineses to return to Mottstown. It also confronts Byron with reality and prepares him for his decision, which eventually delivers him from entrapment in *was* and provides for a change in Lena's station from a prisoner of the automatic kindness and secret cruelty of strangers to an open situation in which she can move by her own volition to her own ends. In terms of freedom and the freeing of individuals, the birth is as significant as Joe's death is in terms of final entrapment.

To insist upon a double surface structure resolves most of the apparent confusions of the ending. Our most intimate glimpse of Hightower and his most realistic view of himself must come at chapter 20 because it must be triggered by Joe's death. But more important, it has to come there because it must come after it is too late to do any good for anything or anyone at all except perhaps Hightower himself (and, of course, the book). It moves Hightower into a tragic measure (depending on how one reads the permanence of his realization and the prevalence of his tendency to madness) and provides the book with a time lapse in which what has happened has time to sink in—that we have been less moved by the whole event than by each of the individual narratives of its parts, that what we have seen has told more than it revealed at the time, that meaning here is a matter of making a number of leaps of faith. Then Byron and Lena must get together in the last chapter, at even greater distance from us, and escape.

The ending is more than Jane Austen's tidying up in the last chapter and sending all the Bennet sisters down the road into the future. It is an escape which we must hear about from a distance because for us as for Hightower, the past and what has happened have become more important, and form more of the core of the meaning of

8. To take either as the ultimate significance of the book is to make the error Faulkner warned us of, to mistake the pattern of nails for the structure of the house (*Univ.*, pp. 48–50, 61; see above, p. 6).

our experience of the book, than they have for anyone who has escaped. We retain everything they have lost in the process. The ending does not even bring us to an apt tidying up, but indeed to a point beyond any surface ending.

This sort of unity is no answer to Cowley's reading, of course. But it is to my colleague who puzzled over the book's aura of evil. And for this the narrative devices which indicate the particular origins of a particular past are less significant than the structures of the whole which act to frustrate any such fictional certainty. *Light in August* is, after all, less a definition of the origins of good and evil than it is a profound moral and philosophical ambiguity. What falls into place in the book, the climaxes of decision and motivation, seem to be attempts at solving the *why* which events have raised rather than just bringing to conclusion the *whats:* hence the backward movement of each of the discrete parts in the slow chronological movement forward. As Faulkner traces back through a sequence toward a cause or back through a biography toward a root event, we discover that he is giving us only so much and no more. Faulkner continually indicates—in narrative structure, in time disjunction, in the overt statements of the narrative presence—that we should seek explanation and answer in the cause rather than in its effects, in the source which (he indicates) the reader has perhaps slighted in his rush to conclusions. Then he traces out a pattern of multiple roots and continual conditioning which finally suspends moral and philosophical certainty between the opposed mirrors of multiple cause and magnified effect. The time structure and its searchings for cause in individual pasts are continually building up our information, accumulating more and more materials for subjective understanding. Our alliance with particular individuals grows as the book proceeds. At the same time a rudimentary alliance with the community of the town, established early in Armstid and Varner and in the sawmill group's examination of Joe and Lucas, gradually decays. In other words, the time structure and the progress of individuals reveal a growth of the subjective and internal, the whole and the groupings reveal a structure of the objective and distant. Our search for general principles is frustrated by our knowledge of particular exceptions.

Sanctuary dealt with an amoral cosmos: the stock good of innocence in Temple and the stock evil of corruption in Popeye are unaffected either by the immanent force of Nature's traditional order or the justifying redressal of the society's established forms. The effects were ironically detached from their causes in a mythical universe of mistaken execution and accidental blooming, arbitrary reward and punishment. Gratuitous circumstance led to arbitrary fate. *Light in August* is neither so ironic nor so detached. There is a sense here that a cause exists for every effect, but its source may be rather accidental and cause wildly disproportionate effect. Everyone in the book pursues his own ends in a world filled with combinations and patterns in other humans which may at any moment turn against him. Each plows a mined field without a map: apparently no conventional guide to virtue will see him safely through. The community proves that it is not enough to mind one's own business, but in taking up with Percy Grimm, it questions the advantage of an abstract ideal. Bunch finds that even caring can be carried too far—into a form of blindness, and Hightower concludes that there is no haven in the present or safety in the future. Our sense of relief in following Byron and Lena out of the book at the end is not just a product of our identification with them, but the strong feeling that having escaped from the community they (and we with them) have escaped from the world of the book.

Light in August gives us at once a growing faith in our knowledge of details and a profound chaos in structure. We can always approach the truth about the characters and the events and the meanings in the book, continually coming closer and closer; but the surrounding meetings, confrontations, and combinations between individuals retain their essential and evocative mystery, the ambiguity of life. What the book makes for us while we are reading it differs from what it makes after we have read it and are away from it. It combines *As I Lay Dying*'s satisfaction of pattern with *Sanctuary*'s mythic and brooding world.

Tour de force I suppose it is not (in spite of the characters of Joe and Hightower) because, as with any product of literary genius, it is impossible to maintain the assumption that it was written by one man who intended all the meanings and structures which emerge from it. But if it is possible to maintain a binocular vision—to see with one eye Old Bill snapping his galluses and talking about storytelling and with the other to see objectively the effect upon us of the death of Christmas—then literary genius must exist.

7 *Absalom, Absalom!*

Yes, shadowy; a myth, a phantom: something which they engendered and created whole themselves; some effluvium of Sutpen blood and character, as though as a man he did not exist at all.

Absalom, Absalom! *p. 104*

The problem of discussing *Absalom, Absalom!* is a problem of where to start. As the novel is (to borrow from Robert Frost) "simply made of metaphor," perhaps a rather crude metaphor taken from the novel's most memorable atmospheric moment would not be out of place. It is like wistaria, that strange plant which thrives and proliferates when you try to kill it, whose blooms know to seek its own extremes, whose seedpods will not simply drop but must burst with a loud explosion. It is a much of a muchness, too much book for its length. It continually goes too far, throws the reader back upon his own control and order to try to resolve its paradoxes poetically. Sutpen's design in its final failure becomes simply inflexible and pathetic like Ike McCaslin's or Addie Bundren's; but at the outset and for most of the book it is simply too big for his imagination or ours to take in. The metaphors—the sherbet that is Judith, Bon the racehorse, Henry the photographic plate, Ellen the butterfly, and all the others—lurch out of control: each moves to its own end until the narrative line seems so cluttered with objects that we as readers have to brush them away to find out where we are. The distorted chronology, excessive rhetoric and style (strongly individual to this novel, but so extreme that it defines what belligerent critics have termed "Faulknerese" once and for all), the scattering of facts and clues and the ratiocination of gathering and sifting them—all seem to direct us as readers to proceed on a headlong drive for solution of this peculiarly cluttered puzzle.

This rush to proceed from the documents, the letters, the scratches on the tombstones to what "really" happened can obscure what is suspended in between. The book's "whodunit" qualities can fasten the reader on Thomas Sutpen as an instance of the American Dream, a Jay Gatsby in patchwork gray. This he surely is, even as Emily Grierson is surely Southern womanhood. But the book is more.

As novel, *Absalom, Absalom!* traces the South. More clearly than any of Faulkner's other novels it is an attempt to deal with the roots of the South's historical neurosis. As myth it is certainly a version of the American Dream. Sutpen is too heroic and too American not to fall into the shapes and dimensions of that rutted category. But more important to a coherent understanding than this theme or this myth is the book's process. To begin to understand *Light in August* is to gain an intermediate mastery, a position from which the book's deeper complexity may be perceived. To begin to understand *Absalom, Absalom!* is to accept the book's process, to move beyond what may seem to be the centers of the book—a hero, a story, a dream, a myth, a tragedy—into the process of narrative itself by which these apparent centers are revealed. Telling and hearing are constant; treatment and focus shift. Could not telling and hearing themselves be at the heart of the book?

A rather arcane analogy for this might be found in Wordsworth: reading *Absalom* is somewhat like reading Wordsworth's *Prelude*. *As I Lay Dying* is complex, but it continually gives the reader encouragement along the way, a feeling that he is approaching a solution, just as "Ode: Intimations of Immortality" does. *Light in August* is a puzzle, perhaps like the "Lucy" poems: any one thread can be worked through but unity is something else again; intermediate solutions reveal greater ultimate complexity, but progress is possible. For *Absalom, Absalom!* it is necessary, as for *The Prelude,* to get away from the surface attractions, distractions, and events to perceive the rhythm of the process. In *Absalom* it is not the figure in the carpet but the process of weaving and knotting that is both essence and subject. To use a somewhat cruder formulation, the book is not about what happened but about arriving at or understanding what happened.

Myth is less important here than failures to realize myth: the distance between the intention and the realization of myth, the distance between the organic myth which all the characters develop together and the private myth of each, the distance between the substance of myth and the process of making it. The way Faulkner gets at each of these distances is to examine the limits of fiction, to ask what is fiction, what are characters, what is narrative—and to have his characters and his narrative ask the same questions of the act of narrative and the act of characterization at their formation. In other words he brings the process of formation downstage, outlines beliefs, standards, and ideals for the narrative, and makes them not just part of the drama but the main attraction. It is a narrative about narrative.

Herman Melville tackled some of these problems in *The Confidence Man* in a very different way. A strong narrative presence constantly shifted his ground, changed his mind, exposed his own lies, deceptions, and failures to us as readers—in short, not only questioned the verity of his own narrative but eventually undercut the act of fiction by exposing himself as the true confidence man, playing upon our confidence in him to tell it straight, have it out and be consistent. Faulkner doesn't go this far and does not depend on so pushy a narrative presence. But Shreve and Quentin play fast and loose with narrative truth, replace the facts they are given with assumptions which better fit their developing design, fool around with time schemes and generally undercut the fiction we assume Faulkner is arranging in the Sutpens. Melville ultimately betrays the narrative act, but there is a margin for safety here: Quentin and Shreve are characters too—they are free to play fast and loose in a way that Faulkner or a surrogate narrative presence would not be.

But getting at *Absalom* and at the fictive process it imitates is much more complicated than this rather simple comparison indicates. As in *Light in August,* the strategy for narrative makes use of confusions and barriers to coherence as well as ordered structures and coherent schema. The confusions and barriers are perhaps the simpler to deal with.

Chronological disjunction can be rather quickly disposed of.[1] The book begins with Rosa's monologue and ends just after the discovery of Henry at Sutpen's Hundred, the burning of the place, and a bit of dialogue between Quentin and Shreve, all circa 1910. In between, the basic pattern is a forward progress through the hun-

1. Chart 1 in Appendix C deals with this much more efficiently.

dred-odd years which the book covers. Chapter 2 retraces half of 1, 3 retraces the other half and moves beyond, 4 and 5 retrace parts of 3, and 6 advances from Sutpen's death where 3 more or less left off. Chapter 7 moves back beyond the beginning of 1 to trace Sutpen's beginnings and take up some points of special interest—Christmas 1859 and Sutpen's proposal to Rosa. Chapter 8 continues this pattern of spots of time, turning again to the Christmas interview, dealing with Bon's beginnings, tracing the progress of Henry and Bon beyond Christmas, and ending with Sutpen's death. Chapter 9 moves to the anchor point, the summer and winter of 1910, in which every chapter (except 5) has begun. The basic chronology is established by 1–3; 6 moves beyond that, and 7 takes up an earlier period.

The ordering logic behind this series of jumps, disjunctions, and revisitings is that of the necessity of withholding information for timed revelation. Chapter 2 fills in one hole of 1 (how Sutpen got Mr. Coldfield's daughter), 3 creates new ellipses (the Christmas interview, the death of Henry, Sutpen's proposal to Rosa). Chapter 4 takes off on one of these traces (Bon's miscegenation), 5 takes another (the proposal). Chapters 6 and 7 provide endings for these which embody some new questions and some new beginnings—including one very big suspended question (Bon's parentage), to be puzzled over and resolved in 8 (the incest). Chapter 8 also takes up all the unresolved ellipses of 3, 4, 5, and 6. Chapter 9 moves the basic action of 1910 to its climax in the discovery of Henry and beyond in the burning of Sutpen's Hundred, Rosa's death, and Shreve's questioning of the whole thing.

In one sense, then, the dislocations of chronology serve the cause of timed revelation much as they would in a tale of ratiocination: they provide another powerful incentive to read for solution. But this dislocation also serves the examination of the narrative process. Telling moments are visited and revisited, come back again and again like favorite songs. Yet the repetition is not primarily to serve rhythmic or revelatory structures but to expose us to a sequence of narrators using the same raw material. The narrative advances (indirectly) in a linear chronology, but at the same time—by its beginning *in medias res* and by its overlappings—suggests layers of knowledge, of understanding, of meaning. This shape is borne out by other structures in the book. Once we see that mystery-solving will bring us no closer to the heart of the novel, we move not so much through the book as we do down into it.

Mystery-solving brings us to another peculiar barrier. Suspense omission and accumulation of evidence are familiar to every reader of mystery stories. But there's something funny here. Narrative intensity, textual density and suspense mechanisms ought to underline crises or lead up to revelations—here they seem to heighten what leads up to crises or, anticlimactically, to draw out what leads away from them. What we expect to take a lot of time takes very little, and what we expect will just go bang, goes on and on. The book's rhythm refuses to be dramatic; indeed, it is almost insistently antidramatic and anticlimactic. The patterns of revelation and connection continually and consistently frustrate conventional suspense and stock fictional expectations.

Take, for example, the ending of chapter 5. The chapter has seemed to build to a point of climax in Sutpen's death and the revelation of what Sutpen said that brought about Rosa's hasty exit from his household. But on the chapter's last page, after some metaphorical complication which seems to be leading toward an expected break and Faulkner's characteristic downhill run to the climax, Quentin gets distracted and interrupts, "because there was also some thing which he too could not pass," the killing of Bon, and the curious similarity of Judith's and Henry's faces. The distraction keeps him from hearing (and us from knowing) whatever climax Rosa's narrative has reached, because the next thing we hear is Rosa, switching our attention back to her story, to the "something living. . . . in that house" (*Absalom,* p. 172). Faulkner is having some ghost-story fun: suspense that is itself suspended improves even conventional suspense. But this sort of fun recurs again and again—whole chapters follow coherently from preceding chapters, but the end of one is not followed up by the beginning of the next—until the reader must reach the conclusion either that Faulkner is more intent on fun than on narrative, or that he has some aim other than conventional narrative build-up, suspense, and climax.

The opening of the book is an even stronger example of the combination of conventional fictional devices and unconventional barriers to frustrate the reader in pursuing his stock responses. The first two paragraphs are heavily atmospheric—we are transported to Miss Havisham's chamber—but they are also heavy with adjectives (forty-nine in the first and seventy-six in the second). Just at the point Faulkner might be expected to want to speed us up, to soar and zoom and pull us into the book, verbal excess slows us down. This is apparently no accident, since the effect is repeated to introduce Quentin's room at Harvard (the first paragraph of chapter 6). Similarly, Rosa Coldfield is oddly chosen as first expositor. She runs off at the mouth, which may permit the novelist more exposition per square inch than he could normally get away with, but since this book is predominantly exposition anyhow, this is no advantage. Rosa's run-on, breathless delivery introduces further confusions in a runaway suspense-omission: her overliteral, overspecific mind assumes that we already know the main outline, and she maddeningly embroiders details. Omission for suspense has seldom left such gaping holes. Her poetic mode and her high rate of metaphor are not calculated to persuade us to read on, and as the narrative itself is at this point cloudy and full of holes, what must metaphors based in that narrative be? Even her grammar is insidiously deceptive—her open-ended clauses give us nowhere to stand.

As she talks, we hear with Quentin. We share his impatience with her indirection, with him we want it over and done with. This empathy underlines our conventional response to exposition: to our deeply felt "why is she telling us all this?" he adds his ironic answer, *"It's because she wants it told . . . so that people . . . will read it and know at last why God let us lose the War"* (p. 11). Quentin still half believes his immediate suspicion that Rosa really wants him to write it up for a magazine.

This is very nearly a parody of how not to start a mystery story—yet its devices and order, its carrot and stick seem to indicate that it is meant to be one. The confusion and barriers of the opening are characteristic of the whole. The confusion exists in the surface, in what is told; coherence and consistency are found in the method, the process, the characterization of the Teller and the completeness of detail in the rendering of telling. The confusion remains confusion only so long as the reader assumes that he must solve the puzzle. To accept this assumption that the book is driving toward completion or solution is to be happy in the dark. The narrative is frustrating only so long as one assumes that a deep understanding of Thomas Sutpen lies at the end of the road, for all of its individual devices will thwart him. If instead he accepts the book's rhythm, the confusions do not disappear, but rather they support and enhance the process. Thickenings and complications and barriers, misplaced in the conventional structure, take on force and purpose in a structure aimed not at solution of what is told but rather at understanding of the telling, the hearing, the narrative, the fiction itself.

The central barrier to a contented and comfortable reading of *Absalom* is metaphor, and this works in concert with the frustration of conventional suspense structures. *Absalom, Absalom!* is Faulkner's most metaphorical novel, and metaphor is more central to its meaning than to that of any of his other novels, because after a time metaphor is the novel's customary form of statement. This alone would be reason enough to devote some space to it. But detailed examination of the metaphors demonstrates that they also determine the narrative's tempo, pace, and rhythm. If the reader is conscious of any dragging in the pace, he notices metaphor. The structure of frequency and density of metaphor is here at the heart of narrative strategy.

The metaphors of *Absalom* have a certain consistency. They cluster heavily around general themes, but these general threads differ from the thematic strands of *As I Lay Dying*. In that novel, metaphors convey meaning (in the definition of individual formulation and abstraction), character relationships (in the shared and unshared patterns), and rendering. Certain sets of images are clearly limited to what farm people could know; others (such as the elements of vertical and horizontal and some of Darl's images of form and shape) go far beyond. In *Absalom, Absalom!* metaphors may define abstract individual formulations (as in Judith's loom of time, p. 127),[2] but shared or unshared is not the issue. Metaphors function in rendering, but rendering here goes far beyond the simple presen-

2. This results in, among other things, the rather elaborately developed conceits (Judith the sherbet, Bon the racehorse, etc.). One of the book's red herrings is the conventional expectation that pursuit of the conceits will resolve the book's general patterns of imagery. It does not. The racehorse could be considered to be distantly connected to Sutpen (even as Jones sees him as a black stallion) but this would stretch the image to fit the theory. There are other scattered instances of food imagery, but it is far from being a dominant pattern—the sherbet stands alone as intensive use of food or drink as a vehicle. The set-pieces perform their function and are gone. The dominant patterns—lacking the individual intensity of the set-pieces—have perhaps equivalent impact on the reader but are not directly related to them.

tation of physical reality and into the realm of metamorphosis and invention, as Quentin and Shreve, largely by means of metaphor, take the novel out of the hands of the novelist.

Quentin and Shreve are the novel's chief makers of metaphor. To them it is a humanistic tool of understanding: under their hands metaphors combine into myth and can transform gossip into poetry. That they are continually conscious of the shifting sands of meaning (in this book meaning is never constant but shifts and advances, not as facts reveal themselves, but as understanding deepens) leads them into something of a stopgap approach to metaphor. As it is a tool, metaphor must first of all be pliable, flexible, so that it can enforce momentary immediate meaning or even a shift in meaning in the passage at hand. Some of this immediacy is seen in the epic embroidery of epithets (the "iron" snow of Cambridge, Rosa's and Shreve's "demon" Sutpen), but generally even the most convenient or frequently repeated metaphors are subject to development. Some begin with one tendency of meaning, evolve through the book, and emerge with quite another meaning. One character takes over another character's metaphor and changes its tone and purpose. Rosa sees herself as one who lacked a childhood; Mr. Compson develops this further in description, and finally several images in chapter 9 render her as a child in old age. Rosa sees Sutpen as a real demon out of a real fairytale; Shreve turns this "demon" ironically, developing his rather pathetic, humanized Sutpen, and finally turns his transformed "demon" against Rosa to comment upon her sensibilities.

As might be expected, when every narrator turns poet and metaphors are the common currency, there is a confusion between tenor and vehicle. There is, for instance, a tendency in Sutpen—as in everybody in the book, or everybody in the South, or (witness today) just everybody—to blame everything on the war. So metaphors of attack, strategy, and things military aptly suit the nature of Sutpen's assault on respectability and the inexorable qualities of fate. The actions of an unseen fate become more tangible and understandable to Quentin and Shreve when they can transform Sutpen's West Indian wife and her lawyer into master-strategists planning the counter-assault on Sutpen's newly conquered respectability. War is the condition of Sutpen's world and becomes the condition of Quentin's and Shreve's inventions: metaphor passes into fact and fact into metaphor as Sutpen, the metaphorical warrior, and Bon, the product of the metaphorical strategists, both proceed to real tents on a real battlefield. The mixing of tenor and vehicle becomes a pathway between the world of event and the poetry of abstraction.

In the conventional metaphorical patterns of death there is a similar productive slippage between tenor and vehicle, past and present. The tomb is the metaphor for Rosa's room, for the airlessness of living in the past, and for Quentin's and Shreve's room, for living in the academy. For Sutpen death is the metaphorical and real source of his time-fixation, the reason he has to see life as a race. More than a simple thematic thread of image, this intermixing of metaphor and event has relevance to the narrative strategy of fictive process. Until Sutpen is dead Quentin and Shreve cannot have him, and they must be given him by a "living ghost" out of the "tomb" so that they can re-create him in another "tomb."

A more complex poetic confusion is perhaps even more important. Long chains of the images Quentin and Shreve seize at the moment become patterns in which the vehicle of one tenor becomes the tenor of the next vehicle, sometimes stretching out to a chain of four distinct metaphors possessing only five elements between them.[3] This makes chapter 7 particularly difficult to read (and even more difficult to analyze for the number of its metaphors).

3. For example, pp. 222–23: "So he had hardly heard of such a world until he fell into it. . . . They fell into it, the whole family, returned to the coast from which the first Sutpen had come, . . . tumbled head over heels back to Tidewater by sheer altitude, elevation and gravity, as if whatever slight hold the family had had on the mountain had broken. . . . And now the whole passel of them . . . slid back down out of the mountains, skating in a kind of accelerating and sloven and inert coherence like a useless collection of flotsam on a flooded river, moving by some perverse automotivation such as inanimate objects sometimes show, backward against the very current of the stream, across the Virginia plateau and into the slack lowlands about the mouth of the James River." The basic metaphor (family's return = falling backwards = mountain = climbing) is a simple metaphor made more specific, changing somewhat in transition. But the next complication (family = falling backwards = skaters = sloven . . . coherence = flotsam = automotivation of inanimate objects) adds five more vehicles, each of which becomes the tenor for the next vehicle, and the final complication (objects . . . against the current = westward flow of expansion = water flowing into lowlands) seems to bring us back closer to the original tenor—falling—from which the metaphors seem to have distanced us. Rather than a curious excessive conceit, this kind of movement of developing and proliferating branched metaphor seems more characteristic of the metaphor in the book than any simple one-step equivalencies.

But it is more than Faulkner's primitive poetic crudeness: it is part and parcel of Quentin's and Shreve's narrative strategy, and thus of Faulkner's. The two roommates move freely between fact and analogy and from one analogy to an analogy for it. They believe more firmly in their metaphors (the lawyer and the racehorse) than they do in the characters, so the metaphors become characters, and action can be more consistently followed as it emerges from metaphorical development than it is in whatever may be found in this book of real characters performing real actions.

The strongest general threads of metaphor do not stand independently. The pattern of chains of single images is repeated in interlocking clusters of imageric threads; again there is productive mixing. The two simplest patterns are, of course, human and animal vehicles. In this book they are frequent not just because they are convenient frames of reference—that they lower humans and raise animals, as in the master-metaphors of beast-fable or the semimetaphor of bestiality—but because of their relationship to slavery. The "monkey nigger" plays upon Sutpen's "wild niggers" in several senses —on the lowered dignity and domesticated tricks, and probably on the costume of the organ-grinder's animal. Bond's animal-like howlings are returns and recurrences of the same "wild" slaves. Beyond the bestial reductions of the slaves (which also works in the opposite direction, to comment upon the masters' degraded view of human chattel and their own bestiality) there are other reductions. The war has made humans act and live like animals. Individually, Rosa's automatic outrage and Sutpen's unconsciousness of the fruits of his actions and the results of his causes are characteristic of the actions of a lower form of life. Ellen's cycle as a butterfly, taking on the inexorable seasonal change, metamorphosis, and decay of the insect is a measure of the same reduction of human control over its destiny and a measure of Ellen's lack of consciousness (compared to Rosa).[4]

A strain of metaphor connected to this in its relevance to slavery (to recur even more powerfully in *Go Down, Moses*) is seen in ve-

4. At the tenor end of metaphors, the characters are dealt with by these vehicles with a frequency which suggests the importance of each in the book, just as one might expect. Sutpen, of course, is far in the lead, with more than twice as many images as any other character and more in a single chapter (7) than the total images applied to any other single character. Then, as might be expected, comes Bon, followed by Rosa, Henry, Judith, and Quentin.

hicles of money and accounting. In Ike McCaslin's story and that of the Snopeses the metaphor becomes physical reality in ledgers. Here the ledger is an invention bodied forth by Shreve and Quentin, General Compson, and even Sutpen himself. This class of images has a traditional function—crudely rendered in the Puritan concept of the "great golden book," or in Jehovah's exactions of seventy times seven.[5] Allusions to classical tragedy connect here, too, in the returns which fate exacts. All involve double-entry bookkeeping, either of offense and punishment, virtue and its reward in another coin, or something similar to the familiar human drive of "getting my due." In the South the ledger mentality has particularly relevant application: humans are sold for money and the simplicity of the bookkeeping masks the moral complexity of the system. This finds a clear parallel in Sutpen's "bookkeeping," his innocent assumption that everything is simpler than it is.

The most forceful use of the metaphor concerns Sutpen's West Indian wife. Quentin and Shreve invent a lawyer to help her out and a ledger in which he can keep the books—the most concrete way to handle in understandable terms the powerful accidents of coincidence or fate which destroy Sutpen's design. The invention of the lawyer is not an oversimplification which glosses over damaging conclusions (as some of Sutpen's inventions and simplifications do), but rather makes understandable an accidence which could not be believed were it left as simple coincidence. Another group, legal and criminal metaphors, and those of hunting and horsemanship, connects to this cluster of general threads with, again, some slippage between tenor and vehicle. The former culminates in the image of the slightly corrupt lawyer, the greatest single metaphorical invention of the book. Sutpen's West Indian wife couldn't possibly be bright enough, relentless enough, or heartless enough to calculate the destruction of his design: there must have been a lawyer there somewhere. The relationship between the hunting of the planters and their fighting as soldiers, between the two aspects of hunting—barbaric reconstruction and aristocratic pursuit (themes

5. Judaeo-Christian reference is as automatic to Faulkner as his complicated financial deals, and more automatic to literature than classical allusion. The pattern perhaps does not need to be related in detail to the themes of the book, but a quick reminder of the fully articulated Biblical patterns in *Go Down, Moses* will suggest the particular relevance of Biblical patterns to ownership and slavery.

again fully developed in *Go Down, Moses*)—are particularly appropriate to Sutpen's story. Wash Jones's image of Sutpen as a stallion finally combines animalism, respect, aristocracy, the military, and the barbaric. As in Judith's image of people's strings tangled with other people's, the imageric threads touch, connect, cross, and twine about each other.

Discussion of such threads might seem more proper to an *explication de texte* than a discussion of narrative. I dwell on them because I am convinced that they are properly a part of narrative strategy. To tell this story, build this corner, realize this germ, Faulkner needed an ordered complication of Teller and Hearer, a confusion of "fact" and surmise. The tale was to be found more in belief than in action, its results to ensue more in the beholder or the hearer than in the participant. Only the narrative strategy he chose—the lengthening shadows of mythic distance, the freedom and flexibility of poetic interpretation, could be the proper net to capture so elusive an essence.

Metaphor's narrative function is perhaps clearest in doubling, an element Faulkner has previously used for ambiguity, here forged into an instrument of enriched meaning and flexible narrative. In *The Sound and the Fury* Caddy was confused with caddie, Quentin with Quentin. Here the doubles and twins of the book—young and old Sutpen, his rational and his emotional self, young and old Rosa, the innocent and the experienced Judith—regularly confront each other. The large number of references to children, games, and toys grows out of this juxtaposition of past with present and the way doubles and twins operate. Sutpen's innocence finds its most telling appeal for sympathy in his rendering of the formation of his design in childhood. And to the late adolescents, Quentin and Shreve, childhood is the most accessible metaphorical frame of reference.[6] Also from the world of innocence and childhood come the elements of knighthood and fairytale, as surely as they grow out of the South's false image of itself, the Waverley syndrome. Rosa and General

6. Accessibility also determines the number of references to science—chemistry, physics, biology, mechanics. These are Quentin's and Shreve's preoccupations at Harvard, and students tend to talk out of preoccupation, even as they tend to abstract enthusiastically as they build on one another's abstractions. Beyond that, physical law has something about it of the inexorable qualities of tragedy and retribution. Gravity, too, turns the wheel of fortune, and principles of scientific design sometimes determine the behavior of the infernal machine.

Compson choose this as their genre for casting the tale; Quentin seeks it out because incest takes on a kind of acceptance in that deep past. The aristocracy of that nonexistent age of chivalry hunted, fornicated, and fought, all in the golden glow of a reflected ideal which seemed to forgive it much. Thus the fairytale is suited to Sutpen's innocence as well as to his villainy, to Shreve's youth (in his "demon") as well as to his student's irony, to Quentin's romanticism and to the fancy of his invention.

The complex apex of doubling is reached in the "two, now four, now two" Quentin–Henry and Shreve–Charles. Shreve and Quentin begin as geographically contrasting reflections of each other, but as Quentin sees Mr. Compson take on some of Sutpen's qualities (further enforced by Quentin's incest-fixation, in which Quentin–Caddy becomes Henry–Judith), and as he moves deeper and deeper with Shreve into the distant events of fifty years ago, these doubles take on real substance in the double-doubles of Quentin–Henry and Shreve–Charles.

This doubling of the protagonists and spectators is carried even further by the theatrical imagery. Rosa's reference to Sutpen's "raree show" (p. 18) establishes it, but the pattern goes beyond the simple point that Sutpen is Jefferson's favorite spectator sport. Sutpen's tragedy has rather melodramatic theatrical trappings, an artificial excess. The book's time scheme and its shifting scenes are theatrical, as the sets for the antebellum Sutpen's Hundred and the South are struck and the stage reset with new decor. Henry's, Bon's, and Sutpen's qualities of performance, criticized as such by Quentin and Shreve as they imagine and invent them, become plays which change from performance to performance, as Quentin or Shreve insists on altering scenes we have seen played before. The thread of metaphor emphasizes the artificiality of psychological scene-making, the element of mask in human behavior and its re-creation, in short, all of the more subtle implications of the "doubling" process.

Because of these impersonations and because of the acceleration of the metaphorical process of invention, Quentin's and Shreve's distance from events and witnesses gives chapter 7 more metaphors than any other. The farthest distance from "fact" brings the high point of metaphor, even as the greatest distance from source brings the high point of myth. But this is only a part of a consistent pattern of metaphorical density, the development of which throughout this novel of thwarted conventions and complex excess provides perhaps its strongest consistent structure. The opening, Rosa's chapter, is thicker with metaphor than any of Mr. Compson's narratives (2–4), but his chapters have fewer metaphors than any others in the book. Chapter 5 (Rosa's return) is even denser, then Quentin and Shreve take over and peak density is reached. The most metaphors of any one page and of any ten pages turn up in the passage in which Quentin and Shreve are almost independent of source and have taken off on their own to invent the relationship between Bon and his mother and the lawyer at the beginning of chapter 8. This whole chapter, though, represents a slight decline from the high point in 7, and 9 declines even more, in a curve which corresponds to the anticlimax of the myth-making as the suspense pattern is resolved in the action of 1910.[7] The high point in 7 is a function of progressive density—how far we have moved in metaphorical development, how many metaphors per square inch we have been conditioned to take in, but also a function of how far we have moved from the "factual" beginnings, the many tellers and re-tellers between the "facts" and us. It also corresponds, almost paradoxically, with the long-awaited appearance of the protagonist's own voice as he talks to General Compson on the architect-hunt.

Metaphorical rhythm is, I think, a unique experiment here. Slowing the reader down is an odd function to single out for critical praise, but if *Absalom* lacked this progress of density—to determine our tempo, establish rhythm, force us into the layered structure, quite literally to determine how the book is to be approached and read—it is just possible that the other functions of metaphor would not operate. Without it, the book might well be read as some critics (and most undergraduates) insist it must be, as the failure of one American Dream. The parallel *Absalom* offers for the narrative act, metaphor's function in determining our distance from events and our closeness to the myth, its function as shaper of the book's characteristic rhetoric, its function as a path

7. I remembered 9 as almost completely straightforward, with almost no metaphors except those which served description, and I was right in the latter but wrong in the former. There is a clear switch here from conceptual and imaginative metaphor (as in Quentin's and Shreve's inventions) to visual metaphor which serves the rendering; but metaphors are remarkably thick—there are more per page and per ten-page unit than in any chapters except 7 and 8, although the total count is near the level of chapters 1–4.

through the confusing time scheme, are all organized by metaphorical density.

The profusion and complication of various strands of metaphor make the book seem a mare's nest even though, as we are reading it, it makes rather good sense. I think the sense depends upon the economical and precise characterization of the voices which inhabit the book, the sources for Quentin's and Shreve's mythologizing: Rosa, Mr. Compson, General Compson, and Sutpen himself. Rosa gives us too much too soon, running from one point to the next in a frantic effort to get it all in, a narrative which either carries us, confused and fascinated, into the book, or puts us off completely. Mr. Compson's tales to Quentin are more orderly, more measured. The immediate impression is of a thoughtful, careful narration; the ultimate impression is of a questionable, self-serving one. Rosa returns in chapter 5 with more of the breathless anxiety. Quentin begins his recension for Shreve in 6 and establishes a clear tone of curiosity and reverie, not so much an anxiety to get it told as an anxiety to understand it. His rendition in 7 of General Compson's tale becomes a compound of all the tones and methods of his several informants: Sutpen's innocent puzzlement, General Compson's rather more leisurely modesty, and some of Mr. Compson's moralization. Then Quentin and Shreve, vying with each other for insights, take over again, leading finally to Quentin's reverie—part experience and part imagination—of his visit to Sutpen's Hundred and its end. Throughout, then, there is a kind of growing peace and thoughtfulness in the telling as early ellipses and anxieties give way to later connections and assurance.

But this is a just representation only of the tone of the Tellers, not necessarily of our responses to what they say and how they say it. Dramatic frustration begins to make itself felt at the end of chapter 1. The book's immediate effects and short-term aims (which call up our conventional fictional responses) work at odds with the book's order and progression in chronological and tonal structure. This conflict, I think, enforces the layered vertical structure. Our progress must be impeded. Every sort of barrier must be set up lest we be taken by the solving of its puzzle. And the barriers only enrich the characterization of the voices.

Rosa Coldfield at the outset tips us off to one of the most important things to remember: we can never tell when we are being told the truth. Rosa is looking for vindication of her actions. In order to justify what she was and what she did, she must make Sutpen a demon and transform the rest of his family into the characters of a melodramatic fairytale. She must insist that the whole story cannot be properly told but still try to give her part so that someone can tell it eventually—three words are too many and three thousand are too few because she cannot organize her material. She is unable to get beyond the events which strike her dumb with outrage so that she may deal with the significant details which might make sense of the outrage. She exists somewhere in limbo between *is* and *was*. She had no childhood. Unlike Hightower she can never be *was*. She has been trapped by circumstances in an obsessive dwelling upon that time when she was not, so she is incapable of becoming *is*. She is trapped as a ghost is trapped, between two clearly defined states of being. She is the chief of many ghosts Quentin encounters in the course of the book, and after his initial uncertainty he greets her with an eagerness which can only lead us beyond the book to his time-obsessed quandary in *The Sound and the Fury*.

At first this characterization seems nothing deeper than caricature. She is the perfect stereotype of the Southern lady (which Faulkner emphasizes by having Mr. Compson define that stereotype, p. 86), sitting in her Havisham-chamber, talking, talking, talking. But the comic elements in Rosa become increasingly serious as it becomes apparent that what she is telling—or something like it—really happened and really matters. As her subjects' fairytale masks begin to fall away to reveal some of the human substance beneath them, as we become convinced that *something* was going on, even though we don't know what it was, the effect becomes for us precisely what Quentin says it is:

> that logic- and reason-flouting quality of a dream which the sleeper knows must have occurred, stillborn and complete, in a second, yet the very quality upon which it must depend to move the dreamer (verisimilitude) to credulity—horror or pleasure or amazement—depends as completely upon a formal recognition of and acceptance of elapsed and yet-elapsing time as music or a printed tale. [*Absalom,* p. 22]

Time begins to operate on us. We not only share Quentin's simultaneous impatience and fascination but begin to perceive that voices tour through time: Rosa still carries that hint of the child (particularly in metaphor), we see Quentin in Mr. Compson as he tells of listening to *his* father talk of Sutpen. In an indirect way the narrative—the power of these voices telling—overcomes the antinarrative of obscurity and overcomplication, false plot and deceptive appeal for conventional response. As Rosa continues we grant her more credence, not because her story grows any more interesting, but because she has planted concepts with us—even the shape of the "demon"—in spite of our unwillingness to take her seriously. Part of Rosa's credibility emerges from just that quality which cripples her narrative truth: she is a participant. As participant she is the one least capable of selecting and organizing what has happened to her, the one most subject to the feelings and memories rather than the thoughts which might grow out of the story of Sutpen:

> *That is the substance of remembering—sense, sight, smell: the muscles with which we see and hear and feel—not mind, not thought: there is no such thing as memory: the brain recalls just what the muscles grope for: no more, no less: and its resultant sum is usually incorrect and false and worthy only of the name of dream.* [*Absalom,* p. 143]

Mr. Compson restates this hint in his letter on Rosa's death:

> *And if aught can be more painful to any intelligence above that of a child or an idiot than a slow and gradual confronting with that which over a long period of bewilderment and dread it has been taught to regard as an irrevocable and unplumbable finality, I do not know it.* [*Absalom,* pp. 173–74]

Rosa's version of the matter of Sutpen deals with the participant's handicap as narrator: entrapment inside the body and skin immediately involved, the inability even later to escape the muscular memory of participation so as to be able to qualify this subjectivity with objective detail. Mr. Compson's restatement relates a second handicap: beyond body and skin, participation is an entrapment in the long time of continual contact, experience, and memory of every moment of an event, a resultant inability to abstract, to gain distance from moment to moment. To a more objective observer the event could have a beginning and an end and not just a continual curve of increasing and diminishing presence.

Despite her handicaps, Rosa's closeness to the proceedings, the force and consistency of her voice, her breathless involvement persisting all these years after Sutpen's death, do manage to get us into the book. The latter part of the first chapter is strong, comparatively straight narrative, the first such in the book, and we begin to think in our limited empathetic adoption of her situation that she is perhaps something more than the stereotyped panicky, prudish spinster.

Mr. Compson comes on, more consistent in his continuity and more consistently inventive in development. The image of the butterfly captures precisely his tone of resignation and his rather distant vicarious resignation for Ellen Coldfield. His skeptical view of morality is seen in the development of Henry's photographic plate, as Bon exposes it bit by bit in progressive moral relativism. Both images perhaps fit Mr. Compson's patterns better than they suit the subjects of the metaphors, but they, together with a continuo of minor supportive metaphors, are nonetheless congruent with Judith's own very moving figure for human involvement, the strings tangled with other people's strings (p. 127). The distance, the resignation, the objectivity are similar.

Such distance—the psychic distance between us and events we are told about—is not the same as our informant's distance from the events. Rosa was participant in much of what she tells, but her narration moves us no closer to the heart of the action because she has already mythologized it to make it bearable. To this distance of indirection is added the distance imposed by ellipsis in her narrative (caused by what she thinks Quentin already knows, what she cannot know or what she cannot face).

Mr. Compson does not have her kind of protective mythology. He has nothing to lose because he is never directly involved. Apparently much of his information was gathered from his father (how much we don't really know, but chapter 7 suggests that it was quite a bit) and some from various informers in the town. This unspecified group narrative (or more accurately, group information) is used here to fill in the gossip, rather than (as in "Emily") to form our attitude or to engage us in a particular way. We share none of the town's community outrage because we are suspended between subjectivities at an objective distance, learning rather than taking sides. We listen with Quentin and put pieces in place. Mr. Compson picks among subjective opinions and forms his apparently objective amalgam.

This results, if anything, in a greater effective distance from the events than in Rosa's narration. Her mythology at least gives a sense of urgency, a feeling that Sutpen represented a force of evil and that his cause (and his effects) had to be combated. Mr. Compson's peculiar fixations distance his information even more than his remote sources will account for. His heavy emphasis on realization, his concentration on his own powers of ironic observation, his affected moralization lead to overcomplexity and oversubtlety, and ultimately to cold remoteness.

The tone of his telling is almost precisely consistent with the conversations he has (and does not have) with Quentin in *The Sound and the Fury*. He is an ironic moralist for whom assumption and subtlety have replaced curiosity and a sense of (or even a need for) a general design. His narration makes clear a second false aim for a narrator. Rosa's showed that the participant is not necessarily the best narrator, corresponding to Faulkner's development from first- to third-person narration in the short stories and in the sequence of novels leading up to *Light in August*. Mr. Compson demonstrates that the Teller must seek the outlines of the story rather than the outlines of his response to it if he is to find the true design for narration. Mr. Compson is trying to sell his brand of resigned, ironic morality more than he is attempting to grasp the shape of the Sutpen story. His narrative is undertaken for the wrong reason: he wants the fiction to fit his rather tired philosophical bromides so that he can feel superior not only to the story but to the men and women who originally enacted the events which form it. If we were to depend upon him or upon him and Rosa for the book, we might have a *Sartoris* but never an *Absalom*. Partly as a result of his incapacity, Mr. Compson's chapters (2, 3, 4) fill up holes that we don't even know about yet. Rosa delivers a chronicle of ellipses, he fills up some of hers and goes on to fill holes in a chronicle which has yet to be formed.

General Compson as narrator errs in another way, in strong contrast to his son and Rosa. Far from imposing his own design or being involved as participant, he only records and transmits. Even Mr. Compson's moral embroidery (which must have been a part of the tale as Quentin first heard it) has disappeared in this rendition. He is a transparent medium and speaks in his own voice only to comment on the quality of Sutpen's telling, enters the picture only as the narrative presence of a third-person narrative might, to comment on the process of narrative itself. Some of this objectivity, of course, is the product of his distance from us. As Shreve hears of the architect-hunt from Quentin, he hears him tell what his father told him that *his* father told him that Sutpen told *him*. Our distance from the participant is more extreme here than anywhere else in the book, unless Quentin's and Shreve's conjectures and inventions are put somewhere on the scale. Certainly Quentin has begun the conjectural process here as he relates Sutpen's, his grandfather's, and his father's tellings to Shreve; but the conjectures upon the nature of the story and Sutpen's tone as he was telling it seem to be based in something General Compson said at the time he was telling it: "He just stopped, Grandfather said, flat and final like that, like that was all there was, all there could be to it, all of it that made good listening from one man to another over whiskey at night. Maybe it was" (p. 255). He emphasizes that Sutpen is not operating on Rosa's "muscle-memory" but rather using selection, omission, and objectivity to make that memory anecdotal—that his whole narrative is a series of anecdotes. This is further developed (whether by General Compson or by Quentin is not entirely clear):

> . . . a very condensation of time which was the gauge of its own violence, and he telling it in that pleasant faintly forensic anecdotal manner apparently just as he remembered it, was impressed by it through detached and impersonal interest and curiosity which even fear . . . failed to leaven very much. . . .
>
> And I reckon Grandfather was saying "Wait, wait for God's sake wait" about like you are, until he finally did stop and back up and start over again with at least some regard for cause and effect even if none for logical sequence and continuity. . . . And still it was not absolutely clear—the how and the why he was there and what he was—since he was not talking about himself. He was telling a story. He was not bragging about something he had done; he was just telling a story about something a man named Thomas Sutpen had experienced, which would still have been the same story if the man had had no name at all, if it had been told about any man or no man over whiskey at night. [*Absalom*, pp. 249–50, 247]

Sutpen as narrator is able to overcome Rosa's handicap as narrator—perhaps by virtue of his innocence, which involves more than a little unconcern for ramifications, complications, and long-term results. He can step outside muscle-memory and combine the best of subjective intimacy and tangibility with objective continuity and tempo. He masters a fundamental strength of good fiction, its freedom and flexibility: "Getting himself and Grandfather both into that besieged Haitian room as simply as he got himself to the West Indies by saying that he decided to go to the West Indies and so he went there" (p. 246). He apparently is able to master it because of that quality of monomaniacal objectivity in his style of life.

In order, then, we have a progression. We begin with Rosa's ogre-demon and then see enough of Rosa to start adjusting the image. Mr. Compson adds human background as he moralizes the tale and pursues his complex digressions. We become accustomed to this because our plate has been exposed long enough now for us to be able to understand what is being told us—to see where the story lies. Sutpen's story and General Compson's telling of it complete the set-up for Shreve and Quentin to make their myth, using all these parts and all these methods. They accept Rosa's demon and Mr. Compson's digressions where the information is useful. They accept General Compson's humanistic Sutpen and integrate it with their own responses until they emerge with a rather human, rather pathetic ogre—for whom even the cruel comment to Milly about the stable is somehow a plea for sympathy.

General Compson's section is the narrative and metaphorical watershed. Rosa's and Mr. Compson's metaphors, like their narratives, are self-justifying, an elaborate form of rationalization. Quentin's and Shreve's metaphors, again like their narratives, are open-handed, with nothing self-indulgent or self-serving about them, aimed only at the perfection of the pattern Sutpen suggests. Rosa's and Mr. Compson's metaphors are psychological, reshaping reality so that it may become bearable and didactic in turn—Quentin's and Shreve's are poetic, devoted not to the easing of an internal wound but to the fulfillment of an external pattern. The collaborative narration becomes more real and pertinent for them than its sources:

> though neither Shreve nor Quentin believed that the visit affected Henry as Mr Compson seemed to think. In fact, Quentin did not even tell Shreve what his father had said about the visit. Perhaps Quentin himself had not been listening when Mr Compson related it that evening at home; perhaps at that moment on the

> gallery . . . Quentin took that in stride without even hearing it just as Shreve would have, since both he and Shreve believed—and were probably right in this too—that the octoroon and the child would have been to Henry only something else about Bon to be, not envied but aped if that had been possible. [*Absalom,* p. 336]

Notice the distance the narrative presence takes from these proceedings, his indifference to hard positivism. Even as the narrative presence of *Light in August* (in the "perhaps" device) suspends judgment on what is going through Joe's head in some of the most ambiguous actions, here the presence suspends judgment on what the facts really were. There are two aims to this: to maintain productive ambiguity in the actions on the Sutpen level, and to emphasize that "facts" are not as important as understanding is to Quentin's and Shreve's assimilation of them in collaboration.

Finally Quentin and Shreve come to a point at which one of the knowns will not work:

> He said it was Bon who was wounded, but it wasn't. Because who told him? Who told Sutpen, or your grandfather either, which of them it was who was hit? Sutpen didn't know because he wasn't there, and your grandfather wasn't there either because that was where he was hit too, where he lost his arm. So who told them? Not Henry, because his father never saw Henry but that one time and maybe they never had time to talk about wounds . . . and not Bon, because Sutpen never saw him at all because he was dead—it was not Bon, it was Henry; Bon that found Henry at last and stooped to pick him up and Henry fought back. [*Absalom,* p. 344]

The passage imitates the interaction between writer and reader in the best of fiction. The writer plays it straight, invents something better than what life has to offer, something that works better, is more apt or fits better; the reader assents and accepts that fiction can establish such inventions beyond the shadow of a doubt, that belief in fiction can become stronger than belief in fact. The process of collaborative understanding and mutual narration has become more important than anything else. In chapter 8 the conventional structure of timed revelation comes to the point at which it can reveal that fear of miscegenation has been a part of Henry's doubts and it comes as a distinct nonrevelation. We as readers already know this in the way that Quentin and Shreve do, by having arrived at it, absorbed it, and become more interested in other things. Yet the book places it where a revelation ought to go (and has gone in earlier chapters) and insists it is more important than a real revelation, the source of Bon's resentment (parallel to Jones's resentment of Sutpen). Again, the book maintains a conventional suspense pattern leading up to the revelation of the identity of the "someone" at Sutpen's Hundred in 1910, but Quentin has tipped us off to the truth earlier, near the end of chapter 8: *"Nor did Henry ever say that he did not remember leaving the tent. He remembers all of it"* (p. 355). If we have been following Quentin's narrative and its clues, this hint is enough.

The strange thing, I suppose, is that Faulkner has bothered with the conventional suspense structure at all. I think there is very good reason for it. The book falls into two overlapping halves. In the first half (chapters 1–5) our principal attention is drawn to Sutpen and his story. We think the conventional suspense pattern will produce the meaning of the book. The second part begins with the introduction of the room in Cambridge in chapter 6, but doesn't really get moving until Chapter 7, and includes some conclusions to the conventional suspense patterns. More important, though, it introduces the plot of Quentin's and Shreve's ratiocination, and this finally represents for us such a depth of involvement that it constitutes our primary allegiance. Quentin and Shreve have taken over the all-important function of *becoming* in the book. They have become protagonists, in the stead of their doubles of the first half.

The characterization of the roommates, and our identification with them, gives the collaboration its life. The contrasts between them are perhaps more important to its success than their similarities. The first is geographical, and Faulkner plays on it continually in their responses to the cold, tomblike room.

> Shreve, the Canadian, the child of blizzards and of cold in a bathrobe with an overcoat above it, the collar turned up about his ears; Quentin, the Southerner, the morose and delicate offspring of rain and steamy heat in the thin suitable clothing . . . brought from Mississippi, his overcoat . . . lying on the floor where he had not even bothered to raise it. [*Absalom*, p. 346]

But it is less the archetypal differences than the individual and functional differences that separate them. *Absalom* pulls in *The Sound and the Fury* in much the same way "That Evening Sun" does. Each of the three Quentins is independent of the others, and each is legitimately read only in the light of his surrounding narrative. But Faulkner supports our temptation to see all three as one by subtle turns of the narrative. Quentin, in moving freely through his and Shreve's flexible—almost loose—narrative, raises the ante on incest and returns to it again and again (the door he cannot get past at the end of chapter 5). Shreve, free of such associative or analogous parallels, is a freer agent to manipulate the story.

The chief functional contrast is between Quentin the Teller and Shreve the Hearer. Quentin functions for Shreve as guide (in the manner of Ratliff in "A Bear Hunt"), as initiator (in the manner of Ratliff in *The Town*), as collective community conscience (in the manner of the narrator of "A Rose for Emily"). As they move through their collaborative chronicle, Quentin must bring Shreve up to the level of information required—not just in the matter of Sutpen (which Quentin has learned about rather recently), but in more general matters of the South and its consciousness. Shreve has, or attains, equality of information but never of consciousness. He must always be meeting the foreign as if it were familiar rather than, as Quentin, the familiar in foreign form.

Shreve maintains his function as Hearer and performs its duties. He wants a neat package; he wants the rough edges of incoherent fact smoothed off because he wants to be shocked at the South and the strange practices of the foreigners. His sensationalism matches Rosa's personal sensationalism on a national or regional scale. Even as he moves toward familiarity (Shreve, after all, by the end of the book, knows more about Sutpen than anyone except Quentin and we as readers) he continually tries to distance the setting for these familiar events and people so that he can retain their shock value. It is he who keeps coming back to Rosa's epithet of "demon" even as he realizes how inadequate a personification it is for Sutpen. Long after his "demon" has become an ironic term, he remains true to his function and its duties, desiring the awful, yearning for the disaster, just as we do and just as we did, cozened by the narrator of "Emily."

In spite of these contrasting roles, they share a coherent attitude toward narrative and myth. Shreve's desire for outrage works in perfect concert with Quentin's desire for a kind of precision, for depth and richness. Their basic desire is to make it work. Their sifting of the evidence is the most purely objective—free of Rosa's axe-grinding and Mr. Compson's emblem-making, free even of General Compson's narrative parentheses. They work toward the design as a whole, attempting to make a perfect arrangement which will realize all the potential and nuance of what they know. It is unselfish (except for that touch of Quentin's obsession with incest), aesthetic, precise in historical reason, and, considering how young they are, rather free of cant. When a sequence lacks a fact they find one and insert it, or assume one, or invent one—but always with a central regard for historical, biographical, and emotional consistency. For instance, they try out the idea that Bon knew that his father was Sutpen, that he had been told by his mother at some time——then that he must have been told before he was old enough to take it in. Neither of these produces enough fullness or depth, so they invent the lawyer who invents the boy as instrument of revenge. Their drive is to supply the fitness of the perfect accidental conclusion with fit intentional causes in individuals' actions, and to combine both harmoniously in a single design. Shreve invents what Sutpen said to Rosa. It won't stand, but its effect is clearly right in terms of the pattern.

The "doubling" of metaphor passes into the characterization. Quentin and Shreve as two become one:

> It was Shreve speaking, though save for the slight difference which the intervening degrees of latitude had inculcated in them (differences not in tone or pitch but of turns of phrase and usage of words), it might have been either of them and was in a sense both: both thinking as one, the voice which happened to be speaking the thought only the thinking become audible, vocal; the two of them creating between them, out of the rag-tag and bob-ends of old tales and talking, people who perhaps had never existed at all anywhere, who, shadows, were shadows not of flesh and blood which had lived and died but shadows in turn of what were (to one of them at least, to Shreve) shades too, quiet as the visible murmur of their vaporizing breath. [*Absalom*, p. 303]

There is the suggestion here not just of the geographical contrast but also of the contrast in their roles as makers of fiction: Quentin as Teller, Shreve as Hearer, eager to keep his original shock intact and find new shocks. This is extended by the roles Faulkner gives them in his habitual narrative structure: Quentin is the insider, supplying, and Shreve is the outsider, demanding information. Shreve is being initiated. The roles are even carried into the metaphor through which they become Henry and Bon:

> So that now it was not two but four of them riding the two horses through the dark over the frozen December ruts of that Christmas Eve: four of them and then just two—Charles–Shreve and Quentin–Henry, the two of them both believing that Henry was thinking *He* (meaning his father) *has destroyed us all.* [*Absalom,* p. 334]

Quentin must be Henry because he has a visible father and an important sister, Shreve must be Bon because he is the alien outsider. This seems at first to deal confusion to the narrative roles. Should not Quentin be the one to expose Shreve's photographic plate gradually to the image of the South? Perhaps, and perhaps this discrepancy in pattern reveals that Faulkner was not quite as deliberate or neat in the laying out of his pattern as we always want to make him appear to be. But in another sense, the arrangement as we find it is right. Quentin is moving through the Sutpen story to a realization about himself and the South—a shocking realization about the most familiar native ground. Shreve is the alien reflector, emphasizing the demons and maidens and outlandish events of the matter of Sutpen because he must maintain the extremes in order to retain his sensationalism. He is in a sense exposing Quentin's plate to the realization that must come at the end of the book. Quentin doesn't kill Shreve, but Shreve forces Quentin to an understanding deeper than just an understanding of Sutpen: what he always held but never fully comprehended. He forces him to face up to himself. And, of course, this is supported by Quentin's realization that Shreve is "just like Father." Quentin, seeing the understanding Shreve has forced him to, begins to understand his kinship with him in a way which parallels the real blood relationship between Henry and Bon.

The second half of the book—the collaboration—moves not so much toward an understanding of Sutpen or the completion or realization of the pattern set forth in the first half's conventional suspense structures (it does this, too, of course), as it does toward an understanding of the process. Indeed Quentin's and Shreve's collaboration not only completes the myth but carries the fiction and the process of constructing it beyond the point of completion, beyond the fiction's initial données or the realization of its patterns to attack the next question: what happens to the fiction once the author's neat little package has been released to the reader?

Throughout the canon Faulkner is talking about the flux of fiction: the process of invention and the product it can make of initial raw materials. What sets *Absalom* apart from the other novels is its concentration on the fictive process and this process's final phase—or indeed, on that which follows the fictional process. The collaboration of novelist and reader (or Teller and Hearer) goes on to make the fictive product an occasion for abstract reasoning, to move its patterns beyond the product and into conjunction with other fictions or lives or events. Fiction's approach to humanistic understanding is a mutual effort of Teller and Hearer.

Quentin's room at Harvard is a place set apart, a place for understanding rather intractable, mystifying, and complex interacting patterns:

> In the cold room (it was quite cold now) dedicated to that best of ratiocination which after all was a good deal like Sutpen's morality and Miss Coldfield's demonizing—this room not only dedicated to it but set aside for it and suitably so since it would be here above any other place that it (the logic and the morality) could do the least amount of harm—the two of them back to back as though at the last ditch, saying No to Quentin's Mississippi shade who in life had acted and reacted to the minimum of logic and morality, who dying had escaped it completely, who dead remained not only indifferent but impervious to it, somehow a thousand times more potent and alive. [*Absalom,* p. 280]

The passage makes a clear distinction between living, telling about, and making a fiction. Sutpen lives and has little to do with the logic and morality which have been applied to his story by those who saw him and heard about him. He has even less to do with what Quentin and Shreve supply or attribute to him or even assume and invent, at such distance from his life. Miss Coldfield told about him, was in a sense making a fiction, but her fiction failed because it was essentially dead. It allowed the demon but none of the more interesting and less extreme human motivations Quentin and Shreve figure out, intuit, or invent. Their re-creation is better than the original because it has a wealth of human meaning that the living man lacked, even for those who knew the living Thomas Sutpen. And it is better because their making the fiction is safer than Sutpen living it. As Aristotle suggests, *Oedipus* is safer than the real event for both the protagonist and the spectators—for the protagonist because real results are now just the ending of the play, for the spectators because there is a possibility for pity and terror rather than just shock. Logic and morality directly applied to the living Sutpen could have inflicted even more damage on those around him than he did himself without logic and morality. Logic and morality applied to his shade can enhance, deepen, and even alter his story for the better. At this distance, in this abstraction, they make it more accessible to human emotion than the *"slow and gradual confronting with that which over a long period of bewilderment and dread it has been taught to regard as an irrevocable and unplumbable finality."*

And safety is just part of their distant advantage.

> It would not matter here in Cambridge that the time had been winter in that garden too, and hence no bloom nor leaf even if there had been someone to walk there and be seen there since, judged by subsequent events, it had been night in the garden also. But that did not matter because it had been so long ago. It did not matter to them (Quentin and Shreve) anyway, who could without moving, as free now of flesh as the father who decreed and forbade, the son who denied and repudiated, the lover who acquiesced, the beloved who was not bereaved, and with no tedious transition from hearth and garden to saddle, who could be already clattering over the frozen ruts. [*Absalom,* p. 295]

There is a freedom of movement, a freedom born of distance and imagination, an innocence of the kind of details that might impose limits. They can shift people about, they can inhabit each of them in turn. If they become the characters for one moment they can at the next cease, cut off the impersonation and return to a more general contemplation of the whole, even as Quentin and Shreve do: "two, four, now two again, according to Quentin and Shreve, the two the four the two still talking, . . . —the two the four the two facing one another" (p. 346). If dogwood is called for in winter, then move the dogwood outside the window, because the shape of the events and their meaning is more important than any of the facts which might have given those events their origin.

Four of them who sat in that drawing room of baroque and fusty magnificence which Shreve had invented and which was probably true enough. . . .

The two of them in leaf-faded gray, a single candle, a crude tent walling them away from a darkness where alert pickets face one another and where weary men sleep without shelter . . . yet in a second tent candle gray and all are gone and it is the holly-decked Christmas library at Sutpen's Hundred four years ago and the table not a camp table suitable for the spreading of maps but the heavy carved rosewood one at home with a group photograph of his mother and sister and himself sitting upon it, his father behind the table and behind his father the window above the garden where Judith and Bon strolled in that slow rhythm where the heart matches the footsteps and the eyes need only look at one another. [*Absalom*, pp. 335, 353–54]

Again the narrative presence will not take a stand on the relative truth of the invention as compared to what was, what "really" happened, because freedom improves his game, too. Not only do Quentin's and Shreve's inventions and ratiocination build the narrative presence's narrative, the story of Sutpen's dream he originally set out to tell, but he could never have achieved this depth, this meaning, this moral commentary without their intercession. Their intercession and their re-creative process have become the main line of the novel—understanding has replaced event at the center of the stage.

I would emphasize the shadowy nature of their creation of Sutpen (noted in this chapter's epigraph). Sutpen takes on substance only when abstracted. In life he can be only Sutpen to be seen by Jefferson and told about by Rosa or by various Compsons to designated hearers. Once abstracted and invented upon he can be fully realized as a character, in the way a fictional character takes on more than life. Even as one of his actions can be used by the makers of his fiction to epitomize the texture of his day-to-day life, as one anecdote in biography can exemplify a characteristic quality—just so can he in his patterns epitomize any man's innocence or design or revenge or despair.

The power of this shade is not fully realized until the collaboration completes it: "And the other said *Wait. Wait. You cant know yet: you cannot know yet whether what you see is what you are look-*

ing at or what you are believing. Wait. Wait." (p. 314). The creation must be a collaboration between the maker of the fiction and the faith of the reader. He cooperates in responding with expectations which arise from what he is told; he collaborates as he alters the substance of the myth, as he identifies with it or not, responds to it, reshapes it in the hearing to suit his own ends.

> That was why it did not matter to either of them which one did the talking, since it was not the talking alone which did it, performed and accomplished the overpassing, but some happy marriage of speaking and hearing wherein each before the demand, the requirement, forgave condoned and forgot the faulting of the other—faultings both in the creating of this shade whom they discussed (rather, existed in) and in the hearing and sifting and discarding the false and conserving what seemed true, or fit the preconceived—in order to overpass to love, where there might be paradox and inconsistency but nothing fault nor false. [*Absalom*, p. 316]

Quentin and Shreve, in their mutual telling and hearing, their contrasts of native and alien, outsider and insider, familiar and shocking, make visible a process which generally starts only after the novel has passed out of the novelist's hands and into the mind of the reader. It is a process which the novelist must continually imagine and project (What will the reader think? What do I want him to do?), but over which he can have no control. Here it becomes a part —and I think a most important part—of the novel itself.

Essentially *Absalom, Absalom!* is another answer to the problem posed by Quentin in "A Justice": "I was just twelve then, and I would have to wait until I had passed on and through and beyond the suspension of twilight. Then I knew that I would know. But then Sam Fathers would be dead" (*SS*, p. 360). The abstraction of fiction makes it possible to combine the freshness of first experience with the maturity and finality of something understood. Fiction cannot be life but must be as the dream of Quentin's metaphor, that "logic- and reason-flouting quality of a dream which the sleeper knows must have occurred . . . in a second." Here Faulkner has not only blended the verisimilitude of events as experienced with the abstraction of the telling, but he has moved a step beyond that to an exposure and detailed examination of the manipulation of the maker. Under his hands events must be not only shaped but altered to become fiction.

The achievement of *Absalom, Absalom!* is better judged in its soaring, its complex ambition and the grand scale of its attempt at a total understanding of the narrative process, than in its emotional impact or formal perfections. Its imperfections and blunt oversimplifications are everywhere apparent. It cannot stand beside the mystery of consciousness achieved by *The Sound and the Fury* or *Light in August* or the simple perfection of *As I Lay Dying*, but its ambition and its overreaching, and most important of all, its examination of the fictive process, stand alone in Faulkner's canon in the grandeur of their attempt.

> "Yes," Quentin said. "The two children" thinking *Yes. Maybe we are both Father. Maybe nothing ever happens once and is finished. Maybe happen is never once but like ripples maybe on water after the pebble sinks, the ripples moving on, spreading, the pool attached by a narrow umbilical water-cord to the next pool which the first pool feeds, has fed, did feed, let this second pool contain a different temperature of water, a different molecularity of having seen, felt, remembered, reflect in a different tone the infinite unchanging sky, it doesn't matter: that pebble's watery echo whose fall it did not even see moves across its surface too at the original ripple-space, to the old ineradicable rhythm* thinking *Yes, we are both Father. Or maybe Father and I are both Shreve, maybe it took Father and me both to make Shreve or Shreve and me both to make Father or maybe Thomas Sutpen to make all of us.* [*Absalom*, pp. 261–62]

8 Uncertainties: *The Unvanquished* and *Go Down, Moses*

Absalom, Absalom! is an end-point of one development of Faulkner's narrative experiment in much the same way that *The Golden Bowl* is for Henry James's. It is clearly a terminus for the fictive self-examination which embodies its synchronous examples as it goes along. To have gone farther would have yielded diminishing returns (as some held that *Absalom* did), or at the very least, would have led to repetition—even more uncharacteristic of Faulkner.

The Hamlet turns a corner, in method, narrative development, and subject matter, but the two books that bracket it in the chronological sequence, *The Unvanquished* in 1938 and *Go Down, Moses* in 1942, are of interest not so much for their own experiments as for the light these two strongly contrasted books shed on this transition. Each is worthy of consideration in its own right. *The Unvanquished* has purity and simplicity in its evocation of the past and a near-perfect narrative realization of surface action; it also represents the most extended development of Faulkner's use of the child's point of view. *Go Down, Moses* is a continuation in substance and theme of many of *Absalom*'s concerns but cast in a much simpler narrative structure; it is also Faulkner's most successful attempt at a generic middle-ground, the short-story compound, and clearly an attempt to justify this as a self-sufficient genre.

But in comparison with *As I Lay Dying, Light in August, Absalom,* or *The Hamlet,* both seem somehow a bit weary. They are almost mannerist books in a way, as is often the case with transitions. Their direction and design have the uncertainty born of a lack of conviction. Both yearn to be done with the past, so each must have yet another go-round with that, repeating thematic concerns of earlier books. One chooses reminiscent evocation, the other seeks, in a final working-through of guilt, possession, and blood, to have it over with once and for all and to get on to the equally difficult present and future. At the same time, both show impatience with the kind of detail Faulkner employed in earlier novels to construct his past and a decided tendency toward peculiar generality. Each reflects in its individual way the sharp shift—indeed, the shock—that *The Hamlet* represented for Faulkner, a shock to both his habits and his development. The shaping confidence is taking up a new direction there, but here it can't quite bear to have done with the old.

The reader's sense of time is strikingly different in each of these, and both are different from *Absalom, Absalom!* This provides a key, at least, to the characteristic distinctions of *The Unvanquished. Go Down, Moses* covers a span of time as great or greater than that of *Absalom:* 1859 to 1942 or from The Beginning to 1942 (if the conversations of section 4 of "The Bear" are taken seriously). The range of *The Unvanquished* is much shorter. But range gives little sense of the shift the reader feels when passing from one to the other. In *Absalom, Absalom!* we are clearly allied with the present, looking at events of the past, aided by the testimony of a survivor who bridges the span between. With Quentin and Shreve our distance from the events is always more significant than our intimacy with the participants. In *Go Down, Moses* a framing device (the opening paragraphs of "Was," taken up again by the opening of "The Bear") attempts to unite all the events and stories in one man's lifetime, but this has only a formal success: despite the attempted frame, we are in Cass's consciousness in "Was" and throughout; at the same time our reading of the stories depends sometimes on distance, sometimes on intimacy, sometimes on a balance between the two. In other words, we move through time here in a way very different from the way we do in *Absalom.* Our movement forward and backward has a lot to do with the way a book makes its impact.

In *The Unvanquished* the past is immediate and present and apparently so uncomplicated that only thorough examination makes it seem worthy of critical attention. The book is cast as Bayard Sartoris's boyhood reminiscence, but as reminiscence it makes no attempt to keep one firm foot in the present. Lucius Priest's narrative in *The Reivers* is determined and shaped by considerations of the present. The old Lucius is making a reading of the young Lucius; when the young Lucius takes over in moments of action, the old Lucius is clearly performing an impersonation. In other words, for *The Reivers,* the present is in control. In *The Unvanquished,* Old Bayard is less a constant or a base than he is an intermittent reminder. The old narrator does not take on the persona of the young narrator, but takes the rather cold view that a narrative presence might take toward his protagonist, letting the young narrator do the talking but dissociating himself from what he feels or sees, and even, here and there, introducing verbal complexities and polysyllabic generalizations that the young narrator could never have had (something like the early statements of the narrative presence in "Barn Burning" before Sarty's "older / still older" consciousness has taken over his functions). The old narrator adds his pontifications and metaphors more or less as objective commentary, rather than as a deliberate link to connect his *now* with his *then* self.

The past, then, impersonates the present. The narrative's strongest consistency is found in the young narrator's actions and perceptions. Our sense of the past realized and rendered is stronger than our sense of Old Bayard's present, and our identification is most strongly engaged with Young Bayard's sense of the immediate. We move through the book on the surface in a narrative which is not so much shallow as it is too swift to have the leisure to allow depth or distractions. "Ambuscade" sets up a tension (in Loosh's destruction of the children's play-Vicksburg) of something concealed, but we remain on the surface of the action. Something is about to happen, but we are sure it will happen where Young Bayard can directly and immediately perceive it (unlike, say, our feeling in "That Evening Sun"). We move from point to point always on the surface, by pursuing the sequence and the action-to-action connection, the immediately attractive appeals of action. Plot in the conventional sense is at the heart of *The Unvanquished* in a way that it cannot be in *Absalom, Absalom!*

But only details can reveal this book's subtle if rather conventional characteristics. The abstract excuse for the narrative is found in one such detail. Ringo is drawing a picture and has attracted the sardonic attention of a Yankee lieutenant:

> "Oh," the officer said. "I see. You're drawing it like it used to be."
> "Co-rect," Ringo said. "What I wanter draw hit like hit is now?

> I can walk down here ten times a day and look at hit like hit is now. I can even ride in that gate on a horse and do that." [*Unvanq.*, p. 160]

"Like it used to be" is what the narrative is seeking. If the later rationalizations of the Old Bayard are permitted to take over, the narrative has failed in its design. But "like it used to be" is as elusive as "like it is." It involves not just concrete, immediate perception but the distortion of this perception that results from the boy's self-protective alterations of fact to suit his fancy: "When you thought of Father being on Jupiter it was as if you said. 'Together they will be too big; you won't believe it.' So you didn't believe it and so it wasn't" (*Unvanq.*, pp. 10–11). Belief, not fact, is the key to whether something is or not. The book finds its center in defining the balance-point between the fiction in the child's belief and the factual, hard, and sometimes bitter action suspended by that softening mist, a product of both his sensory participation—his muscle-memory—and the delicate adjustment of momentary belief, the measure of what he can at this moment manage to believe.

The passage quoted above is followed by a transition which distinguishes between the Young Bayard's way of seeing and Old Bayard's:

> that odor in his clothes and beard and flesh too which I believed was the smell of powder and glory, the elected victorious but know better now: know now to have been only the will to endure, a sardonic and even humorous declining of self-delusion which is not even kin to that optimism which believes that that which is about to happen to us can possibly be the worst which we can suffer. [*Unvanq.*, p. 11]

The older perception undercuts the younger's rampant idealism, puts it in perspective and reminds us that this is a book about defeat which needs to keep on hoping that it is about victory. But it offers a choice. If we have to choose between the boy's self-delusion and the old man's moralistic and abstracted irony, we'll take the boy's. Of course, it's not a free choice: Faulkner made the decision in the book's design.

Faulkner's variations upon this simple suspension between belief and hard fact for the most part are produced by simple devices. He appeals to us with some of the usual stereotypes familiar from his other fiction of childhood: the trading of roles, for instance ("then I would have to be Grant once so Ringo could be General Pemberton or he wouldn't play anymore," p. 7). Lewis Carroll's touchstone, the metaphysical implications of size, is called up, too. For Bayard a moment can alter the size of his father on his horse or of Granny, or can lengthen or telescope space (as he runs toward the house after shooting the Yankee, p. 30). Perhaps more significant to this narrative, one moment can also transform what comes before it and what comes after: "like when once the musket decided to go off, all that was to occur afterward tried to rush into the sound of it all at once" (p. 31). But not all these appeals are so familiar or so overt. Ringo is perhaps Faulkner's most successful emulation of Mark Twain's Jim: " 'Then hit's so,' he said. 'If somebody tole you, hit could be a lie. But if you dremp hit, hit can't be a lie case ain't nobody there to tole hit to you. So we got to watch him' " (p. 23). The lie must have a human agent, and this implies that evil is caused by wicked humans, a view of the world which conveys both wisdom and self-delusion. The child's (and in particular the wiser black child's) cosmos is economically rendered.

The tone of the book conforms to this surface of childhood. Indulgent, sunny toleration is its humor, allowing for little dangerous slowing-down in the events. The irony and cruelty of *As I Lay Dying* (a far funnier and a far more serious book) would give us pause, and Faulkner cannot afford to let us have a moment's pause. In the strong sequential impetus and powerful momentum of surface narrative, Faulkner allows few intermittent undercuttings of doubt. These are a bit hard to see—indeed, it's hard to see that there's anything to *The Unvanquished* except movement and charm. But without these momentary doubts the book would lapse into simple nostalgia. There must be some preparation for the hard events of the last one-third of the book.

Doubt—or the interruption of happy belief—tends to occur as part of a sequence, and the sequence of variant devices is more characteristic of this book than are individual narrative tricks.

> Then we listened. We heard: the names—Forrest and Morgan and Barksdale and Van Dorn; the words like Gap and Run which we didn't have in Mississippi even though we did own Barksdale, and Van Dorn until somebody's husband killed him, and one day

> General Forrest rode down South Street in Oxford where there watched him through a window pane a young girl who scratched her name on it with a diamond ring: Celia Cook.
>
> But we were just twelve; we didn't listen to that. What Ringo and I heard was the cannon and the flags and the anonymous yelling. That's what we intended to hear tonight. [*Unvanq.*, p. 17]

The whole passage sets up an expectation (similar to the boy's expectation of Christmas in "That Will Be Fine") that Bayard's father will tell stories, which he turns out to be too tired or too defeated to do. The opening sentence imitates aurally the melody and spell of such stories and the next observation makes clear a part of the stories' power (that the names are foreign to Mississippi). The next ends us up in a very concretely realized moment (whether realized by the Old Bayard or the Young we're never quite sure): Celia Cook has seen Forrest and scratched her name on a window. The burden is fact, but it's enveloped in wishful legend. In the next paragraph we are deep in the consideration of the power of belief, the boys' power to hear what they intend to hear.

The basic order for such sequences is that seen in the opening of the first story: "that summer. . . . this afternoon. . . . at last it was damp enough. . . . Then suddenly" (pp. 3–4). Generally the sequence locates the moment in time and all the participants in space. In the process of location there is usually some rendering—not necessarily of the most important feature of the surroundings, but characteristically, of just that feature the boy might fasten on. This is followed by a "suddenly" moment for which the boy's point of view forms the core. These act as do freeze frames in a film, concentrating on this detail and then that, to tell about each as it is fastened by perception in the intensity of a moment of violent action. Locating and rendering frequently focus on commonplace surroundings in which nothing much is happening (as in the building of the stockpen in the swamp), but even these passages become a part of the dominance of sudden action, because they establish a background of the everyday against which the sudden urgency of uncommon event can be better perceived.[1] This not only intensifies the opening and other points of crisis but provides the essential im-

1. See chap. 2 above, the discussion of "Shingles for the Lord" and "Shall Not Perish."

petus by which the compelling surface continually drives us forward:

> Perhaps it was the dark or perhaps we were the two moths, the two feathers again or perhaps there is a point at which credulity firmly and calmly and irrevocably declines, because suddenly Louvinia was standing over us, shaking us awake. She didn't even scold us. She followed us up stairs and stood in the door to the bedroom and she didn't even light the lamp; she couldn't have told whether or not we had undressed even if she had been paying enough attention to suspect that we had not. [*Unvanq.*, p. 20]

Our participation in any of these is so immediate, the narrative is so swift, that we seldom pause to examine what it is doing to us. The telescoping of time passes into rendering and the rendering into the breaking of routine and sudden action with such ease and freedom—it is worked with such skill by Faulkner—that we suddenly find ourselves in the midst of danger, and our surprise is much the same as that of the boys:

> She made her bed down in the wagon by the chest and Joby slept under the wagon with the gun beside him like when we camped on the road. Only it would not be exactly on the road but back in the woods a way; on the third night Granny was in the wagon and Joby and Ringo and I were under the wagon and some cavalry rode up and Granny said, "Joby! the gun!" and somebody got down and took the gun away from Joby and they lit a pine knot and we saw the gray. [*Unvanq.*, p. 63]

Stasis and routine pass directly into flux and chaos. A description of the library which mixes the older Bayard's total recall with the younger Bayard's jumbled logic can be interrupted by allusions to the past or comments on function. These don't just promote our initiation as insiders by making us familiar with surroundings, they put us directly within his sense of time:

> We waited until Father was settled in his chair in the room which he and the Negroes called the Office—Father because his desk was here . . . and where the dogs could come and go with impunity, to lie on the rug before the fire . . . —these whether Mother, who died when I was born, gave him this dispensation before she died or whether Granny carried it on afterward or whether

> Granny gave him the dispensation herself because Mother died I don't know: and the Negroes called the Office because into this room they would be fetched to face the Patroller . . . and which Granny called the library because there was one bookcase in it containing a Coke upon Littleton, a Josephus . . . a thousand and ninety-eight page treatise on astrology, a History of Werewolf Men in England, Ireland and Scotland and Including Wales by the Reverend Ptolemy Thorndyke, M.A. (Edinburgh), . . . a paper-bound Dumas complete, too, save for the volume which Father lost from his pocket at Manassas (retreating, he said). [*Unvanq.*, pp. 17–18]

The boy wants to tell us everything at once, and one measure of Faulkner's skill in impersonation of this eagerness is that he can arrange the narrative to accomplish this in such a way that we are never bored, never indifferent, but tend not to notice what he's doing to us. We never feel that we are a captive audience for irrelevant background or genre touches, but at the same time we don't feel that we're being manipulated.

Because we are so much on the surface, Faulkner can afford to bring us closer to the war in *The Unvanquished* than he can in *Absalom, Absalom!* or *Go Down, Moses.* Faulkner was nervous about the Civil War. This may sound outrageously wrong—but try, if you will, to recall just how much of that war really takes place in his fiction: a bit in *Light in August* and *Sartoris* and even less in scattered stories ("My Grandmother Millard" and "Mountain Victory"), and all these actions are really tangential to the war. The war brought out a bit too much of the Hightower in Faulkner—the flash and crash of cavalry and the vague odor of gunpowder mingled with jasmine. The real meaning of the war—that the anchovy-raid was a feint in the midst of a defense of slavery, that the glory was based on an overreaching which, like Sutpen's, was humanly heroic but, in order to be so heroic, had to transform humans into chattel—was deep in his consciousness and neither glorious nor honorable. The child participant thus provides a good excuse. The war, the glory, the gunpowder, and Confederate jasmine stay on the surface, and Faulkner can avoid being dragged into the deep concerns he might be forced to consider if Old Bayard mixed in his current feelings, or if he himself became involved in meanings beneath the surface.

In *The Reivers* Lucius Priest, swept up in the events in Memphis, suggests that if he stopped to think it through he would be miserable. The same might be said of Faulkner's war: the immediate attraction and swift sequence as perceived by the child are fixed and must remain fixed on the surface, lest the implications of all that this surface conceals should break through.

The most remarkable of the war sequences is a moment in a side-effect of war, the intensely visual experience of the sea of freed slaves in "Raid." The passage opens with a grand simile, more literary than visual, but the poetry quickly becomes experience: "We never did overtake them, just as you do not overtake a tide. You just keep moving, then suddenly you know that the set is about you, beneath you, overtaking you, as if the slow and ruthless power, become aware of your presence at last, had dropped back a tentacle, a feeler, to gather you in and sweep you remorselessly on" (p. 116) The sense of movement and scope is joined by an unearthly sound, the more terrifying because the simple metaphor is incapable of doing it justice.

> It was like we all heard it at the same time—we in the wagon and on the horse, they all around us in the sweat-caking dust. They made a kind of long wailing sound, and then I felt the whole wagon lift clear of the ground and begin to rush forward. I saw our old rib-gaunted horses standing on their hind feet one minute and then turned sideways in the traces the next, and Drusilla leaning forward a little and taut as a pistol hammer holding Bobolink, and I saw men and women and children going down under the horses and we could feel the wagon going over them and we could hear them screaming. And we couldn't stop anymore than if the earth had tilted up and was sliding us all down toward the river. [*Unvanq.*, p. 118]

The passage has the surface attraction of a movie spectacular—wide-screen writing. What are later proved to be real people can appear for the moment to be ants or water or some less affecting form of chaos. But the scope never interferes with the focus of consciousness in the boy's perceptions. We experience the sea with him and from his sheltered consciousness as we have adopted it, sense with him the discovery that individual human wickedness will not explain all the ills of the world, that beyond the shelter of Granny's skirts lies a world in which cause can be made irrelevant by mass suffering, in which the pushing and pulling of mass desire and mass irrationality make individual guilt or intention beside the point.

It is well that the surface attraction of *The Unvanquished* is so powerful, because structurally the book leaves something to be desired. The connections between stories are immediate and sequential. These stories are not complex parts of a whole, with multiple connections to each of the other stories, but just segments or installments. The subtleties of the short-story compound must wait for *Go Down, Moses.* The basic sequence builds to Granny's death and tone and effect are sharply reversed. There have been hints that this would come, but—perhaps because of the power of our identification with Bayard and Ringo—we are unprepared for this and its meaning. Its implications for the book are never satisfactorily put in perspective.

"An Odor of Verbena" is set apart, still only a segment, but somewhat out of sequence. Here Faulkner seems suddenly to perceive the possibility of a double structure for the book, the possibility that "An Odor of Verbena" might by thematic suggestion draw the book to the implications of the story, bring us to rethink our premises and enrich the whole. But this fragmentary and cursory double structure only frustrates. The final story cannot carry the book away because of Granny's residual force. She is as hard to get rid of in the book—as organizer of action, center of whatever little thematic and sequential structure the book has—as she was to get rid of in life.

The Unvanquished is wonderful while it is going on, but it resists critical reduction. It is neither a failed *Absalom* nor an unrealized *Go Down, Moses.* It pursues a narrative which escapes from theme dominance and ignores structural complexity. In the Trilogy Faulkner ultimately rejects the avenue of escape offered by simple, swift action narrative, but he incorporates there much of what this swift surface has taught him. The experience stands him in good stead only when he has finally found an open form which can combine such surface ease with a structure which can support more fictional weight than *The Unvanquished* ever aspires to.

If one took *Absalom* to be a spinning-out of the proposition, "Thomas Sutpen made this design and these are the results," then one could take *Go Down, Moses* to be a development of the proposition, "Lucius Quintus Carothers McCaslin spawned this and these are the results." *Absalom* represents a more conscious and deliberate debacle, *Go Down, Moses,* a more organic growth of accidence, but "the sins of the fathers" dominates both. In *Absalom* a plan constitutes one heritage of disaster and in *Go Down, Moses,* a plan is devised to expiate another. Except that neither paraphrase really works: *Absalom* is not about what happened to Thomas Sutpen and his plan but about the ways of understanding what happened to them; *Go Down, Moses* is not so much about a cause and its effects (we are kept at an even greater distance from Old McCaslin than from Sutpen) as about the comparative effects of a cause in various spawn, both "white" and "black," as they emerge in individuals and develop through time.

What I am trying to suggest is that there is good reason for this book to be a compound of short stories—beyond just that a compound is simpler than a novel [2] or that Faulkner was uncertain about going back to leftover themes. To deal over such a span of time with a set of characters not only influenced and altered by the passage of time, but themselves obsessed with questions arising from the nature of time, the short-story compound offers very attractive economies. And of Faulkner's three short-story compounds (four, if *Big Woods*'s rehash is included), *Go Down, Moses* is the only one which does not have to make a case for its generic consistency either on the power of its individual stories or on some compromise or relaxation in standards normally applied to the novel. Faulkner found a shortcut in technique for *Absalom*'s long way around and in the process produced a remarkably flexible literary form: it commands the respect due a novel's unity and cohesion and at the same time conforms to the standards of concision and impact in its short stories.

The stories of *Go Down, Moses* are sequentially disjunctive but thematically parallel. The freedom of this double structure permits some of the more baroquely complex echoing, retracing, and recapitulation of *Absalom* without having to bother with its attendant obscurities of style and structure. Every story grows out of "Was" in two ways: every cause that has an effect in the book and every

2. The choice of short units should not, of course, be heavily interpreted as a yearning for simplicity. A novelist sometimes needs short fiction the way a painter need watercolors after or before oils or acrylics—not so much as a change motivated by weakness as a change for the sake of variety.

pattern that develops through the other stories can be found there. "Was" is at the same time its own discrete cosmos: it points out its own immediate causes and runs to earth their results, it develops its own crisis and denouement; neither its function as story nor its function as a part of the whole compromises the other.

Perhaps this is the greatest achievement of "Was": that Faulkner can so successfully arrange the divergent narrative appeals necessary for the story to work without miscalculating any of its necessary precalculations for the book. Cass is truly a boy, with only a boy's understanding and perception, but he can give us, frequently without realizing it himself, exactly the information Faulkner knows we need to fill the holes left in the story's narrative by suspense-omission, and at the same time, without appearing to do so, introduce the causes of effects we can only recognize when the book is finished.

The story rests upon an elaborate scheme of breathless, headlong involvement in action, sometimes not unlike the surface attractions of *The Unvanquished.* This conceals an exceptionally subtle pattern of suspense by omission and timed revelation. It is perhaps not until a third reading that we come to realize that Tomey's Turl is in a conspiracy of some sort with Miss Sophonsiba. The overcomplication of the wagers (which at first appears to be just more of Faulkner's vicarious adoption of Cass's innocence, or just his weakness for ornate chicanery) becomes richer and richer the more we come to realize how little of the complication is accidental, either on the characters' parts (the first wager, p. 15, is a case in point) or on Faulkner's.

The headlong involvement, centering in Cass's consciousness, keeps the surface consistent but does not prevent the same narrative from suggesting to us some darker hints beneath the surface. The book's innocence is another touchstone of comparison to *Absalom, Absalom!* This is not a mythic innocence or the South's frantic search for some rationalizing dream of chivalry out of *Waverley,* but rather an innocence which persists in the face of myth-destroying fact. That the board on the porch of Warwick is rotten, that Sophonsiba is keeping up appearances with a horn-boy atop the gate, that it "would sound as if she and Mr Hubert owned two separate plantations covering the same area of ground, one on top of the other" (p. 9), all this can maintain its own innocence, but let us know what's going on. At the same time Cass provides the story with an elusive tone on which it and much of the book depends. That the chase of Tomey's Turl is a "good race," that Buck and Buddy are charming, boyish eccentrics, that the child is having a whale of a good time conceal only for the moment that human beings are the quarry in the chase and the ante in the card game. That Uncle Buddy becomes no more than a property to be wagered by no means equalizes his state with that of Tomey's Turl, but on the contrary only enforces Ike's eventual conclusion. An individual's innocence in a system he never made is beside the point, because the system and the individual collaborate to treat humans as chattel. Ownership itself degrades not just the chattel but the owner as well. Such delusive innocence and ironic good nature deal more forcefully with the antebellum South's self-delusion than could any amount of hoop-skirts and anchovy-raids and the graves of our Glorious Dead. What an antidote for *Gone With the Wind* or, for that matter, for certain elements in *The Unvanquished.* And that the world of Warwick and Buck and Buddy is to serve in a sense as the book's Golden Age, that what follows is to be a falling away from this mark, indicate how unconventional a book this is.

So central is our identification with Cass here that it is possible to remember "Was" as a story cast in the first person. Faulkner, up to his old tricks, has used the child's mind so skillfully that we ignore the simple adoption of the child's point of view and his subjection of this to a third-person narrative. We make a thorough adoption of the child's consciousness: technical success converts the story in memory to the first person. The book throughout is an exercise in varieties of the third-person narrative, but an exercise remarkably different from similar experiments in *Light in August* and *The Hamlet.* As in these books, variations can be laid out on the scale of narrative distance—our distance as readers from the actions, established by variation in point of view, abstracted remoteness, dramatic qualities, or the immediacy of narrative presence. The variations do not form a sequential pattern but rather make their points by contrast or surprising juxtaposition. The intensely directed third person can achieve an intimate identification with the protagonist (Lucas in "The Fire and the Hearth") or develop a more casual familiarity (Ike in "The Bear"); the former is reminiscent of Joe Christmas, the latter, of Sarty Snopes. The intensity, familiarity, or kinship themselves do not make the point, but rather the connections and contrasts between one and the next or one and the other.

"The Fire and the Hearth" is, like "Was," an exercise in reduced narrative manipulation, but in quite a different way. We begin deep in Lucas's mind, making a smooth transition from the intense point of view at the end of "Was." Exposition deals with the immediate past, but even the exposition seems to replicate the workings of Lucas's mind. Faulkner develops an almost invisible technique to render Lucas's thought-processes, continually transmitting significant but subtle shifts between one train of thought and the next. In order to realize the subtlety and sophistication of this one has only to cast back to the mechanical devices of Benjy's transitions, or even Quentin's, in *The Sound and the Fury*. Here there is a refinement in the narrator's humanistic sharing of the protagonist's conscience, of the minor details of how a mind works.

The resultant narrative does not simulate the first person as "Was" did. The exposition demonstrates the narrative presence's freedom—it can break free of the protagonist's thoughts at any point. Cass's child's consciousness makes him a slave of the immediate in "Was." But Lucas's thought-processes determine narrative timing: we are given what occurs to him at the time it occurs; we move through the present at Lucas's speed and into the past when he decides to travel through time. Lucas, in other words, exercises more control over the narrative presence's selective attention than Cass's point of view does in "Was." But Lucas has less control over the narrative presence's comments on what he is doing.

The result here is a chronological flux which replaces the cause–effect flux of "Was." We move in a chaos of dates, ages, "years since" and "years ago," calculated to force us to construct a chronology for ourselves. There is some conventional omission-suspense as unexplained events are introduced, but the greater part of the narrative's suspense rests on time flux and the concealed parallelism between a set of actions in one story or framework and actions in another.

Once Lucas's thought process and the parallelism are established, the narrative presence can break into Lucas's intense point of view with moments of insight into the other characters. These appear the more striking because of the power of Lucas's flow. A great proportion of the story then can become dramatic reporting. But I think the force of the story is not so much dependent upon drama or immediacy or event or juxtaposition as it is upon the basic framework of Lucas's process of mind and our identification. We identify and then we begin not to like what we are about. Our distance from Lucas is greater at the end than in the beginning as we come to realize, more and more, that he is obsessed. We buy out of the alliance at the same time that the narrative frees itself from the dominance of the intense point of view.

Then (when we begin to look at things objectively) Molly becomes central. She has been a distant Caddy-figure in the story—too touching to be heard in her own voice. She is a figure of mystery in the events of Edmonds's original offense, but as she begins to assert herself in the third chapter she persuades us that her distance in that part of the story (the narrative of 1898) was just a by-product of our identification with Lucas, our entrapment in his mind. Perhaps we saw so little of her not because Lucas failed to understand her but simply because he failed to take her into account. Molly's importance at the end has a double function. She steps in to protect her hearth. Her reasons differ from Lucas's, but her determination is parallel to his earlier action. Her emergence in the end suggests that we were mistaken in our way of looking at earlier actions. The ending, then, functions as I think the ending of "Uncle Willy" does (and as the ending of *The Unvanquished* tries and fails to do): not only does it resolve the issues raised by the story's données, but it casts such a light on such issues that we are forced to change our mind about the story's premises.

"Pantaloon in Black" works in an identification structure which contradicts this at almost every point. For intensity and intimacy there we have here a rather calculated and cold distance. At the end no alternate center is offered around which we might be able to form a new synthesis. It ends in an emptiness. If the story has any place at all in this book it seems to me it must be found in contrast: Rider's distance from the whites (and from us as readers) must contrast evocatively with Lucas's almost Machiavellian manipulation of human relationships. Rider's end must demonstrate in its objectivity and in its meaninglessness a zero-point far below Joe Christmas's end. It involves negation of family, possessions, guilt, blood, and heritage, all of which give echoes to Lucas's accommodating management of the whites.

The "Pantaloon" of the title suggests that the story will be a drama and a stereotype, distanced by artificiality. It is, but not quite in the way we might expect. Here is the same alternation between apparent intimacy and objective drama found in "Dry September," but here the alternation finds little of the intensity of that story in either of its modes. It lacks the hermetic atmosphere which impelled "Dry September" and never attempts to fasten our attentions on Rider as the day-to-day details fastened us upon Minnie. Like Hemingway's "Big Two-Hearted River" (a story with a similarly ironic title), "Pantaloon in Black" chooses negation as its mode to contrast itself to the stories that surround it. We must read it in terms of what it lacks and what its protagonist does not do. It is an outline for speculation rather than a direct appeal to sympathy or a manipulation of our identification. The speculation is productive because the story's negations are designed to fit, point by point, the surrounding stories' fullness and intensity. It operates on parallelism by contrast.

"The Old People" and "The Bear" move out of the point-of-view dominance of the first two stories (not to say that point of view disappears, far from it) and into what is more an exercise in stylistic distance than it is distance determined by purely narrative devices. The child's point of view recurs from "Was," but another recurrence, the litany-like verbal pattern of the opening two paragraphs of the book, seems more important than the child's responses. The omniscient narrative presence seems to be firmly in control, crowding out much of the intimacy and identification of a simple sharing of the child's view.

Style and verbal patterning are not my province in this study, so I might better have avoided comment on *Go Down, Moses* altogether, because it seems to me that the book's effect is finally dependent in large part on variations in style. But because style forms the reader's patterns of response it falls legitimately within the domain of narrative structure. I am on a rather shaky footing with recent developments in stylistic analysis, but I must proceed to some rather amateur observations on style if only to contrast the workings of this fiction to the workings of others determined by more purely narrative calculation.

In *Absalom* the complexity of the style and verbal excess is a symptom and a direct result of the narrative experiment, but here verbal pattern and innovation are a replacement for narrative innovation and fullness. This constitutes the most important shortcut to *Absalom*'s hard-earned narrative complexity. Like the return to the more controllable short-story unit, this shortcut attempts to replace organic complexity and the novel's spacious development with comparatively unearned and unintegrated thematic and emotional force. Compare, for instance, the rather lengthy series of metaphors dealing with young Sutpen's geographical progress (*Absalom,* chap. 6, pp. 222 ff.) with this from *Go Down, Moses:*

> And as he talked about those old times and those dead and vanished men of another race from either that the boy knew, gradually to the boy those old times would cease to be old times and would become a part of the boy's present, not only as if they had happened yesterday but as if they were still happening, the men who walked through them actually walking in breath and air and casting an actual shadow on the earth they had not quitted. And more: as if some of them had not happened yet but would occur tomorrow, until at last it would seem to the boy that he himself had not come into existence yet, that none of his race nor the other subject race which his people had brought with them into the land had come here yet; that although it had been his grandfather's and then his father's and uncle's and was now his cousin's and someday would be his own land which he and Sam hunted over, their hold upon it actually was as trivial and without reality as the now faded and archaic script in the chancery book in Jefferson which allocated it to them and that it was he, the boy, who was the guest here and Sam Father's [sic] voice the mouthpiece of the host. [*GDM,* p. 171]

There is an immediate difference apparent: the passage in *Absalom* reflects immediately the tone, logorrhea, and slant of Sutpen's autobiography, a strongly narrative effect. The passage from *Go Down, Moses* originates in the narrative presence with only a slight nod toward the boy's point of view. The statement does not so much emerge from the narrative itself as it is applied to it by the narrative presence. Echoes of the King James Bible and the rolling, continuous rhythm, as if from some dark source in legend, are similarly brought to the narrative rather than emerging from it. The breathless continuity of sentence to sentence and the simplicity of compound transitions from period to period can call up the evocation of a Golden Age seen in the Indian point of view of "Red Leaves."

The preceding distinction is stated in a way that may seem calculatedly prejudicial to *Go Down, Moses.* I don't intend it as such, because the purely verbal movement of this book—the litany of the introduction, the legend of this story and that of "The Bear" embody what is perhaps Faulkner's strongest claim to be called an accomplished stylist. And that this style has a firm purpose which it accomplishes is certainly no criticism of the book. I state the distinction only for the purposes of comparison of this book with the more integrated and organic styles in others—styles which emerge from narrative necessity. Verbal and aural patterns, in that they exercise their power in an addition to substance (although I will not agree with many that they are independent of substance) must always be, to some extent, appliquéd, not organic, always striving for something not "earned" in the way that integral narrative structure and fictional technique works for and "earns" its effects. Style appeals to our senses and, by its allusiveness, to our intellect. The strongly stylistic passages of *Go Down, Moses* deal with our senses and intellect so effectively that they persuade us to a thematic profundity which the book arranges and outlines but never really works through.

"The Bear" is a deliberate myth, written with the style and the confident design of a writer who knows precisely what he is doing. It is practically a copybook example of what can only be admired, the full confidence of a man at the top of his form. The string-pullings and strivings of narrative technique seem to disappear because the power of a storyteller in the act of telling has taken over so authoritatively that critical comment is almost forestalled. I could not, even in the most jaundiced mood of reductive comparison, refer to the opening of this story as unearned or appliquéd or as an exercise in applied rhetoric (as it surely is) because to do so would be to abdicate the critical responsibility of balance. On the balance, the story's confidence and competence earn its impact as it goes along, justify the litany of its introduction. None but the most stubborn advocate of the "natural" narrative can object to the ordered and well-designed clicks of integral pieces falling into place.

They give the sensual pleasure of listening to a fine camera do its work: the quietest, most efficient, reduced whir of pieces designed to do just what they are doing and only that.

Section 4 of "The Bear," however, can be criticized. It is clearly calculated, clearly an overt manipulation of us as readers to serve the book rather than the story. In this section, perhaps more so than at any other point in the book, Faulkner can be charged with the deliberate manufacture of meaning. Its method is a distraction in terms of the book's generic structure and the consistency of its parts. Each of the stories of *Go Down, Moses* satisfies its own unity while contributing to the integrated and organic unity of the whole. Aside from section 4[3] and the introduction to "Was," nothing in the book compromises either part or whole.

Once section 4 is singled out, it is easy enough to make it a scapegoat for the book. Then one can reduce *Go Down, Moses* to a moment of uncertainty, a narrative turning-point filled with leftover substance. Passing from 3 to 4 is an unassimilated transition: we pass immediately from straight storytelling into something more like chapters 7 or 8 of *Absalom, Absalom!* There is a significant connection between section 4 and chapters 7 and 8 in the relationship between Quentin and Shreve, and Cass and Ike. Section 4 has both Teller and Hearer, but both tell and hear. There is sharing and lack of sharing. Ike is an insider (to be inside here is to be obsessed by a way of looking at things, rather than, as in *Absalom,* to be native-born to a body of tradition) and Cass an outsider trying to understand. Cass is trying to maintain the sensational value of the revelations, but for a more directed purpose than in *Absalom*—in order to persuade his cousin that the course he has chosen is mad. Even more than Quentin and Shreve, Cass and Ike argue like college freshmen grown heady on the panoply and scope of the Saga of Western Man. Both have the self-confidence of rather parochial autodidacts, of men "ignorant of the ignorance of the world" who thus feel free to range more freely and leap more frantically with the intoxication of their untested wisdom.

But section 4 must be where it is. "The Fire and the Hearth"

3. Faulkner admitted that section 4 was exceptional in an interview. This is implied in his omission of section 4 in its other publications: it was not included in *The Saturday Evening Post*'s original publication and was omitted from *Big Woods.*

rests upon what it will reveal of L. Q. C. McCaslin's estate in the coffeepot. Without all this—even the Gospel (or perhaps the Pentateuch) according to St. Ike—"Delta Autumn" would lack the bitterness it gains in overturning section 4's high idealism. Perhaps the section should have been a story in itself: by so arranging it, Faulkner would have gained by one almost perfect story ("The Bear") and by an improved structural consistency for the whole book. The short-story compound's structural dilemma is here evident. Faulkner had to have 4 where 4 is for practical reasons: the seeds of the inflexibility of theory in Ike's plan must be contained within the book's highest fable. Even though it forces the book into a premature peroration, the most important exemplum must have its high ideal juxtaposed with its application. This is matched by a contrast in the texture of the book's prose: 3's elegiac simplicity passes into 4, and from 4 moves back into the pure storytelling of 5.

Section 4 is a miscalculation in story unity and generic consistency, perhaps it is an alien excess in style and method, but even this miscalculation and inconsistency can be seen to have a justice to them—the rightness of exception in a book formed by its exceptions. And there is another, more complicated justification. What fails for Ike is his plan. He formed it in reaction to Old McCaslin's sins, and it fails, as surely as Lucas Beauchamp's more accommodating reaction to those sins, because it forgets love and, perhaps more important, forgets that times change while human slipperiness remains constant. There is no more reason to criticize Ike's plan than there is to rail at Addie Bundren's design. Each is such a plan as man loves to make—full-blown, self-consistent, locked into place without a thought that the world in which it finds itself will prove its undoing. Not the plan but the world fails, a world which will not stop turning, containing people who will not stop being people, subject to all the weaknesses, changes, and evolutions people are subject to.

The plan is popped in in section 4. The book then fails it as the world fails to live up to the plan: the book goes its way, coherent in its parts, its parts relating consistently to the whole—except for the introduction and section 4. Looked at critically they may seem out of place: this is book-making or the manufacture of meaning, to patch up a sequence of stories which turned out not to mean quite enough on its own. But looked at as a structural imitation of just the situation they treat—the unfitness of this world for a perfect abstraction—the two sections must be misfits. Even as Cash Bundren's coffin is obscenely defaced by Vardaman's love and set off balance by the family's absurd concern for Addie's wedding-dress, the inflexible legend-narrative of the introduction and section 4 are defied by the free-form of the rest of the book's interrelationships. That section 4 is the book's true peroration is right, too. Now is the time for summary, quickly, now, before the plan goes all to pieces in the sloppiness of human actions, accidence, and love.

After section 4, it's downhill—not Faulkner's downhill run to climax, but Dilsey's vision of unending decline. That "The Bear" has no clearly calculated strategy of point of view (such as that in "The Fire and the Hearth") leads to the conclusion that the book progressively grows more objective. "Delta Autumn" bears this out. After the feast of ideals, legend and near-allegory in "The Bear," after the antagonist/embodiment, god/victim is met and destroyed, "Delta Autumn" brings the incursion of practicality, the comedown, the falling-off, the hangover. It does not bring the death of the ideal, because such an ideal, once formulated, will not die but only gradually erode, like the coffeepot legacy. Even the manifestations of nemesis—from the railroad in "The Bear" to the auto and the land-grab of "Delta Autumn"—are appropriately practical and modern. Quite a few intervening years have elapsed between the end of one story and the beginning of the next, so as to give the shock of the comedown some verisimilitude. Ike's marriage is only glimpsed for a moment in section 4.[4] Ike is now at a distance. Not only does he have to get to the Wilderness in a car, but on the way he has to hear not just the talk of non-Wilderness (he who had cherished the best of all talking) but foreign intrusions from across the water. And as if Faulkner had arranged that we should share this much of his alienation, the contemporary intrusion comes as a shock to us, too, locked in our fictional dream as Ike is in the dream of an ideal which has been his life. World War II was not Faulkner's war. Even more is it not Ike's.

He clings to his dream. There's no need here for the elaborate distancing apparatus of "The Fire and the Hearth" because Ike's distance is established at once in the contrast between the end of

4. I've always felt that this was something of a throwaway and wished that Faulkner had chosen to develop a story enlarging it.

"The Bear" (or the end of section 4, to be slavishly chronological) and "Delta Autumn." "Delta Autumn" brings him finally, almost cruelly, to his cot in his underwear to play his big scene. This is less narrative than it is dramatic or rendering pressure, but it is as sure a choice as any of Faulkner's tricks. The shrillness of Ike's tirade is in direct contrast to the tempered flow of his fullblown theory in section 4. He is confronted by a product which demonstrates to him, again dramatically, that his ideal was a dream, a living embodiment of his failure to stop the world. As if that were not enough, the embodiment speaks to him the words which can bring even him to realize that the act of devising a plan was an empty, limiting abstraction: "Old man, . . . have you lived so long and forgotten so much that you dont remember anything you ever knew or felt or even heard about love?" (p. 363). He ran counter to the force of life. Lucius Quintus Carothers McCaslin has won.

Of course he hasn't, but the balance between what remains of our strong identification with Ike and our present objective distance from him is so surely calculated that we can have our cake and eat it too: feel the subjective defeat vicariously and see the other side objectively at the same time. We find ourselves, in other words, in Ike's dramatic situation in "The Bear": the animal in order to live must die. In order to gain force as an ideal, Ike's design must go sour, must be tested out and fail. Addie is admirable and courageous and wrong. Ike is righter than that, but unlike her, will not be spared as she was the bitter realization of his plan's failure.

In "Delta Autumn" and "Go Down, Moses" the book drifts off. The last story ties up the loose ends of McCaslin's black spawn. Perhaps it does not tie them up the way we would like them to be, certainly not as satisfactorily as the end of "The Fire and the Hearth" tied up that story's ends, without putting an endstop on anything. But it realizes the story's premises without a false note and better serves all the book's premises.

Misunderstanding, a constant theme, persists in the last story. Gavin Stevens thinks that Molly wants a parade and we know she does not. Gavin and the town conclude implicitly that Samuel Worsham Beauchamp is a victim of his own inferiority, that he has paid the price of leaving the county and its benevolent restriction, when we can see (in the black's Chicago experiences, another of Faulkner's exercises in cinematic summary) the warfare of an irrevocably split society. This again constitutes defeat for Ike's scheme, but a defeat perceptibly lightened by a touch of Faulkner's faith in endurance. With all of Gavin's blundering and misunderstanding he has not forgotten love. What the town thinks it is granting Molly is a parade permit, but it is really granting recognition of her fellow-citizenship, kinship in the family of residence, at least. The granting of it is grudging and mistaken, it is more blunder than gesture, but it's there.

Molly in her own quieter way is exercising Lucas's hard-won art of manipulation, and the conclusion of the book seems to point back to him, to the advantages of accommodation and flexibility over the adherence to ideals. Lucas's accommodation was as rooted in L. Q. C. McCaslin's heritage as Ike's ideal was. Ike's ideal rose to theoretical triumph and dwindled in defeat, but Lucas's—without much more than a momentary setback—lives in Molly to accomplish something at the end. Samuel Worsham Beauchamp could not have done this for himself, any more than Rider could have. Perhaps Lucas made the same mistake Ike did. He forgot about love too, or at least about the mutuality which, when it was threatened, first started him on a career of manipulation. And some qualified or limited mutuality—mistaken in intent on both sides—seems to be the strongest force that emerges at the end of the book.

Innocence is another constant theme—it appears in each of the stories: the innocence of Lucas, Rider, Ike, Boon, the naiveté of the Old Ike and of Gavin Stevens, reaching a climax in Molly's perhaps calculating innocence. I think that this innocence is one reason that this book seems to have emerged from an earlier century, somewhat as Faulkner's public letters seem to. It stands, as they do, as the attempt of a reasonable, moderate Southern white to understand black men as sympathetically as he can without actually putting himself in their place. The novel goes on to the reconstruction of the whites by the blacks and to parallel this reconstruction to a highly idealistic self-reconstruction in one white. In terms of the Black revolution, *Go Down, Moses,* of course, is already a historical document, a tombstone for the white moderate and the just-let-us-go-about-this-in-our-own-way principle. Up to the end of "The Bear" the book is a slightly sad recognition of the Southern white's idealism and the Southern black's flexibility. Lucas's use of adopted white methods and his adaptation to white morality may perhaps save him (when he learns to apply them in moderation) but these resources are simply not available to Rider.

But such a political view proves its own weakness in the last two stories in the book. If one were to assume that Faulkner was a white racist, and that *Go Down, Moses* is his racist pamphlet, to make it work one would either have to reject the last two stories of the book as defective or else manufacture an elaborate schema which could allow for the white Southerner's lust for self-defeat. This would necessitate a built-in rhetorical shift. One would have to say that the book was started in apologetics but ended in hopelessness as the author is forced to let the defeat emerge.

This is one reason I have such a hard time making sense out of Faulkner as a racist pamphleteer. I don't think he was very interested in fiction as a platform, or that he was even a spokesman-in-spite-of-himself. The fictions are more important than opinions of their author: this is one of Faulkner's most deeply held literary principles. Even without using his overt theoretical statements, it is easy enough to demonstrate that he could not sustain pure exposition of principles long enough for a whole fiction. They aren't interesting enough in themselves. Even in the unfortunate *Intruder in the Dust,* where overt statement of moderate principles abounds, the fiction demands more twists than a pamphlet would allow—it takes too much to itself to be regarded as just a tool of opinion. Faulkner's strength is not in wisdom or the overt statement of ideals (that is, the books' conclusions), but in embodiments and complex interactions, the books' experience. This will account, perhaps, for some of the disappointment of *Go Down, Moses.* There remains, no matter how ingeniously section 4 is justified, more than a little unresolved tension between the flux of event and the inflexibility of plan. The book's ambiguities do not quite dominate its certainties. Too much of Faulkner's mind has been made up: he can no longer float as free of the dogmatic as he did in *As I Lay Dying, Light in August,* or even *Absalom, Absalom!* He cannot move easily from the hangups of the past into the numbing complexities of the present, and perhaps *Go Down, Moses* transfers too much of the heritage of the past's barely manipulable chaos on to the present's intractable continuum of problems. Uncertain about a solution to the past, how can he seem so satisfiedly certain in confronting the blank enigma of the present?

But none of this—how dated the book seems, the destruction of its central ideal, the lack of any emergent ray of hope save the rather muted one of limited mutuality—damages the book's effect. All this is grudging and muttering—both beside the point when it comes to the triumph of parts in this book. "Was" is as good, as characteristic, and as funny a story as Faulkner ever wrote. It looks forward to the impossibly complex chicanery and scheming of the Snopeses and back and forward to what we might label (if we didn't get distracted) as Faulkner's most craftsmanlike achievement, the mastery of fiction rendered from the child's point of view. "The Fire and the Hearth" is a solid accomplishment of a character who can be favorably compared to any character in the canon, the more amazing because he is black. "The Bear," even when smothered by its explicators, is still almost as good as they say it is—and this test, the trial by the fire of multiplied ingenuity, is perhaps the most severe test fiction can be subjected to. If we can still read the story and it can still give pleasure after what it has been through of stretching and pulling this way and that, then it must be pretty good. The whole is as close as Faulkner ever comes to combining his two chosen genres into a distinct and almost independent third. The compound of short stories for the most part is remarkable in the self-sufficiency of the stories and their simultaneous connection into a rather complexly unified whole. Each makes its own meaning and contributes to the whole. And this is so tricky an achievement that it is difficult to come up with other successful attempts (except Faulkner's own) to which it can be compared.

Then too, the whole is as close as Faulkner ever gets to integrating his world—putting blacks and whites on a single stage and making them function as cogs in the same machine (Dilseys and Nancys notwithstanding). The book here again stands at midpoint, between the completed development of the narrative experiment of individual consciousness in the earlier novels and that of the fully functioning fictional world of the Trilogy. That *Go Down, Moses* compromises each is only testimony to the courage of its striving for both.

9 Faulkner's Failure: *Intruder in the Dust, Requiem for a Nun,* and *A Fable*

"I hate this," Miss Habersham said.

Intruder in the Dust, *p. 101*

After a certain amount of concentrated study a reader finds himself drawn in his admiration of novels or a novelist into a process over which he has little control and more than a little doubt. A novel liked, studied, and still liked becomes a novel explained, excused, and defended. He finds himself less and less willing to find any fault which affects the book's achievement, more and more like an author quarreling with what he feels is a stupid review—indeed the investment of author and constant reader are similar: both have put their time in, have blessed the text with their labor.

If there is a constant progress toward perfection in the eye of the beholder, there is a geometrical progression in disaffection for less favored books by favored authors. Every perfection found in the one makes the imperfection of the other loom larger. There is an almost personal sense of betrayal in a weak or bad book. First: "I've defended his prolixity and rhetoric where I found it justified, but this is just indefensible." Then: "How could he do this to me?"

And the doubts which assail a growth of unconsidered affection are nothing compared to the doubts which attack the Faulkner- or the Wordsworth- or the Joyce-enthusiast when forced to comment on bad Faulkner or bad Wordsworth or bad Joyce. He finds himself repeating the easy pattern of a lazy, nay-saying sophomore, doing the Mark Twain gig on Fenimore Cooper, then warming to the task, drawing up charts to prove how bad one book is as assiduously as he charts the perfect geometry of another.

Unfortunately, bad Faulkner narrative also illuminates the essential issues of the good: technical control, measure, taste, the sureness of timing and the fitness of "corner" or "box" to substance. It has to be done, but if I pass too quickly over some complex texts, let it be understood that it is because necessity never quite measures up to the distastefulness of the task. The enthusiast avoids reading some early Keats and some late Wordsworth because of the threat posed by them: he may come to believe his doubts.

Edmund Wilson was right. *Intruder in the Dust* is an unsuccessful pamphlet. But I am far less interested in its rhetoric or its stance than in the way these concerns divert its narrative. A successful character, a plank hewed from the "still-living tree" is plucked out, trimmed down, and gussied up to serve as a what-not for things of the moment. Lucas Beauchamp, Uncle Tom though he may be, is at least consistent in *Go Down, Moses,* the vehicle for some moments of undeniable power in "The Fire and the Hearth." Here not only is that consistency and strength betrayed, but his character becomes the plaything of plot and the exemplum of a faltering sermon. Wouldn't the Lucas of *Go Down, Moses* have taken more pleasure in triumphing over the whites in his own good time than he would (as he does here) by sitting on his information until the plot is ready for him to reveal it? This Lucas becomes the object of action where that Lucas was always originator. Of course he is older, of course the "corner" is a different one, but is it not unthinkable for him to become so quietistic, such an object?

I seem here to be denying a basic principle of form and function espoused earlier, but I think not in the long run. This is no momentary forgetfulness or vacillation on Faulkner's part—not the same as the fancy tie-store in New York City he finds for V. K. Ratliff. Faulkner is not succumbing to overfondness for a character but rather using the character for a purpose which defies his nature, valuing his usefulness before his essence. Remaining true to the original might not have permitted the overt detective-story shape, but it would certainly have made a better story.

There is an even more central rule being broken. Faulkner is preferring what he can say to what he can embody, "wisdom" over storytelling. After years of embodying the South of his mind, peopling his imaginary county with essences and ideals whose imaginary shapes can construct precisely a powerful moral structure, he suddenly sets out to tell us about the "real" South. It's no more real than the South of his mind's eye, of course, far less so because it is rooted in the time of the telling and mortally fixed in Faulkner's opinions of the time of the writing. It is as if he suddenly believed that what he had been doing all along was what Cowley had said he was doing—or worse, that he was becoming what the second *TIME* cover-story said he was: sociological delineator, social critic, conscience of his land.

Some of this arises from hindsight. Racial attitudes of gradualism and moderation—especially even the most moderate forms of moderation—are poor leftovers. But worse than this is the tone Gavin Stevens gives them (presumably a tone Faulkner has consciously calculated). When Ike McCaslin preached from his camp cot in his underwear in "Delta Autumn" the reader could keep him objective, assign the speech to senile screaming, feel better about the book in that this ranting moved Ike's design into line with the other failed designs and plans of Faulkner. Here Gavin is decently dressed, respected by Chick (indeed, too much tolerated), sitting in his office above the square preaching some of the same stuff. There are good reasons for readers to be attracted to Faulkner, but I hope never to meet the reader attracted by Gavin's speeches.

Perhaps these aberrations could be glossed over if the narrative functions of the book did not so clearly support a conclusion that Faulkner was here engaged in telling for effect and not engaged in telling to its own end. The book is a compendium of old tricks lifted from other books. My quarrel is not with the fact that they are tricks, because device is the measure of narrative, nor that they are old, because it's not easy to invent new ones in such a runnelled field, but that they are lifted, and in the lifting their context is ignored. It is as if Faulkner has lost the key to his structure in which parts fit other parts and the whole, in which all parts are timed and measured. Here the choice of method seems a matter of, at best, convenience, at worst effect or expedience. The expedience ignores the function the devices served in their original context and seems to assume that any narrative trick is equally applicable to any narrative, no matter how it functions in conjunction with other tricks or with the substance of the story.

For instance, there is a touch of the time dislocation of "Barn Burning." In that story it constituted a stretching of the boundaries of short story toward the novelistic. It allowed for a mature presence to comment on Sarty's present immaturity, for the scope of final judgment to be applied to presently unjudgable events. Here the initial assumption seems to be the same.

> That unmistakable odor of Negroes—that smell which if it were not for something that was going to happen to him within a space of time measurable now in minutes he would have gone to his grave never once pondering speculating if perhaps that smell were really not the odor of a race nor even actually of poverty but perhaps of a condition: an idea: a belief: an acceptance, a passive acceptance by them themselves of the idea that being Negroes they were not supposed to have facilities to wash properly or often or even to wash bathe often even without the facilities to do it with; that in fact it was a little to be preferred that they did not. But the smell meant nothing now or yet; it was still an hour yet before the thing would happen and it would be four years more before he would realise the extent of its ramifications and what it had done to him and he would be a man grown before he would realise, admit that he had accepted it. So he just smelled it and then dismissed it because he was used to it. [*Intruder,* p. 11]

But as the novel develops there is no excuse offered (as there was in "Barn Burning"), for the maturity revealed in narrative presence's mind-reading. Chick is evidently a shape to be filled, waiting for any thought, rhetorical complexity, or metaphorical excess that the narrative presence or Faulkner can think up. Truth to the individual limitations of the character is evidently less important to Faulkner than the consistency of the whole argument and statement of the pamphlet, which is all very well until one wonders why he bothered to introduce the device in the first place. Was it just for a momentary effect of innocence for which he is not willing to pay the price or even to acknowledge its limitations? The scheme is brought full circle by the end of the novel, but there is still nothing to deny this sad conclusion:

> By the simple mischance of an old Negro man's insomnambulism and then having got away with that by means of a plan a scheme so simple and water-tight in its biological and geographical psychology as to be what Chick here would call a natural, then to be foiled here by the fact that four years ago a child whose presence

> in the world he was not even aware of fell into a creek in the presence of that same Negro insomnambulist because this part we dont really know either and with Jake Montgomery in his present condition we probably never will though that doesn't really matter either. [*Intruder,* pp. 228–29]

Evidently we were taken on this buggy ride only to show us how far we had come, and it turns out we hadn't really been anywhere.

The device does, however, achieve a perhaps pointless intensity in our experience of the action through Chick. This is enforced by a device lifted from another novel—the "thinking . . . thinking" pattern of *Light in August.* Here it is employed in a significant way only for Chick, and it operates on a much more superficial level than in its source. It is used impressionalistically, with no consistent variation between the first and successive instances of "thinking," and without the ordered variation seen in Joe's "thinking" between knowing, thinking, remembering, and the like. The use extends throughout the book (more than seventy instances, in a cursory listing), but it seems to be directed to no very elaborate or exceptional purpose beyond the initial aim of the device in *Light in August*—to balance a third-person narrative with some first-person immediacy.

> This time Lucas looked straight at him, straight into his eyes from five feet away and passed him and he thought *He has forgotten me. He doesn't even remember me anymore* until almost the next year when his uncle told him that Molly, the old wife, had died a year ago. Nor did he bother, take time to wonder then how his uncle (obviously Edmonds had told him) happened to know about it because he was already counting rapidly backward; he said thought with a sense of vindication, easement, triumph almost: *She had just died then. That was why he didn't see me. That was why he didn't have the toothpick:* thinking with a kind of amazement: *He was grieving. You dont have to not be a nigger in order to grieve.* [*Intruder,* pp. 24–25]

There is then, something of the same attitude implicit in the use of this device: it worked there, why not here? And there is, as in the "Barn Burning" borrowing, some of the same lack of concern for the relationship of part to part and parts to whole.

Beyond these, there is some plain and fancy metaphor work—

neither so extensive nor so ordered as the metaphors of *Absalom, Absalom!* but clearly deriving from, vaguely, the same aim—a calculated impediment to the reader's progress through the novel's actions. But where in *Absalom* these were set within a carefully calculated and timed order which justified the excess—the slowing of the reader almost to a halt in chapter 7—here the metaphors reveal only a pattern of mounting and diminishing excess, perhaps corresponding to a sequence, but a sequence of mounting irritation:

> By nightfall the whole land would be hung with their spectral intact tallowcolored empty carcasses immobilised by the heels in attitudes of frantic running as though full tilt at the center of the earth. . . .
>
> Bursting out of the thicket ahead of the dog, the small white flare of its scut zigzagging across the skeletoned cottonrows like the sail of a toy boat on a windy pond. . . .
>
> He flung himself bodily with one heave into a kind of deadly reasonableness of enraged calculation, a calm sagacious and desperate rationality not of pros and cons because there were no pros. . . .
>
> He thought how it was not really a paucity a meagreness of vocabulary, it was in the first place because the deliberate violent blotting out obliteration of a human life was itself so simple and so final that the verbiage which surrounded it enclosed it insulated it intact into the chronicle of man had of necessity to be simple and uncomplex too, repetitive, almost monotonous even. . . .
>
> This land was a desert and a witness, this empty road its postulate (it would be some time yet before he would realise how far he had come: a provincial Mississippian, a child who when the sun set this same day had appeared to be—and even himself believed, provided he had thought about it at all—still a swaddled unwitting infant in the long tradition of his native land—or for that matter a witless foetus itself struggling—if he was aware that there had been any throes—blind and insentient and not even yet awaked in the simple painless convulsion of emergence. . . . [*Intruder,* pp. 4, 17, 82–83, 89, 96–97]

The painfulness of such extracts is connected to what I said at the outset—to take Faulkner out of context is the last thing an admirer wants to catch himself doing—but it has more to do with the failure of the narrative than the prolixity of the prose. Such passages are made worth the effort by the context of *Absalom, Absalom!,* justified by the reader's involvement and the effort in that narrative. Here they neither fit the context nor justify their complexity.

Such disconnected and abstracted lifting argues that Faulkner is here involved in simple bookmaking. The "lumber-room of the memory" takes on a rather rueful meaning—in this novel he seems to be reaching back there not for the memory and experience with which to form "flesh-and-blood" embodiments, but for bits and pieces to tart up what is essentially a rather plain and straightforward narrative.

Why couldn't he (the fatal question for a critic) have stuck to a narrative center of baldly perceived action, a strong surface of stopped-motion sequence perceived through the eyes of a child? *The Unvanquished,* of course, lends some of its manner here, too, especially in the graveyard.

> "Pah," she said and took the reins from him and before he could even brace his hand for her foot she put it in the stirrup and went up as light and fast as either he or Aleck Sander could have done, onto the horse astride so that he had just time to avert his face, feeling her looking down in the darkness at his turned head. "Pah," she said again. "I'm seventy years old. Besides we'll worry about my skirt after we are done with this:"—moving Highboy herself before he had hardly time to take hold of the bit, back into the road when Aleck Sander said: "Hush." They stopped, immobile in the long constant invisible flow of pine. "Mule coming down the hill," Aleck Sander said.
>
> He began to turn the horse at once. "I dont hear anything," Miss Habersham said. "Are you sure?"
>
> "Yessum," he said, turning Highboy back off the road: "Aleck Sander's sure." And standing at Highboy's head among the trees and undergrowth, his other hand lying on the horse's nostrils in case he decided to nicker at the other animal, he heard it too—the horse or mule coming steadily down the road from the crest. It was unshod probably; actually the only sound he really heard was the creak of leather and he wondered (without doubting for one second that he had) how Aleck Sander had heard it at all the two minutes and more it had taken the animal to reach them. Then he could see it or that is where it was passing them—a blob,

> a movement, a darker shadow than shadow against the pale dirt of the road, going on down the hill, the soft steady shuffle and screak of leather dying away, then gone. [*Intruder,* p. 99]

The trouble is that the action narrative can never dominate with the pastiche of distractions, pieces, and liftings, the heavy hand of Rosa Millard imitation (as in the introduction of Miss Habersham, p. 76), the appliqué even of Rosa's climactic nonclimax (p. 104) or the rhetorical impetus of random moments from various novels all mixed up: *Light in August* "thinking" meets *Absalom, Absalom!* metaphor. No action narrative, no matter how pure or exciting, could compete with this kind of fragmentation. And as if he is afraid that the collage will be less than complete, we are even given a moment of the cosmic morality of *Go Down, Moses:*

> *This time. Maybe this time* with all this much to lose and all this much to gain: Pennsylvania, Maryland, the world, the golden dome of Washington itself to crown with desperate and unbelievable victory the desperate gamble, the cast made two years ago; or to anyone who ever sailed even a skiff under a quilt sail, the moment in 1492 when somebody thought *This is it:* the absolute edge of no return, to turn back now and make home or sail irrevocably on and either find land or plunge over the world's roaring rim. [*Intruder,* p. 195]

Rhetoric, manner, metaphor, device from every sort and condition of context in the novels are brought together in a mad summary—as *The Reivers* seems almost to be racing against time to unite all the Yoknapatawpha genealogies, so does *Intruder* work to complete itself as a fallacious Reader's Guide to Faulkner. This might be merely sloppy if it were not for the pamphlet. Gavin runs on and on (pp. 153 ff., 199 ff., 238 ff., 242 ff.), and the growing conclusion of constant reader, regret it as he will, is that this has malice aforethought. The pamphlet is being tricked out with good melodrama and bad arty touches, but it's still pamphlet.

Clarence Brown's film, although an improvement on the novel in some respects, convinces us even more of this sad conclusion. Faithful to the book almost to the point of literary enslavement in the early sections, in its middle improving on the action sequences in the manner of *The Unvanquished* (as only film could), ultimately it must call a halt to what could have been good and straightforward (if perhaps a bit too literary) film in order to let Gavin pronounce just a bit of his pamphlet. The last section of the movie is a good lesson in adaptation: it is the strongest possible argument for leaving the literary text on the printed page. But it's more. To introduce even the little bit of Gavin that it does is to recognize that the book (and hence the film) is a construct devised to this deliberate end: that even a stripped-down, disciplined filmic realization in the movie is incomplete without this overt statement. The story has been a container to sell a product, and the pitch completes it.

Perhaps constant reader should be grateful for such a powerful example of what Faulkner was so often thought to be and so seldom was: one sermon to prove that the other novels are not, one deliberate product to set the others in perspective. How ironic, though, that Faulkner should mount all this on a lynching story, that hoary cliché he generally avoided, save to redeem it once in "Dry September" and transfigure it in *Light in August*.

Requiem for a Nun is a different sort of problem. I have already spoken (in the discussion of "That Evening Sun") of Faulkner's failures as dramatist. Much of what goes wrong here can be traced to that. And there is Gavin Stevens again, more abstract here than in *Intruder*, but still droning on and on. But the real problem lies beyond these.

The book falls into two halves, much as *The Wild Palms* does (in spite of Faulkner's protests that the Old Man and the story of Charlotte Rittenmeyer were created together). Sometimes the almanac supports the drama in odd, abstract, poetic ways—as in the history of the courthouse and the jail—but more often the two go their separate ways. But for each there is a rather distressing uncertainty: we are tempted to ask, as we do of bad expository monologue, "Why is he telling us all this?" I think he's telling either half for a bad reason, but in each case a different one.

The almanac is the answer to Malcolm Cowley's dreams. As in the appendix to *The Sound and the Fury*, the text synopsizes other fiction already written and in a congruent style and tone, summarizes what might become more fiction yet to be written. It makes very pleasant reading. The doubt about it is, I suppose, partly a regret—that Faulkner never got around to spinning all this out, never managed to embody it fully. There is also some nagging doubt similar to that of the artist who takes too many commissions: is he painting what he wants to or what he has been told he should? Faulkner's time was his own, and he was free to decide for himself. Perhaps he was filling the time between things, or working on the Trilogy at the same time. Probably it was all very useful. Do we then need to be given it to read?

But this is just testiness. As I said, it's good to read and that's that. The drama is more disturbing. It is less sequel than explication; it doesn't so much continue *Sanctuary* as it attempts to alter it. And this involves a lapse of taste and a failure of judgment. It implies that *Sanctuary* needed this kind of improvement, when it is just those questions and ellipses and silences that we most value *Sanctuary* for, and it asserts that such improvement is possible: that mystery or myth or nightmare can be improved by an explanation. Would we be grateful if the person from Porlock had never knocked at the door, or closer still, if Coleridge had suddenly remembered later what it was that led up to or away from that fragment? *Sanctuary* is not "Kubla Khan," but its power is neither rational nor capable of explication. *Requiem* does worse damage to *Sanctuary* than Caddy's adventures with the Nazis in the appendix does to *The Sound and the Fury:* there, at least, Caddy is kept at arm's length. Temple is brought downstage and, as with Lucas Beauchamp, her second appearance does not convince us that we are watching the same person.

I think some of my complaint is connected with that foreword to *The Mansion,* some late but cherished misconception by Faulkner that what he was doing was creating discursive truth or wisdom. Of course there was more to be said on the subject of Temple Drake, but this kind of thing will never say it. She is made less by the addition and by the explanation. I think that the book's failure cannot all be put down to the stilted dialogue of Faulkner's failed drama, or even to Gavin's boring qualities, but must, some of it, be credited to Faulkner's change of heart. *Knight's Gambit, Intruder in the Dust,* and *A Fable* are *Requiem*'s nearest chronological neighbors, and all tend to corroborate at least a momentary change in Faulkner's aims for fiction.

A Fable is for me the most difficult of Faulkner's failures to write about: hopes were so high, praise was so great, and it is so bad. I shall not indulge in biographical guesswork: it takes no guesswork to assert that *A Fable* must represent at least as much outside influence upon Faulkner as do the appendix to *The Sound and the Fury* or the *Almanach da Jefferson* of *Requiem.* "Why don't you write something really important, Bill?" rings in the ears, whether it was ever really said or not.

Some of the difficulties arise from the borrowed devices, as in *Intruder in the Dust.* The parent novels are, again, *Light in August* (cf. *Fable,* pp. 24–27, 38, 40, 47, 49, or chap. 3, 4, 6, 7 passim, and end of 8) in the "thinking . . . thinking" patterns. In this novel it is not so difficult for him to keep the words of these thoughts characteristic of their thinkers, but they still give the effect of device appliquéd to a text rather than natural development or organic growth of device carefully nurtured for the purposes of this book. There is also a complexity of description and exposition, similar to the metaphorical and textual complexity of *Absalom, Absalom!* (cf. pp. 250 ff.), but which here appears not only unearned, but unassimilated. The difficulty of the text is random, not calculated to impede in a developing sequence. This argues at least for a neglect of narrative means, if not for simple obscurantism or plain bad writing.

But the most interesting borrowing—because it indicates an even greater narrative dilemma—is the cinematic treatment of crowds with which the novel opens and which recurs now and again throughout:

> Only it was the people advancing on the cavalry. The mass made no sound. It was almost orderly, merely irresistible in the concord of its frail components like a wave in its drops. For an instant the cavalry—there was an officer present, though a sergeant-major seemed to be in charge—did nothing. Then the sergeant-major shouted. It was not a command, because the troop did not stir. It sounded like nothing whatever, in fact: unintelligible; a thin forlorn cry hanging for a fading instant in the air like one of the faint, sourceless, musical cries of the high invisible larks now filling the sky above the city. His next shout though was a command. But it was already too late; the crowd had already underswept the military, irresistible in that passive and invincible humility, carrying its fragile bones and flesh into the iron orbit of the hooves and sabres with an almost inattentive, a humbly and passively contemptuous disregard, like martyrs entering an arena of lions. [*Fable,* p. 5]

In *The Unvanquished* the sea of slaves is presented in a narrative shift, from close-up to wide-angle. It has a distinctly remarkable impact, a force similar to the force of the slaves. *A Fable* adopts distant focus as its norm, shifting from it into the closer examination, the dialogue, the "thinking . . . thinking" patterns. The novel never really manages to alter this distance of narrative once it is established as the norm. Only part of it is a function of the narrative presence and his attitude toward the characters (as in part of "Red Leaves," similar to Joseph Conrad at his most godly)—much of it is attributable to the grand style, the sweep of the announced time-scheme, clearly meant to carry heavy significance. The result, I think, is a failure of empathy.

> It crossed in its turn the *Place de Ville,* where the three generals still stood like a posed camera group on the steps of the *Hôtel.* Perhaps this time it was the simple juxtaposition of the three flags which were just beginning to stir in the reversed day wind, since certainly none of the other three who were not Frenchmen, and possibly none of the whole twelve, seemed to remark the significance of the three dissimilar banners, nor even to see the three starred and braided old men standing beneath them. It was only the thirteenth man who seemed to notice, see, remark; only the gaze of the corporal in passing as he and the old supreme general, whom no man in any of the other lorries could say had ever looked definitely at any one of them, stared full at each other across the moment which could not last because of the vehicle's speed—the peasant's face above the corporal's chevrons and the shackled wrists in the speeding lorry, and the gray inscrutable face above the stars of supreme rank and the bright ribbons of honor and glory on the *Hôtel* steps, looking at each other across the fleeing instant. [*Fable,* p. 17]

We are never given a narratively determined reason to be looking at what we are looking at. We look at it because we are told to, and the narrative presence seems to be directing our attention there for very good reasons known to himself even though none of them are vouchsafed to us. I think this is a legitimate reader's complaint. As exemplified by the passage quoted above, the surface of the texture lacks both the plenitude and the attractiveness of the Trilogy (and this passage is one of the better passages in terms of appeal to the reader); it may be strongly end-determined, but we are given no *narrative* or internal clue as to where that end may lie. It is neither old narrative nor new, and while it is going on, the reader can get the strong impression that there is nothing determining the text's selectivity beyond either a desire for fine writing or perhaps a simple desire for picture-making. The end-determination ultimately is to be found in the allegory—and again this seems to me to be grounds for a legitimate complaint by the reader.

Perhaps the uniformity of the text, the lack of empathy, the distant focus would eventually have its effect on us and we would be able to read the book as a piece of legend, a tale in the allegorical manner, were it not for the crippled racehorse. At page 151 the style alters sharply and the narrative impetus picks up, moving toward a given end with a clear narrative reason, with the accustomed movement of familiarization to engage our empathy, with some of the swiftness of direct action narrative. Some of the tag lines are transferable to the book's normal manner: these make the racehorse *seem* to fit, but it is clearly different. And the trouble with this is not that the racehorse story is irrelevant to the burden of the text, or that it is so apparent that it was written separately and stitched into place, but that the rest of the book is not enough like it. End-determined narrative impetus which is moving toward some resolution in action can be as comfortable for the reader as the well-made, end-determined plot. We feel a distinct lift. Except for this bit of excitement, empathy, swiftness, I find no reason to read *A Fable*. But on the other hand, without this story, the novel would perhaps be less apparently flawed and failed.

The tendency of Faulkner's career to strong contrasts—between apprentice and "main range" and chronicle, between early concentration on consciousness and later interest in society—is repeated in this sort of uncomfortable analysis of "flaws" and "failures": even as he demonstrates great gifts, it is held, so is he subject to perversely bad habits. The argumentative model is to blame, I think. Instead of considering consciousness and society together, or taking the clearly layered characteristics of a career usually depicted as linear, strength and weakness have been carefully isolated from each other. What this obscures is that something which seems to be a weakness or liability at one time can turn into a strength at another point in his career because of changed circumstances, a change in design, Faulkner's development in the refinement of the narrative art or his laziness in applying what he knows so very well. Weaknesses, far from being nervous tics or bad habits, are, I think, self-recognized tendencies or habits Faulkner worked with in an attempt to turn them to his advantage.

Of what are usually termed his weaknesses, probably his susceptibility to overblown rhetoric and purple passage comes most immediately to mind. Narrative strategy not only can cover the traces of this as weakness, but can sometimes turn the weakness to strength by providing the passage with a context which justifies the verbal baroque (or can seem to justify it) or at the very least can distract the reader's attention from the passages by making verbal pyrotechnics a function of a larger pyrotechnical design. Like the plots of some of Faulkner's wagers, deals and I.O.U.'s (the poker game of "Was," the mule transaction of "Mule in the Yard"), narrative strategy can create a deliberate mare's nest of prose as readily as it can of plot.

His weakness in the coherent argument of literary, philosophical, or moral concepts, the lack of consistency in theme, lies beneath the surface of many of Faulkner's strategic decisions. The more frequent choice, taken in most of his books, prefers the embodiment of principles to the bald expression of opinion or overt statement. I think Faulkner's reluctance in the interviews to stipulate the "message" of a given work is proof that he knew direct statement was a weakness and clear evidence that he tried to avoid it or to cover the traces. Statements on symbolism and symbol-hunting in the Virginia sessions and the demonstration of his susceptibility to easy bromides or pushy personal opinion when carrying the black passport at Nagano are others; he could not have created a Gavin Stevens or a Mr. Compson (to take the semicomic and semitragic extremes of this impetus) had he not been both prone to the weakness and at the same time aware that it was a weakness.

Narrative strategy makes possible the indirect embodiment: by suspension and personification he can take a position, let the structure, imagery, shape make statements that he knows he should not voice directly. The enclosure of a carefully articulated design and shape in "Dry September" (to take an overtly shaped, heavily structured short story) or the deliberate sucker-bait of the carefully designed nostalgic opening and *non*-closing (or anti-ending) of "That Evening Sun" (to take a more subtle story as example) bring the reader to construct Faulkner's statement for him—to do the work himself. If consecutive thought or coherent argument is to be had in these stories, it is the reader who produces it. The strength he found in his weakness for direct statement was suspension: the net, the appropriate "urn or shape," the meaning which hovers around the edges or in the depths of a carefully constructed "corner." Embodiment and suspension is a most attractive and flexible alternative to the pushy meaning-mongering which Faulkner can sometimes be subject to (as in the stories of World War I, *A Fable,* or *Intruder in the Dust*).

Faulkner has been criticized for some of his "categories" of characters. It has been argued (as Walter Scott argued of Lord Byron) that most of Faulkner's characters are variants of a standard stereotype: the mould-made haunted young man, the bustling granny, the strange, doomed woman persist through many different names. He can, in off-days, create such character clichés—racial, sexual, or age stereotypes; but at his best the variety he imparts by strategic calculation of voice, of rendering, or of the time-structure which surrounds the character can make any of these stereotypes take on a unique existence, make it live in his terms of "flesh-and-blood, living people," but strangely strengthened by its closeness to the stereotype. Minnie of "Dry September" is a stereotype which, in the hands of William Inge (*Picnic* et al.) and his imitators has become a mainstay of bad drama. Because of the formal distancing of the design and her open-ended actions in the story Minnie becomes herself, a one-and-only—only Minnie, only for this story. Similarly Faulkner did the job almost too well in "A Rose for Emily." Out of a Southern gothic stereotype he made a story which fits its purpose, builds archetype to become an individual's prototype—much different from the universal stereotype for the Southern gothic victim, but clearly capable of replacing the universal stereotype in the minds of readers. The Compsons, Temple and Popeye, Joe Christmas, and Flem Snopes function in something of the same way; that is to say, such archetypal development is a part of their power over our memories, even if it is not a complete or thorough explanation of their success as characters. Such characters extend theme, the poetics of meaning or of the didactic.

But Faulkner's ultimate constant characteristic is his firm roots in the oral tradition, and it is similar to the other constants: it can feed either strength or weakness. The garrulousness of some characters, the fictive power of gossip, some of the sweep of purple passage and baroque phrase are explained and justified by this, the firmest foundation of his art. His overfond patronizing of some characters and some narrative blunders can likewise be blamed on this. But the wildest complications of theme, psyche, and plot, the deepening maelstrom of consciousness are all made accessible only by virtue of the surface of oral immediacy and vocal link. This is a quality that critics have had trouble with. The plain fact is that if something in Faulkner appears to be incoherent or inexplicable (with the possible exception of some of Benjy's or Quentin's sections of *The Sound and the Fury*), the reader has only to read it aloud, and usually not more than once. The surface is sure, direct, connected. Critics have trouble with this because they are habitually more at home with complexity and apparent disconnection than with sure oral coherence, narrative skill, and apparent flow. A reader can seem to understand everything in Faulkner's fiction once it is read aloud—which says less perhaps about Faulkner's hypocrisy of accessibility or the critics' hypocrisy of "meaningfulness" than it does about the sure and confident strength of the work. No classicist claims to understand the *Iliad* and no Americanist (in his right mind) would claim to understand—to comprehend completely—*Light in August,* but any of them can hear and hear it plain.

Which, I think, brings us to *The Reivers.* If tested by comparison to the "main range" novels, Faulkner's last novel is clearly a lightweight entry. It avoids consciousness and skirts evil, it plays with old characters and restrings almost all of the old genealogies, it escapes into Faulkner's fondest hunting ground in a nostalgic trip to the halcyon past in a halcyon motorcar with a halcyon ne'er do well, a halcyon black, and a halcyon child, and it is, as he demonstrated at West Point and elsewhere, meant to be read aloud. Faulkner's love for fine words is not neglected. Yet with all of these returns, one cannot conceive of a better way to end a full career, short of, say, another *Light in August.* To trace this novel's narrative strategy in detail would not be to the point. In part one would have to repeat much that was said about *The Unvanquished* and more generally about the nature of his late return to the freer subject matter of the short stories. But a more important reason to leave the novel uncharted and unanalyzed is that much of its achievement rests on a successful escape from just the devices, the patterns, the more overt necessities of narrative precalculation which can be successfully charted or analyzed. Keats's *Ode to Autumn* must needs be taught, but *Nightingale* offers more returns for the teaching. I think *The Reivers* is Faulkner's *Autumn*. Elaborate solutions of the past are now in the past. The vacillation between weakness and strength, the tension between craftsmanship and "flesh-and-blood" are resolved here.

10 Snopes

The Hamlet is a fresh start in Faulkner's fiction, but far from looking fresh, it seems like rather old stuff, the appearance of perpetual return—to old short stories, to straightforward chronicle, to simple people. The proof of the "fresh start" is not to be found so much in subject matter as in the new mastery of subjects already covered in the short stories and in a new organization of narrative. *The Hamlet* moves beyond "Mule in the Yard" even as *The Sound and the Fury* moves beyond "That Evening Sun." That the subject matter and tone of this fiction can be traced to the short stories of the late twenties and early thirties is perhaps the strongest testimony that this new beginning is deliberately chosen. That in spite of its "straight" appearance the Trilogy manifests what can only be called a "new narrative" is perhaps more difficult to prove. And it would be a mistake to attempt to reduce the "newness" of this narrative to critical abstraction at the outset. Much of the new and the finesse lies in the process, the continual interaction, of one device with the next. How we are led along is the key to the process. I think the clearest way to explicate here is simply to trace the opening of *The Hamlet* in rather exhaustive detail.

The beginning seems hackneyed. The narrative presence is telling us things. This shadowy figure, generally so elusive in the major novels, steps forward almost as if he had been leaning against the proscenium of *Our Town*—more loquacious than ever, ready to tell things straight out and in their proper order, ready to look at everything at once—history, change, locality—not just to stick to one family but to skip around among various individuals. He seems to choose to tell us what he does because he wants us to see, not because it is in some obscure way relevant to a narrative design as yet unrevealed. We've seen this sort of introduction before, of course, in "Mule in the Yard" or "Spotted Horses"—but even there the principle of selection was different: what we were told was relevant to the development of the story at hand, or relevant to a body of data which Faulkner suspended at the beginning to reveal as he went along. Here the narrative presence seems to be aiming at nothing in particular and seems to hold nothing back. The apparent principle of selection is so familiar that it can hardly be dignified as a narrative device at all: he seems to be setting a scene.

It is unaccustomed overtness. It is the kind of leisureliness which even Faulkner must have felt was old-fashioned and artificial because he uses it so seldom. The narrative sections of *Requiem for a Nun,* to roughly the same purpose, come all tricked out in elision, disconnection, document- and almanac-imitation. This, by contrast, is an exercise in the uncalculated and uncalculating, an easy wandering from point to point in which the points passed determine what we are told, not some distant thematic or structural purpose.

But the opening is offhand only up to a point. We find very quickly that the casual stage-manager also serves the novelist, focusing down for a moment of intense physical rendering for the Frenchman's Place, then seeming to relax into a reverie on immigration, a litany of names, something of the Revenue laws. We are stopped short (right on target) at Will Varner: "the present owner of the Old Frenchman place, was the chief man of the country" (*Hamlet,* p. 5). The tone becomes more affectionate, familiar; we are given our first clue as to the nature of the power structure and the psychological threats which serve as its medium. Power, in a sense, is the unwritten theme of the Trilogy, and the first instance is representative of what we are to see of it: "came to him, not in the attitude of *What must I do* but *What do you think you would like for me to do if you was able to make me do it*" (p. 5). The impact of this suggested power is enhanced by our momentary sense that the narrative presence knows more than he feels free to tell us: "of a Rabelaisian turn of mind and very probably still sexually lusty" (p. 5). Varner's horse and his chair are casually brought to our attention, but they will return to the narrative later, like weapons in an epic, touchstones of this suggested power, converted by Flem into landmarks in his conquest. The name of Ratliff is dropped just as casually (p. 6), but at once we are given a sense of his importance in similar terms of power: "It was only to an itinerant sewing-machine agent named Ratliff . . . that he ever gave a reason." Perhaps, he's not telling us everything we need to know about Ratliff, either.

We then slide effortlessly into Jody. Again the overt "was" rings sharply because we are so little used to it in Faulkner: it is out of a once-upon-a-time narrative. The imperfect tense in *Light in August* moved us to a different end. There it enforced a feeling of fatal coincidence ("In the town on that day lived a young man named Percy Grimm," *Light*, p. 425); here it seems more a measure of how conscious a Teller the narrative presence is. He gives only a physical description of Jody, without any mention of Will's kind of power. Jody's power is at best illusory and occasional, but neither Faulkner nor the narrative presence needs to tell us that now—it might spoil what follows.

By page 7 Faulkner is ready to get us into the present, to let the action of the book take over from the exposition, and the suddenness of the transfer (bridged by "one afternoon he was in the store") is covered by a description of Jody's actions as Ab Snopes approaches. He is looping bights of new cotton rope onto a row of nails in the wall of the store. In this, in the mock-epic description of the making of Will Varner's barrel chair, throughout the book, there is a constant sense of what people do with their hands, with their time, how they fill their days. Not only does this expand the simple action of the book into a fully articulated world, but it becomes the framework of Ratliff's anecdotes, the arena and medium of Flem's mysterious rise, the central factor in the frenetic action which accompanies comic structure. It is also an anchor for the book's mythical yearnings. Cash's carpentry is thematic and Cora Tull's cakes extend her character, Burch's illegal liquor is more or less just filler. Some of the habitual occupations and movements here move to such ends. But generally they go farther, become an independent leitmotif. There is so much doing, work, know-how, and it is treated with such loving detail, that it needs no external excuse in theme, character, or plot. Everyday pursuits are another of the book's central subjects.

The Hamlet continually surprises us with this kind of pleasant discovery. We find ourselves moving through a bit of narrative, a detail, or a digression in the same casual way in which it is offered; but we discover gradually that what seems to be simple, conventional storytelling has a subtle covert purpose. Faulkner's achievement of narrative richness here is doubly successful. The covert and suspended is not in the foreground (as in *Light in August*) but concealed beyond an overt and direct surface. In other words, we have the sense of a remote significance beyond the surface even as we are enjoying the comfort of an open-handed, fully articulated surface narrative. This is a step beyond *Absalom*'s interrupted surface, the picture-puzzle qualities of omission suspense and sequential elision. For instance, Jody's scene with Varner ends and he is left standing on the gallery of the store. In what appears to be simple rendering we see the group on the gallery (as direct as an old cover of *The Saturday Evening Post*) and hear one of them speak. But this group of observers, this audience, begins to displace the heavy-handed narrative presence, begins to resolve our relationship as readers of the action in a more integral way, and begins to become the locus of moral judgment. The group has been set in place and set in motion as casually as Ratliff was earlier. A second voice emerges from the group and it takes on life; it knows more than Jody does, and in this situation, knowledge is a kind of currency, a very real power. The voice turns out to be Tull because it can't be Ratliff yet. Ratliff knows too much and would have to give Jody more information than he should have at this point, maybe even enough for him to be able to avoid what is coming. Jody's presumption, mostly bluster, leads him to the false conclusion that he has the situation under control, only to discover that he hasn't even found out what the situation is. But the group, even without Ratliff, suggests its function perfectly and economically: it is guardian of a body of knowledge and instrument of the community's attitude of controlled, understated amazement at the chicanery on the one hand, and the dupedom on the other, of the men who are performing this drama for it.

Faulkner used this device and this tone for the sawmill group of *Light in August* to establish in us a momentary kinship and community of reaction to the outsiders, but he has never used it before as the basic structure for an entire novel. Ratliff's and Tull's understatement (" 'Sho now. So that's him,' " p. 9) produces a comic superiority in us—superiority to Jody in this case; later, superiority shared with them in the ability to read Flem's understatement, and indirect clues, such an important part of his threat of alien and unknown motivations. The group develops our desire to outsmart others, to be on a par with the brightest and most informed of the natives, to work as a poker player among poker players. Understatement is the mode and superiority is the aim.

Jody's discussion of the tenant with his father has the clearly practical purpose of setting up for us a sense that he wants to rival his father for caginess—the chip is eager to outdo its block. But again the conversation is not offered in isolation, but enclosed in an environment—supper with the Varners. The casual rendering gives us more of a sense of Mrs. Varner than we get anywhere else and, just sitting at the table, Eula. She is introduced with a set of metaphors which seem excessive on first reading or until we get to know Eula, but which in retrospect suffice even for Eula ("apparently not even having to make any effort not to listen," p. 10).

The sense of full rendering Faulkner has established by this point is a very delicate structure. He has very nearly put his narrative presence out of business: for him to step in at this point with a "meanwhile" or a "two months later" would be intrusive. One of the burdens of such apparent ease with detail is that its development is irreversible: once established, the narrative cannot slide back into artifice or shortcut. Neither Faulkner nor the narrative presence can now afford to lower a curtain to denote the passage of time. So the narrative stays firmly fixed on Jody, and time passes as we accompany him, not only to give the Snopeses a chance to move in but to give us the chance to doubt Jody's bluster and determination. Then as Jody, contract in pocket, encounters Ratliff on the road, he is even more liable (in his strengthened determination) to the new doubts that Ratliff introduces.

Omission suspense here is in the mind of the immediate protagonist. Everyone who turns up seems to know more than he does. The same people may know more than we do, too, but we forget how ignorant we are because it is continually made so easy for us to feel superior to the protagonist. We join anyone who has new information and forget our own ignorance in the revelation of the protagonist's even more dramatic ignorance. Ratliff in *The Hamlet* is a conscious creator of comedy, not just in the timing and delivery of his stories, but in the manipulation of anyone liable to be affected by his information. His understatement ("I dont know as I would go on record as saying he set ere a one of them afire. I would put it that they both taken fire while he was more or less associated with them. You might say that fire seems to follow him around, like dogs follows some folks," p. 13) and his spinning out of facts into his casual running account are calculated as surely to the end of torturing Jody as they are to the end of good storytelling. And Jody is the perfect victim. His ignorance is comic, because it cannot help him learn what to do next time or even let him see what he is—it only drives him inexorably to see how foolish he has just been.

The narrative presence steps in for a moment to give us Ratliff's background as a sewing-machine salesman and demonstrates that he shares Ratliff's tone and attitude. He has supreme confidence in the rightness of what he is doing and the order in which he is doing it. He controls us as surely as Ratliff controls and plays the changes on Jody. He has the ease (but not the uneconomical means) of the eighteenth- or nineteenth-century novelist's chatty persona, and all the qualities he accords Ratliff are equally appropriate to him: "pleasant, affable, courteous, anecdotal and impenetrable," with "a pleasant, lazy, equable voice which you did not discern at once to be even more shrewd than humorous" (p. 13). This simultaneous description of himself and Ratliff is the signal of his abdication and the orderly transfer of his functions to Ratliff, to go on with the authority he had at the outset but to carry it more casually and economically.

Ratliff's measured description of Snopes does not exhaust the comic possibilities. When Jody meets Ab we discover that the old man too can twist the knife, every bit as skillfully as Ratliff, whether consciously and ironically or accidentally and innocently we never know: " 'I can get along with anybody . . . I been getting along with fifteen or twenty different landlords since I started farming. When I cant get along with them, I leave. That all you wanted?' " (p. 21). The conclusion of the chapter brings another turn. Jody realizes that Flem was standing just where nobody could see him from the house. He's not sure what this means ultimately, but immediately it is one more piece of the evidence piling in upon him that unmistakably tells him he has underestimated his adversary. He will need more than that bluster to escape with his skin. To us it is a signal, as casual and as ineradicable as that first metaphor for Eula, that Flem is setting up in business for himself. The true antagonist has arrived.

The opening has the characteristics of the whole. This is no massive assault, no burning of the old Burden place about which we will continue to make discoveries, no end-point toward which the whole structure will be organized, but rather an easing into things. Ratliff, Eula, and Flem have all been introduced in a quiet, almost offhand way. Ratliff has his prior information, Eula her metaphors, and Flem his unidentified threat to mark their places in our minds, busy as we are, listening to what seems to be another story. There is some suspense by omission (such as Ratliff's relationship to Will Varner's power) but the richness of the surface almost keeps us from noticing. We never have to shift into a defensive posture or feel the necessity to work at the narrative puzzle. Rather than omitting the connections necessary to make a sequence or a set out of what we've been told, the narrator omits what comes next. In no other of Faulkner's narratives is there so manifest a feeling of balance between material and method, of efficient craftsmanship blended with the natural ebullience of a storyteller who enjoys equally the story he is telling and the process of telling it involves.

I dwell on details of the mechanics at such length because it is so easy to dismiss all this as accidental writing—Faulkner getting old and more relaxed, sitting on the porch, spinning tales. His manifest enjoyment of what he's doing here is surely a significant part of the texture of the narrative, but its ease is deceptive. It is the mixture of this ease and relaxation with a covert complexity, a new kind of storytelling, the fresh start that I would emphasize. Characters seem to wander on and off. They do in *Light in August,* too, but there the casual introduction of characters is ultimately followed by tight connection to a stong central scheme of theme, structure, and plot. Their initial wanderings are strongly determined by an end-point known to Faulkner at the outset. The wandering seems to serve only a minimal verisimilitude of accidental encounter and then it is abandoned. Here the wandering is part and parcel of the nature of the narrative. He is not enforcing a theme of accidence by the wandering, but rather building a texture of everyday familiarity. Movement is not determined by a column of smoke drawing everyone forward toward an end but by a series of footprints or successive monuments, by a sequence, not a landmark. It is true flux. In *Light in August* there must be the appearance of flux, but it is always in control of the end-point.

Sequence here seems more determined by the characters or events than it is a product of thematic or structural design. Meaning seems to develop and is interpreted as it is developed, rather than being revealed slowly, step-by-step, from a predetermined locus of meaning toward which the structure moves. This is an exaggeration, of course. Faulkner surely did not know at the outset every meaning that *Light in August* would embody. But the structure of that novel is such that it can seem at the end that he did: the effect is of controlled significance, of managed meaning. *The Hamlet* conveys a feeling of continuing surprise—not just to us but to the author. The surface answers less to thematic or structural connection, or the appearance of it, than it does to the variety of plenitude and the power of random events and people to develop meanings as they go along, to collide accidentally. It is the turn of the kaleidoscope, not the pulling of the strings. The pieces are carefully designed to make beautiful connections, but when they make them there is little feeling of precalculation, but rather of happy accident. This is a most difficult form of suspension, especially for a Faulkner who has constructed *As I Lay Dying, Light in August,* and *Absalom, Absalom!* It is almost as if a Mondrian suddenly decided to become Jackson Pollock. That the Trilogy later declines from this high measure of suspension and this open structure to the level of authorial self-indulgence is all the more reason to stress the balanced achievement of *The Hamlet.*

By the beginning of the second chapter Ratliff is in control and will remain in control for most of the rest of the book. Exceptions are the Eula section (much concerned with the past) and Ike's pursuit of the cow (cast in its own style); both of these are interludes, rather long interludes to be sure, but departures from our central structures of identification. Basically Ratliff is our center. In a variety of methods ranging from omnipresence through intense point of view to internal monologue, he is our representative. When he leaves town time passes, when he returns there is a reconstruction of what has happened. He is our locus and our receptor.

He is the perfect figure for the center of this rather odd comedy. His control of tone is almost flawless. He won't laugh while he's telling it or anticipate his own punch line. His canniness and calculation transfer readily from the careful construction of anecdotes to the equally careful arrangement of human situations (like the sale of the machine to Mink) in order to find out something he (and we) need to know. This element in his narrative function raises some questions about his human ethics: he is malevolent in the sense that he feeds on what other people do while remaining safely divorced from such actions himself, and there is a certain amount of sadistic delight involved in his stringing along of Jody or Will or Mink as he does in order to bring them to comic peak. Faulkner perhaps felt this too (at least in this volume of the Trilogy) because he cannot let Ratliff pass through unscathed: he too must finally fall victim to the kind of *hybris* which leads a man to think he has it over a Snopes. He must buy the Frenchman's Place in a sense as expiation for what he has had to do to keep us entertained.

In the Pat Stamper story the full force of Ratliff's abilities is joined with the fully realized function of the front-porch group. That group's compulsion to watch the raree-show Flem is making of Jody Varner's operation of the store matches our compulsion to move through the fiction and Faulkner's to make the fiction: you've got to make your own fun around here. Ratliff feeds out the Stamper anecdote; the porch-group is his audience. We hear it too, but we hear it as it is enhanced in the hearing as well as the telling. The story of Pat Stamper's trades with Ab is the funniest and most unified passage in the book, but in itself it is neither short story nor chapter—it could never stand alone. It must be heard by an audience to gain its tone, ambience and effect. The story by itself might leave something to be desired in the way of verisimilitude: without the audience we might stop to ask whether one could really do that to a horse with fishhooks (or with a bicycle pump), and without the fishhooks and the bicycle pump the story wouldn't even make it as an anecdote.

The operation of the basic narrative structure of the book is almost perfect here. The best teller is telling about the best swap in the history of the county's greatest manipulator (Pat Stamper is to Flem Snopes as the anecdote is to the book). He is telling it to the book's natural audience with their comments to interrupt him and to egg him on (fiction is to life as the men on the porch are to us). The book's close attention to the everyday actions of work or livelihood—how to drive a mule, how to drive a bargain, how to sell a sewing-machine—is here fully integrated with Ratliff's story. The narrative of doing here calls upon a kinship in abilities between the Teller and the listeners and an assumed kinship in abilities between the Teller and us. In order to understand what's funny we have to know (or act as if we know) something about driving and trading mules. We become a part of the community of interest, training, and familiarity because without that kinship the story would not be as funny, and we want more than anything for this to be the greatest story of being bested in a deal we've ever heard, because a Snopes is on the losing side. "It won't sound very funny, you had to be there to see it," is the excuse of a storyteller who cannot render the audience for a given series of actions. "I don't get it," is the despair of a man without the expertise (or a man unwilling to fake some) to see the point of what's funny. Here everything builds on everything else and the narrative method of the book, only suggested before, is operating at full power.

The tale ends with Miz Snopes's pleasure in her new toy, the separator, her pleasure in mastering a machine, whether she needs the milk separated or not, and again we are cast into a situation which calls upon our kinship with the group within the book. The everyday is commonplace until it is shared and built upon and developed in a community of telling and hearing, analysis and response. The narrative technique is objective third-person, even though we tend to convert our close association with the porch-group into direct experience. This is the basic technique throughout *The Hamlet:* "the gallery, where already a dozen men, Ratliff among them, lounged" (p. 52). Some rather distant reminders of the group technique of "Emily" appear here and there: "someone noticed," "those who saw him," "it was told of him later" (p. 58). But the group is kept at arm's length, remains in a sense *them.* I think this offers Faulkner a kind of freedom. *The Sound and the Fury* and "A Rose for Emily" take a more complete or perfect identification of ourselves as readers with the community of the town and convert it into guilt. Guilt or our knowledge of ourselves is not what Faulkner wants here: Ike Snopes and his cow do not call forth the same response as Emily and Homer. We can voluntarily join the gallery-group and share with it up to a point. Faulkner wants a social consciousness and a sense of our kinship with the town as audience, not our guilt and the personal self-knowledge which might result from a more completely developed association. We have to be ready in a moment to drop one allegiance and take up another. "Then in September something happened. It began rather, though at first they did not recognise it for what it was" (p. 59). "The cold surmise which now began to dawn upon them was that—" (p. 60). "Now they just watched, missing nothing" (p. 61). All eyes are focused on the spectacle. This is no hermetic tale of the past and its heritage reaped by a few oversensitive members of a single family. Sutpen was best as raree-show for those at a distance from him, next best for those who lived alongside him, least for those who actually knew him. And he was an aristocrat by design if not by birth. The "fresh start" has this influence upon subject matter. The past and the aristocrats are over and done for. It is in a sense just Flem's *lack* of heritage that makes him so attractive to the gallery-group and to Ratliff. Snopeses don't share the guilt of the land because they haven't owned any. They burn bridges as well as barns behind them. In this sense the Snopeses are pastless, as are the Bookwrights, the Tulls, the Armstids, and Ratliff. Eula and Flem give this new community its identity, just as the former aristocratic center of the community—the Sartorises, the Compsons, and McCaslins are departing (although they are brought in late in the Trilogy for a series of last gasps). Quentin can look at a Sutpen but Bookwright and Ratliff need a Snopes. The New South demands a new kind of hero.

But the new hero—essentially an alteration of subject matter—does not so much determine the narrative as the narrative is designed to be appropriate to it. Snopesism is the greatest comic invention of the book, a positively original contribution to American literature. Snopesism found a unique and highly complex narrative strategy as its voice. It is a compound of the various narrative tactics and devices traced in the novel's opening, but takes in several other functions not yet discussed. We begin to encounter how-to-do-it narratives similar to the "work" passages. We follow Ratliff on one of his mysterious hegiras (p. 56) and learn not only how diversified his dealings are but also one reason why he is so laconic about what he has been doing while he has been out of town: it is too complicated to understand and considerably too detailed to be useful as anecdote. We get a parallel but even more obscure description of the process by which Flem and his factors can make a bad blacksmith pay off (p. 67). Both of these depend on a sequence of interlocking steps as complex as the interlocking wagers in the poker game of "Was," and for some of the same reasons. Deals are a form of entertainment, both in performing them, working them out, and telling about them afterwards. A Ratliff can profit twice from a shrewd deal—once in the money and once in the telling—and timing is every bit as essential in spending the telling as it is in spending the money. Information and money are both coins of the realm in this world and complicated information is the best currency. The smallness of the profit in sewing-machines does not deter Ratliff from his rounds, because the nature of the merchandise gives him entrees he might not otherwise have and, besides, the act of dealing and the gossip that accrues while dealing are more central to his real business than money is, anyway. Complicating the deals promotes both enterprises. At the end of the blacksmith story we get a clear indication from Jody that the "deal" is at the heart of life in the hamlet, as it is the basic organizational unit of the book: " 'Just what is it going to cost me to protect one goddamn barn full of hay' " (p. 68). Small deals are the fabric of the everyday chronicle and the source of community power (as in Will Varner). Large interlocking deals are the locus of gossip and eventually (in Flem Snopes) the stuff of the "progress" of the legend.

This "progress" or "rise and fall," one of the oldest of narrative old saws, is superimposed upon the community chronicle. Flem has been a distant object for the community. Ratliff's claim to authority as Snopes-watcher is his two years of Ab-watching when he lived on the same place (pp. 26–27). Then Flem was just worth a mention alongside Sarty, now vanished, perhaps "mislaid in one of them movings." To a certain extent Flem's distance in the first two chapters persists throughout the Trilogy. His speech takes on an exceptional, rather Sybilline quality, probably as a product of our eagerness to understand, fostered by our association with the porch group.

The basic structure which eventually brings him out of the shadows is an involved series of manipulations, the backbone of Snopesism, the origin of which might be rendered as a two-man poker game with Jody. The necessity of covering his bets (and his traces) brings a lot of other people into the game, including Ratliff. Ratliff's game (at the outset no more than a side bet to the main event) is to engage even more secondary characters in deals which might reveal the secrets of Flem's game, perhaps eventually even maneuver Flem himself into a revealing wager—test his aims, try his skill, tip his hand, or at the very least provide evidence which might support Ratliff's shifting theories about him. In order to do this Ratliff has to get around the complicated results of Flem's first game with Jody, and that game is more complex even than Ratliff bargained on. Threatening the barn, of course, is just the first round, not the name of the game. As in a poker game, Flem's surface strategy makes no sense until the submerged aim—the nature of the strength or the nature of the bluff—is revealed, and Flem plays his game very close to the chest.

Ratliff is the first to discover that it is a game, with its own rules. The gallery-group simply assumes that Flem is at the head of an army, bent on the siege and occupation of Jefferson. Ratliff discovers that Flem is far beyond this, that Snopeses are less an army than they are Flem's bag of tools; he will use individual Snopeses as long as he can control them, as long as they don't get in his way or embarrass him, as long as they don't interfere with the profits of the main action (whatever that may be). The gallery-group's assumption is that Flem wins because he is subject to no rules, that he can play fast and loose and leave the community behind, surrounded by their shattered laws and codes. As the novel and the Trilogy proceed, it becomes clear that this apparent lawlessness is instead a constitution of practical power and pragmatic aptitude, every bit as hierarchical as Miss Reba's whorehouse or Popeye's enclave at Frenchman's Bend. Snopeses are selected for tasks which fit their abilities (or disabilities) and their desires. When their usefulness ends they disappear or are removed. And the beauty of it is that in Snopesism success looks the same as failure to the gallery-group. It is seldom clear whether a minor Snopes has been removed from the scene because he has broken the rules or because he has accomplished his assigned task and has been moved on.

It becomes clear [1] to Ratliff that Snopes-watching is not just a matter of finding out what Flem hopes to gain and how he's going to get it, but of discovering how far he's willing to go to get it. Sometimes Flem will emerge from the bushes for a moment to adjust things after a particularly noticeable individual gaffe, but even then (as with Montgomery Ward's jail sentence) it is never perfectly clear whether this was individual Snopes enterprise exceeding the mark or just Flem's proper use of a particular tool which he knew and anticipated would malfunction in just the right way.

1. Not really at a particular point in the Trilogy because Ratliff's process of discovery is continual, involves shifts and continual guesses and adjustments, but somewhere in *The Town* around the time of Atelier Monty.

It is an almost perfect framework for comedy. The initial wager (and subsequent ones such as Armstid's treasure-hunt) permits us comic superiority; the covering actions of minor complication permit the fast enter-and-exit routines of outrageous characters with stock-comic names, engaged in the kind of frenetic and apparently motiveless motion so essential to comedy. Ratliff's campaign of espionage translates much of this into the classic American language of understatement and at the same time provides the first of the Trilogy's endless cycles—the outsmarters outsmarting the outsmarter and the victim outsmarter outsmarting in return.

"What's Wrong with this Picture?" is perhaps the best general image for the book. The group on the gallery is frame, audience, victim, and control for these events. Their interaction and the pattern of their everyday work, their dealings, what they eat and how they eat it, where they sit and what they watch, their automatic actions and reactions, form (like the mules reversed in the traces) the picture for which Flem continually provides the What's Wrong. The picture has directness, simplicity, the commonplace elements of the child's puzzle with the lightbulb screwed in upside down, the horse hidden in the tree. We watch as one thing after another wrong or out of place appears in it: a bad blacksmith who turns a profit, a horse in a parlor, a man in love with a cow providing a street-show for an otherwise moral citizenry. In the picture birds sing and trees bloom, spring and winter come and go. Flem is the cause of the What's Wrong and himself the chief example: he's wrong in the sense of the town's expectations—a tenant farmer/bank president. But the puzzle after a while becomes not just to find the What's Wrong (which is usually more than readily apparent) but to trace the strings from the What's Wrong back to Flem and to figure out why he's pulling them, what's in it for him when it goes wrong. Ratliff's other master-image, the quarry in the bushes (by the time the bushes shake Flem has already gone on), is parallel to this. And it comes closer to the secret of the book's perpetual motion: before one What's Wrong can be solved the next one has appeared; before one shaking bush is seen shaking and traced back to Flem, the next bush has begun to shake.

The end of the first section is a copybook example of the way Faulkner keeps this chained sequence suspended. Ratliff, put out of circulation by his operation, has returned, and he gets together with other members of the gallery-group in the restaurant to catch up on what he's missed. In perhaps the book's most brilliant example of total integration the narrative, atmospheric rendering and character, relevant recapitulation, irrelevant cattle drive, and a lot of sloppy eating are mixed into one flowing continuum. Ratliff thinks he has maneuvered Snopes into position for a direct engagement. Then Flem burns one promissory note and is elusive about the second (thus expressing his mysterious power at the same time he is shaking the next bush). Suddenly the narrative turns to Mink and Houston and their nagging property dispute, planted earlier by Faulkner but never quite raised to the level of the surface narrative. This, by omission suspense, provides plenty of unknowns to carry us over to the next section. One of the men on the gallery delivers the curtain-line: " 'It was Flem Snopes that was setting in the flour barrel' " (p. 92). Flem has moved again.

The mastery of movement in the narrative is not just the juggler's trick of keeping a certain number of oranges or cigarboxes in the air without dropping any. Each development must seem natural, each shaking of the bush must seem possible to have predicted after it happens but not before, and each must be teased right up to the edge of solution just in time for the next bush to shake or the next What's Wrong or the next orange to distract us from this solution in the implications of the next for what has preceded. The movement is always forward; we learn to keep up with the group and with Ratliff, to manage as well as they do to handle each new development as it is tossed to us. The narrative continually looks to the future.

"Eula" shifts us out of all this developing scope and depth of Snopes and town, performer and audience, picture and What's Wrong, into an interlude with its own kind of peace. Hustling toward the next footprint or the next landmark in Flem's progress is forgotten for a moment as Faulkner develops one of them at leisure—perhaps the most mysterious and awe-inspiring of the lot, Flem's conquest of Eula.

The choice of method is familiar; biography. When in doubt Faulkner falls back on it, and here he offers no excuses but suddenly abandons the functions of Ratliff and the gallery-group he has so carefully nurtured as casually as he first introduced them. He moves to a direct depiction of character in a narrative which moves step by step with the same kind of inexorable progression which marked

Flem's early rise. But there is an important difference. Flem is an operational enigma. Each of his actions must seem to begin to reveal a bit of his motivation but end less in revelation than in puzzle. Eula is less an enigma than she is a heroic commonplace. We know *what* she is: what remains to be revealed, step by step, is that she is beyond any other in that class: more woman, more Eve, more everything than any earth-goddess we have encountered. Flem's constancy of purpose is not revealed until the end of the chronicle, after many false solutions. Eula's constancy is a given—the surprises are its manifestations. Eula satisfies fully—even to excess—every expectation of her mythic and feminine archetype as surely as Flem frustrated every expectation in enigma.

The story of Labove depends on another group of familiar old tricks. We begin (p. 102) with a story within a story, move (p. 103) to a story within that, and then (p. 108) reach one of those points at which the reader has to pause to sort out digressions. He finds he is reading a story within a story within a story within a story, and all this narrative complication and indirection seem intended to no grander purpose than to provide background for what appears to be a secondary character. This seems at first to be a distraction: why are we dealing in such detail with Labove? Is his development to be justified later in the book in some way?

What Faulkner is getting at here is the story itself and not (as in *Absalom*) the loss or gain involved in transition between Teller and Hearer or Teller and Reteller. He explores the ramifications of Labove's story as they can be traced back into their sources. Labove must embody what Eula is by reflection, her effect as we see it in him. The epic proportions of Eula's archetypal woman might demand this kind of narrative elevation or deflection: we gaze on the Medusa in a mirror; the lover fully worthy of Eula is, must be (if not a giant) a complex and subtle man.

But Labove progresses toward a dying fall, not a worthy complexity. His story is another of Faulkner's exercises in the sickness which is love—similar to Joanna Burden's "phases" in *Light in August* without her pathological decay, similar to the obsession of Byron Bunch without its fortunate end. Labove is sick with nothing but love—not age or doubt or guilt—and such love is not a blessing but, as Hightower and Byron indicate, an irrational seizure.

So large a hunk of apparently independent interlude in an otherwise unified narrative suggests that it be read thematically. Extended in this way the interlude connects to other thematic threads of the Trilogy to provide a countertheme for Flem's progress in an anatomy of love. Ratliff is at one extreme by virtue of Faulkner's continual references to his ascetic, monastic, celibate existence.[2] Gavin Stevens is almost a whole anatomy in himself, ranging from thumb-chewing over Eula through frustrated father-figure–Platonic-lover of Linda to his temporary loss of even Melisandre Backus. Hoake McCarron, Manfred and his back window (to say nothing of Tomey's Turl), the nonmarriage–marriage of Linda and Kohl provide the extramarital center. Ike and his cow stand alone in the class of accomplished romantic love, and marriage is dealt with in variety: Houston and his wife, Mink and his, the Mallisons, the Varners, the Tulls, the Armstids. We even have a moment of Miss Reba in *The Mansion* with Fonzo and Virgil Snopes trotted out again for their famous soft-shoe routine to provide something of a sidelight on love's social dimension.[3] Love ranges from absurd to tragic, from frustrating to ennobling.

Tracing it out makes the anatomy seem rather too neat, a bit too pat; but when put alongside other elements of the everyday—the working, the eating, the deals, and the progress of day and season—it becomes impossible to dismiss it as an artificial structure because it is a part of the integration of this total world. And it is more central to the spectator sport of Snopesism than any other. Here for a moment in "Eula" is an island of concentration in which it is possible to see the theme working in isolation and to perceive its centrality for the book and the Trilogy. The "Afternoon of a Cow" is similarly set apart, not because it is irrelevant to the central narrative, but to command for a moment an independent attention.

"The Long Summer" picks up teasers from the end of "Flem," and the book proceeds on its basic narrative almost as if we had never been away: we proceed to more deals, more loves, more work, and more nature. A case might perhaps be made that "The Long Summer" is the serious harvest of the comic premises of "Flem." At least Ike's punishment, Zack Houston's death, and the duping of Ratliff, Bookwright, and Armstid here cause us to reflect on the

2. Epithets used (for different reasons) for Ike McCaslin in *Go Down, Moses.*

3. And to give some anchor to yet another of Ratliff's images for Flem's actions, the whorehouse money pinned in the underwear.

serious consequences of comic premises. But I think tragicomedy would be wide of the mark. This is comic-with-doubts. The structure is consistently comic throughout, even in the interludes, but it follows the mechanics of a Tinguely self-destroying machine rather than that of an infernal machine. The treatment of Ike is perhaps the best case in point. When we come to the loose clapboard and move to peer in, we find that, even though we have not been suckered in and condemned with the rest of the people of the town, we do want to look through the hole. Faulkner, with Ratliff (and with our better judgment), nails back the clapboard and won't let us look. Our open-ended association with the gallery-group at this point (we wanted to look, but we can still condemn them objectively) makes us question a number of things: bestiality, the cruelty involved in the humanistic punishment of animalism. The punishment is an act of decency but it seems excessive, probably because we have shared the love. Making Ike eat the cow is more like black magic than enlightened decency, and no amount of argument over who is going to pay for the animal in that jolly front-gallery bonhomie is going to distract us from that inhuman punishment of beast-man and man-beast.

This is a function of the way in which the book continually sets up an anti-ideal for every ideal, the way in which it manages at least to look at the other side of an abstraction or to question it experimentally with other examples rather than simply pronouncing it. *The Hamlet* is getting at the difference between what humans are as individuals and what they are in groups in a way very different from *Light in August.* Every ideal is provided with an anti-ideal and every abstraction or generalization with its exception. The book questions every one of the group's clear moral stances in one or another of the alliances with individuals it has cultivated. The result, I think, is yet another fresh start: a way of dealing with humans in a new form of suspended fictional judgment. *As I Lay Dying* and *Light in August* each questioned its own moral standards but depended upon an external moral sanction. *The Hamlet* embodies both "offense" and "punishment" without any such appeal to the external. It is an independent cosmos in a way that they are not. But *The Hamlet* is the high point. The second and third volumes of the Trilogy fall back on the external sanction.

The definition of fictional suspension in general is difficult to make without appearing to be either anti-intellectual or antiformal. In a sense, to single out this particular quality for praise is to extol Faulkner for something he perhaps was not even trying to do or for something his book did without his knowing it. In these moments, the particular données of narrative—metaphor, theme, and moral aim—dissolve in a narrative which goes beyond the need for any of these tools, goes beyond any striving for immediate ends. One such moment is the rather long scene at the corral during the auction of the wild spotted horses from Texas. The immediate aim is the depiction of a kind of chaos, an animal version of the Snopes tribe's disregard for mores and traditions. In terms of plot it is yet another What's Wrong, another shaking bush, another opportunity to try to see what Flem can gain, how he'll get it and how far he'll go. It supports the character development of the book by serving as a participatory center in which the village can, one citizen at a time, betray its expertise about taming wild animals by its eagerness to snap up a bargain. The event is also the perfect vehicle for the frantic comings and goings, chases and points of calm which exemplify comic inertia. But while it is going on the passage seems to strive for none of this. And it adds to all these functions the strong basic continuo of people doing, eating, desiring, dealing—the deep pulse of the everyday—in such a way that the immediate aims and functions lose their individual identity in the total impact of the passage.

Flem is clearly identified with the horses and Buck Hipps at the outset. He rides in with him, crosses the porch and says one word. This is enough to excite speculation in the gallery-group about his possible profits from the venture and for them to make the obvious connection, which Buck Hipps can studiously ignore. The horses thus become not only a circus, a break in the everyday, but a spectacle of the Snopes enterprise, something subject to continuing analysis, study, and endless adjustment. It's the kind of setup on which Flem thrives. A little suspicion about his part in it only fulminates speculation, providing a better smokescreen for his real intentions and motivations than any amount of secrecy would.

The scene develops cinematically, a series of metaphors which never really take on individual shape: the horses are like the circling tigers in an illustration for *Little Black Sambo,* a rendition of streaks and colors with ears. The gallery-group is the focus and Ratliff is its star. It not only provides speculation on Flem's connection with all this but manages to anticipate for us, to raise our expectations as they might not otherwise be raised because of our ignorance of horse-maelstroms: " 'How you reckon he ever got them tied together?' Freeman said. 'I'd a heap rather watch how he aims to turn them loose,' Quick said" (p. 278). This expectation is then gratified as Hipps manages (again in a rendition of blurs) to grab one of the horses by the nostrils, to deliver his line of patter (" 'Pretty lively now . . . but it'll work out of them in a couple of days,' " p. 279), to warn the group that he is about to let them go and to get the back of his vest severed from top to bottom. The individual action of the horse increases our respect for the herd and anticipates the comic possibilities of the sale with its promise of individual man-to-horse combats spreading all over town.

Wallstreet Snopes comes into the group to find his father (whom Ratliff has been pumping for information about Flem's possible profits, which it turns out Eck simply does not have) and we are called in for supper. Ratliff returns and pronounces some overconfident general truths, imprudent words that escape him because he's been too happy eating and feels too good after supper. They are (even as Jody's were in the beginning) a statement of *hybris:* " 'A fellow can dodge a Snopes if he just starts lively enough' " (p. 281).

Nature, as it has throughout the book, makes a series of carefully timed appearances. The pear tree is rendered in terms complementary to the metaphors for the horses: "In full and frosty bloom, the twigs and branches springing not outward from the limbs but standing motionless and perpendicular above the horizontal boughs like the separate and upstreaming hair of a drowned woman sleeping upon the uttermost floor of the windless and tideless sea" (p. 281). A mockingbird, as night falls, sings from the same tree, which brings it into the gallery-group's discussion.

> "First one I've noticed this year," Freeman said.
>
> "You can hear them along Whiteleaf every night," the first man said. "I heard one in February. In that snow. Singing in a gum."
>
> "Gum is the first tree to put out," the third said. "That was why. It made it feel like singing, fixing to put out that way. That was why it taken a gum."
>
> "Gum first to put out?" Quick said. "What about willow?"

> "Willow aint a tree," Freeman said. "It's a weed."
>
> "Well, I dont know what it is," the fourth said. "But it aint no weed. Because you can grub up a weed and you are done with it. I been grubbing up a clump of willows outen my spring pasture for fifteen years. They are the same size every year. Only difference is, it's just two or three more trees every time." [*Hamlet,* p. 282]

Isolated from the scene this moment of digression would be no more than a genre piece, a bit of local color, and it probably represents (as surely as one could guess), a bit of dialogue overheard in Oxford's Square. Taking another bent, a critic might identify it as obscure metaphor and praise Faulkner for his subtlety in turning all things to the shape of Snopeses. It is all of these but not clearly any, any more than it is only testimony to the general commonsense of the gallery-group, shortly to be contrasted to their madness in crowds at the auction. Nor is it exclusively applied to the allegorical function of the horses in representing the forces of spring seen all about us (pp. 281–83, 304, 314, 316). It is all, but not trying very hard to be any, and a case cannot be made that it is more one than another. Everything is working, but none of it looks as if it is trying to work.

The integration of nature, gallery-group, work, skill, the turnings of the day that surround the maelstrom of horses, Hipps the stranger, the everyday with the exotic, is practically perfect. Faulkner can even—because he is so sure of what he is doing—get away with putting a peachblossom in the mouth of one of the townsmen and then identifying a speech coming from "the man with the peach spray" (p. 316). Something exciting—as in the Stamper story—is rendered by its integration and reflection in the everyday of the village: Armstid bidding against his wife's wishes, the child and the ginger-snaps, Mrs. Littlejohn and her laundry. There are two interludes in the midst of this. Ike walks through the street (p. 317) and all other motion seems to stop, even as Eck's boy, in mid-bite, stops, stares, watches him out of sight, and bites again. We are at once carried back to the cow and the cruelty of Ike's punishment, but there is too much going on for us to pause for long. Then there is a sudden manifestation of the narrative presence to rush Jody and Ratliff to the ends of their lives and as suddenly to disappear:

> Save for the clerk in the background, they were the only two standing, and now, in juxtaposition, you could see the resemblance be-

tween them—a resemblance intangible, indefinite, not in figure, speech, dress, intelligence; certainly not in morals. Yet it was there, but with this bridgeless difference, this hallmark of his fate upon him: he would become an old man; Ratliff, too: but an old man who at about sixty-five would be caught and married by a creature not yet seventeen probably, who would for the rest of his life continue to take revenge upon him for her whole sex; Ratliff, never. The boy was moving without haste up the road. His hand rose again from his pocket to his mouth. [*Hamlet,* p. 324]

The suddenness of the appeal to another dimension is a theatrical coup, not unlike the sudden prophecies of Thornton Wilder's Esmeralda in *The Skin of Our Teeth.* There is no excuse for it in the fiction and no excuse is offered, because it works. It works in the same way Ike's appearance does: it isn't trying and it won't be pinned down but remains slightly mysterious. Like the final image in some of Matthew Arnold's poems it stands open to a number of potential connections but demands no one in particular, insists on nothing dogmatically but suddenly strikes in the imagination a rather deep chord of distant association or moving juxtaposition.

The moment of integration (like the unification of the Bundrens in *As I Law Dying*) hovers for a moment and is gone. The horses are sold and dispersed as the threads of the book are gathered up and then scattered again. It is a moment of cohesion in the midst of frantic action and a certainty among uncertainties. The lawsuits arising from the horse auction segue into the long-awaited trial of Mink (bearing a greater burden of action to come than of action accomplished). Ratliff goes off to be duped, fulfilling the promise of his *hybris* but throwing our identification with him into some confusion. Armstid is left limping about at the treasure site like an animal and Flem faces his move to new worlds with a simple "Come up" to his horses. The other two novels of the Trilogy cannot possibly achieve what this one does in this kind of suspension because what it can suspend they will have to pin down and tie up, what it surmises they will have to conclude, and what it promises they must inevitably disappoint.

The Hamlet yearns toward epic, toward the power of compound myth. Of classical development there are only hints here—the cow, Mink's checker game and a glimpse of Eula at Varner's window (pp. 311–12). Metaphor generally grows from the individual consciousness; it stops short of taking on the autonomous existence it had in *As I Lay Dying* and *Absalom, Absalom!* Faulkner seems to be saying, "This is the stuff that myths are made of, but I won't." In the other volumes of the Trilogy, Gavin Stevens steps in to draw all the parallels, overstate the examples, and turn potential myth into mythology. Here we have only hints and hints that, again, suggest rather than strive. But the country must give way to the town, and primary freshness yield to secondary restatement.

In *The Hamlet* Faulkner is working without a dominant metaphorical or a limiting narrative structure. We are free but directed by the gallery-group toward conclusions. As they watch the Snopes performance they are attempting to make sense of disparate facts, and we as readers are trying not only to make sense of the same facts, but also to make sense of the senses they make of them. The town is creating its consciousness and we are creating our consciousness of it in a joint response. Faulkner has here made out of fairly barren material—casting himself adrift from the incests and guilts of odd families, the rich associations and dark hints of the aristocratic past—a world which engages the reader in a way that is more than thematic, imageric, characteristic, or simply novelistic. His interest extends to what is going on beyond just the efficient completion of a structural design or the neat embodiment of thematic meaning. Relevance to theme or end does not determine the shape of the fiction, but rather disjunctive sequence and disparate events establish their own relevance. There is the feeling of an easy, inexhaustible supply of men, manners, motion, love, deals, an abundance or plenitude of what's going on. The mystery that emerges is that of a world in which all the events seem relevant to the narrative but never reach a point of synthesis or imposed meaning which might explain (or be explained by) order or lack of order. Practical adjustments dominate the method rather than grand designs. The narrative does not require the reader to understand it abstractly (except insofar as it is made up of words), but it does require him to pursue it in its own terms.

In *The Town* Faulkner moves away from some of these freedoms by hardening or codifying some of the devices he had invented for *The Hamlet.* He retains the open-ended narrative flux and the movement toward the future. *The Town* is no more plotted (in Dickens's sense of plot) than *The Hamlet* was, and it is no more rooted in the past. Faulkner wants the sense of community, but for the larger arena of the town he opts for an elite group of Snopes-watchers as opposed to the gallery-group under Ratliff's casual leadership. He casts the narrative in a mixture of their first-person accounts which consequently forces him to abandon the shape and underpinnings of *The Hamlet*'s fully integrated work and motion. If Ratliff, Mallison, or Stevens sees something being done, a meal being eaten or a tree blooming, it tends to be seen to some purpose, noticed to some end; it is not just there for its own sake. It is a natural result of the first-person technique that each individual narrator must select details because they are relevant to his particular narrative, and this, of course, eliminates the grandeur of the suspended world.

But the method of *The Town* is not without its own merits. The narrative, perhaps because it is cast in a simpler technique or because it can build upon the world already established by *The Hamlet,* seems the most unified of any of the novels of the Trilogy. Its impact is immediate. I think this is in part explained by the carefully specified distinction between one teller and the next and a rather peculiar suspension of the listener who is assumed to be the hearer for all these narratives.

Chick is the first and last to speak and has the most to say.[4] He is the teller with whom we have and are intended to have the most in common. Partly this is because he is less pushy than the others and thus more able to move toward objectivity; but it is also, quite simply, because he is a child, subject to the objective freedom and subjective limitations peculiar to the child-narrator. He is able to observe transparently because he has his eyes open and is not subject to the adult bias of selection. The third-person narrative of *The Hamlet,* of course, could be freer in choice than any first-person or combination of first-person narrators could be, to blend objective with subjective, mix group identification with group-alienation. Chick is free in this way only insofar as he is more fallible than an adult: he is unformed, not yet subject to the overabstracted, participatory limitations which beset Gavin Stevens and the rather know-it-all cracker-barrel philosophy that Ratliff sometimes slides into in *The Town.*

As learner, Chick is very close to us. Like him, we are coming to

4. Faulkner also retains in him some elements of the now-abandoned gallery-group: "So when I say 'we' and 'we thought' what I mean is Jefferson and what Jefferson thought" (*Town,* p. 3). "Then we learned . . ." (p. 15).

this narrative late: he isn't born until six years after his starting-point in the narrative, and the book (as all good trilogy or tetralogy segments should) assumes that we haven't read the first volume and carefully brings us up to date. We are second-hand hearers: we hear from him; he has been told so that he may catch up. His lack of involvement in the proceedings—as messenger-boy, as Gavin-substitute for Ratliff during the war, as the little pitcher with big ears—makes his narratives the most convenient medium for traditional suspense structures and for Faulkner's favorite device of suspense by omission. The amount that he cannot know or finds out too late or is too small to understand serves the cause of timed revelation, because then Ratliff or Gavin can step in with the answer or the analysis or the conclusion, satisfying our reader's urge for fictional didactic. Mallison is the anchor of the book not only in the prevalence of his sections but also in the way in which his attractiveness can cover weak transitions.[5]

Gavin Stevens is the most deeply involved as participant. He most frequently holds the answer to a question asked in the other narrators' sections, holds a note we haven't read, or is privy to a scene which only he has witnessed. But as participant he is also the narrator most subject to the Rosa Coldfield limitation, the obsessive distraction of muscle-memory, the confusions of entrapment in moment-by-moment participation. Even as he holds more exclusive information, so too (more than either other narrator) does he come up most often with the wrong answers. To differentiate his verbal style from Chick's norm and Ratliff's backwoods dialect, Faulkner settles on one of the least attractive devices in his bag of tricks: compound sentences filled with polysyllabic abstract words. In combination with Stevens's moralizing tendencies and his way of working within obsessive patterns which alter reality to suit his inner landscape, Gavin can talk to others (and himself) and sound like either Quentin or Mr. Compson. This is appropriate to combine his rather boyish naiveté and susceptibility with his frequently sententious generalization.

The most unfortunate part of this is that Stevens, here as well as in his appearances in *Intruder in the Dust, Requiem for a Nun,*

5. Five of his sections begin with no direct connection to the section preceding. All of Stevens's have some connection. Two of Ratliff's have no direct connection, but one of these is directly connected to the previous Ratliff narrative.

and *Knight's Gambit,* sometimes gives the impression that he is speaking for Faulkner too. Some of the guff is strikingly similar to the Nagano Faulkner and the Eternal Verities persona of West Point and Virginia. This leads us to an even less attractive speculation: that Stevens is (or at least that readers might think Stevens is) Faulkner's mouthpiece.[6] I don't believe it, any more than I can believe that Ike McCaslin, clad in his underwear, trapped and screaming in his cot, screams for Faulkner; but the threat of this reading is hard to escape in both *The Town* and *The Mansion.* Gavin, looking down on his town from the heights and mouthing his overt pronouncements on the differences between men and women, comes uncomfortably close to the sound of Faulkner.

Ratliff's importance in the book is not well represented by his own narrative sections.[7] As in *The Hamlet* he is the center of information, theory, and evaluation even though Chick has displaced him as our closest alliance. He pronounces on the Snopeses as often as Gavin and more accurately. Even as Gavin steps in to deliver his exclusive information, Ratliff appears with statements (generally correct) that, no matter how much Lawyer thinks he knows *he* doesn't, Lawyer is wrong. He is the greatest force for continuity in the Trilogy.

One can carp about the book in comparison to *The Hamlet* by fastening upon details, by suggesting points of lost vitality and decline, or by fastening on internal consistency (which must always rule in favor of the first novel, and the succeeding novels err whenever they diverge from it), by examining, in other words, the limitations Faulkner imposed on himself for this book, which seem ponderous when compared to the apparently effortless suspension of *The Hamlet.* But the fact remains that *The Town* is good to read and that Faulkner is getting at something new here. The first-person technique limits his power of objective balance but makes possible a new avenue of narrative experiment of its own. *Absalom* began on a track of traditional suspense structures and conventional character and event revelation. By the time we finished the book we discovered that the suspense structures were empty and the conventional characters a kind of sideshow or exemplification of the main

6. This conclusion is generally arrived at in an unfair way, as a shortcut to literary understanding—witness all the productions of Bernard Shaw's plays in which the protagonist is seen with a fiery red (or worse, a long white) beard, with the actor striving to imitate recordings of Shaw's voice.

7. Thirty-three pages, or 9 percent of the total, and six chapters or 25 percent.

attraction—the unconventional process of fiction-making and the embodiment of fiction-theory in Quentin and Shreve have replaced them. *The Town* does not aim at *Absalom*'s high mark and is not designed to dig so deep into human motivation or the sources of the act of fiction. But *The Town*'s first-person narrative has opened up even farther the structure's potential for plenitude and at the same time retained its open-ended comic impetus. To *The Hamlet*'s open system of narrative relevance Faulkner has added the complex possibilities of a narrative which is apparently being invented by its characters. The openness of sequence and connections is now enforced by another freedom, the apparent disappearance of narrative presence and authorial presence from the work.

I think the alternating first-person narrative also sets up a tension between traditional and open structure in *The Town,* suspended between the forming consciousness of each of the various narrators—what each wants to make of the story, what's in it for him, what he is aiming at—and Faulkner's more traditional shapings of the book behind the scenes, beyond their powers. I think this tension (rather than sloppiness or lack of planning) accounts for the peculiarly unformed qualities of the narratives' assumed hearer. Faulkner's large sense of chronicle yearns for continuity and cohesion between one narrator and the next, but at the same time all the narrators must appear to be operating independently of this large aim: each must appear to be pursuing his own ends of communication, self-justification, independent analysis, and just plain showing off. In *As I Lay Dying,* a completely different narrative situation, the narrators (with the possible exception of Darl) all seem to be unconscious of the form of the whole. Their narratives contain no indication of the kind of telling and hearing we see in *The Town.* There they seem to address their words more to themselves than to any hearer. Faulkner managed to get around some of his problems of distribution of narrative by inventing Darl's prescience and Addie's immortality and employing them with great flexibility. The closest approach to this sort of thing here is Ratliff's superior experience and analysis which always stop short of prescience.

The narratives are all delivered as if spoken aloud, to be heard by an interested receptor. Perhaps Faulkner's idea of this hearer was no more specific than something like "the reader." The projected hearer is certainly not specified or coherently articulated. The relationship between one narrative and the next and the relationship between the several narratives of a single narrator shifts and changes in the course of the book, and it is only on close examination that a definition of this hearer emerges. In chapter 2 Stevens takes up by a kind of fakery where Mallison left off. Mallison tacks on two lines of a dialogue between Ratliff and Stevens at the end of chapter 1, about another of Ratliff's images, the whorehouse money pinned in Flem's underwear. Chick adds this because it takes one step farther the idea of the monument/footprint of Flem's brassy water tank. He seems to have the sense that the narrative he is finishing here will be continued later, that it is a part of a longer whole he is helping to form. Then Gavin steps in at the beginning of his chapter and says "He hadn't unpinned it yet" (*Town,* p. 30). We know exactly where we are, but we think we've been given a dramatic situation when we haven't. The book at this point seems to be a front porch or a minstrel show, each character listening to the others, taking up his story where the preceding narrator left off, listening patiently while another talks, then talking himself, giving us the information he's gathered or been given, while the others listen. There is a similar link between chapters 3 and 4 (pp. 77–78). Ratliff answers or confirms Chick's guess and moves it farther: "Gowan said you would even have thought she was proud of it." "She was." But at the end of chapter 4 the nature of these happy continuations begins to become clear. If Faulkner is to get the value out of having three separate narrators, he must separate them: give one a goodie the others don't have, give one some secret and let the others yearn for it. Ratliff takes the Eula–Manfred story down to the point of Gavin's not-so-civic-minded lawsuit. Ratliff sees the light in the office above the square and guesses that Gavin was not alone but doesn't say it. Gavin picks it up by saying, "The poets are wrong of course" and proceeds to give us the scene in his office.

Up to this point the dramatic situation between narrators could be just as I have suggested—the minstrel show or the front porch—with one important difference: they have agreed to reveal all, and they are hearing some of what they are hearing for the first time. Gavin has just recounted one of his "exclusives," the scene with Eula in the office. Ratliff picks up in chapter 6 without reference to it, chronologically we are where Gavin left off, but no farther along in knowledge than his own narrative at the end of 4. At this point it is apparent that not all the narratives are shared, even though they seem to be spoken aloud. In *As I Lay Dying* the assumption was that the monologues were private, and we later discovered the exceptional shared moments (through imagery, Darl's prescience, through the forces which bring the family out of their individual tracks into action as a unit). Here we have assumed a sharing which turns out to be illusory.

Between chapters 6 and 7 Chick does not make a direct connection to what Ratliff has said about Helen but recalls that Ratliff "once said" this. It's apparent from other references throughout the text that Ratliff says it all the time. Between 7 and 8 there is a connection that, again, appears to be direct because it is a repetition of a verbal formula; but again it turns out to be a familiar, oft-repeated phrase in town: the sharing of bits of knowledge or consciousness rather than mutual knowledge. At the end of 7 Chick begins to tell of Gavin's first encounter with Linda after his return from the war. Gavin's abrupt interruption with his narrative can have the appearance of continuity by virtue of verbal repetition, can appear to be delivered in Chick's presence by virtue of the sudden interruption (almost, "Here, let me tell this part"), but at the same time can have the advantage to character, the advantage to the sense of character-formed narrative, of being again an exclusive, the statement of data held by only one individual.

In that we do not know who the hearer is, it is not a perfectly articulated narrative device, but we sometimes know who the hearer is not. The ambiguity and suspension of the narrative scheme makes the shape of the novel unique and gives it both a clear function in the structure of the Trilogy and a place in Faulkner's continuing narrative experiment. Ratliff's interruptions at 9 and 11 (which share with *Tristram Shandy*'s short chapters the comic parody of novelistic form) continue the perfect suspension of the scheme of mutuality. We can hear Ratliff telling Stevens that he doesn't know, but Stevens can't and probably Chick can't. Whether Ratliff can hear directly (that is, hear Chick's narration of 10 after he speaks 9 and before he speaks 11) is in doubt. He wouldn't have to. It could be just more of the mutuality of knowledge or data. Gavin has an "exclusive" for the office and what happens there because he throws Chick out in chapter 13. Chick returns in 14 and tries to figure out from physical clues what took place.

In chapter 19 Chick hands Gavin the note. We want him to read it but he doesn't. In 20 Gavin tells us what was in it. At the end of 21 Chick is again sent out of the room for 22's interview in the Mallison house. The partial overlap between the end of one narrative and the beginning of the next is repeated in the overlap of information. The literal overlap of events narrated indicates this, and dialogue taking place within the narratives and the quotation of one narrator by another, bear it out. The range of the connections between chapters follows the same general scheme seen in *As I Lay Dying:* they begin with close connection, overlapping, and apparent continuity early in the book and later give way to time-lapse, ellipses, and lack of connection. As we are made accustomed to the nature of the sharing and nonsharing and are familiarized through synopsis and association, it becomes less and less necessary for the narrative scheme to point out its connections to us, more and more possible for it to work on our unconscious. The narrators' involvement in the action and how it affects what they tell, their calculation of how best to tell and when best to reveal, give a dynamic surface to the novel which, although different, cannot automatically be judged inferior to that of *The Hamlet.*

What the narrators are working with, what they are telling us about, is to a certain extent banal, boring, and everyday. But what they tell us is not. This kinship with us (a totally different kind of kinship from that established in *The Hamlet*) and their vying with each other as story-tellers make a whole in which the parts strive with each other for dominance, in an organic relationship. The action of striving, the interrelationship of tellers, provide a second level of significance to play against the everyday level of narrated events. *The Town*'s aims and effects are so removed from the aims and effects of *The Hamlet* that qualitative comparison on the basis of method is no more than casuistical guess. There is a possibility that the shift in method corresponds to the change in the community's consciousness. *The Hamlet* begins the process, an integrated whole, an unfragmented consciousness of cohesive community attention for the drama in its midst. This, perhaps, must shift as the community changes in *The Town:* its first-person approach—individual explanations and individual interpretations of the several voices forming themselves into the self-appointed community conscience—is more appropriate to the complexity of an emerging community. The novels pass from rural into semi-urban concerns and from a size which is almost familiar to a size which can no longer be described as a village, and the narrative design repeats this shift. The shift between *The Town* and *The Mansion,* then, would represent in the changed method a breakdown of our own certainty and that of the community conscience as to the reliability of individual solution. The individual voices of *The Town* lend credence to a vestigial community agreement, but the mixture of first- and third-person narratives and the peculiarly disconnected order in *The Mansion* testifies to a fragmentation and breakdown even of this tentative certainty. The chaotic order of narrative method in *The Mansion* reflects the chaos of a community which has outgrown its identity.

Once again at the beginning of *The Mansion* we are tempted to odious comparison. We begin to see compromise on every quarter. Working on Mink's consciousness in the third person seems to be an attempt to drag us bodily back to the world of *The Hamlet.* This has a bonus effect that is somehow thematically right: a great portion of Mink's power is his force as an absurdly anachronistic nemesis. But chapters follow with speakers italicized at their heads which could have come from *The Town,* and we begin to think Faulkner is just writing a sequel. There are a few chapters (13–16) that do neither but seem designed to be stop-gap connectives between the two methods.

There is more order to the structure than this comparative niggling will allow. The three divisions of the book continually increase in length [8] and each is clearly distinctive from the others in technique. "Mink" begins in the third person with an intense point of view located in the criminal, turns to two chapters of first-person narration (Ratliff's, and one by a newcomer, Montgomery Ward—so successful an experiment in first-person Snopesism that one wonders why it is unique) and returns to Mink's point of view in a third-person narration. "Linda" works on the analogue of *The Town* [9] with some of the "exclusives" of that book but little of its other rhythm or design. Then "Flem" moves the narrative into the third person for its entire length. Variety is provided only by switches between a third person dominated by Mink's point of view

8. Mink, 103 pages; Linda, 147 pages; Flem, 177 pages.
9. Two Ratliffs, two Mallisons, a Stevens, and then a third Mallison.

(pp. 259–93, 396–416, 434–35) and objective third person with some mind-reading by Mallison and Stevens. Throughout "Mink" and "Flem" there is a rather disorganized use of the "thinking-thinking" patterns familiar from *Light in August* which, when applied to Mink, seem to bring him closer to Joe Christmas than the other obvious parallels. It is an attempt to deal with the hermetic and subverbal thoughts of a mind pursued.

The structure, then, is not a mishmash but a mixture, not necessarily compromise, but perhaps flexible combination. What makes me uneasy about the book is another kind of compromise, harder to get at and even more difficult to pin down because it slides into critical impressionism. It is in the nature of things for endings to be judged by their beginnings rather than vice versa—for the first volume of a trilogy to be not only a unit in itself, a novel, and a beginning, but to form premises and données for the whole project. The second volume, although it must be a unit, can lope along as middle without being much criticized because we have to suspend judgment: we don't know what the end is to be. As long as the second supports the premises it is doing its job. But the third volume must be a unit, must continue the second, and must fulfill the promise—and more difficult, all the premises, of the first.

The Mansion is, properly, a book of returns. We began as we end in a section called "Flem"; our second was "Eula" and our penultimate is "Linda." Mink, the Trilogy's shotgun, is dragged on to the stage in act 1 and fired in act 3. We have seen the beginnings of Flem's rise, have followed his progress, and here have a stabilization and inevitable fall. The outrageous methods of the rascal's beginnings cannot possibly be matched in the solid propriety of the bank president's end.

Faulkner seems aware of the problem of cohesion natural in a trilogy begun in 1929 and finished in 1959 (to say nothing of a trilogy which probably didn't know it was a trilogy until some time after the first volume was completed). He underlines the problem in a prefatory note which borrows its metaphor from Malcolm Cowley and its tone from some of the more universal of his own universal generalizations.

> Since the author likes to believe, hopes that his entire life's work is a part of a living literature, and since "living" is motion, and

> "motion" is change and alteration and therefore the only alternative to motion is un-motion, stasis, death, there will be found discrepancies and contradictions in the thirty-four-year progress of this particular chronicle; the purpose of this note is simply to notify the reader that the author has already found more discrepancies and contradictions than he hopes the reader will—contradictions and discrepancies due to the fact that the author has learned, he believes, more about the human heart and its dilemma than he knew thirty-four years ago; and is sure that, having lived with them that long time, he knows the characters in this chronicle better than he did then.

The statement is graceful, determined, succinct. It counters the claims of *The Hamlet*'s premises by affirming the authority of *The Mansion*'s conclusions. So 1959 takes precedence over 1925, 1931, or 1940. By this formulation *The Hamlet* (like Benjy's section of *The Sound and the Fury*) is a failed sketch improved by the later additions. Faulkner seems here more satisfied with the end of this than he ever was with any of the attempts (even that in 1945) at ending the Compsons. He holds that wisdom is the criterion he was aiming at all along, not invention or consistency.

It seems to me unlikely that he is just excusing the giving of forenames to Ratliff or the changing of Houston's or any other of the idiosyncratic surface discrepancies. He has done this all his life and never found it worth a public statement. I suspect he is very conscious of the distance between *The Hamlet* and *The Mansion,* not in years but in power and suspension and scope. And I suspect that he knows the feeling of comedown inevitable in the drawing to a close of so powerful a beginning, to say nothing of ending something which was so much fun while it was going on.

But change in details is a red herring. What is significant is a subtler change in attitude. I think Faulkner in this book betrays his own creation in a way which, though perfectly understandable, is difficult to define. He has come to like Ratliff too well and to tolerate Stevens too much, to let Mallison stumble along as a gap-filler, an ageless Little Orphan Annie, never seeming to mature with the passing years. Ending gambits are understandable, but that Faulkner here softens his insight and dulls the edge of his characters in order to arrange his ending undercuts the integrity of the work, and that he then dignifies all this as the growth of wisdom makes him suspect of deviousness.

Differentiation between the three narrators in *The Mansion* is far from sure—one slurs into another. The lack of variety in sequence (Ratliff–Ratliff, 6–7; Mallison–Mallison, 8–9) indicates that their independent functions and individual responses have become less important. Chick has moved closer to Ratliff in humor; years have brought him little maturity but a coarsened outlook. The objective child we counted on as antidote to Stevens and Ratliff has become a rather narrow and bitter adult. Ratliff's dialect seems more extreme (perhaps made so since that's all that separates him from Chick now). Perhaps these are excusable in the terms of change Faulkner proposes for "living literature." But what is not is the game-playing he indulges in with Ratliff: the forenames, the tie-buying, the Country Mouse in the City. Faulkner condescends to Ratliff as he never has before. Ratliff in the New York sequence becomes no more than another Fonzo or Virgil.

There ought to be a critical term for the author's fondness for his characters—some term to distinguish between an attachment which carries the character beyond the author's donnée into a realm of independent action, freeing him from the author's conscious premises, and that fondness which can mislead an author into sequel-making, the frame of mind which can produce V. K. Ratliff at the tie shop as easily as Victor Appleton can produce *Tom Swift and His Electric Runabout.* Faulkner must indulge his whim, no matter what Ratliff has become on his own, or what dignity our respect for him as master, as victim, as fully formed human has produced. Of course if the Ratliff of *The Hamlet* had been confronted with the tie shop we would have a very different story. But the impulse which makes Faulkner think the tie shop a good idea is the same impulse that makes him incapable of letting Ratliff be what he was. Ratliff's brilliant interim conclusions of *The Hamlet* and quick strokes of almost accidental wit must here become punditry, quick sense become wisdom, the covert originality become overt. Rosa Coldfield could make of Sutpen whatever she wanted as long as he was her exclusive property: she could demonize to her heart's content. But once her testimony became just so many bits of data to be judged by other data, she lost the right. Faulkner does not recognize that Ratliff is not only his creation but our property. He is *not* free to make of him what he will.

The novel suffers because the characters have to a certain extent become pawns of Faulkner's authorial self-indulgence. He no longer seeks the characteristic for its own sake but the characteristic as a function of a genre-piece. The difference between Ratliff in *The Hamlet* and Ratliff in *The Mansion* is the difference between a good Flemish portrait and a bad Greuze.[10] Faulkner has given over the authorial in favor of that mixture of possession and authority which makes up the least attractive clichés of what we think of as "fatherly."

This kind of carping comes of looking at *The Mansion* as the last novel of a rather successful Trilogy. But *The Mansion* is also a novel. As such it stands or falls on quite another element: the character of Mink. Mink is some kind of triumph. Elsewhere in this book there is the same sort of narrative uncertainty which marked *Light in August* and *Absalom, Absalom!*—the *perhaps* syndrome, that which rendered ambiguous Joe Christmas's most significant gestures and automatic responses:

> They was wrong of course; hadn't nothing happened yet. I mean, I prefer that even that citadel was still maiden right up to this moment. No: what I mean is, I wont have nothing else for the simple dramatic verities except that ever thing happened right there that night and all at once. [*Mansion*, p. 122]

Ratliff makes attempts—some of them false—to read Chick's mind (p. 113), he invents thoughts and speeches for Linda (pp. 143–44); Chick has similar uncertainty when he tries to imagine what Gavin wrote on Linda's slate at first ("maybe what he wrote was simpler still," p. 200) and suffers an attack of *maybes* when working on the possibilities of Gavin marrying Linda (p. 205). The device here is less sure than in the other novels: it is not ambiguity to a given end, but ambiguity which only builds the general uncertainty of interpretation. But there is none of this uncertainty between the narrative presence and Mink. Mink is Rip Van Winkle: surrounded by confusion and doubt he finds his certainty within. His internal resolution and his law—all he can bring to bear to face not just a

10. Or, to bring it closer to home, Lucas in "The Fire and the Hearth" and Lucas in *Intruder in the Dust.*

world he never made but a world remade while he was out of it—is what he knows from his inner experience while sealed off from the world. He is frozen in the certainty of his own consciousness. It is the strongest characteristic carried over from his appearances in *The Hamlet* and this calm and common sense of internal self-rationalization here seem even more reasonable, even more justified than in the earlier book. We know that Mink is in a way mad, but at the same time we recognize obstacles placed in his path by the town's guardians as ineffectual and in a way, irrelevant.

Because Mink is so consistent and so true to his own certainty we side with him and see the vacillations of the guardians for what they are. This is the effect of a narrative strategy: a third-person version of the alliance we formed with the narrator of "Emily." We must prefer the consistent and tough-minded immediacy over the mumbling and chaotic voices in the background. But our alliance here is not directed toward disillusionment in the denouement: there is no comedown to follow the buildup. Mink dominates this book in a way unmatched elsewhere in the Trilogy. What comes first and what comes last matters more in a trilogy than it does in a single novel. The first novel has the freedom to make the premises and the last is under a compulsion to make some endings. That Mink comes last matters a great deal.

This contrast between uncertain pundits and a certain and determined criminal brings us to a case for the book's undeniable strength: an absurdly stupid nemesis is powerfully and sympathetically portrayed, party because the town's guardians are so civilized, educated, and ineffectual in their attempts to stop it. It may very well be that Faulkner is working this last bit of deception upon us. We watch what we think is the main attraction, the guardians of public probity fumbling about, repeating to each other their rather set and clearly outdated formulas for combating the Snopeses while the book's promises of community virtue, of rascality in the Snopeses, even Linda's promise as Helen's daughter—run ever and more disappointingly downhill. Faulkner is again working on the sideshow rather than the main event. Even Flem—our best hope for vitality—has declined from the variety and invention of his beginnings. At least his nemesis (subject to none of Flem's new dignity) can be nemesis worthy of the name of Snopes, one of the old sort. It is possible to accommodate Faulkner's authorial fondness in this scheme. To cover his traces, Faulkner made what seemed to be the main attraction seem even more so—made the guardians into Super-Guardians—by attaching to them the deceptive authority of his own fondness and familiarity. Could he not be playing another game with the reader? He drops into place in a freehanded manner all the magic names from other parts of the Yoknapatawpha canon, so that the reader thinks he is still reading the same book, only to discover by the end that he is pursuing a new track of rather perverse vitality, of absurd anachronism. Mink is shoved on from the wings with a cheap pistol to do a job and then die. He does it, but he doesn't die. Seen this way, the book offers a nemesis out of the *Sanctuary* landscape stalking upon *The Unvanquished*'s friendly turf.

This reading is too ingenious and there are too many obvious objections to it for me to be entirely serious about it, but it does establish another point about the book: some of its endings and returns work better as independent functions of a new kind of narrative than they do as endings and returns of the old. Faulkner's decline or fondness cannot account for all the reasons the book seems weaker than *The Town*. Some have their source in a new and freer sense of invention and variation, and perhaps even a sense that the present, his new subject matter—won't stop changing as he writes.

The first time Flem puts Mink away he does it as a kind of reflex action—even nonaction: not to move to help him is to be rid of a tool which has outlived its usefulness. The second time he has to employ Montgomery Ward, another outmoded tool, in a manner almost baroque in its calculation and intricacy. The first action is characteristic of the young and comparatively unformed Flem; the second of his middle period. The catch is that things put away tend to pop up again (as Sutpen discovered), but also that Flem, by doing it not once but twice, has planted himself a time-bomb. He can age and mellow and soften, but the nemesis in Parchman stands still, where time stands still, sealed to bring forth revenge out of due season—not as revenge might be now, but as immediate revenge would have been had it occurred in its time. Faulkner's development of Mink is a perfect extension of the solitary Mink of *The Hamlet*. He takes the stupidity, stubbornness, and pride of the small-time killer through the refining and concentrating process of the convict's contemplation and emerges with a human image which, perhaps even more clearly than his portrait of Joe Christmas, demands our censure as it commands our respect for human consistency and strength.

But because we have so far accepted Stevens, Ratliff, and Mallison as interlocutors, and because they are pointing at Flem instead of Mink, we proceed to the conclusion that Flem's end is improperly resolved, instead of thinking that its accidental, bad-dream quality —even Linda's last, curious, ambiguous aid and comfort—is a gratuitous tying up of a thread, instead of seeing as we might a productive ambiguity beyond us, beyond the self-appointed guardians of community, beyond Flem and beyond Mink.

It is an ambiguity similar to Mink's rather crude estimation of Old Moster, Earth, Fate. His end reminds us that the operations of endings sometimes move beyond the fulfillment or disappointment of their premises into considerations of the nature of ending itself: the fury of the nemesis which was seeking him out, called off when a church fell on him in Mexico.

> Because he was free now. A little further along toward dawn, any time the notion struck him to, he could lay down. So when the notion struck him he did so, arranging himself, arms and legs and back, already feeling the first, faint gentle tug like the durned old ground itself was trying to make you believe it wasn't really noticing itself doing it. Only he located the right stars at that moment, he was not laying exactly right since a man must face the east to lay down; walk west but when you lay down, face the exact east. So he moved, shifted a little, and now he was exactly right and he was free now, he could afford to risk it; to show how much he dared risk it, he even would close his eyes, give it all the chance it wanted; whereupon as if believing he really was asleep, it gradually went to work a little harder, easy of course, not to really disturb him: just harder, increasing [*Mansion*, pp. 434–35]

So Mink is assumed bodily into the earth and Faulkner tacks on, as if for good measure, "Helen and the bishops, the kings and the unhomed angels, the scornful and graceless seraphim" (p. 436). Again we are cast into doubt because the last lines move to weak ending and parodic game, to literary motto-for-the-wall, to overt and self-conscious moralizing, and to the absurd excess of life's mixture.

I suppose that in order to convince myself of the quality of *The Mansion* I would have to cross the boundaries of criticism and appeal to some intentional fallacy—even as this immediate discussion has seemed almost to praise the accidental and to favor a perverse reading over a reasonable. But I do find that if I am to value the Trilogy as a whole I must have something to suggest that the ending is not an ending.

Mink is as perfect a characterization as Lucas Beauchamp is. But beyond his human form he is that rough beast that, like Samuel Worsham Beauchamp, lurks outside the realm of just endings for fictional premises. His human yearnings and his evil represent just that mixture of human endurance and perversity which Faulkner so often talked about in interview and infrequently embodied in fiction: an ultimate ambiguity on any conventional scale of good and evil. Mink is so powerful an emblem of man's contemporary doubts about his future, and particularly of Faulkner's certain doubts and uncertain gropings about the future in general, that he demands an attention independent of his place in the fiction. The proper ending of a book or even a Trilogy sinks to insignificance next to such a literary invention.

In such a scheme *The Mansion* is the third of the Trilogy's series of successful, though mutually contradictory, suspensions. In *The Hamlet* the covert structure is suspended behind the overt surface narrative of the everyday. Its narrative employs any narrative effect that comes to hand but seems to strive for none and succeeds in catching a sense of life's fullness and vitality. In *The Town* the open-ended order is maintained in a new suspension of character-formed narrative exchange, the process of mixing character and narrator is superimposed upon the difficulty of human interpretation, the problem of pattern and structure to what is at best a confusing flux of whim and oblique motive. In *The Mansion* this same complexity, in turn, is retained in a vitiated form to act as red herring to a new suspension. While we are watching the decline of a group of well-intentioned but inept guardians, a new force of accidence and perversity in the form of Mink is replacing the old force of chicanery and oblique motive as seen in that bush-league Machiavelli, his cousin Flem.

Conventional narrative surprise is overwhelmed by the shocks to our expectations of what the narrative structure ought to be doing—or what we have been led to believe the narrative structure ought to be doing. Our formal disappointments in expecting any book to follow or fulfill or complete the preceding are overcome in wonder as one after another defies all the structures of its predecessor to move toward a truth in human nature—or perhaps a prophecy of human nature—beyond the reach of form or consistency or ordered structure.

It is the dilemma of the formalist always to want to find familiar shapes, but always to be disappointed when all the shapes work out perfectly. Because the formalist, in order to keep his self-respect, must continually recognize that finding a shape is only a means to understanding, and that making a shape must for the maker always remain secondary to the total understanding, the total artifact, the total impact offered by the fiction. And he must be ready to accept the shape to come when it appears, even when it may seem to represent the end of shape entirely.

11 The Search for Freedom

The aim of this study is not to reveal any figure in the carpet, but rather to attempt to identify a pattern common to all of Faulkner's works, the centrality of narrative. I suggest that what needs to be understood is not a theme or a character or an ideal, but a constant concern for narrative craft and the fictional art which continually derives from and returns to immediate narrative need. Faulkner is first and foremost a narrator, a storyteller. From this central fact emanate almost all the other concerns of his fiction: had he not been attempting to find new ways to embody stories we should not have had the series of technical experiments of the "main range"; had he not been aware of the artificiality of fiction and its devices there would have been no *Light in August* and no *Absalom;* and had he not believed in the connections between "story" and living, we should not have had Yoknapatawpha County at all.

His claim to priority as an innovator in fiction and his place in twentieth-century experimental fiction may both be traced, rather strangely, directly back to his firm roots in the oral tradition. His connection with the mainstream of American fiction is an odd combination of his firm belief in "natural" storytelling and his insistence on the necessity of artifice. He shares with Melville a rather innocent willingness to break the rules and re-make fiction in order to obtain the instrument capable of telling the story he wants to tell. With Hawthorne he shares a determined abstraction and the dominance by some of his darker themes, with Twain he shares the background in the oral tradition and American humor usually characterized as "frontier." Finally, his implicit theory and his complexity share common ground with the overt theory and complexity of Henry James.

As I have tried to indicate among his "failures," the humble origins and roots in the oral tradition can be a mixed blessing. Some of his overt rhythms, the big words, the purple passages, are a direct result of his experience as autodidact. Again, Faulkner shares this with Melville: a rather naive approach to the classics, to philosophy, to "great words" can be directly attributed in both cases to the reading in a vacuum which all autodidacts go through. From the same source, of course, comes their zealous belief in the mystical power of the word, which makes them dare to make prose into litany-like incantations.

And from this too, perhaps, comes the digressive element, responsible in Melville for much of his allegorical richness, responsible in Faulkner for effects ranging from the free association of *The Sound and the Fury* to the open comic structure of the Trilogy. The innocence of the anecdote about his first novel and Sherwood Anderson reminds us that at least this much of the gallus-snapping persona was legitimate: he was self-educated, well-read, and chiefly influenced in his fiction through his reading, yet self-taught and unaware of much that experimental fiction had already accomplished. In a sense, he wasted time re-inventing what had already been invented.

We can find most of the problems of Faulkner's fiction somewhere along a line drawn between homely roots and sophisticated development. These two poles were for Faulkner the horns of a personal as well as an artistic dilemma. In chapter 1, I concentrated on craftsmanship and artifice, but even there the interviews quoted indicate clearly that Faulkner very much wanted the appearance of the self-taught, natural storyteller. That he was a primitive was a point of pride. But at the same time, if he were seen only as a primitive, much of his fictional accomplishment would have to be seen as no more than happy accident, and that prospect left him far from happy. He needed recognition of the accomplishments he knew he had made, but he did not want to be caught claiming them for himself. The best images that I have found for this are two portraits—the first that of the first *TIME* cover story—Whitmanesque workman's shirt, galluses, no tie, and a rather sullen demeanor—the second that of Cartier-Bresson's pictures made at West Point—three-piece suit, bowler hat, bumbershoot, and the air of contentment of the literary lion. The humble portrait depicts the man who makes fiction of his life's blood, the "I-couldn't-stop-writing-if-I-wanted-to" pose familiar in Thomas Wolfe. The sophisticated portrait is the international man of letters, the craftsmanlike cabinetmaker, the man who put it all in intentionally, no matter how happily accidental it looks when it is read.

The description of *As I Lay Dying* as a "simple *tour de force*" belongs to the Faulkner of the humble portrait. Even if the novel were a simple tour de force, one is tempted to ask what is so simple about a tour de force? But the apparent disavowal of one of his best novels is also an indication of the schizophrenic tension in the man of both portraits. The phrase *tour de force* is a catch-all for Faulkner in the interviews. Once it is knowing "exactly what I wanted to do" (*Lion,* p. 226). Another time he says it is "technique charg[ing] in and tak[ing] command of the dream before the writer himself can get his hands on it," adding. "But then, when technique does not intervene, in another sense writing is easier too. Because with me there is always a point in the book where the characters themselves rise up and take charge and finish the job—say somewhere about page 275" (*Lion,* p. 244). This sets up a distinction between "technique" taking over and characters taking over: "Once these people come to life they begin—they take off and so the writer is going at a dead run behind them trying to put down what they say and do in time. . . . they have taken charge of the story. They tell it from then on" (*Univ.,* p. 120). When technique "charges in," it is tour de force; when characters "take off" it is not. There are other spot definitions: in *A Fable* he seems to hold that tour de force is a strong idea; for Boon Hogganbeck at the end of "The Bear" it is manipulated literary contrast; [1] at other times, tour de force seems to be the ability to predict the last word when writing the first (*Univ.,* p. 207), opposing the Bundrens with all the forces of nature (*Univ.,* p. 87) or simple narrative tricks, such as Darl's clairvoyance.

All these statements point to one or another element of precalculated artifice, but they point with some disdain: *As I Lay Dying* was tour de force because Faulkner knew how it was going to come out and managed through technique and tricks and contrasts to

1. "Suppose that had been Christ again. . . . That He would naturally have got crucified again, and I had to—then it became *tour de force,* because I had to invent enough stuff to carry this notion" (*Univ.,* p. 27). "That made the tragedy of the dog and the bear a little more poignant to me. That's the sort of *tour de force* that I think the writer's entitled to use" (*Univ.,* p. 60).

make it come out that way with a certain lack of "agony." *The Sound and the Fury* apparently was not tour de force for the opposite reasons: he did not know how it was going to come out, the characters took over, and no matter how much technique he employed he could not get it "told right," and "agony" ensued. He claims he wrote it in "six weeks," but in spite of this folksy declaimer, the sum of his statements on *As I Lay Dying* give the impression that he thought it was a pretty good novel: in 1931 he described it as "his best book" (*Lion,* p. 8), and he later said, "It was not easy. No honest work is" (*Lion,* p. 244).

He emphasizes tour de force, I think, because he felt somehow cheapened by deciding what an end should be before he—or before his "charging" characters—got there. He must have felt a bit like Cash, perhaps, to know an ending, or be willing to say there was any ending. The heartlessness of narrative calculation, the cold act of fictional deception or prearrangement of narrative effect made him nervous. Ought not his characters run away from him and his story defy the telling if he was a true natural genius? "That's just a trick," is spoken by a phony persona, but this persona is very close to the center of Faulkner's very real dilemma between the "natural" of experience and memory, of "flesh-and-blood people" and the artifice and craftsmanship of the "box," the "corner," the "urn or shape."

The tension between artifice and "flesh-and-blood" comes down to a problem of mimesis. In order to make the thing work (as Faulkner very clearly realized by the time of the short stories of the thirties) he had to calculate his order, his voices, his arrangements, and his effects. But he found such artificial means to be at odds with his end and aim, the passion and blood of the story at hand. Without the artifice they wouldn't work. Without the blood it didn't matter whether they worked or not.

I think one of his pragmatic solutions for this perpetual tension was to compartmentalize some resources of fiction in one area or the other, some in artifice and others in some form of the "natural." Time schemes clearly belong to artifice: they are designed, arranged, may even accomplish their function in a manner completely independent of the substance of the stories being told (as in *Light in August*). But the scope of the time covered by novels and stories seems almost always to have been chosen according to a storyteller's simple necessities. *As I Lay Dying* and *The Reivers* take place between the beginning and the end of a journey, *Light in August* between a cause and its effect, the Trilogy between a point just before Flem's entrance and a point just following his exit. *Sanctuary* occurs between an impulse and its result (a shorter interval than that of *Light in August*), *The Unvanquished* between the beginning and the end of the time of war, *Go Down, Moses* between the offense and the failure of the expiation. *The Sound and the Fury,* somewhat more difficult to define, takes place somewhere between the beginning and the end of a single family. *Absalom* (on one level) between Sutpen's plan and its collapse and (on the other) between first perception of myth and its full-blown form. No matter how complex the chronology or the time-warps of the narratives, the boundaries of the time covered by each are set according to a simple scheme. It is as if Faulkner conceived of this definition of narrative scope as an envelope, a clear and simple enclosure separating the artifice from the flux of life.

Faulkner's endings are another matter, and belong to artifice: they are art rather than life. They tend to be disconnected in a poetic way, like the endings of some of Matthew Arnold's major poems—but beyond this they demonstrate a formal resolution to the pattern of what has gone before. *The Sound and the Fury* ends with a metaphor for the book, "each in its ordered place," as Benjy circles the square; *As I Lay Dying* in the rather beside-the-point accomplishment (considering the agonies we have been through with Darl and Addie) of the family's lesser aims—burial, marriage, teeth, and bananas—and these lesser aims comment ironically on the heroic coming together at the book's center. *Sanctuary,* with Temple in the Luxembourg Gardens, ends with something like Bartleby's blank wall, a proof of the novel's ultimate ambiguity, more sure a proof perhaps than Popeye's ambiguous demise. *Light in August* returns to Lena's remark near the opening for a resolution of the book's open ending which, again, comments ironically on Joe's closed ending. *Absalom, Absalom!,* too, ends in its second structure, with Quentin's and Shreve's realizations of where they have been—the framing device has become the novel in a narrative readjustment similar to the adjustment of premises at the end of "Uncle Willy." These novels of the "main range" have perhaps less conventional endings than the later novels. *Go Down, Moses* gives a glimpse of the future in Samuel Worsham Beauchamp, *The Hamlet* has a non-ending in Flem's "Get up" to his horses, more another beginning than an ending. *The Town,* after the distractions of Eula's funeral and monument, returns to the guardians' central concern for the Snopes menace as they pack off Byron's wild Indian offspring, and *The Mansion* has either a resolution that fails to resolve or another glimpse of the future in Mink, similar to that at the end of *Go Down, Moses. The Reivers* ends in more conventional and more absolute narrative resolution than any of the others.

How big a slice Faulkner cuts for himself seems to be determined pragmatically; how to end the exploration of that slice seems determinedly abstract, formal, poetic. Both are indicative of his theoretical concept of what narrative does. The story or the novel is an envelope containing a certain amount of event, a certain development to a perhaps unexpected end. It has a beginning and an end determined by the development, the moment, the "germ" he wishes to capture. Narrative is imitation of moment, of life, of time, of place—this is a function of the "natural" storyteller. But narrative in order to succeed must calculate its devices, deal abstractly with time, render development less in what is seen than in what is not seen, anchor the chosen moment to a measure of meaning partially predetermined, partially self-generated. It must deal in abstraction, in the patterning of artifice, in the unification of recurrent theme, in the ordering of a disordered real world. It must impose an artificial beginning and end, an artificial structure, an artificial form on what, in its natural state, is meaningless flux. In terms of his interview metaphors, the "germ"—the muddy drawers, the gray hair—is predominantly a matter of the natural storyteller. It comes from that storehouse of experience and passion, the lumber-room of the memory. Rendering comes from this, too, a certain amount of dialogue, cues for character. Building the box or the corner or the cabinet are of the more sophisticated side of the novelist—his craft, his artifice, his sleight-of-hand.

The ideal compromise between these two contributive elements, compartments, or resources, is not just a matter of art imitating life or life imitating art but a free passage from one to the other, a texture in which the seams and joints disappear so that we cannot tell artifice from reportage, so that we do not know when we are being manipulated. Ideally in the natural passage of one event as cause into another event as result, we cannot distinguish between the arrangement of artifice ("I knew how it was going to come out and made it happen") from the accident of development ("the characters rise up and take charge and finish the job").

Achievement of a perfect compromise is impossible, but to seek it is to seek freedom for himself as author and freedom for us as readers. The burden of the rules of Teller and Hearer is that we want to be manipulated, but the other, perhaps more ancient rule of imitation, mimesis, verisimilitude amends this: we want to be manipulated, but we want not to know when it is being done. We want to think we are moving with the freedom of an observer rather than the close attention of the explicator. The tourist with a hired guide has less pleasure because serendipity becomes impossible if too much is pointed out.

The search for narrative freedom in both "natural" storytelling and the experiment of artifice is the development in Faulkner's career that I would stress most because it makes the most coherent sense. Faulkner usually seems to be trying to escape the particular constriction the narrative of his latest book has imposed on him. Access to this freedom is found (in the early years) in experimental innovation and (later) in cautious return to an earlier simpler, direct narrative. Experiment is never a total departure and return is never a slavish retreat.

The first constriction, common to the novels of the apprenticeship, is a thematic or substantive entrapment which leads to narrative rigidity. The early books are overwritten. The substance is of a generation lost: it's society's fault. This lostness is embodied in various individuals in differing ways, but they have a common cause, so common that it becomes repetitive. The substance determines the manner: since the force is in the generation's realization of its lostness, the fiction becomes rather narrowly focused on direct statement of opinions for those characters who realize what is happening to them and satirical treatment of those who do not. The novels tend to tell more often than they embody. Calculation of narrative design seems either completely random or else determined only by a minimal desire for narrative impetus or force.

The second phase or "main range" contains so much variety of constriction and subsequent access to freedom that it can hardly be generalized upon without describing each novel as a distinct subphase. All of them are characterized by form and experiment in technique. One result of the technique (or perhaps its accomplished aim) is greater objectivity about characters and careful, detailed anatomy of consciousness. Turning inward gives the novelist and his characters immediate freedom from the constrictions of generational lostness: individuals here are isolated by the community's animosity rather than generational or societal trauma. The central empathy is with *them* rather than with *us*. Form and technical experiment produce powerful internal cohesion. Time becomes freer because internal time is more important than societal time, and internal time takes on a measure of relativity. Isolation and compulsion bring a need to explain their causes; the burden of the past and the agony of past becoming or influencing the present become central: inheritance, tradition, and the family.

But the new freedom soon develops into new constriction. We know more about each of the successive narrators of *The Sound and the Fury* than about any of the characters in the apprenticeship novels, but we know this because the novel's technique entraps us for a significant period in each consciousness. We can make the connections between characters by virtue of the same depth of experience. The experience convinces us, first-hand, of the entrapment of individual Compsons, and by extension, of the entrapment of man in his consciousness. But that they are so very hermetic, that we stay so long in each, also indicate Faulkner's entrapment in his chosen structure. The familiar statement on the novel ("I wrote it once . . . I wrote it again") implies that each section was conceived as a self-sufficient entity to contain the meaning of the muddy drawers, that he tried each in succession and each failed. He is trapped in a particularly rigid first-person method and trapped in his failure to make a whole of the sections. There is no way to end the book because one of its themes is the process of dwindling and wasting away which cannot end.

In *As I Lay Dying* some of the isolative effects of the first person are offset by modifications. The Bundrens moved through time (which none of the Compsons within his own narrative could) and through space (for the Compsons the inner landscape obliterated everything outside). First-person consciousness once set on the road and made free to grow in time is no longer hermetic. Development is opened up by splitting the single monologue into small segments and ordering them in the time of the dying and the journey. First-person narratives of observers outside the family are introduced. The ordering of the segments is more crucial than the ordering in *The Sound and the Fury* but not as rigid. Division of each monologue into segments makes possible a complex order, not only of precedence and juxtaposition but also of outsider to insider, of alive to dead, of multiple one-to-one contrasts. This has not, of course, achieved freedom. That Faulkner refers to the novel as tour de force indicates that the temporary solution has imposed a new constriction, this time a constriction connected to his nervousness about artifice.

Sanctuary was undertaken, he said, to "boil a pot." Again Faulkner states a kind of truth, implying that he resorted to sensationalism to make some money when he was exploring the uses of sensationalism (and its freedoms) for its own sake. Feeling the constriction of subjective closeness, Faulkner tries the enforced distance of third-person narrative. But here distant does not mean objective. It is still wholly dependent upon consciousness, but a consciousness concealed: it is an exercise in the control of characters' self-revelation. Intrusion into point of view is strictly controlled. The treatment of consciousness is a perpetual tease without climax, without final answer. The book continually says more than it reveals and implies more than it says.

Faulkner here explores the Caddy side of things. She was "too beautiful and too moving" to speak. The aim of *Sanctuary* is to apply the pressure of circumstance and excessive, almost expressionistic atmosphere to bring forth just enough of the concealed world and no more. Some of the rendering devices are similar to those of the apprenticeship novels—visual extremes, extended expressions—but here nature, city, and town, like the concealed consciousness, are far more profound in enigma than they could be in explication. Sensationalism continually promises more than it delivers; what we eventually get is not exposé but revelation of a still deeper enigma. The whorehouse is revealed and we see its society and its rules to be more dependable and sensible than those of Horace's Jefferson. Yet Temple's imprisonment takes place within these laws and Popeye's powers are transferred from one set of laws to the next: enclave to whorehouse to dancehall. Calculated enigma is the aim; the result is enigma within enigma and nightmare upon nightmare.

Yet the narrative is freer here than in *The Sound and the Fury* or *As I Lay Dying*. Some of what Faulkner gains, though, in this freedom of the third person he must give up (again as in the apprenticeship novels) by virtue of traditional plotting, structure, and cross-cutting between one narrative line and another.

Light in August can be seen as a combination of part of the method of *As I Lay Dying* (the suspension between insider and outsider) and part of that of *Sanctuary*. Distance is manipulated more freely with a greater variety in third-person technique. We are given almost total objectivity or almost total mind-reading—here carried farther than in any of Faulkner's other novels in the modified first-person device which sets forth several layers of the unspoken, from the almost-spoken to the almost-unverbal. Because of this and the greater freedom of distance, the book's impact is more a result of participation in things shared with the characters than even the first-person books. This is something of a mystery because there are strong elements—in Joanna's autobiography, in what we are told of Percy Grimm, in some of the narrative presence's ambiguous renditions of Joe's actions—which resemble *Sanctuary*'s effects of concealed consciousness. There are some conventional suspense-structures and conventional plotting, but on the whole *Light in August* is certainly freer of these than *Sanctuary*. Faulkner has found a way to end the book before he sets out (as he had *As I Lay Dying*) but in Lena and Byron and in Hightower he has found an avenue of escape from the constriction of end-plotting in establishing what amounts to an anti-ending.

In *Light in August* elements of narrative discipline offer maximum pressure and elements of narrative freedom give maximum leeway. The inner sanction of pleasing himself here works best together with the external sanction of what a novel "should be" so that the result is the apparent effortlessness of self-justifying fiction. There is a freedom from the necessity of exposition in beginnings and string-pulling in ends. *Light in August,* perhaps more than any of the other novels, gives the impression of a self-willed narrative, establishing speed, rhythm, variety, and world on its own terms and to its own ends. It has confidence and independence from narrator's determination. Faulkner can move to his highest point of confidence and his most profound exploration of consciousness.

Absalom, Absalom! uses variant narrative distance and devices to a completely different end. It exaggerates distance by keeping the characters who provide the action at arm's length. Faulkner gains a double, if rather bizarre, freedom: the tellers, Quentin and Shreve, move to a level of perfect narrative freedom on which they are not even bound to respect facts given them by firsthand participants, and Faulkner gains not only this freedom from authorial responsibility but also the freedom they make available to him to change the course of the book midway, to develop the frame of the tellers into a fiction itself. The Sutpen line has a traditional plot, conventional suspense, and timed revelation; the Quentin line has a rather freer structure. It can run merrily along for half the book without looking as if it is a fiction at all but only a frame for another fiction. Again, there is a double ending: the book has one ending similar to that of *Light in August* or *As I Lay Dying,* ending where he intended it to end from the outset, in Sutpen's death and the lingering of his generations; the Quentin line ends simultaneously and brings to a climax Quentin's and Shreve's realization. Instead of *Light in August*'s anti-ending, there is a parallel and simultaneous open ending.

Go Down, Moses and *The Unvanquished* mark a breaking point between this phase of Faulkner's fiction and the third, and both represent attempts to escape from the dominance of structure and deep consciousness which were the hallmarks of the "main range" novels. Thematic focus and depth can be as constrictive, apparently, as subjective or technical entrapment. *Go Down, Moses* tries shortcuts, opting out of the complexities of *Absalom*'s narrative maelstrom by borrowing its themes without, in a sense, earning them, and opting out of the complex narrative a novel would need to earn these themes by substituting a loose interrelationship of stories, each with its own (sometimes rather complex but nevertheless simpler) structure. *The Unvanquished* pursues a different course toward freedom, the open, accessible action-narrative viewed by children, and the book almost miraculously frees itself of the burden of the past (in terms of guilt and inheritance) by dispensing with even the poetic sort of thematic shorthand of *Go Down, Moses.* A new premium is placed on the reader's demands for swift narrative (and the writer's relish for its directness and simplicity) and with this comes again the framework of traditional plotting and structure so comfortable for the reader and the abandonment of more complex experiments in which Faulkner pleased himself by craftsmanship.

But *The Unvanquished* does not define the third phase of Faulkner's fiction so much as it indicates (as *Go Down, Moses* does) a road not taken. If Faulkner had continued to pursue this simplistic return to the action narrative, then it might be legitimately said that in the third phase he was over the hill. But the Trilogy and *The Reivers* seem to me more a new beginning than a return to the old. They apparently move toward formlessness (as compared to the "main range"), so it is too easy to think that this deliberate shift in design represents the abandonment of form. But the form beneath the formlessness affords a better explanation of the fictions. I think the governing principle of this underlying form is plenitude. Faulkner wanted a shape into which anything would fit and he settled on two of the oldest shapes known: the "progress" or "rise and fall," and he set them at the center of not just the family chronicle of the Snopeses, but also a chronicle of the community's coming of age, from almost rural to almost urban. The two are interrelated: the chronicles provide evidence for the progress, the progress predetermines elements of the chronicles, but all are open structures, (at least until it comes to the problem of ending the Trilogy). With this rubric, openness is not just a lack of restraining structure. An aim of plenitude provides that everything attached to the structure is of equal relevance and that the structure can sustain the addition of any number of incidents or characters. For instance, the issue of narrative distance and intimacy of consciousness becomes irrelevant to the narrative of the Snopeses. Everything is in focus because there is no focus. Nothing is irrelevant once attached because its attachment to the chronicle (and its implications for the "progress") constitutes its relevance.

The principle of selection then must become liveliness, not relevance. Events, actions, characters, are included because they can carry their own weight, earn their own place, so as to attract our immediate interest and engage our attention. The central aim is to make the surface attraction uniformly engaging rather than to interconnect parts. A part cannot be made more attractive by its significance to the development of meaning, but must qualify itself for inclusion on its own merit. It is the kind of leisurely grace of meaning that Herodotus knew—that everything, true or false, comic or tragic, whether it fits some preconceived order of meaning or builds to some end or not, whether it leads to anything or follows upon anything, would be news to the reader and thus grist for the writer's mill.

The basic engagement of us as readers is the same as that for many of the short stories. We move into town and want to learn all we can and there are interpreters and reporters in plenty to tell us all they know. The order in which we learn things is a function of the openness of the narrative. Lineality and sequence replace connective interaction, and chronology replaces relative time. The narrative has all of the freedoms sought by *Light in August* (except perhaps that rather inhibiting freedom of total access to consciousness with none of its obligations).

This openness extends from narrative design to narrative technique. The aim of chronicle is to show how a story changes as it runs through time, the aim of a "progress" is to show how the subject changes, shifts, and develops. The static quality of the conventional teller of a "progress" (say, one like Cavendish's persona in his *Life of Wolsey*) becomes dynamic as the teller becomes an active learner, subjected to the same developmental time scheme and opportunity for change as the subject. It is difficult to gain insights into the subject of a "progress," so the teller's job becomes double—to find out and to reveal. We already share with the narrators the learner's role and we adopt the teller's role as we move faster or slower than the teller himself through the clues that he relays to us.

The difference between this arrangement and what Faulkner is doing as far along in his career as *Absalom* calls up the "natural" resources of the novelist: imagination, observation, and experience. All three are actuated by technique as it enables him to put these resources to practical and effective use. In performing his task, in creating the cosmos in which imagination, observation, and experience can have a free rein, he is something of a show-off. He must be a virtuoso of impersonation—in voice, in character, in verbal patterns—which call up shapes and parallels to exercise control of us, he must overreach human limits and in a godlike way pull events toward the end he has devised for them and make it seem an inexorable movement. As painter he must provide backdrops which fool us immediately and become an integral part of the world he has invented.

In *Absalom* Faulkner turns over impersonation and rendering and a part of the end-determination to characters, makes them the showoffs, while at the same time demonstrating that they are on rather uncertain ground—thus tipping the surrogate novelist's hand and pointing out the strings being pulled. In a way it is an endpoint for narrative. Once the tricks have been exposed, what act can follow?

In the Trilogy (especially *The Town*), Faulkner again makes the characters the showoffs, but the uncertainty of their ground is not of the novelist's world but of the world in which the characters find themselves. They don't know their story's outcome, so their pulling of it toward an end or an outcome keeps shifting constantly. They sometimes have an end in mind which, it turns out, just won't work. And then they have to go back and adjust their premises. They are not so safely removed from the realm of action as Quentin and Shreve are. A twist in the narrative can throw them off balance or (as in V. K.'s treasure-hunt) harm them directly.

The essential difference here is that Quentin and Shreve are presented as conscious artists of fiction, subject to the laws of the guild and willing—perhaps even too willing—to develop their narrative along the lines of a well-made fiction, creaking cogs and mechanisms, dark intents and conscious connections, cause and effect to the fore. Ratliff and the gallery-group and later Ratliff, Mallison, and Stevens are artists but accord themseves to the rules of fiction only insofar as the rules of fiction overlap the rules of anecdote and gossip.[2] But they are less conscious and have less freedom to invent and change and fool around because they are, for the most part, in the immediate presence of the events, with the outcome unknown and with themselves frequently cast as instigators, detectives, motivators, victims, or spear-carriers, and their narrative must adapt (and frequently adapt in sudden jumps) as the events dictate.

This difference could be inadequately and mistakenly dealt with by comparing the artificiality of the substance of *Absalom* with the realism of the substance of the Trilogy. An analogy, faulty as analogies tend to be, perhaps comes closer. *Hedda Gabler* and *Breathless* (or *Jules and Jim*) are similar in the sense that both are performed in order to realize their potential. One is a well-made play, the others *nouvelle vague* films. The essential difference between them is their differing attitudes toward narrative. *Hedda* pleases itself (and pre-

2. In *The Mansion,* this is carried a bit farther in the direction of the rules of formal fiction.

sumably Ibsen and even sometimes us) by playing according to the rules, setting up the dueling pistols and firing them in order, bringing all the right people together at the right time and keeping the wrong people out of the room at the right time, treading the line of fortuitous circumstance which permits all its designed parts to function together in a timed sequence so it can do what it is designed to do: bring Hedda to a crisis, say something more general (about a woman or women or men and women or people or society or something) and manipulate us in our expectations, satisfactions, and discoveries so that we come to a point of understanding, in a development which roughly approximates Hedda's development in the course of the play. The play is end-determined—not just in that Ibsen knew what the end would be and aimed for it, but in the way in which almost everything is calculated to lead to this end. It is end-plotted: pieces fit adjacent pieces and serve the development of the advance to the end. The characters take on importance in respect to their function in moving Hedda: important characters put pressure on her, trigger her decisions; less important ones deliver messages to her, let her know what she has to know when she needs to know it, or come in so that she may tell them or imply what she thinks just when we as audience need to know it. Dialogue is directed at these pressures, triggers, and timed sequences of information. She remains something of an enigma in that all of this, through the predetermination of literary artifice, is calculated to reveal to us an enigma of a woman for our contemplation or pity or terror. There is, in other words, a literary effect that is not predetermined or foreordained, but everything surrounding it *is* predetermined. Our pleasure is in this enigma and our secondary pleasure in watching the dueling pistols go off on schedule, seeing the cogs turn, hearing all the doors shut on her escape. It was designed to do just that and it does it. Its ambiguities are calculated ambiguities and its certainties arranged certainties.

Breathless makes a virtue of accident where *Hedda* made a virtue of arranged circumstance. *Jules and Jim* deals in the sequence of unconnected incident rather than the interaction of connected events. It is end-determined in that its aim is to show a progress, a change or development in time, but it is not end-plotted. Ambiguity occurs not just in its end or its central characters, but in all the events which lead to that end, as side-effects of the disconnection or ellipsis between one event and the next. Certainty is a function of the character's consistency and the immediately engaging qualities of the incident or the immediate intrigue of unexplained ellipsis as we perceive it flashing before us, rather than being the calculated product of the timed revelation of end-determined hints. The product is what is put together from what has been shot of a given sequence of events—ellipses and accidents become a part of the aesthetic. *Hedda* calculates and predicts what our response will be at a given moment in a calculated structure of expectation and revelation.

The analogy is overstated, of course. *Hedda* is subject to accident of performance and interpretation even as *Breathless* is subject to the rather more complex precalculation of juxtaposition, angle, and rhythm. But it is overstatement, I think, to the point. Faulkner was a screenwriter and we perhaps take him too much at his word when he says that all he got out of it was the money. *The Big Sleep* (and I recognize the quicksand which lies before me as to who did what and with which and to whom when it comes to the artistic contributions to a film) was described by Howard Hawks as a plot-ridden mishmash—perhaps too well made to be understood. He has said in interview that he realized if he could retain the impossible complexities of the plot in its transferral to the screen ("Neither the author, the writer, nor myself knew who had killed whom") [3] he would have a successful picture. Whoever was responsible, they did it.

The point is that the extreme of plottiness comes close to becoming the accessibility of open structure. Once the plot is impossible to follow, the connections impossible to make, the viewer or reader is thrown back to surface attractions. As in the "Was" poker game, impossibility of understanding lends a fascination to the surface. Between the suspense-omission of the opening and the centrality of the impossibly complex wagers, the reader retreats to the surface: it's "a real good chase" and perhaps he can come to understand the bets the next time around. In the case of *The Big Sleep* every little movement has a meaning all its own, but an immediate meaning and not one that can be carried over into a reading of a motivation or an obscure connection to the ultimate solution of the events or

3. Peter Bogdanovich, "Howard Hawks," Museum of Modern Art monograph, 1962.

the prediction of an outcome. Bogart getting into a car or walking down a corridor eventually becomes as important as the plot developments because of the split between visual events we can follow and verbal events we cannot. The essence of the film, then, is very similar to the essence of the Trilogy, the continual entertainment of the surface, the delight in the immediate rendition of what's happening, our synchronous involvement (not far removed from the child's delight at the burning of the church in "Shingles for the Lord") in what's happening right now, seen through the eyes of fiction-makers as confused as we but apparently responsible for judgment, narration, suspension, creation. It does not need the outside sanction of relevance to a greater end or greater point or greater effect to excuse it: simply that it is happening is its justification.

The narrative can support any digression because of the nature of the town's curiosity and the nature of Flem—anything that happens ultimately leads back to (or is thought by them to lead back to) Flem. Once everything is relevant, anything is as important as anything else. Since the "progress" of Flem is measured in footprints and shaking bushes—development which takes place outside the consciousness—there is no need for a firm hold on the principal or his consciousness. The freedom is threefold and corresponds to the three elements Faulkner tried to keep in balance. In an escape from end-plotted narrative he found a new way to satisfy the expectations and demands of the readers without resorting, as in *Sanctuary,* to the slavery of nineteenth-century plottiness. In a new concentration on community, familial and individual consciousness, he does justice to the subject and escapes from the hermetic enclosure of deep consciousness (another way of describing the retreat to the surface) just as he is breaking out of the narrative restrictions of experimental storytelling into the direct narrative. He satisfies himself in a new sort of craftsmanship—predominantly a progress sequence rather than a design to fit a given end—and the somewhat less technical narrative challenge of a design which depends on perpetual invention. If freedom is what he was after (and I think it was), he found it.

For the sake of definition I have overvalued the engagement of our senses and intelligence in the surface and too much devalued distant significance and the power of an end-determined pattern. All this distortion of literary values can appear to be nothing much more than a salvage operation: to praise the minimal qualities of the

Trilogy after demonstrating the formal complexity of something like *Absalom* or perceiving the psychological and human depth of *The Sound and the Fury* or *As I Lay Dying* can be parlously close to an effort to cheer up the left hand by praising the right. And it might be, were Faulkner's career a strictly linear development. But, like *Absalom* itself, his career is as much a layered series of simultaneous levels as it is a progression or sequence. Any level of concern may rise to the surface at any point. And everything he learns or tries is available at any point. The short stories of the late twenties and early thirties establish the areas of his substantive and technical exploration in fiction and all the concerns reflected there continue to be simultaneously present in the roughly chronological periods of development which follow. Technical, structural, and thematic hallmarks of one or another central concern come to the fore in a fairly systematic way, but he is at work on *Light in August* as he develops *The Unvanquished,* he completes *The Hamlet* as *Go Down, Moses* is developing, he completes the Trilogy while deep in *A Fable. The Wild Palms, Pylon,* and *Knight's Gambit* don't fit in a categorical scheme if taken at their chronological position.

But the accepted description of Faulkner's career continues to be Cowley's: more "planks . . . cut, not from a log, but from a still living tree," [4] the completion of the organic unity of Faulkner's legend, the exercise of epic-filling, chronicle, the continuing effort to flesh out the County and make the canon whole. A corollary to this, implied by the phrase "main range," is that he took up busywork once the experiments in consciousness reached their natural end in *Absalom, Absalom!* Certainly Faulkner had fears that he was later in his career becoming "burnt-out":

> The last thing any writer will admit to himself is that he has scraped the bottom of the barrel and that he should quit. I don't quite believe that's true yet. But it's probably not tiredness, it's the fact that you shouldn't put off too long writing something which you think is worth writing, and this I have had in mind for thirty years now. [*Univ.,* p. 107]

"This" was the Snopes Trilogy. The bigness of the chronicle would make it, naturally, something he might want to leave for later leisure, and the action of filling in, filling out, completing, is the arche-

4. *The Portable Faulkner* (New York: Viking, 1946), p. 8.

typal movement of the tired writer. Faulkner regretted (in the Cowley letters and interviews) that *The Portable Faulkner* had come along when it did: "I planned to get out a book like that myself some day, when I was all written out" (*Lion,* p. 60). That so many shorter pieces turn up again in this phase, warmed over and recast in the Trilogy, that he put together *Big Woods* mostly out of spare parts lends credence to an argument for decline.

But fear of decline seems to satisfy the evidence better than decline itself. He had certainly returned to an earlier manner of narrative; he had clearly given over the complicated technical striving and complex exploration of consciousness; he was not as angry, and apparently was quite content to write books that stated ideas (*Intruder in the Dust*) rather than embodying them in "flesh-and-blood" people. But "burnt-out" is an adjective that should not be applied lightly—for instance, just because later books seem different from earlier, or because their writer seems at the time more concerned with his whole cosmos than with the individual technical experiment of the moment.

There is a somewhat obscure comment on this in an earlier statement about style: that in his earlier career he had too much "pushing inside him to get out . . . to bother with style" (*Univ.,* p. 77). The "too much" might be seen as the experiments with consciousness and technique rather than, as the statement would have it, what he had to say about the agony of man. There is a rather plaintive element in another statement:

> I don't say that style is not important, there are people to whom style is very important—Walter Pater, for instance. . . . But there are other people that are too busy writing about men and women, human beings, the human heart in conflict with its self, with its fellows, or with its environment, to have time to bother with style. I wish that that were not so. I wish that I did have a good, lucid, simple method of telling stories. [*Univ.,* p. 88]

A conscious return to the narrative method of the short stories is an attempt to get at what he here terms a "good, lucid, simple method," and the statement as a whole implies a period of openness in which he could afford to reflect and consolidate. He knew narrative was what he could do, but he was not necessarily doing just straightforward narrative. Beyond saga-completion and canon-filling the novels of the third phase embody a more subtle exploration of the aims and uses of narrative for its own sake, the giving over of experiment in consciousness and technique, the examination of guilt, time, and expiation, in order to pursue the mysteries of telling, knowing, and event, the mysteries of the storyteller.

No one can call *The Hamlet* a book of clichés either in substance or method. A writer too busy with innovation to bother about style is also, apparently, a writer too accustomed to innovation to abandon it. The Trilogy and *The Reivers* introduce new aims, new combinations, a totally new structure of plenitude, and, I think, a sense of the fictional world which represent a revolutionary change in narrative.

But insofar as two totally unlike entities can be compared, it is apparent to any sensible reader that the Trilogy and *The Reivers* are not as "good" as *The Sound and The Fury, As I Lay Dying, Light in August,* or even *Absalom, Absalom!* But this again is not so much a question of the comparative achievement of one group or the other as it is a question of the length of time available to Faulkner to develop the earlier strain and the prejudicial hangover in us of long-standing habits of judging fictional quality according to conventional narrative models. Recall for a moment Faulkner's generic standards from the interviews. The narrowest, that for the short story, is impossibly perfectionist because of the high premium he places on condensation. That for the novel operates on an exclusionist principle of coherence and self-consistency. All of Faulkner's stated generic standards are judgments based upon condensation. My point is simply that, while he was working in the "main range" and in the early short stories, he was striving and judging himself against deeply held and deeply felt objective and almost arbitrary standards; while working in the newer open narrative he was judging himself by assumptions about his readers. In both areas he sometimes judged aright. But in the former he did not even know that his standards were impossible. His achievements, thus, self-judged, were on a measurable scale. For the latter he could never know, and his self-measurement was necessarily impressionistic and relativistic. The habitual underpinnings of relevance and condensation were denied and all he then had to go on was his guess about his readers, the engaging qualities of the immediate surface narrative and his taste in selection, arrangement, and the balance of severity and excess. Seen this way the change in direction was an act of courage and constituted a remarkable achievement in guessing right so often and making his balance so true.

The tension between artificial craftsman and natural storyteller also had a substantive parallel, never directly related, but of a corresponding opposition. Of Faulkner's most constant themes—inheritance, possession, guilt—the strongest perhaps are those of isolation and community. The two run throughout the canon, frequently opposed to each other, as I have indicated in the several discussions of *us* and *them*.

The completion of this pattern by the later work might best be exemplified by contrasting some characters: say, Emily Grierson and V. K. Ratliff. There is an apparent sociological contrast—isolation seems to run to the upper classes, community to the lower—but this is not by any means an absolute. But the sociological is far less significant than the contrast in narrative approach. If Caddy is set beside Emily and Lucius Priest beside V. K., perhaps the point is clearer. The contrast defines opposite poles, the isolated individual and the representative of community, the laconic and the chatty, the doomed woman and the child. Caddy was "too moving" to tell the story of the Compsons in her own voice; so is the older Drusilla, young Bayard (of World War I), Temple, Popeye, Charlotte Rittenmeyer, Elly, Minnie Cooper, Nancy in "That Evening Sun." All are isolated, set aside by their community or themselves, alone. The narrative may find its aim in concern for one of them, or find its center in his consciousness, but it treats all of them as *other*. Concern for *them* reaches an apex in *Light in August* as Faulkner's series of experiments in the revelation of consciousness reaches its high point. Individuals, of course, vary, but the lonely, the lost, the doomed, the gothic grotesque, the recluse, the pariah, the self-center of Addie Bundren—each dwells in his loneliness unviolated by the crowds that surround him. The community representative varies, too: V. K., Chick, Gavin, to a certain extent Horace Benbow in *Sanctuary,* Miss Reba in *The Reivers,* Quentin and Shreve in *Absalom,* Bayard and Ringo in *The Unvanquished.*

The lonely ones tend to be aberrations: they demonstrate by how they differ from us what we share in common with them. The community-figures are norms: in their resemblance to us they demonstrate our desire to depart from their norms. As I have suggested, the isolated ones are not good tellers. In their mouths first-person narrative is distorted (as in *The Sound and the Fury,* parts 1 and 2) or fragmentary and poetic (as in *As I Lay Dying*). Third-person narrative takes on elaborate complication and involution in an attempt to deal with their isolation. The community figures are natural Tellers; telling is a part of the norm they represent, telling about the isolated ones is self-protective for them, as well as a part of their identity, their currency, and frequently their power. Our adoption of the norm they establish, our adaptation of ourselves to their way of seeing things, is the aim of their telling, and it follows that this adoption, adaptation, or the norm itself constitutes a threat to our individuality. What we hold in common with them of group ideal, misconception, myth—or more important, what they *cause us* to hold in common with them—constitutes a failure of our individual uniqueness.

When we find that we have a common cause with the isolated, it is a surprise, and it has been arrived at by covert narrative calculation. When we find we have a common cause with the community-figures, we have arrived at what we expected to arrive at all along, and it has been accomplished overtly. It is difficult to assign the child-narrator to either pole, but I suspect he belongs more easily with the builders of the norm: our identification with him is sure, ingrown, immediate; its appeal is overt. If we fail to identify directly with a child telling a story it is exceptional. Vardaman Bundren is an example to the contrary, demonstrating the possibilities for isolated children.

But either identification we make, whether with isolated loneliness or gregarious community-yarnspinner, is accomplished by means of conventional devices and narrative appeals, the manipulation of our *us*ness and *them*ness from moment to moment by the identifications, rhythms, and shapes of the narrative at hand.

A necessary part of the "particular corner" or the "urn or shape," then, is the calculation of this allegiance. Faulkner is careful of the relationship between the fiction and the reader's empathy not just because he respects narrative craftsmanship but because this abiding interest in the poles of loneliness and community demand narrative calculation: meaning, theme, and nuance are part and parcel of the means of conveying them. Telling is here not just the manner or the form or timing of a story but a part of its import. To group Faulkner with the legion of twentieth-century artists pursuing the themes of alienation and dislocation is true enough, but it is only half of the truth. He is at the same time pursuing a theme of community, perhaps not as determinedly domestic or familial as that of Dickens, nor so organized as Mann's *Buddenbrooks* or Cheever's *Wapshot*. But community is the pole at which he ends his swing, and as such it is a necessary completion rather than a simple relaxation or denial of what has gone before.

In the course of the career, family and individual consciousness give way to the community and the community becomes a replica of society. With the dominance of community comes gossip, no longer allied (as in *Sanctuary* and *Light in August*) with the forces of the lynch mob and group fear, but here at the center of the narrative, the instrument of empathy, binding us as readers to the *us* of the town. The observer, the group, the big picture, the *us* have taken over center stage. There are still isolated characters, but they are no longer the chief targets of our empathy; they have become more clearly *them*. The lost woman, for instance, survives, still a victim of repression and an icon of compulsion, but here she plays out her role to a chorus of gossips and chroniclers, for the edification and terror of the community.

These two matters—the tension between artifice and storyteller and the pendulum between the isolated individual and the community—contain, I suppose, the crux of my impatience with Cowley's scheme of the "still-living-tree." He praised Faulkner for far less than he had accomplished. Faulkner was an artist of powerful American substance and variety, but he accomplished this substance, this County, this epic at the same time that he was pursuing a personal search of continual formal, structural, and philosophical narrative experiment. The means are more remarkable, at least in American letters, than the ends. Yoknapatawpha is rich, amazing, rewarding, full, but the greater amazement is that the stories and novels that make it up are each so satisfying a completion of their own premises, fulfillments of their own designs, and that together they develop from one to the next through such a variety of theme and substance with such clear continuity of narrative aim, variant method, and experiment. This must precede, in our admiration, the fact that most of Faulkner's writings, when all piled together, make one big book.

A writer's aim or his theory or his development, in any event, is of use only as it can demonstrate its aptness to the work, not as it can explain it. Its failure to explain or encompass the totality of what the work accomplishes is the proof that literature lies beyond theory, criticism, or career. The use of theory or shape is found in the explication it can offer of premises, not results. Unlike the "particular corner" Faulkner builds in fiction, which can suspend a moment and capture meaning, the particular corner of the critic can prove little beyond whether it is well-designed or ill-made. Even Faulkner's fragmentary theory is not much better. It is good only in that is can tell us clearly that he cannot tell us what he made.

Appendix A–Narrative Structure of *As I Lay Dying*

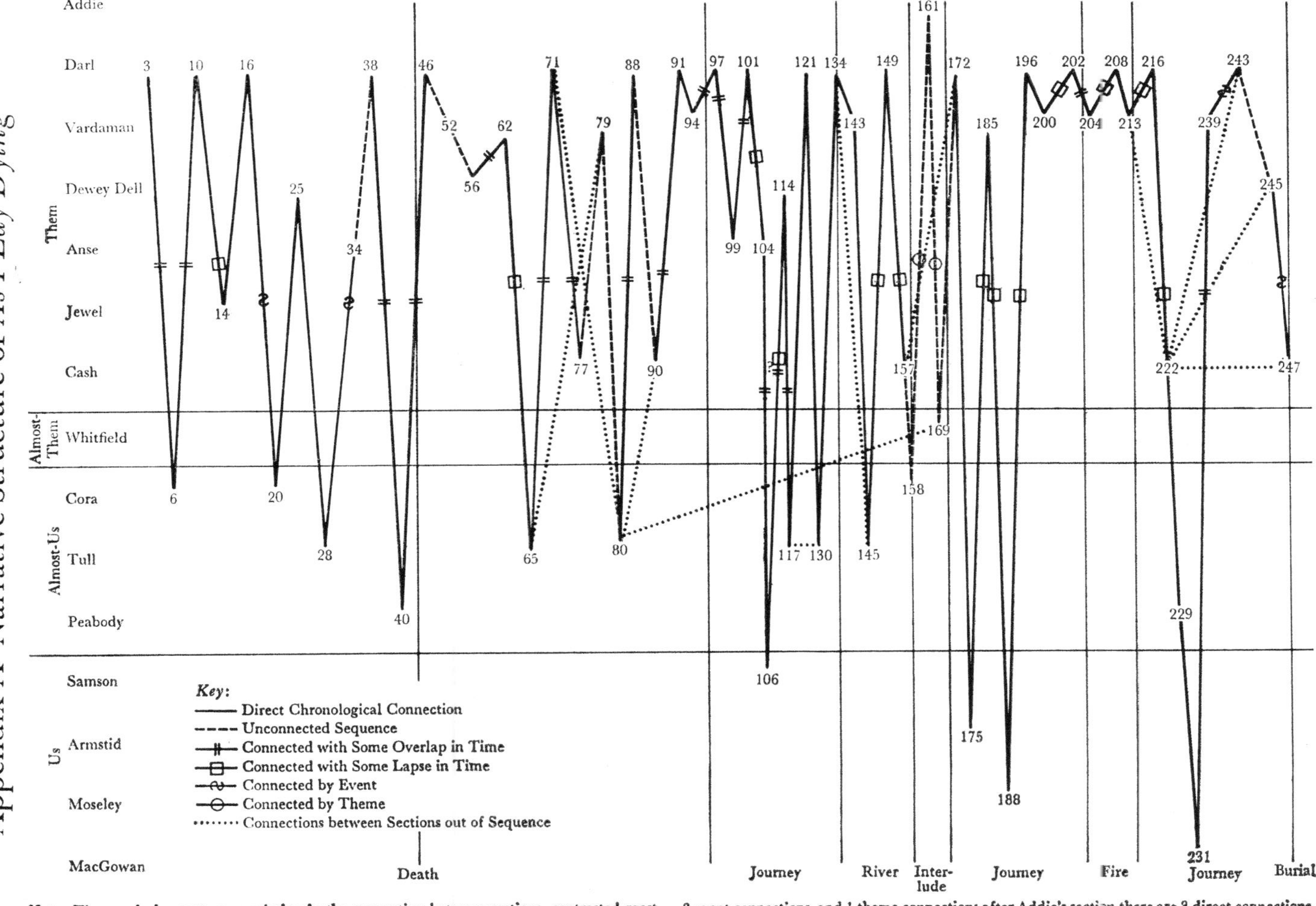

Note: The graph demonstrates variation in the connection between sections, contrasted most strongly by a comparison of the sections before Addie's section and those sections which follow: before Addie's section there are 8 direct connections, 5 unconnected, 16 overlaps, 4 time lapses, 3 event connections, and 1 theme connection; after Addie's section there are 3 direct connections, 3 unconnected, 2 overlaps, 7 time lapses, 2 event connections, and 1 theme connection.

Appendix B *Light in August*: Progressive Cognition

Needless to say, of the 322 patterns of sequential cognition appearing in *Light in August* (comprising a total of 815 thinking, believing, remembering, knowing, saying verbs), those cited in chapter 6 are very simple examples. The complexity of the patterns varies from a single "thinking" to combinations which can run up to a sequence of ten verbs (*Light,* p. 225). All of my tabulations are based on a reading record which would surely be corrected by a systematic concordance, which I hope someone or some machine is preparing.

I expected to find a clear differentiation between one character's thought patterns and another's. A systematic examination of the progression from level to level of thought within each sequence would yet, I suspect, reveal differences between one character's thought and another's, even as a careful stylistic analysis of the statements of these thoughts certainly would. But beyond increasing complication and frequency of the device as the book proceeds (there are four "thinking" patterns in the last ten chapters for every three in the first eleven chapters), and an increase in the use of the device at particular points of crisis (Joe has 74 such verbs in chapter 8, the encounter with Bobbie, 106 in chapter 12, in which he kills Joanna; Byron has 78 in chapter 17, the pursuit of Brown; Hightower 70 in chapter 20), there is not much that can be said about any individual character's consistency. Progressive cognition is used for Joe's consciousness in 17 chapters, for Byron's in 9, for Hightower's in 6, and for Lena's in 8. Instances which involve "thinking" are employed for Joe 162 times (392 verbs in all), for Byron 40 times (195 verbs), for Hightower 72 times (146 verbs), and for Lena 5 times (7 verbs). Comparison between Byron and Hightower shows, I think, a distinction between the occasions each has for ventures into consciousness: Byron's "thinking," more frequent, seems to go deeper; Hightower's, less intense, is a more continuous process.

An analysis of the verbs other than "thinking" demonstrates a similar pattern.

	Byron	Hightower	Joe
believe	6	1	28
know	13	4	35
remember	4	3	13

This narrative device enforces the way in which the past determines the present in the book, as the frequency of such verbal patterns laid out in a chart according to chapters demonstrates:

Chapter	1	2	3	4	5	6	7	8	9	10	11	12	13	14	15	16	17	18	19	20	21
Joe					28	36	17	74	27	34	43	106		27							
Byron		19	12	4									27			9	78	46			
Hightower		1		2									31			12	30			70	
Lena	24																	3			

Descents into the past for Christmas (chaps. 5–12) and Hightower (chap. 20) make patterns of progressive cognition of their conventional narrative for such segments, while for Byron the pressure of the present in the birth of Lena's baby and the pursuit of Brown have this effect. In all three cases character revelation is not limited to the end-result or logical conclusion each arrives at, but this self-realization is seen in the light of the specific process of thinking, knowing, remembering, believing that brought him to this point. This includes what each believes without knowing, why and what each once "knew" but has now forgotten in the pressure of new thinking, knowing, or believing.

There is a further complication, too. Even as (in *As I Lay Dying*) Darl's questions of essence (or *is*) are sometimes resolved by considerations of *is-not,* Joe's "thinking," "knowing," and "believing" are not just the product of complex combinations with other verbs ("thinks . . . thinking . . . believing," "thinking . . . believes . . . believes," "thinking . . . says . . . thinking," "thinks . . . remembers"), but of combinations of "not-thinking" (23 instances, all Joe's), "not-believing" (10 instances, 6 of them Joe's), and "not knowing" (27 instances, 14 Joe's).

Appendix C–*Absalom, Absalom!*

My assumptions about *Absalom, Absalom!* at the outset were impressionistic, and in order to substantiate or disprove them, I undertook a systematic study of the imagery. I began by abstracting the metaphors of the book (as far as this was possible) on cards. I then noted the metaphors by location in the book, by subject of the tenor and by subject of the vehicle. Thus a single metaphor could appear as only two points or as many as eight or ten points on the record, depending on the number of characters or subjects covered in the tenor and the breadth of possible subject interpretation in the vehicle.

Metaphor, especially the metaphor of this book, is not reducible to chart or graph. The images are usually inextricably mingled and it is almost impossible to find what one could surely call a "single" metaphor. Take, for example, the extended metaphor analyzed in chapter 7, note 3. To deal with such complexity in fully analytical form would be to construct a text far longer than *Absalom, Absalom!* itself. The rather simple formula I used permits some charting of the incidence of metaphor and a rather accurate guide to metaphorical density, perhaps the most useful information that emerged from the study, aside from the sense of metaphorical movement that I tried to trace in the chapter itself.

Chart 1–Chronological Structure of *Absalom, Absalom!*

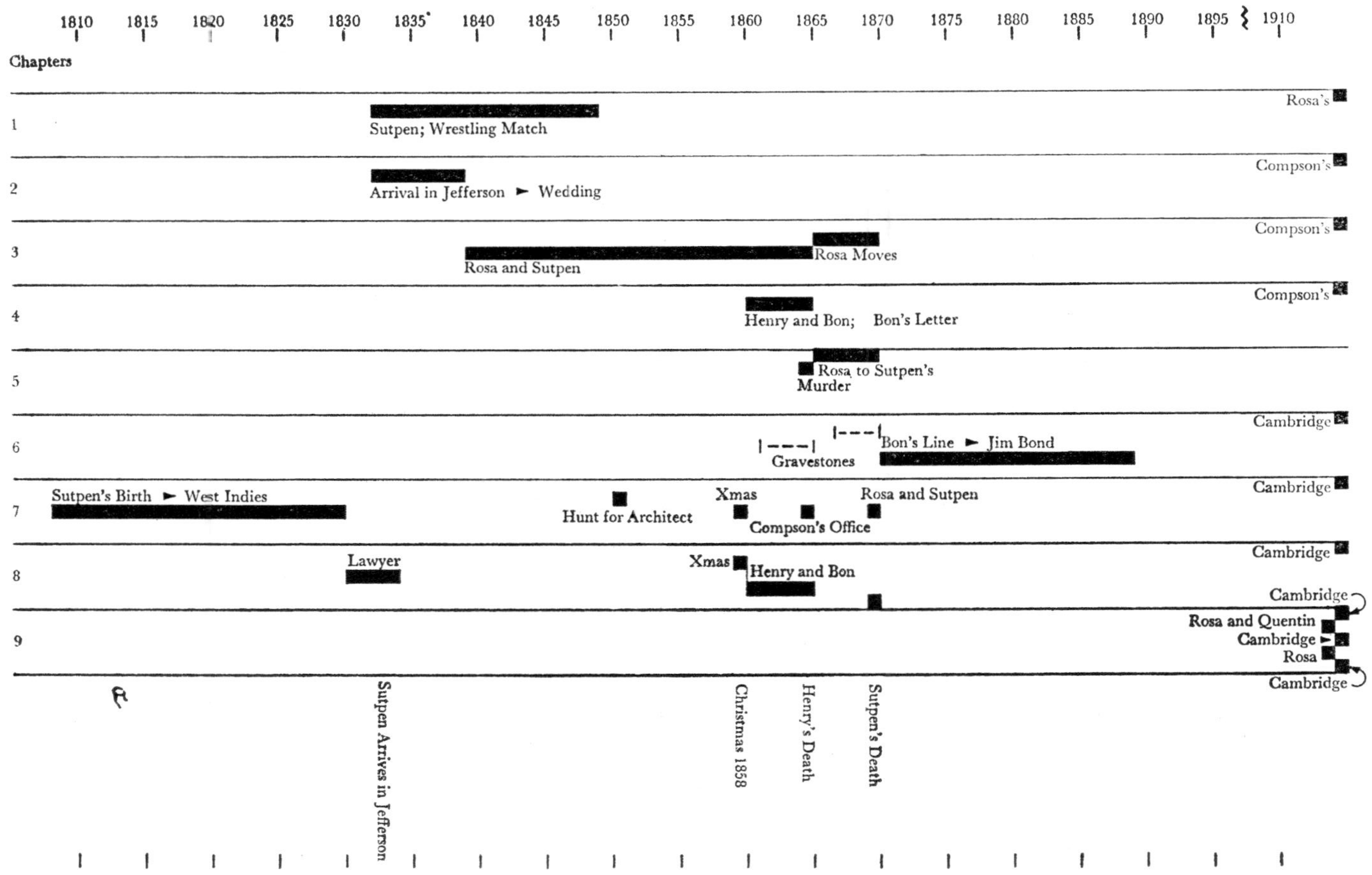

Chart 2–Density of Imagery in *Absalom, Absalom!*

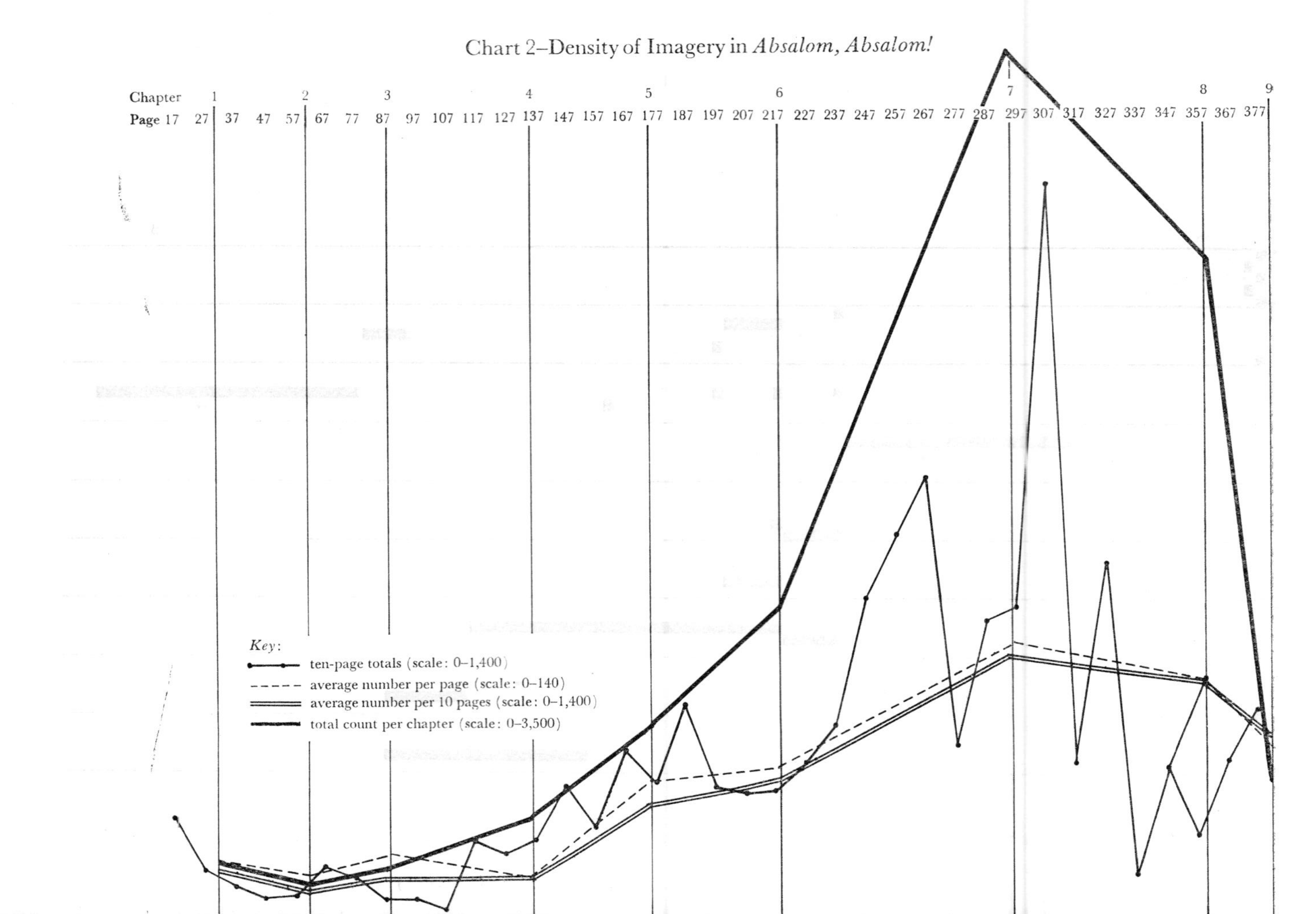

Index

Page numbers in italic indicate primary discussions of particular works.

Absalom, Absalom! 12, 20–21, 29, 118, *145–75*, 176–78, 185–87, 194, 199, 207–08, 211, 221, 225, 233, 240, 243–44, 252, 258, 262, 267–68, 270–71, 275, 277–78; Civil War in, 18, 183; as expository novel, 150; the South in, 146
action. *See* Narr. action
Adams, Nick, 23
Aeschylus, 55
"Afternoon of a Cow." See *Hamlet, The*
Albee, Edward, 14
Aldrich, Thomas Bailey, 39–40
Aleck Sander (*Intruder*), 207
allegory, 69, 259; in *Fable,* 213; in *GDM,* 196; in *Hamlet,* 238
American Dream, 146, 158
American literature, 34, 228, 258, 280
American Myth: Regeneration through Violence (Richard S. Slotkin), 62*n*
Ames, Dalton, 78
Anderson, Sherwood, 259
Anne ("Artist at Home"), 41
Appleton, Victor, *Tom Swift and his Electric Runabout,* 251
Arcadia, 68
archetype(s), 38; in *Absalom,* 168; in *Hamlet,* 233; in *Light,* 130–31, 134, 141; in "A Rose for Emily," 215
Armstid, Henry, 87–88, 121, 123, 134, 143, 231, 234, 238–39
Armstid, Martha, 121
Armstids, the, 228, 234
Arnold, Matthew, 239, 262
artifice. *See* Narr. artifice
"Artist at Home," 41–43, 55
As I Lay Dying, 7, 48, 58, 75, 80, *84–113,* 121, 134, 139, 144, 146, 151, 175, 176, 180, 199, 225, 235, 239–40, 244, 246–47, 260–62, 265–68, 275, 277, 279; time-scheme in, 113; as tour de force, 84–85; verticals and horizontals in, 102–04, 106–07
Atelier Monty, 230
atmosphere: in "Dry September," 191; in *Hamlet,* 232; in *Sanct.,* 266
Auden, W. H., 83
Austen, Jane, 142

Backus, Melisandre, 234
"Barn Burning," 43–46, 50, 55, 98, 121, 205
Barron, Homer, 15–16, 18, 227
"Bartleby the Scrivener" (Herman Melville), 262
Bascomb, Maury, 76
Basket, Herman, 22, 47
"Bear, The." See *Go Down, Moses*
"Bear Hunt, A," 24–26, 34, 63, 135
Beauchamp, Hubert, 187
Beauchamp, Lucas, 23, 177–78, 188–90, 195, 198, 205, 210, 252, 256; as Uncle Tom, 202
Beauchamp, Molly, 190, 197–98, 205
Beauchamp, Samuel Worsham, 197–98, 256, 262

Beauchamp, Miss Sophonsiba, 187
Benbow, Horace, 60, 64–66, 70–72, 115, 266, 278
Benbow, Narcissa, 71
Bible. *See* King James Version of the Bible; *Go Down, Moses*
Big Sleep, The, 273
"Big Two-Hearted River" (Ernest Hemingway), 191
Big Woods, 73, 186, 276
Blackmur, R. P., 55–56
blacks, as slaves, 18, 31, 33, 154, 167, 182–84, 198–99, 204–05, 211–12
black bodyservant ("Red Leaves"), 47–48, 55, 61
black revolution, 198
Bland, Gerald (*S & F*), 78
Blotner, Joseph L. See *Faulkner in the University*
Bobbie (*Light*), 114, 120, 130
Bobolink, 184
Bogard, Capt. H. S., 26
Bogart, Humphrey, 273–74
Bon, Charles, 21, 145, 148–49, 151*n,* 153, 154*n,* 157–58, 162, 166–67, 169–70, 173
Bon, Eulalia, 158, 169
Bond, Jim, 154
Bookwright, Odum, 228, 234
Bookwrights, the, 228
Boswell, James, 5*n,* 49
"box-building." *See* Craftsmanship, carpentry metaphor for
Brand Pluck'd out of the Burning, A, (Cotton Mather), 62*n*
Breathless, 271–73
"Brooch, The," 56
Brooks, Cleanth, 15*n*
Brown. *See* Burch, Lucas
Brown, Clarence, 49, 208
Browning, Robert, 48
Buddenbrooks (Thomas Mann), 280
Bull Run, 180
Bunch, Byron, 73, 115–19, 121, 123–28, 133, 135, 137, 139–42, 144, 233, 263, 267
Bundren, Addie, 11, 85–87, 89–91, 93–98, 100–10, 145, 195, 197, 244, 262, 278
Bundren, Anse, 90–95, 97–98, 100, 102–03, 105–10
Bundren, Cash, 7, 84, 86–88, 90–98, 100–03, 105–09, 196, 220, 261
Bundren, Darl, 20, 40, 84–110, 113, 123, 128, 139, 151, 244, 246, 260, 262
Bundren, Dewey Dell, 84, 86, 88, 91, 92–97, 99–105, 107–10
Bundren, Jewel, 84–85, 88, 91–99, 103–05, 107–08
Bundren, Mrs., 103
Bundren, Vardaman, 34, 38, 84–89, 92–96, 99, 101, 103–05, 107, 109, 195, 279
Bundrens, the, 20, 80, 84–88, 92, 97, 99, 103, 106–07, 110, 114, 134, 239, 260, 265
Burch, Lucas, 116–17, 120, 122–23, 125, 135, 143, 220
Burden, Joanna, 113–14, 118–20, 129–33, 135–37, 233, 267
Burden House, 116, 118, 224
Burdens, the, 113–14, 133
Burr, G. L., 62*n*
Byron, George Gordon, Lord, 2, 215

Caldwell, Erskine, 59
Calvinism, 119–20
Candyman (film of *Sanct.*), 61
Carlyle, Thomas, 5
Carroll, Lewis, 180
Cartier-Bresson, Henri, 1, 259
Cassandra, 15
Cavendish, George, *Life of Wolsey,* 270
"Centaur in Brass," 23
character(s), 1, 3–4, 7, 9–10, 14, 21, 24, 40
  in Faulkner's fiction, 4, 16, 202, 204, 215–16, 261, 263–65, 270–71, 276, 278
  in *Absalom,* 145, 147, 150–52, 154, 159–60, 167, 169, 172–73, 243
  in *As I,* 84–86, 89, 94, 100
  in "Dry September," 54
  in *Fable,* 212
  in *GDM,* 186–87, 195, 200
  in *Hamlet,* 220, 224, 231–32, 236, 244
  in *Intruder,* 204, 207

in *Light,* 112–13, 115, 117–20, 133, 140, 142–44, 224
in *Mansion,* 252
in "Red Leaves," 212
in *Reivers,* 217
in "A Rose for Emily," 15, 19
in Sanct., 58, 72–73
in *S & F,* 75
in *Town,* 245–46, 256, 271
in the Trilogy, 250–51
Chaucer, Geoffrey, 81
Cheever, John, 280
Chekhov, Anton, 9
Childe Harold, 82
child(ren) in Faulkner's fiction, 3, 31–32, 34–41, 43–46, 180, 279
in *Absalom,* 156, 161
in *GDM,* 38–40, 42, 187–89, 191–92, 200
in *Intruder,* 207
in "Shall Not Perish," 36–37
in "Shingles for the Lord," 37
in "That Evening Sun," 32–34
in *Town,* 241
in "Two Soldiers," 37
in *Unvanq.,* 176, 179–81, 183–84, 188
Christ, 142, 260
Christmas, 35, 77, 181
Christmas, Joe, 20–21, 38, 113–25, 127–35, 139–44, 166, 188, 190, 205, 215, 249, 252, 254, 262, 267
chronology, time-scheme, time-disjunction, 9, 261–63, 270, 272, 275
in *Absalom,* 145, 147–50, 157, 159–61, 177
in *As I,* 85, 87, 90*n,* 104–06
in "Barn Burning," 43–45, 203–04
in *Fable,* 212
in *GDM,* 46, 177, 181, 186, 189, 197
in *Intruder,* 203–05, 207
in "A Justice," 29
in *Light,* 112–18, 121–23, 125, 128–29, 132–33, 141–43
in *Reivers,* 178
in "A Rose for Emily," 14–15, 19
in *Sanct.,* 59, 115
in *S & F,* 76–77, 82
in *Town,* 245, 247
in *Unvanq.,* 177–78, 182
cinema, cinematic. *See* Film
city, the, in *Sanct.,* 69
Civil War, 152–54, 183–84. *See also* Bull Run; Faulkner, William; Manassas
Clarissa (Samuel Richardson), 75
climax, 13, 18, 25
in *Absalom,* 148–49
in *Light,* 143
in "A Rose for Emily," 14
in *Sanct.,* 60, 266
coherence, cohesion, 9, 265
in *Absalom,* 147, 150
in *GDM,* 186, 195
in *Hamlet,* 239
in *Light,* 123
in *Town,* 244
in the Trilogy, 249
Coke, Sir Edward, 183
Coldfield, Ellen, 145, 148, 154, 162
Coldfield, Goodhue, 148
Coldfield, Rosa, 24–25, 147–50, 152–54, 156–65, 168–69, 171, 173, 242, 251
Collected Short Stories of William Faulkner, 12–57, 121, 174
comedy, comic, 65, 219
in *As I,* 85, 88–89, 94, 97
in *Hamlet,* 222–23, 225–27, 231; structure 220, 226, 228, 234–37
in *Light,* 124–25
in *S & F,* 78, 83
in "That Will Be Fine," 35
in *Town,* 244
in the Trilogy, 259
community, town, 15, 278–80
in *Absalom,* 162
in "Dry September," 51, 54
in *GDM,* 198
in "Hair," 26
in *Hamlet,* 221, 227–30, 240, 247
in *Light,* 117, 119, 123, 126, 129, 133–44
in "A Rose for Emily," 14–16, 18–20
in *Sanct.,* 64, 71, 266
in *Town,* 240–41, 247–48
in the Trilogy, 253, 269
"our town" technique, 16, 19, 38
in "A Bear Hunt," 24–25, 34
in "A Courtship," 22

community (*continued*)
  in "Hair," 25–26
  in "That Evening Sun," 31
  in "Uncle Willy," 39
Compson, Benjy, 38, 75–83, 189, 216, 250, 262
Compson, Caddy, 3–4, 12, 20, 31–33, 74–78, 156–57, 190, 210, 266, 278
Compson, Caroline Bascomb (Mrs. Compson), 32
Compson, Jason, II (General), 155–59, 162–66, 169
Compson, Jason, III (Mr. Compson), 31–32, 152, 157–63, 165, 169–70, 172–73, 175, 214, 242
Compson, Jason, IV, 31–33, 74–76, 79–83, 108
Compson, Quentin, 20–21, 23, 29–34, 44, 46, 73–83, 89, 94, 110, 147–50, 152–75, 177, 189, 194, 216, 228, 242, 244, 262, 268, 271
Compson, Quentin (Caddy's daughter), 74
Compsons, the, 20, 31, 33–34, 76, 80, 83, 88–89, 173, 215, 228, 250, 265, 278
Confidence Man, The (Herman Melville), 147
Conrad, Joseph, 47, 212
consciousness. *See* Narr. of consciousness
Cook, Celia (*Unvanq.*), 181
Cooper, Miss Minnie ("Dry September"), 20, 50–51, 53–55, 87, 191, 215, 278
"Courtship, A," 22
Cowley, Malcolm, *The Portable Faulkner,* 21, 112, 143, 203, 209, 249, 275–76, 280
Coxswain, the ("Turn About"), 55
craftsmanship, 1, 2, 9, 12, 258–61, 263, 268, 274, 278–79
  of Cash Bundren, 96, 103, 105
  in *Hamlet,* 224
  in *Reivers,* 217
  carpentry metaphor for, 30, 59; "box-building," 5, 7–8, 10–12, 56, 202, 263; corner-building," 6–8, 10, 12, 19, 21–22, 25, 34, 40, 55, 156, 202, 215, 261, 263, 279, 281; "lumber room," 207, 263; "nails–house," 142; "tools," 7. *See also* Form, "single urn or shape" metaphor

deception in Faulkner's narrative, 261; in the Trilogy, 253–54. *See also* Fiction as lies
Delta, 67
"Delta Autumn." See *Go Down, Moses*
Deluge, The, 80
design. *See* Narr. design
deSpain, Manfred, 234, 245
development. *See* Narr. development
devices. *See* Narr. devices
Dickens, Charles, 44, 114, 240, 280
Dictionary of American Biography, 114
Dilsey, 31, 33, 81, 83, 196, 200
distance. *See* Narr. distance
"Doctor Martino," 26, 55
Donne, John, 56
"doubling." *See* Narr. doubling
Dracula, 72
Drake, Temple, 20–21, 60–65, 68, 70–71, 115, 143, 210, 215, 262, 266, 278
drama, dramatic, 29, 48–49, 80, 209
  in *Requiem,* 210
  in "That Evening Sun," 33
"Dry September," 12, 20, 50–55, 191, 209, 214
Dumas, Alexandre, 183
Du Pre, Virginia Sartoris (Aunt Jenny), 60, 62, 71

Eden, 68
Edmonds, Carothers (Old Cass), 20, 194
Edmonds, Zachary (Zack), 190
"Elly," 55, 278
empathy 3, 38, 265, 279–80
  in *Absalom,* 150, 162, 207
  in *As I,* 85, 88–89, 92, 94, 97
  in "Barn Burning," 43–44
  in "Dry September," 51
  in *Fable,* 212–13
  in *Hamlet,* 227
  in *Light,* 133, 140–41
  in "A Rose for Emily," 13–21, 25, 27
  in "Red Leaves," 55
  in *Sanct.,* 72–73

in *S & F,* 76, 78–79
See also Identification
ending(s), 262–63, 267–69
entertainment, pleasure, 8, 9, 11; in *Hamlet,* 228–29; in *Sanct.,* 63
entrapment. *See* Narr. entrapment
Esmeralda, 239
evil: in *Absalom,* 163; in *Light,* 119–20; in *Unvanq.,* 180
experience as "raw material" for fiction, 5
experiment. *See* Narr. experiment

Fable, A, 201, 210–13, 215, 260, 275
failure. *See* Narr. failure
Fathers, Sam, 21, 23, 47, 174, 192
Faulkner, William
and Civil War, 183–84
interviews of, 214
literary principles of, 199
personas of, 1–2, 4–5, 27, 58–59, 144, 224, 243, 259–61
racial attitudes of, 199, 203
as screenwriter, 273–74
as self-educated man, 259
as social delineator, 203
Faulkner in the University, ed. Gwynn and Blotner, 2, 4, 5–7, 9, 27, 59, 84, 112, 260, 275–76
fiction. *See* Genre; Narrative
fiction as lies, 2, 4, 25, 30
Fiedler, Leslie, 34, 59
film(ic), cinema(tic), 49, 63–64, 72, 81, 115, 181, 184, 271, 274
in *Fable,* 211
in *GDM,* 197
in *Hamlet,* 236
of *Intruder,* 208–09
Light as, 132–33
of *Sanct.,* 61
See also *Breathless; Jules and Jim; Gone With the Wind; Rashomon;* Brown, Clarence; Hawks, Howard
Finnegans Wake (James Joyce), 56
"Fire and the Hearth, The." See *Go Down, Moses*
first-person. *See* Narr., first-person
"Flea, The" (John Donne), 56
form, "single urn or shape" metaphor, 1–2, 7, 8, 56–57, 215, 261, 279
"Fox Hunt," 56
Fox, Matt ("Hair"), 25
Freeman (*Hamlet*), 237–38
Frenchman's Bend, Frenchman's Place, 64–66, 71, 115, 219, 226, 230
frontier humor, 258
Frost, Robert, 1, 145

Gatsby, Jay, 146
genre 9, 29
of *GDM,* 200
in *Sanct.,* 60
in the Trilogy, 252
ghost story: "A Rose for Emily," 12–14, 17
mystery story: *Absalom,* 149–50
novel, 9, 20
poem, 9
short story, 9, 12, 17–18, 21–22, 25–26, 34, 74, 192, 195, 261, 275–76
short-story compound, 9, 186
trilogy, 249–50
"germ." *See* Narr. "germ"
ghost(s), 84, 160
Go Down, Moses, 20–21, 75, *176–200,* 208, 228, 234*n,* 262–63, 268–69, 275; Biblical patterns in, 155–56; child narrator in, 38–40, 42; Civil War in, 183; innocence in, 198; metaphor in, 154; misunderstanding in, 197–98
"The Bear," 9, 21, 46, 177, 191, 193–98, 260
"Delta Autumn," 195–97, 203
"The Fire and the Hearth," 188–89, 194–97, 202, 252*n*
"Go Down, Moses," 197–98
"The Old People," 191
"Pantaloon in Black," 190–91
"Was," 177, 186–89, 191, 194, 200, 214, 273
golden age, 31, 188, 193
Golden Bowl, The (Henry James), 79, 176
Gone With the Wind, 188
Goodwin, Lee (*Sanct.*), 61, 65
Goodwin, Ruby (*Sanct.*), 61–62
gossip, 24, 26–27, 30, 216, 280
in *Absalom,* 152, 162
in *Hamlet,* 229
in "A Rose for Emily," 14

gossip (*continued*)
in *Town,* 271
gothic, the, 7, 13, 18, 78
Grand Guignol, 60
Greene, Graham, 58
Grenier, Cynthia, 74
Grierson, Emily, 14–19, 25, 30, 87–88, 117, 127, 146, 227, 278
Grierson, Mr. ("A Rose for Emily"), 15, 18
Griersons, the, 16
Grimm, Percy, 117, 127, 134, 138–39, 144, 220, 267
group(s), fictional grouping, 20–21, 30
in *Absalom,* 162
in *As I,* 85, 94
in "Dry September," 53
in *Hamlet,* 227, 230–32, 235–36, 238
in *Light,* 26, 113, 119, 134–36
in "A Rose for Emily," 16
in "That Evening Sun," 31
in *Town,* 241
in the Trilogy, 26
See also Community, "our town technique"
Grove, Lena, 73, 113–25, 127, 130, 133–34, 137, 139–42, 144, 262, 267
Guardian(s), 254, 256
Gulliver's Travels (Jonathan Swift), 13, 62, 81
Gwynn, Frederick L. See *Faulkner in the University*

Habersham, Miss Eunice, 201, 207–08
"Hair," 20, 25–26, 135
Hait, Mrs. Mannie, 49–50, 55
Hamlet (William Shakespeare), 16
Hamlet, The, 176–77, 188, 218–44, 247, 250, 253–54, 256, 262–63, 275, 277; "Afternoon of a Cow," 234; "Eula," 232, 234; "Flem," 234; "The Long Summer," 234; nature in, 237–38
Hapsburg genealogy, 76
Harvard University, 77, 150, 156, 171
Havisham, Miss, 18, 149, 160
Hawk, Drusilla, 184, 278
Hawks, Howard, 273
"Hawkshaw," Henry Stribling, 25–26, 53–54
Hawthorne, Nathaniel, 56, 258
Hearer and Subject. *See* Teller, Hearer, and Subject
"hearing-seeing." *See* "Thinking . . . thinking"
Hedda Gabler (Henrik Ibsen), 271–73
Helen of Troy, 246, 253, 255
Hemingway, Ernest, 23, 191
Herodotus, 269
Het, Old ("Mule in the Yard"), 49
Highboy (*Intruder*), 207
Hightower, Rev. Gail, 113–16, 118–19, 121, 123–24, 126–28, 133–34, 137, 139–42, 144, 160, 183, 233, 267
Hines, Eupheus, 114, 118–20, 129
Hines, Mrs. (wife of Eupheus), 142
Hineses, the, 113, 142
Hipps, Buck (*Hamlet*), 236–38
Hogarth, William, 73
Hogganbeck, Boon, 198
Hogganbeck, David ("A Courtship"), 22
Hôtel (*Fable*), 212
House of the Seven Gables, The (Nathaniel Hawthorne), 56
Houston, Jack (Zack in *Town*), 234
Houyhnhnms, 62
Hubert, Mr. *See* Beauchamp, Hubert
Huckleberry Finn (Mark Twain), 9, 39
humor, 7; in "A Rose for Emily," 20; in *Sanct.,* 60. *See also* Comedy, comic

Ibsen, Henrik, 272
identification, reader's, 3, 38, 279
in *Absalom,* 167
in *As I,* 246
in *GDM,* 188, 190–91, 197
in *Light,* 139–40, 144
in *S & F,* 83
in *Unvanq.,* 185
See also Empathy
Ikkemotubbe, 22
Iliad, The, 216
image(s), imagery. *See* Metaphor
imagination as "raw material" for fiction, 5, 8
Indians, 20, 22–23; in "Red Leaves," 193. *See also* Narratives of Indian captivity
individual(s), 278–80; and universal, 4
in *As I,* 92–94
in *GDM,* 188

in *Hamlet,* 235–36
in *Light,* 112–13, 116–17, 119, 132, 134–37, 139–44
in "A Rose for Emily," 20
in *Town,* 246–47
Inge, William, 215
initiation, 21, 25, 30
in *Absalom,* 31
in *As I,* 92
in *Unvanq.,* 182
Intruder in the Dust, 49, 135, 199, *201–11,* 215, 242, 252, 276; film of, 208–09
irony, 26, 32–33; in *As I,* 180; in *S & F,* 83
Ishmael, 63, 89, 117, 140
Issetibbeha, 22
is–was, 4; in *Absalom,* 160; in *As I,* 113; in *Hamlet,* 220; in *Light,* 112–14, 122–23, 126, 128–30, 142; in *Unvanq.,* 179
Italian girl (*S & F*), 78

James, Henry, 1, 65, 79, 176, 258
Japan, 2, 19, 60, 80, 214
Jefferson, 16, 38–39, 62, 64, 66, 93, 115, 157, 173, 192, 230, 241*n,* 266
Jehovah, 155
Jenny, Miss (Aunt). *See* Du Pre, Virginia Sartoris
Jerrod, Hubert ("Doctor Martino"), 26
Jesus ("That Evening Sun"), 31, 34
Jew Lawyer, the (*Sanct.*), 71
Jim (*Huckleberry Finn*), 180
Joby (*Unvanq.*), 182
Johnson, Samuel, 49
Jones, Milly, 165
Jones, Wash, 151*n,* 156, 167
Joyce, James, 201
Judge, the (*Sanct.*), 62
Jules and Jim, 271–73
"Just Before the War with the Eskimos" (J. D. Salinger), 48
"Justice, A," 23, 29, 34
Justice of the Peace, the ("Barn Burning"), 43–44

Keats, John, 1, 202, 217
King James Version of the Bible, 192
Kinsey, Albert, *Sexual Behavior in the Human Male and Female,* 16
Knight's Gambit, 210, 275
"knowing." *See* "Thinking . . . thinking"
Kohl, Barton (*Mansion*), 234
"Kubla Khan" (Samuel Taylor Coleridge), 210

Labove, (*Hamlet*), 233
Lawyer, the (*Absalom*), 158
lies, fiction as. *See* Fiction as lies
Life of Johnson (James Boswell), 5*n,* 49
Light in August, 20–21, 29, 48–49, 73, *112–44,* 146–47, 163, 166, 175–76, 183, 188, 205, 208–09, 211, 216, 220–21, 224–25, 233, 235, 249, 252, 258, 261–62, 267–68, 270, 275, 277–78, 280; character-dominated 112, 115; evil in, 119–20, 143; Faulkner pleasing himself in, 267; groups in, 26
Lion in the Garden, ed. Meriwether and Millgate, 1, 3–7, 9, 27, 74, 84, 260–61, 276
Little Black Sambo, 236
Littlejohn, Mrs. (*Hamlet*), 238
Little Orphan Annie, 250
Loosh (Lucius; *Unvanq.*), 178
Louvinia (*Unvanq.*), 182
Love and Death in the American Novel (Leslie Fiedler), 59
"lumber-room." *See* Craftsmanship, carpentry metaphor for
Luster, 81
Luxembourg Gardens, 65, 70, 262

McCallum, Lafe (*As I*), 101, 108
McCannon, Shrevlin (Shreve), 20–21, 147, 152–59, 164–75, 177, 194, 244, 262, 268, 271, 278
McCarron, Hoake, 234
McCaslin, Amodeus (Uncle Buddy), 188
McCaslin, Carothers (Cass), 177, 187–89, 194
McCaslin, Isaac (Ike), 20–21, 29, 34, 110, 145, 155, 188, 192, 194–98, 203, 234*n,* 243
McCaslin, Lucius Quintus Carothers, 186, 195, 197–98

McCaslin, Theophilus (Uncle Buck), 188
McCaslins, the, 228
McEachern, Simon 114, 119–20, 130
McEachern, Mrs. (wife of Simon), 130–31
McGowan, Skeet (*As I*), 87, 134
Machiavelli, 190, 256
McLendon, Capt. Jackson ("Dry September"), 51, 53–54, 139
Mallison, Charles, Sr., 248*n*
Mallison, Charles, Jr. (Chick), 203–05, 241–47, 249–52, 255
Mallisons, the, 234
Mame (*Light*), 120
Manassas, 183
manipulation. *See* Narr. manipulation
Mann, Thomas, 280
Mansion, The, 210, 234, 243, *248–57,* 263, 271*n;* as book of returns, 249; as last novel in Trilogy, 252
Mason, Perry, 71
Mather, Cotton, 62*n*
Max (*Light*), 120
Maxey ("Hair"), 25–26
Melville, Herman, 147, 258–59
memory, reader's, 29, 261; in *Absalom,* 161; in *GDM,* 188; in *Intruder,* 207; in *Light,* 112–13, 119, 128, 131, 141; in "A Rose for Emily," 141; in *S & F,* 77–78; in *Unvanq.,* 179
Memphis, 61–62, 64–65, 68, 72, 115, 135*n,* 184
Meriwether, James B. See *Lion in the Garden*
metaphor, 1, 8, 10, 17, 263
in *Absalom,* 145, 149, 150–59, 161–62, 165, 169, 174, 192, 206, 211, 286
in *As I,* 93–94, 97, 100–01, 110, 151
in "Dry September," 53–54
in *Fable,* 211
in *GDM,* 192
in *Hamlet,* 222–24, 231, 236–40
in *Intruder,* 204–06, 208
in *Light,* 126
in *Mansion,* 249
in "Mule in the Yard," 50
in "A Rose for Emily," 17
in *S & F,* 262
in "Uncle Willy," 40
in *Unvanq.,* 178, 184
See also Craftsmanship, carpentry metaphor for; Form, "single urn or shape" metaphor
method. *See* Narr. method
Millard, Rosa (Granny), 180, 182–85, 208
Millard (Bayard's mother), 182–83
Millgate, Michael. See *Lion in the Garden*
mimesis, 261, 263; in *S & F,* 75
Mississippi, 38, 167, 171, 180–81, 206
Mondrian, Piet, 225
Montgomery, Jake (*Intruder*), 205
Moseley (*As I*), 87–88
Mosquitoes, 6
Mottstown, 142
Mountaineers, 59
"Mountain Victory," 183
"Mule in the Yard," 49–50, 52, 214, 218–19
Mummy, the, 72
"My Grandmother Millard and General Bedford Forrest and the Battle of Harrykin Creek," 183
myth(s), 1, 279; in *Absalom,* 145–47, 152, 156–59, 162–63, 165, 168, 170, 174; in *GDM,* 187, 193; in *Hamlet,* 220, 233, 239–40; in "A Rose for Emily," 17; in *Requiem,* 210; in *Sanct.,* 73, 210

Nagano, Japan, 214
Nancy ("That Evening Sun"), 31, 33, 48, 200, 278
narrative, 1, 5–6
narr. action, 35;
in *Fable,* 213
in *GDM,* 187
in *Intruder,* 207–08
in *Unvanq.,* 178, 181, 185, 187, 268–69
narr. artifice, 42, 258–59, 261–64, 266, 280
narr. atmosphere, 49, 51–54
in *Absalom* 145, 149;
in *As I,* 104
in "Dry September," 191
in *Hamlet,* 232
in *Intruder,* 135

in *Light,* 135
in *Sanct.,* 135, 266
See also Rendering
narr., brief, 9
narr., "cheap" techniques in, 58–59, 61
narr., child's, 38. *See also* Children in Faulkner's fiction
narr. of consciousness in *Light,* 133
narr. design, 7, 56, 213–14
in *Absalom,* 169
in *As I,* 85, 94, 98
in "Dry September," 214
in *Hamlet,* 218–19, 225, 228, 240
in *Reivers,* 269
in *Town,* 248
in *Unvanq.,* 179
narr. development, 263, 265, 270, 276–77, 280–81
in *GDM,* 176, 200
in *Hamlet,* 176
in the Trilogy, 274
in *Unvanq.,* 176
narr. devices, 11, 29–30, 33, 45–46, 50, 54, 56
in *Absalom,* 149–50, 267–68
in *Fable,* 211
in *GDM,* 191
in *Hamlet,* 219, 228
in *Intruder,* 203–05, 208, 211
in *Light,* 117, 122, 128, 143
in *Sanct.,* 72
in *Town,* 242, 246
in *Unvanq.,* 179–80
narr. dilemma in *Intruder,* 211
narr. distance, 30, 39, 41–42, 46, 53, 55
in *Absalom,* 147, 153*n,* 157, 162–64, 166, 168, 172, 267–68
in *As I,* 97
in *Fable,* 212–13
in *GDM,* 188, 190–91, 196
in *Hamlet,* 188, 229
in *Light,* 125, 130, 132–33, 141–43, 188, 267
in "A Rose for Emily," 19–20
in *S & F,* 76
narr. doubling in *Absalom,* 157, 169
narr. entrapment, 30, 54, 264–65
in *Absalom,* 161
of Joe Christmas in *Light,* 126–27, 131, 142
in *GDM,* 190
in *Town,* 242
narr. experiment, 8, 264–65, 274, 278, 280
in *Absalom,* 176, 191–92
in "Artist at Home," 41
in *Town,* 243, 246
narr. failure, in *Fable, Intruder, Requiem, S & F,* 78, 201 ff.
narr., first-person, 28, 30, 33, 46, 48, 55, 241
in *Absalom,* 163
in *As I,* 85, 87–89, 265–67, 279
in *GDM,* 188–89
in *Intruder,* 205
in *Light,* 116, 205, 267
in *Mansion,* 248
in "A Rose for Emily," 13–16, 18–20
in *Sanct.,* 65
in *S & F,* 78–81, 265–66, 278–79
in *Town,* 241, 243–45, 247
narr. "germ," 3–4, 12, 24, 49, 56, 263
in *Absalom,* 156
in *As I,* 88
in "A Rose for Emily," 18–19
in *S & F,* 76
narr. intensity, 32
narr. interference, 32
narr. manipulation, 24, 263–64
in *GDM,* 189–91, 194–95, 198, 260
in *Sanct.,* 73
in "Shall Not Perish," 37
in "That Evening Sun," 33
narr. metaphor in *Absalom,* 151–57, 162
narr., metaphor for: shotgun, 14, 18; "plank" from "still-living tree," 202, 275, 280. *See also* Metaphor
narr. method, 10
in *GDM,* 46
in *Mansion,* 248
narr. objectivity in *Light,* 114, 117, 133, 135, 139
narr., open, 8
narr. pattern, 6, 8–9, 258, 263, 278
in *Absalom,* 149, 151*n,* 153–54, 158, 167, 169–71, 173, 206

narrative (*continued*)
in *As I,* 85, 91, 101–02, 107, 110, 144
in *GDM,* 187, 191, 193
in *Hamlet,* 231
in *Intruder,* 206
in *Light,* 112, 115–16, 119–20, 122–23, 125–26, 128, 131, 134, 138–41, 143–44
in "Mule in the Yard," 50
in "A Rose for Emily" 16, 18, 134
in *Sanct.,* 59, 65, 72
in *S & F,* 79
narr. presence, 24, 42–44, 47, 51
in *Absalom,* 147, 164, 166, 173
in "Artist at Home," 41–42
in "Barn Burning," 178
in "A Bear Hunt," 25
in *Fable,* 212
in *GDM,* 188–89, 191–92
in *Hamlet,* 218–23
in *Intruder,* 204
in *Light,* 114, 117, 122, 124, 126, 128, 134–37, 143
in *Town,* 244
in *Unvanq.,* 178
narr. process, 30
in *Absalom,* 146, 148, 150, 171, 175
narr. puzzle in *Absalom,* 145, 150, 159; in *Hamlet,* 224
narr., reminiscent, 23, 33–34, 44, 46
in "A Bear Hunt," 34
in *Unvanq.,* 177
See also Reminiscence.
narr. rhythm, 259, 279
in *Absalom,* 146, 148–51, 158
in *As I,* 85–88, 91–92, 100
in *GDM,* 192
in *Light,* 267
narr. scheme, 41
narr. selection in *S & F,* 75
narr. shape, 7, 8, 48; in *As I,* 98–99, 101
narr., stopped-action, 18, 35–36; in "Shingles for the Lord," 37
narr. strategy, 8, 10–11, 21, 30, 34, 37, 40–41, 46, 48, 50, 54–55, 214
in *Absalom,* 147, 151, 153–54, 156
in *As I,* 86–87, 110
in *GDM,* 196, 214
in *Hamlet,* 228
in *Light,* 112–13, 117, 133, 147
in *Mansion,* 253
in "Mule in the Yard," 214
in *Reivers,* 216
in "A Rose for Emily," 18, 87
in *Unvanq.,* 216
narr. structure, 10–11, 22, 24, 54
in *Absalom,* 147–48, 151, 158–59, 166, 170, 268
in *GDM,* 176, 186–87, 191, 193, 195
in *Hamlet,* 221–22, 225–26, 234–35, 240
in *Intruder,* 203
in *Light,* 112, 134, 141–44, 225
in *Mansion,* 248–49
in *Sanct.,* 59, 64
in *S & F,* 77
in *Town,* 244, 256
in Trilogy, 256–57, 269, 277
in *Unvanq.,* 176, 185
narr. surface in *GDM,* 187
in *Hamlet,* 221, 232, 256
in *Unvanq.,* 180, 182, 184–85
narr. suspense in *Absalom,* 149, 151, 158, 167
in *GDM,* 189
in *Light,* 116
See also Suspense
narr., suspension of, 214
in *As I,* 267
in *Hamlet,* 235–36, 239, 250
in *Light,* 267
in *Mansion,* 250, 256
in *Sanct.,* 267
in "Shall Not Perish" and "Two Soldiers," 35–36
in "Shingles for the Lord," 35
in *Town,* 246, 256
in *Unvanq.,* 179
narr. technique, 24, 27, 260
in *Sanct.,* 60
narr. theory, 11, 30, 37
narr., third person, 27–28, 30–31, 42–44, 46–48, 50, 55
in *Absalom,* 163–64
in *As I,* 88–89
in *GDM,* 188
in *Hamlet,* 188, 227, 241

in *Intruder,* 205
in *Light,* 120–21, 188, 205, 267
in *Mansion,* 248, 253
in *Sanct.,* 266–67
in *S & F,* 76–77, 82–83
narr. tone, 42
in "That Evening Sun," 33
in "Uncle Willy," 39
narr. tools, 10, 29, 34, 37–38, 42, 48. *See also* Craftsmanship, carpentry metaphor for
narr. transitions in *As I,* 86, 91
narr. tricks, 260–61
narr. truth in *Absalom,* 147, 161, 166, 174
narr. verisimilitude in *GDM,* 196. *See also* Verisimilitude.
narratives of Indian captivity, 61, 64
Narratives of the Indian Wars (Charles Lincoln), 62*n*
Narratives of the Witchcraft Cases G. L. Burr), 62*n*
narrator, 10, 14–15, 29, 39, 113; child as, 34–35, 37–40, 42; omniscient, 55
in *Absalom,* 152, 161, 163–65
in *As I,* 85, 89, 107, 244, 247
in "Barn Burning," 44
in "Centaur in Brass," 23
in "Hair," 25
in *Hamlet,* 224, 247
in *Mansion,* 251
in "A Rose for Emily," 14, 253
in *S & F,* 74–76, 189
in *Town,* 242, 244–45, 247
in *Unvanq.,* 178
Natalie (*S & F*), 78
"natural," the, 261, 263–64, 270
nature: in *Hamlet,* 237–38; in *Sanct.,* 64–73, 144
Nazis, 210
Negroes. *See* Blacks
Newgate Calendar, 61
novel, nineteenth-century, 64. *See also* Genre

objective–subjective, 265–67
in *Absalom,* 161–62, 164–65
in *As I,* 87–89, 91, 94–97
in "Dry September," 191
in *GDM,* 191–92, 197
in *Light,* 114, 117, 121, 133, 140–41, 143–44
in *Town,* 241
See also Narr. objectivity
observation, as "raw material" for fiction, 5
Ode to Autumn (John Keats), 217
Old Man (*The Wild Palms*), 209
Old Moster, 255
"Old People, The." See *Go Down, Moses*
omission–suspense. *See* Suspense by omission
O'Neill, Eugene, 48
oral tradition, 13, 27, 30, 215–16, 258–59; in *Sanct.,* 59
Our Town (Thornton Wilder), 218
"our town" technique. *See* Community
Oxford, Miss., 65, 72, 181, 238

"Pantaloon in Black." See *Go Down, Moses*
Paradise Lost (John Milton), 72
Parchman, Miss., 254
Pater, Walter, 276
pattern. *See* Narr. pattern
Peabody, Dr. Lucius, 87–88, 94–95, 108–09
"Pennsylvania Station," 56
Penrod, 35
Peter Pan (J. M. Barrie), 56
Pip, 44
Place de Ville, 212
Player, the (*Light*), 117
pleasure for reader as aim of fiction, 2, 10, 38; in *GDM,* 200; in "A Rose for Emily," 19. *See also* Entertainment
Poe, Edgar Allan, 13, 39–40
poetry, the poetic: in *Absalom,* 153–54, 156, 165; in *As I,* 89, 110; in *S & F,* 83. *See also* Genre
Pollock, Jackson, 225
Popeye, 59–61, 63–67, 69, 71–73, 95, 143, 215, 230, 262, 278
Portable Faulkner, The. See Cowley, Malcolm
power, as theme in Trilogy, 219, 221
Prelude, The (William Wordsworth), 146

Priest, Lucius, 34, 39, 178, 184, 278
Process. *See* Narr. process
Provine, Lucius, 24–25
pulp fiction, 59–63
Puritan ethos, 62, 155
Pylon, 275

Quick, Solon or Ben, 237

Rabelais, 219
"Raid." See *The Unvanquished*
Rashomon (Akira Kurosawa), 79
Ratliff, V. K., 23–26, 32, 50–51, 80, 168, 202, 219–32, 234–39, 241–46, 248, 250–52, 278
reader's identification. *See* Identification, reader's
Reba, Miss. *See* Rivers, Miss Reba
Red (*Sanct.*), 59, 61, 65
"Red Leaves," 47–48, 61, 193, 212
Reed, Susan ("Hair"), 25
Reivers, The, 23, 28–39, 45*n,* 48, 177–78, 184, 208, 216–17, 261, 263, 269, 277–78
religious, the, in *S & F,* 78
reminiscence, 22–23; in "That Evening Sun," 34. *See also* Narr., reminiscent
rendering, 151. *See also* Narr. atmosphere
Requiem for a Nun, 48–49, 201, *209–10,* 219, 242
Restoration, 60
rhetoric, Faulkner's weakness for, 5, 7, 201, 214
  in *Absalom,* 145, 158
  in *GDM,* 193
  in *Intruder,* 202, 204, 208
rhythm. *See* Narr. rhythm
Rider (*GDM*), 190, 198–99
Ringo, 178–82, 185, 278
Rittenmeyer, Charlotte (*The Wild Palms*), 209, 278
Rivers, Miss Reba, 230, 234, 278
Rodney, Uncle ("That Will Be Fine"), 35
"A Rose for Emily," 12–21, 25–26, 28, 31, 52, 80, 87–89, 95, 117, 134, 141, 162, 168, 215, 227, 253
Rowlandson, Mrs. Mary, 62*n*

Salinger, J. D., 48
Samson (*As I*), 95
Sanctuary, 58–73, 98, 115, 135, 143–44, 210, 254, 262, 266–67, 274, 278, 280; the city in, 69; dirty jokes in, 59–60; film of, 61; Indian captivity narratives and, 61–64; nature in, 64–73; Puritan ethic in, 62
Sartoris, 4, 163, 183; style of, 64–65
Sartoris, Bayard (Old Bayard), 178–83
Sartoris, Bayard (Young Bayard), 177–82, 185, 278
Sartoris, Col. John, 15
Sartoris duel, 131
Sartorises, the, 20, 228
Scott, Sir Walter, 215
Selection. *See* Narr. selection
"Shall Not Perish," 35–37, 181
shape. *See* Narr. shape
Shaw, George Bernard, 243*n*
"Shingles for the Lord," 35, 37, 181, 274
short fiction, 29–57, 186, 200, 218. *See also* Genre
Shreve. *See* McCannon, Shrevlin
Skin of Our Teeth, The (Thornton Wilder), 239
slavery, 33, 154, 155*n,* 183. *See also* Blacks
Slotkin, Richard S., 62*n*
Snopes, Abner, 220, 223, 226, 229
Snopes, Eck, 237–38
Snopes, Eula Varner, 20, 222–25, 228, 232–34, 239, 245, 249, 263
Snopes, Flem, 20, 50, 215, 219–21, 223–24, 226, 228–34, 236–37, 239, 245, 248–49, 253–56, 262–63
Snopes, Ike, 225, 227, 234–35, 238–39
Snopes, Linda, 234, 246, 248–49, 252–53, 255
Snopes, Mink, 225–26, 232, 234, 239, 248–49, 252–56, 263
Snopes, Montgomery Ward, 230, 248, 254
Snopes, Mrs. (wife of Mink), 227
Snopes, Sartoris (Sarty), 43–46, 55, 178, 188, 204, 229
Snopes, Virgil, 59–60, 65, 234, 251
Snopes, Wallstreet Panic, 237

Snopes, name of, 253
Snopeses, the, 154, 200, 222, 228, 230, 236, 238, 240, 243, 253, 263, 269
Snopesism, 228–29, 234, 248
Snopes Trilogy. *See* Trilogy, the
Soldiers' Pay, 56
Sophonsiba, Miss. *See* Beauchamp, Miss Sophonsiba
Sound and the Fury, The, 12, 56, 58, *74–83,* 87–88, 92, 94, 112–13, 163, 175, 209–10, 216, 218, 227, 250, 259, 261–62, 265–66, 275, 277, 279; narrators in, 74–82; time scheme in, 113
South, the, 38, 146, 152, 155–57, 168, 170, 187–88, 202, 203; allegory for, 16; Faulkner's understanding of, 16; New South, 228
Southern naturalism, 7
Southern women, 24–25, 146, 160
Soveraignty and Goodness of God, The (Mrs. Mary Rowlandson), 62*n*
"Spotted Horses," 219
Stamper, Pat, 226, 238
Stevens, Gavin, 5, 23, 26, 197–98, 203, 208–10, 214, 178, 234, 241–51
Stevens, Gowan, 33*n,* 245
story-series. *See* Genre
storyteller(s), 2, 4, 7–8, 10, 13, 22, 25, 27, 30, 193, 195, 202, 258–59, 263, 276–78, 280; *Hamlet,* 220, 224, 227; ritual, in *S & F,* 80; in *Town,* 247; "natural," 258, 264
Strange Interlude (Eugene O'Neill), 48
strategy. *See* Narr. strategy
stream-of-consciousness in *S & F,* 82
structure. *See* Narr. structure
style: Faulkner and, 276–77; in *Absalom,* 145, 191–92; in *GDM,* 191–93, 195
subgroups, 15, 18, 25, 135. *See also* Groups
Subject. *See* Teller, Hearer, and Subject
subjective. *See* Objective-subjective
suspense, 13–14, 22, 29, 55; in *Absalom,* 243. *See also* Narr. suspense; Narr., suspension of
suspense by omission, 22, 39, 41; in *Absalom,* 149–50; in *As I,* 91; in *GDM,* 187, 189, 273; in *Hamlet,* 221–22, 224, 232; in *Light,* 118; in *Town,* 242
suspension of disbelief in *As I,* 90
Sutpen, Ellen Coldfield. *See* Coldfield, Ellen
Sutpen, Rosa Coldfield. *See* Coldfield, Rosa
Sutpen, Henry, 21, 110, 145, 147–49, 154*n,* 156–57, 162, 166–67, 170, 183, 185–86, 192, 228, 251, 262, 268
Sutpen, Judith, 73, 145, 149, 151, 154*n,* 156–57, 162, 173
Sutpen, Thomas, 12, 21, 145–46, 148–73, 175, 254
Sutpen, Mr. (Thomas Sutpen's grandfather), 164–65
Sutpen, Mrs. (Thomas Sutpen's West Indian wife), 152, 155
Sutpen (*Hamlet*), 228
Sutpen's Hundred, 147–48, 157, 159, 167, 173
Sutpens, the, 147
Sybilline quality, 229
symbol, 3, 7, 214

tabloid journalism, 60, 63, 65
"Tall Men, The," 26
technique. *See* Narr. technique
Teller, Hearer, and Subject, 13–14, 19–21, 23–25, 27–30, 38, 42–43, 47, 54–55, 63, 80, 264, 270, 279; in *Absalom,* 146, 150–51, 156, 158–59, 163, 168–69, 171, 174; in *GDM,* 194; in *Hamlet,* 220, 224, 226–27, 233, 241; in *Light,* 115, 117, 140; in *Town,* 241, 244, 246–47
"That Evening Sun," 20, 30–34, 45–46, 178, 209, 214, 218, 278
"That Will Be Fine," 34–35, 37–39, 181
them–us, 20, 265, 278–80
in *As I,* 87–89, 94–95
in "Hair," 26
in *Light,* 140–41
in "A Rose for Emily," 18
in *Sanct.,* 73
in *S & F,* 80, 82
theory. *See* Narr. theory

thinking . . . thinking: in *Fable,* 211–12; in *Intruder,* 205; in *Light,* 122, 124–26, 128–30, 133–34, 205, 208, 211; in *Mansion,* 249
third-person. *See* Narr., third-person
TIME Magazine, 16, 203, 259
Tingueley, Jean, 235
Tom Swift and His Electric Runabout (Victor Appleton), 251
Tomey's Turl, 187–88, 234
Tommy (*Sanct.*), 59, 72
tone. *See* Narr. tone
tools. *See* Craftsmanship, carpentry metaphor for; Narr. tools
tour de force: *As I,* characterized as, 260–61, 266; *Light,* characterization as, 133, 144; *Town* as, 49, 75, 230*n*, 240–48, 254, 256, 263, 271
tragedy, 7, 269; in *Absalom,* 146, 156–57; in *As I,* 85, 88–89, 91, 94, 97; in *GDM,* 260; in *Light,* 124, 127, 142; in "A Rose for Emily," 17; in *S & F,* 83
transition. *See* Narr. transition
Travelling Salesman, 60
Trigorin, 82
Trilogy, the, 9, 20, 26, 38, 46, 50, 185, 200, 210, 212, 218, 225–26, 228–31, 234–35, 239, 240–41, 243, 246, 249, 252–53, 256, 259, 262, 269, 271, 274–77; power as theme of, 219
Tristram Shandy (Laurence Sterne), 246
Tull, Cora, 86, 88, 90, 92, 94–95, 102, 107, 220
Tull Vernon, 86, 95–97, 104–05, 221
Tulls, the, 87, 228, 234
"Turn About," 26, 55
Twain, Mark, 180, 201, 258
"Two Soldiers," 35–37

Uncle Tom. *See* Lucas Beauchamp
"Uncle Wiggily in Connecticut" (J. D. Salinger), 48
"Uncle Willy," 39–41, 190, 262
Understanding Fiction (Brooks and Warren), 15*n*
unity, 1–2, 9, 22; in *Absalom,* 146; in *As I,* 84, 89, 110; in *GDM,* 186, 194–95; in *Light,* 113, 123, 141, 143; in "That Will Be Fine," 35; in *Town,* 241. *See also* Coherence, cohesion
Unvanquished, The, 38, *176–200,* 207–08, 211, 216, 254, 262, 268–69, 275, 278
"urn or shape" metaphor. *See* Form, "single urn or shape" metaphor
us–them. *See* Them–us

Varner, Eula. *See* Snopes, Eula Varner
Varner, Jody, 220–23, 226, 229–30, 237–39
Varner, Mrs., 222
Varner, Will, 123, 134, 137, 143, 219–22, 224, 226, 229
verisimilitude, 3, 13–14; in *Absalom,* 174, 226; in *Hamlet,* 226. *See also* Narr. verisimilitude
"Victory," 55

Wapshot (John Cheever), 280
War. *See* Civil War; World War I stories; World War II
Warren, Robert Penn, 15*n*
Warwick, 187–88
"Was." See *Go Down, Moses*
was–is. *See* Is–was
Waverley, (Sir Walter Scott), 156, 187
Werther, 82
West Indies, 152, 165
West Point, N.Y., U.S. Military Academy, 1, 216, 243, 259
white(s), 33, 190, 202
white slavery, 61, 65, 71
Whitfield, Rev., 36–37, 86–87
Whitman, Walt, 259
Wilder, Thornton, 239
Wilderness, the, 196
Wild Palms, The, 209, 275
Williams, Tennessee, 25
Wilson, Edmund, 202
Winbush, Fonzo, 60, 65, 69, 234, 251
Wingfield, Amanda, 25
Wolfe, Thomas, 260
women, 39, 62. *See also* Southern women
Wordsworth, William, 128, 146, 201–02
World War I stories, 20, 22, 215, 278
World War II, 35, 196

Writer-Reader. *See* Teller, Hearer, and Subject
Wycherley, William, 60
Wylie, Ash (Old Ash), 25
Yankee, the (*Unvanq.*), 178, 180
Yoknapatawpha County, 20, 23, 208, 254, 258, 280
Yeats, William Butler, 1